DATE DUE FOR RETURN

**This book may be recalled
before the above date**

90014

MARSDEN HARTLEY

MARSDEN HARTLEY

The Biography of an American Artist

Townsend Ludington

LITTLE, BROWN AND COMPANY

BOSTON   TORONTO   LONDON

For permission to use materials from their collections,
the author gratefully acknowledges the Archives of
American Art and the Yale Collection of American
Literature, Beinecke Rare Book and Manuscript
Library, Yale University.

Excerpt from "Ash Wednesday," in *Collected Poems
1909–1962* by T. S. Eliot, Copyright 1936 by
Harcourt Brace Jovanovich, Inc., Copyright © 1964,
1963 by T. S. Eliot, reprinted by permission of Harcourt
Brace Jovanovich, Inc., and Faber and Faber Ltd.

Excerpts from *Collected Poems* by Marsden Hartley are
used with the permission of Black Sparrow Press.

Library of Congress Cataloging-in-Publication Data

Ludington, Townsend, 1936–
    Marsden Hartley: the biography of an American artist/Townsend
Ludington. — 1st ed.
        p.   cm.
    Includes bibliographical references and index.
    ISBN 0-316-53537-0
    1. Hartley, Marsden, 1877–1943.   2. Painters — United States —
Biography.   I. Title.
ND237.H3435L8   1992
759.13 — dc20
[B]   10006(1118 T   91-37621

10 9 8 7 6 5 4 3 2 1

MV-NY

*Published simultaneously in Canada
by Little, Brown & Company (Canada) Limited*

Printed in the United States of America

This book is dedicated
to Gertrude Wells Barney
and Wright Saltus Ludington

"To the Nameless One"

You, who have power over
everything obscure
Listen — come over here, sit by
my side
and let me say the things I want
to say —
I want nothing in the way of artificial
heavens —
The earth is all I know of wonder.
I lived and was nurtured in the
magic of dreams
bright flames of spirit laughter
around all my seething frame.

Marsden Hartley,
from *Collected Poems*

Contents

Illustrations appear following pages 114 and 210

Preface

WRITING in the *Nation* two weeks after Marsden Hartley's death in 1943, Paul Rosenberg, who had recently become Hartley's dealer, declared that the "gaunt eagle from the hills of Maine" had been a "prodigy, . . . an almost gigantic secondary artist." He felt that Hartley had lacked a driving desire for perfection and suggested that a certain "consecutiveness" was missing from his work, but he acknowledged that the artist had been "abundantly talented" and a "very modern American."[1] Rosenberg meant to be extravagant in his praise, and was, but he was not convinced that Hartley had been absolutely of the first rank. Now I believe we are sure, a fact reflected in the price a major painting by Hartley can bring. More important, we understand what he was doing and recognize that his talents sustained him throughout a long career. The more we look, the more we see that each phase of his work has remarkably distinctive qualities as well as an intimate relationship with every other phase.

Rosenberg was correct in emphasizing Hartley's modernity. The painter was deeply committed to modernism and comprehended what it was, asserting in "Dissertation on Modern Painting," an essay written in 1921, that

> The thing must be brought clearly to the surface in terms of itself, without cast or shade of the application of extraneous ideas. That should be, and is, it seems to me, the special and peculiar office of modern art: to arrive at a species of purism, native to ourselves in

our own concentrated period, to produce the newness or the "now-ness" of individual experience. The progress of the modernist is therefore a slow and painstaking one, because he has little of actual precedent for his modern premise. It must be remembered that modern art is, in its present so-called ultra state, not twenty years old, and it must likewise readily be observed that it has accomplished a vast deal in its incredibly prodigious youthfulness.[2]

Modernism may be defined in many different ways, but surely Hartley caught something of its essence in this statement.

It is noteworthy that he was speaking as an American. However much he loved Europe, he wrote and painted out of his American roots, which is one of the reasons for his significance. He was among the most important of a first generation of American modernist paint-ers that included Georgia O'Keeffe, John Marin, Arthur Dove, Alfred Maurer, and Max Weber. Although he spent numerous years abroad, particularly in France and Germany, he had thoroughly American sensibilities. European painters such as van Gogh, Kandinsky, Franz Marc, Cézanne, and Picasso affected him profoundly, but he was no copyist. Rather, his understanding of the modern European masters enabled him to release his native sensibility and express a rich blend of sophistication and naïveté, as well as a sense of the size, the unfettered-ness — even the wildness — of the North American scene, the pri-mary subject of his work.

In 1985, after spending four days roaming about East and West Berlin in an effort to grasp the essence of Marsden Hartley, I drove west through a portion of what was at that time East Germany and then headed south, stopping many hours later in Dinkelsbühl, one of the more charming kitschy towns in Bavaria. I had meant to end up nearer Garmisch-Partenkirchen, in the Alps, but the young man from whom I had rented the car in West Berlin had advised me, overcau-tiously, to get out of East Germany as quickly as I could, and as a result I covered two sides of a triangle rather than taking a more direct route south, via Dresden.

No matter. In Dinkelsbühl by myself, I began to put Hartley into some sort of perspective as I had not been able to before. Exactly why I could do so at this moment is difficult to explain; nevertheless, I knew I was starting to understand him better than ever I had. That eve-ning I began to sort out my own vivid impressions of the past several days and to gain a sense of Hartley that had eluded me. His stay in Germany in 1913–1915 was, of course, the culmination of the first important period in his life. Germany was tremendously significant for him both then and later, with its avant-garde art, its young men with whom he fell in love, its culture, and even its militarism, which for him translated into the bright colors and forms of grand marches, handsome men and women, and the discipline and order of the military.

What he did, all that he was, stood out in my mind amid the Germany I was seeing. Hartley embraced life and people, not collectively but individually; he respected the vitality, the power, of nature; he loathed the misery that mankind perpetually inflicts upon itself; and he feared the pain of illness and the inevitable death that makes us mortal. All these elemental matters one could sense in contemporary Germany, amid the esprit of the West Berliners and the beauty of Bavaria, with its plains and mountains. And yet here also were the Berlin Wall, with the hatreds it symbolized, the lethal barriers that divided East and West, and reminders of Nazi Germany: some 140 kilometers from Dinkelsbühl lies the town of Dachau, itself a profoundly confusing dichotomy, with its beautiful surroundings and the bleak horror of the death camp.

Hartley knew nothing of Dachau, of course, nor of the bitternesses of post–World War II Europe, but he had a great feeling and love for the Germans; and somehow everything that constitutes the nation is what he came to understand about life and rendered in his painting. He was no George Grosz, changing the expressionists' slogan from "man is good" to "man is a beast" and painting scathing caricatures of him en masse. Hartley understood beauty, and cruelty, and love, and death, and like any other great artist, he painted them, in his landscapes and seascapes as in his abstractions, his naive portraits, and even his still lifes. There is a newness about his works, as he would have wished, but they are also about the same old, fundamental matters always, and that is why we keep coming back to them.

Chapel Hill, North Carolina
October 1991

MARSDEN HARTLEY

A Partial Portrait

I

On July 20, 1943, the American painter Marsden Hartley boarded an evening train in New York to travel to Maine. Sixty-six years old, he was in poor health, overweight and suffering from a weak heart. Nevertheless, he was bent on returning to Corea, a small coastal village near Mount Desert Island, where he had lived the previous three summers. Maine was his native state, and after shunning it for many years, during the late 1930s he had returned each summer for a time, staying in such places as Georgetown, Vinalhaven, and West Brooksville before finding Corea, which suited him well because it had the visual qualities and the sorts of people he sought. Nineteen forty-three was wartime, and the train was crowded with military personnel. Porters were not available to help him with his luggage as he changed trains, and the entire trip was long, so that by the time he arrived in Corea he was exhausted.

Two weeks later he sat in the small upstairs room he rented in the modest home of Forrest and Katie Young and wrote to his young friend Richard Sisson, an Army technical sergeant stationed in New York. Hartley was immensely attracted to Sisson, a tall, extremely handsome man of twenty-five with a deep interest in the arts. He told Sisson that his heart fluttered constantly and that he slept little. He was able to move about only with considerable difficulty and was in more physical pain than he had ever been before during a life marked by frequent illnesses. But he sounded cheerful in his letter as he chattered away about many things. He missed his young friend, who during the previous winter and spring had sometimes joined him for dinner near the Hotel Winslow, where Hartley had a small room. Occasionally they had strolled back to the hotel after dinner and continued their discussions for several hours. Hartley had enjoyed his role as sage, and now he remembered "all the dear times we had together and how happy I was with you close to me."

Although a local doctor had told him that he should remain quiet, he expected to paint some and to complete a book of poems and another volume he was writing about the circus. Had Sisson by any chance seen a one-ring circus called Spangles? He must, for it was "a darling show" in which there was a white horse that looked like "a page out of Wm. Blake's prophetic books." And just before leaving New York Hartley had seen the film *For Whom the Bell Tolls,* which was "a BUM film" with a bit of good acting but mostly "hog-wash," with Hartley's "beloved G[ary] Cooper so handicapped by a stupid role he couldn't show up like anything," and Ingrid Bergman too pretty and blond for her part. Hartley's friend Monroe Wheeler had called it "Hell's Bells for Whom." Hartley admitted he would like to take a year away from painting, but, proud to be a member of the "racing stable" of the noted dealer Paul Rosenberg, he knew he must show new work.

He spoke excitedly about the Coptic art he had been collecting, choosing the pieces for their colors. No other painter had a collection like his, he was sure, and he was especially pleased with a Chinese head and three bronzes he had obtained in exchange for several of his paintings. He had given Sisson a small Coptic in celebration of his twenty-fifth birthday, but also "to enlarge [his] esthetic scope." Sisson was an avid admirer of Paul Klee's work, and Hartley wanted his young friend to broaden his vision. "It is nice to like Klee & have some nice ones," Hartley wrote, but the Swiss was of course "a minor artist" whose work lacked "depth of emotion in the larger sense." He was interested to hear from Sisson of a party Wheeler had given for his companion, the novelist Glenway Wescott, to which the poet Marianne Moore had come. Hartley had recently met a "most nice little artist fella" who had agreed to do the cover for his book about the circus. The artist, Hans Moller, would certainly make the cover "light and charming and playful," for that was the tone of the book. A lot of it was written already, and he hoped to complete everything during the summer, especially since it ought to be very salable. Now Hartley wanted to get his note in the mail. "Please call this a letter," he ended, "& know that I love you most dearly — you are very close to me." He urged Sisson to write, and added, "just tell me you love me & I shall be happy."

Sisson, embarrassed by Hartley's effusiveness but sensing his loneliness and real fear of death, responded. Hartley immediately wrote back, "What a lad you are — and do I cherish you! — Yes!!" He proceeded to speak of a fine young doctor near Corea who was testing him for high blood pressure. The doctor assured him there was no danger of a sudden catastrophe. He had been sleeping better — but enough of that, he declared, and he filled the rest of his letter with talk about his distaste for the artist Joan Miró and for the later Picasso "of the two eyed faces," though heaven knew he had done much of the best work of the century. Picasso was "a scholar in the paint itself," as was Rouault. Good painting made a good picture, in Hartley's opinion.

He talked about many other things: his beloved Coptics, having to stretch his own canvasses, his idea of moving soon to the Southwest to paint, the handsome people in Corea, the experiences of his landlady, Katie Young, and his renewed effort to paint despite his weakness. "Well dear one," he closed, "I . . . love you deeply."[1] On September 1 he was taken to a hospital in the nearby town of Ellsworth, where early the next morning he died of myocarditis, inflammation of the heart tissue.

Did this man who clutched so hard to life and companionship — and who was brimming over with ideas and plans — die content? Alfred Stieglitz, the photographer, gallery owner, and supporter of Hartley as well as of such artists as Georgia O'Keeffe, John Marin, and Arthur Dove, thought he did. Hartley had had some recent financial success, had been taken on by the outstanding dealer Paul Rosenberg, and in his last years had been able to do some of the things he had yearned to do. "Hartley is one of the luckiest men that I have ever met. He died at the right moment," Stieglitz declared in a letter, adding that Hartley had been full of life when he left New York for Corea, even though he had become overweight and lacked strength. Still, Stieglitz maintained, he could attend concerts, the theater, and exhibitions "and could walk Fifth Avenue and 57th Street in real Hartley fashion." To the last Stieglitz had enjoyed the other's stories; Hartley was a good talker who would be missed by many people. He would have an important place in American art, Stieglitz asserted, a judgment whose truth time has amply borne out.[2]

II

Hartley's luck had not always been so good, and he had several qualities that made him particularly difficult, among them a tendency to imagine that others were snubbing him, a shyness that was frequently interpreted as hauteur, and a dependence on others that arose from a gnawing condition of poverty. While he had a sense of humor — generally expressed in the form of comments on the ironies of life — he was often painfully reserved, a trait that could throw him into despair when he felt he needed to put himself forward. "Why can't a man like myself be put on his feet in a manner he can respect," he complained to the artist Rockwell Kent in 1920 as he searched desperately for financial support. Hartley was sure he had fine credentials, but he could not bring himself to "go out and play the rotten game now." His situation half prostrated him, so typically he threw himself on a friend.[3] One acquaintance, while liking him, thought that his introversion stemmed from his looks. She remembered him as one of the ugliest men she had ever met — his large nose and jutting chin gave him the look of Guignol, the French puppet.[4]

The critic Paul Rosenfeld captured the complex artist's attractive side when he wrote that reading Hartley's book of informal essays, *Adventures in the Arts,* published in 1921, was like

> having shared in the best of the conversation; of having met him on Fifth Avenue with swagger-stick, gardenia, and Scotch shawl, in a fair mood produced, say, by the news that he had been elected corresponding member of the international society of dadas; of having strolled with him, looked into shop windows, visited a gallery or two, taken a turn at a vaudeville house, stepped into a circus dressing room while commenting epigrammatically on some of the problems present to the modern artist.

He was "a distraught Brummel among the American moderns, seeking to drown himself in a sea of handsome color and animal grace." Rosenfeld, no slouch with colorful language, referred to Hartley as an "elongated person with ... Pied Piper eyes and Emersonian proboscis who very probably dreams of living a sort of Heliogabalus, amid porphyry, purple, and gold, of wearing heavy robes of the Tyrian dye, and strolling languorously down galleries attended by a horde of servants carrying things."[5] Such private dreams Hartley may have had, and when the going was relatively good he liked to dress with a flair — swagger stick, gardenia, shawl, and all — but when things took their not infrequent bad turns, he reflected that too. The son of a friend remembered seeing the same man who liked fancy dress attired, in the early 1930s, in a pajama top and a threadbare coat, with a gaunt, unshaven look.[6]

His temperament was mercurial. One of the things that made him appealing was his appreciation for the vagaries and vicissitudes of life. "My problem is just as dull as yours is," he wrote near the end of his life to his intimate friend Carl Sprinchorn, an artist who had had little notable success during his long career. "I don't care as there is always a moment to finish it," he continued, "and yet how we cling to life — and the clamour of the simple physical self is so strident against all the questionings and philosophizings and faith does not increase with the years." Whatever success Hartley himself had had was "all gaff and hogwash — all that. How grand a sensation it must have been," he supposed, "for a poet like Arthur Rimbaud, who at 20 had created a new impulse in French literature, and then gave it up, never wrote another line, went off to various Orients to deal in rugs and pearls and forget the 'grandeur and the glory of art.'"[7]

As he was toward Sprinchorn, Hartley was frequently considerate, a model of gentleness and humor who could write to a friend's cat and sign himself "Mr. Starshoveller Birdsong."[8] He could also be a paragon of unsureness, however, exasperating even his closest friends with his inability to look after himself and with his consequent demands. Gertrude Stein, who liked him, caught something of his fluttery side and his ubiquitous conversation in an abstract portrait of him in her play *1:*

MARSDEN HARTLEY

A cook. A cook can see. Pointedly in uniform, exertion in a medium. A cook can see.

Clark which is awful, clark which is shameful, clark and order.

A pin is a plump point and pecking and combined and more much more is in fine.

Rats is, rats is oaken, robber. Height, age, miles, plaster, peddle, more order.

Bake, a barn has cause and more late oak-cake specially.

Spend rubber, holder and coal, high, careful, in a pointed collar. A hideous southwest is always a climb in aged seldom succeeded flavoring untimely, necessity white, hour in a blaze.

Break, sky blue light obliquely, in a cut carpet, in the pack. A sound.

MARSDEN HARTLEY

No noon back. No noon settler, no sun in the slant and carpet utterly surrounded.

No pressed plaster. None.

No pressing pan and pan cake. Not related exactly. Not related.

Matter in the center of single sand and slide in the hut.

No account of gibberish. No skylark utterly.

This passage and more from the play were included in a catalogue for a 1914 exhibition of Hartley's paintings at Alfred Stieglitz's famous New York gallery 291.[9]

Georgia O'Keeffe, an intimate part of Steiglitz's circle from the moment in 1916 when he first saw her work, could take Hartley only in small doses. He, fully aware that she was a privileged rival for Stieglitz's attention, was fond of but condescending toward her, regarding her as most male critics did: as a good — even fine — artist, but a woman, after all, and unintellectual, totally intuitive, and unconcerned about the intimacy of her paintings. "One of the exceptional girls of the world both in art and in life," Hartley called her in 1921, and he asserted that her paintings were "probably as living and shameless private documents as exist, in painting certainly, and probably in any other art." From the start she found him too full of "heat and clamor," and the first paintings of his that she saw, the German military series exhibited at 291 in April 1916, struck her as being "like a brass band in a small closet." He "began a painting in a state of great excitement but could not sustain his commitment," she thought.[10]

The poet William Carlos Williams wrote that in the early 1920s Hartley was "a sort of grandpapa to us all — male and female alike — with his taste for tweeds, his broad padded shoulders and loveableness. We all adored him," he declared with a touch of hyperbole. Hartley, however, had a face that doomed him, the nose of a Wellington, enormous, projecting from the edge of his face like a medieval pike's point. . . . Marsden was one of the best men of the group; his small Dresden China blue eyes under savage brows made him look as if he were about to eat you. Which he would have liked, I suppose, to have done. We none of us took him seriously — except in his work. He was too kind.[11]

More than one person had reservations about Hartley. Among these was Eugene O'Neill, who had met him in the summer of 1916 in Provincetown, Massachusetts. In his play *Strange Interlude* O'Neill created a character, Charles Marsden, who has much of the painter Charles Demuth and a touch of Hartley about him.*

He is described as "a tall thin man of thirty-five, meticulously well dressed in tweeds of distinctly English tailoring, his appearance that of an Anglicized New England gentleman." O'Neill revealed something about both men when he gave Marsden a "face too long for its width," a nose "high and narrow," a broad forehead, and the eyes "of a dreamy self-analyst," with "thin lips ironical and a bit sad." The character has an "indefinable feminine quality about him," stooped shoulders, and a fragile constitution. But there is as well a charm and an "appealing, inquisitive friendliness," a desire to sympathize and to be accepted.[12]

O'Neill was not simply mocking the two artists in his portrait but drawing from what he knew to create a character whose timidity and fear of life act as a kind of foil to the tumultuous passions that swirl about him. Marsden loathes sexuality; love should be pure, and platonic, he believes. Yet in some ways he feels disgust for himself, for having been "born afraid . . . afraid of myself." He thinks himself "neither hated nor loved" — liked, yes, but that is all. He is "dear old Charlie" to people, "dear old Rover, nice old doggie,"[13] and his life as he sees it is "cool green shade wherein comes no scorching zenith sun of passion and possession to wither the heart with bitter poisons."[14] It is understandable that O'Neill, with his own scorching zenith suns,

---

*In *Charles Demuth* (New York: Whitney Museum of American Art, 1987) Barbara Haskell, citing Louis Sheaffer, *O'Neill: Son and Artist,* observes in a footnote that Charles Marsden is based primarily on Demuth. But in the next footnote she quotes O'Neill as saying that he had "known many Marsdens on many different levels of life," a remark that "would indicate that the character reflected many of O'Neill's general ruminations" (page 65). Precisely, and reason to think that there is something of Hartley in the character of Charles Marsden.

would find the reserved Hartley thus, whose considerable tribulations were of a different sort.

In the last decade of Hartley's life, the artist and political leftist Fairfield Porter, who knew him quite well, had occasion to write to the poet John Brooks Wheelwright, himself on the left. Porter had recently seen Hartley at an exhibition of his work and found him "hard to talk to because of his deafness, and because he is bitter and contemptuous, so that he turns your remarks into something absurd and silly." Porter had given Hartley Wheelwright's address; Hartley had sneered at it because it was on Boston's stylish Beacon Street but observed that if it had to be there, at least it was on the better part of the street. "He probably prefers the poor and the Proletariat to 'Society,'" observed Porter, "but he is a reactionary just the same, I think. However, he is a real artist, who deserves better treatment from the world." Wheelwright responded that he thought Hartley a good but lifeless painter; Porter pointed out that this was a paradoxical statement, and added, "Hartley's still lifes have more life than for instance Grant Wood's people, even more Humanity."[15]

Porter's term *reactionary* was part of the inflated rhetoric of the time; Hartley did, in fact, sympathize with the poor and the proletariat, but he cared little for politics. When in the early 1930s he admired Adolf Hitler, it was not for his politics — the sordid realities of which Hartley paid little attention to — but for the discipline, order, and dignity that he seemed to be restoring to the German people. When Hartley came to understand what Hitler was about, he detested it and mourned for the Germany he had known before Hitler's rise to power. Hartley had little enough use for capitalism, as it had not treated him particularly well. Socially he may have been snobbish, but it was less a matter of class than of disdain for those who he believed lacked intellectual and aesthetic taste. He admired thinking people and scorned the art crowd, the people with money who followed the dictates of the critics. He disliked those people who seemed to him too conventional, or just too stupid, to comprehend modernism. And late in his life, when he was weighed down with deafness and frail health, his bitterness and contempt surfaced. He made demands on people who sought to help him, and then he either took them for granted or was gruff and ingracious in return. Louise Young, the daughter of Forrest and Katie Young, with whom he lived in Corea, remembered the lack of thanks she received for driving Hartley around the coast so he could study scenes that he wanted later to paint. One Christmas when he was staying with her family she bought a scarf for him out of her ten-dollar-a-week salary, along with presents for her family. Opening his gift, he glanced quickly at it, turned to Louise's grandfather, and asked, "Here, you want it?" When another time she did her best to take some photos of him and they did not turn out well, he stalked away annoyed.[16]

He came to have a strong sense of his own importance in his last years, and it took an understanding person to cope with that. Chenoweth Hall, a young sculptress living near Corea, respected his talent but at the same time found him aloof, haughty, vain, and disdainful. He snubbed her mother when he was invited to see some jeweled watches she owned. At the Youngs' small restaurant in Corea, where Hartley always sat at the same table, he ignored other summer residents who might have a genuine interest in talking with him. It was not uncommon, if he was approached by one of them, for him to put his finger under his nose and walk away. "He was really *not* a very nice man," in Hall's opinion.[17]

It took an understanding person also to tolerate his miserliness. Almost all of his life he scraped along, borrowing, scrimping, and going without everything from new clothes to adequate meals. In complex ways his hauteur late in life was the result of his earlier having had to ask for help. He built up in his mind the idea that others had not been sufficiently responsive — had not recognized his worth, both as artist and as person — and so he scorned all but those he considered close friends. But even when he had money, his longtime habits endured. One good friend, Rebecca Strand, who had been extremely generous to Hartley in many ways, remembered his having small candies that he ate constantly but never offered to others. And Catherine Evans, the wife of John Evans, Mabel Dodge's son, recalled that when Hartley stayed with them in Maine in 1939, he would scoop up the carton's worth of cigarettes that she put in a bowl each week in her front hall. He never thought to replace them, and even after she took to buying him a carton of his own, he would still scoop up the cigarettes in the bowl. One had to be tolerant.[18]

He could be extremely touchy. When William Carlos Williams wrote him a letter that he found overly gossipy and intimate, Hartley bridled. "I hate gossip and I hate intimacy," he lashed out, and then he proceeded to lecture Williams at some length about his imposing too much on their friendship. He had attributed to Hartley some statement or deed that Hartley felt he had not said or done. "You do not allow for the quality of imagination which you will admit is without moral — and for which you have a genuine gift," he wrote. He was offended by what he saw as glibness on Williams's part:

> Just let me tell you Bill — I am never intimate with anyone. I never know anyone so much that I feel I am entirely at home. You baffle me as much as anyone I have ever come in contact with — barring none — and it is because you veil your reality with charm which is the only excuse for talking to or being with anyone. Not that the story you tell me is troubling, but that you assume so much security of attitude. You shall never be able to be specific with me dear Bill — because in my life no one is that real. I can tolerate no one more than for their capacity to "create" themselves in my presence.

In an obtuse fashion Hartley was placing limits upon their relationship by saying that friendship was nonexistent and that acquaintance could be only "a fine fancy in human shape," a fancy that would be "destroyed by the wearer."[19] Hartley's large nose was severely out of joint; at that moment he was being supremely self-pitying — annoying, Williams must have thought, his gestures of intimacy hardly worth the effort. "I really loved the man," he later declared, "but we didn't always get along together, except at a distance."[20]

Hartley's stance was typical of his last years, when he sometimes became the "bitter and contemptuous" person that Fairfield Porter described. But it was a pose that his intimate friends understood, and none more so than Adelaide Kuntz, his closest woman friend from the 1920s on, to whom he wrote, "I get feeling sometimes you are the only one I really can talk to, so just let me jabber and jibber on and think it sounds like sense." A year after his death she wrote to Hudson Walker, Hartley's dealer from 1937 to 1940, to express her annoyance at the critics who seemed not to comprehend Hartley. They treated him as "a sophisticate they dare to patronize," she claimed. In contrast, she saw him, "in spite of a complex nature," as "essentially a simple soul, in that he was uncorrupted, utterly honest, and unpretentious." Her fondness for him prevented her from perceiving his weaknesses, but her portrait is a moving statement about his character and friendships:

> He loved flowers, insects, birds, minerals, children, as well as mountains and music, poetry and painting. He loved spectacles and crowds, as he says, and people great and small everywhere. He highly respected the bourgeois virtues. And the perfect family, he was always seeking out and bowing before. . . . Marsden was a truly dignified man. He had a great respect therefore always for dignity in human relations. He was not really a talkative man — but he saw more with his blazing blue eyes than anyone I ever knew, and he thought constantly and he wrote a great deal. His mind functioned with little rest — he told me once that he always kept pencil and paper by his bedside and that when he woke in the night and couldn't sleep, he could write down what he was thinking. Marsden Hartley was an honorable man, a really loyal friend. He worshipped his friends and never renounced them and he was endlessly appreciative of every crumb of kindness thrown his way. He had self respect and thank God he believed in himself and his talents, and gathered to his heart every word of what he felt was deserved praise — so that one needn't mourn lest he felt unappreciated. He was a very responsive person. You will see in reading his letters to me how the best ones are called forth by what he found to be a cheerful or alive one from me, or else by warmth and stimulation from some other source; more likely new people rather than new scenes. He insisted that he wanted solitude but I noticed that he drooped under neglect and would have been a very lonely man except for his constantly creative mind under stimuli. And he found stimulation everywhere in the most unexpected places and things.

Although his line of thought was "arabesque," she believed it to be consistent. While he was intuitive and instinctive, he found order beautiful and worshiped beauty. She maintained that "all his life he fought fear, fear of starving, fear of death mentally and physically." What she admired was that he had fought and searched for answers and order in metaphysics. "He built up defenses and hid himself from sight at times not only to avoid being hurt but to save his sense of human dignity." She had found him courageous, zestful, and eager for the future even as his health deteriorated. Only at the end, because of physical illness and a touch of "worldly success," had he taken on "an air of ponderousness bordering on pomposity. But remember that Marsden was dramatic," she added, recalling that he had once admitted to acting like a prima donna on occasion. She thought that in his last years he had enjoyed the "role of sage." To her he had seemed unique, "a human being par excellence, friendly and kind, akin to all people, sharing weakness and frailties, but arising above most of them. He was my friend and I shall miss him the rest of my days," she wrote, and concluded gently:

> The last time I saw Marsden was on a hot summer Sunday late afternoon just before he set off on his last visit to Maine. He had lingered late in town as if loath to depart and as if saying many wordless goodbyes. We met by chance in the Museum of Modern Art and I had with me my son, then sixteen, whom he had known from the time he was born, but had not seen for almost a year because the boy had been away in school. Marsden was overjoyed to see him again, and now almost a man, and very formally invited us to dinner "out of doors on a terrace." He finally decided to take us to the roof of his hotel, where we dined in the sunset overlooking "the towers of New York" which he loved. He seemed completely happy and proudly introduced us to some of the inhabitants of the hotel as we went to and from our table. "Now they can see that I am not just that weird lonely man they have thought, but that I have a family too — May I call you that?" It was infinitely touching to me, especially as I sensed his pride in being able at last, after all the years of fear of spending[,] to entertain his friends with some lavishness. I shall always remember him like that, with his extraordinary gaze steadfast under the glow of the late sun in his face.[21]

1

New England
1877 – 1900

HARTLEY WAS BORN on January 4, 1877, in the small industrial town of Lewiston, Maine. Situated immediately below the Great Falls on the Androscoggin River, Lewiston grew up in the 1840s as a utopian mill community along the lines of Lowell and Lawrence, Massachusetts, mill cities that had developed several decades earlier. Benjamin Bates, who founded the Bates Mills in Lewiston, had made his money in Lowell and used the mills there as models for the community he would try to create along the Androscoggin. But by the time of Hartley's birth much of the utopian atmosphere — if ever there had been one — had dissipated amid the huge, redbrick mill buildings, the increasing grime of industry, and the system of class and caste that prevailed among the growing population. The social scale was symbolized by the geography of the residences: on a small rise called English Hill, which overlooked the mills along the river, lived many Britishers who had migrated to the town to work. Below the rise was Gaspatch, home to many of the Irish workers, and below that was Little Canada, inhabited by French Canadians.

Hartley's parents were both English. Thomas, a Lancashire man, came to Lewiston in the 1850s to work as a cotton spinner, and Eliza Horbury, a native of Staleybridge, Yorkshire, soon joined him. They married, and in 1859 their first child, Elizabeth Ann, was born. Eventually there would be eight children who lived through infancy; a ninth, Thomas, died soon after birth, and a tenth, George, died at birth. John, the third child and oldest boy, died in 1874, so Hartley, the youngest, knew none of his brothers; and as the sister next to him in age was almost five years older than he, he was in a sense an only child, with a mother who was "strong, expressive, executive in plain matters, ultra maternal."[1]

Thomas Hartley, whom his son described as "a good, poetic reserved person," had little money, so the family lived not on English Hill but down below on Lincoln Street, near the mills, in a drab, four-story house from which one could hear not only the noise of the mills but also the rush of the Androscoggin below the Great Falls. Born Edmund (he would assume his stepmother's given name, Marsden, in 1906), Hartley thought himself "the most obstreperous, spiritually speaking, the last, the least found, the most troubled." Though dramatized, his description is essentially accurate. He was, as he said, "frail, shy, diffident, and in a child's way suspicious of everything but the sunlight," so that during his years amid the drab surroundings of the mills with their tough youths, the timid boy must have often been frightened and lonely. He recalled in a poem that

> My childhood which was hard, it is always
> hard to be alone at the wrong time,
> brought seizures of intensity to the years;
> the harsh grinding of the mills rang in
> my ears for years — and a sordid sort of music
> came out of it.

In the same poem he remembered that the mills and factories had seemed "gigantic . . . , monstrous, terrifying, prison-like."

But his early years were not unremittingly gloomy. He also recalled playing in Franklin Pasture, a big field partway across town from Lincoln Street that was "the Asia and Africa of our first impressions" and probably the same place where in spring he walked along the edge of a small stream with his reserved father and gathered flowers, and in autumn, mushrooms. In winter there was tobogganing, and at any time the excitement of seeing town characters such as Dr. Alonzo Garcelon, whom the children dubbed "Dr. Gasselon" and who liked to race his buggy through Haymarket Square; Lizzie Janes, a plump, hairy-faced woman with a twitch in her eyes who played the organ at Trinity Church, at the corner of the town green, where Hartley as a child sang alto in the choir; and a gaunt, tall woman nicknamed Skinny Jinny, who was reputed to carry a butcher knife under her black shawl to use on little children, whom she supposedly hated.[2]

The introverted boy's most enjoyable moments were those spent by himself in the Franklin Pasture as he walked to his grammar school. Within the pasture was a wooded area, where near a brook he would dally to study the many flowers until the school bell rang and he had to hurry on to class. His classmates, several of whom he later came to admire, frightened him then.[3] He did not smile much; it is more than a little sad that his not unusual early childhood was symbolized in his mind by the death of a white kitten. He and his sister Lillian grieved for it and, having laid it in a saltbox, carried it to Franklin Pasture, where they buried it on a small knoll surrounded by boxberry leaves. The kitten's death, "a strong love of flowers," and later "mountains, . . . the sea, delicacy, strength, [and] moving forms" were what he saw as "the foundations of all that was to come" in his life.[4]

His fragile ego was crushed when, on March 4, 1885, two months after his eighth birthday, his mother died. According to his niece Norma Berger, he never really recovered from his horror at Eliza's illness and death. Late in his life he spoke of it, about "how he had seen her lying in her bed, her face so white, and she was so quiet, and eventually she was gone and there was this . . . what to him, was the horrible experience of a funeral, a black hearse, and relatives and friends following, going to the cemetery."[5] With her death, most of something that he would crave all his life — a sense of order — was destroyed.

His father was preoccupied with trying to make ends meet; after some years as a spinner at the mills he had taken a job posting bills for a local theater that belonged to Eliza's brother, Charles Horbury. He could not manage the household, so the two youngest daughters were sent to Cleveland to be with their older sister Sara, who was already living there. Hartley went to live with another sister in nearby Auburn, Maine. The result of this family split was, for Hartley, a deepening sense of isolation. After the death of Eliza, "my father succumbed to the general uncertainties," he wrote, "having one different child on his hands, who because of [the father's] absence throughout the entire day, became in psychology an orphan, in consciousness a lone left thing to make its way out for all time after that by itself."[6]

In part Hartley brought his loneliness upon himself; Thomas was an amiable enough man who would have liked to be close to his only living son. But Hartley had been his mother's boy and resented his father, who in his eyes had broken up the family. Only late in life did he realize that the best way for him to gain his father's respect would have been to help support him.* He did not — could not — help, however, and a barrier grew between them from early on.[7]

Hartley's oldest sister, Elizabeth, with whom he lived in Auburn, was the only one who really figured in his life during the years between Eliza's death and 1889, when, on August 20, Thomas married Martha Marsden, eight years younger than he. Hartley accompanied his father when he went to England to fetch Martha and bring her back to America. Many years later, he told Adelaide Kuntz that he had "actually been in the Yorkshire Moors . . . I was eleven then & of course pathetically sensitive as I really am now — my father was over — getting my stepmother to come to us." Hartley was fond of her and referred to her as "the new good stepmother, also an Englishwoman out of Staleybridge," who became "the littlest thinnest part of the reconstructed family" in Cleveland, where she and Thomas moved soon after their wedding to join the three daughters who were already there.[8] Hartley remained behind with Elizabeth. Despite her kindnesses, his sense of isolation was exacerbated; more than ever he felt "left with myself to discover myself amid the multitudinous other and far greater mysteries."[9] The process must have been dreary; he said little about the time between his father and stepmother's move to Cleveland and his joining them in 1893, when he was sixteen. The year before he had dropped out of school and taken work in Auburn for three dollars a week in a shoe factory, where his task was to check the lots of shoes as they passed from one department to another.[10]

In Cleveland he took another job at three dollars a week, this one as office boy at a marble quarry along the muddy Cuyahoga River. The work itself was hardly exciting — sweeping the company offices and running errands for the superintendent — but Hartley was exhilarated by the various marbles: yellow Pavanazzo "veined with

---

*In a poem, "Family Album in Red Plush" (*The Collected Poems of Marsden Hartley, 1904–1943*, page 280), written in the last years of his life, Hartley made a sort of peace with his father, portraying him as good, and average — which was the artist's problem with him from the start, of course. The poem ends:

> [My father] was clean-mouthed, clean-souled, proud of being honest,
>   avoided being conspicuous in any other way
> The finest people in the world are those who act in the right way;
> My mother and father were among them.

purple black"; verde antique, green with whitish veins; and dark and Numidian, as well as Carrara, onyx, and lovely granites. These heightened his taste for color even as he was developing a curiosity about art, which he linked with a growing interest in sex. Because he shied away from "concrete escapades," he later wrote, he "inclined to abstract ones and the collection of objects which is a sex expression."[11] However accurate his reading of his own sexuality may have been, through art he found some release from his frustrations as a shy adolescent.

Hartley continued to work at the marble quarry for the next few years as he became more deeply intrigued by art. The art historian Barbara Haskell sets 1896 as the year when Hartley was one day led to "some gloomy looking art studios on the top floor" of the City Hall building on Superior Street in Cleveland. There he was introduced to John Semon, "a landscape painter of the Barbizon persuasion and by no means a bad painter." Hartley remembered him as "a sort of self-invented cross between Corot and Theodore Rousseau — smoked his pipe incessantly and painted as I recall nothing but beechwoods with their golden bark and spreading roots embedded in luscious mosses."[12] He arranged with his employer to take Monday mornings off to study with Semon, which cost him one of the three dollars he earned each week. Hartley's interest grew; he began other art classes and for a period took a sketching class with six or eight other students. And somewhere during this time — Haskell puts the date in the summer of 1898 — he was invited by Cullen Yates, "a very blonde pink young man of manners of the same hue" who had come to Cleveland "direct from Paris," to join his summer class.[13]*

Sometime during this period Hartley also took a two-week vacation with Semon, who owned a place in southern Ohio. Apparently upon his return he was fired from his job, his superintendent, Hartley thought, recognizing that the young painter would be of little use in the marble or any other business.[14] This probably occurred during the summer of 1898, for Hartley could only have stopped working if his studies were subsidized, which was the case after a wealthy trustee of the Cleveland School of Art saw some of his work for Yates's class. At the Cleveland School the most notable influence on him was Nina Waldeck, the teacher of drawing, who gave him a copy of Ralph

---

*In the 1930s, when Hartley wrote his autobiography, his memory was vague, to say the least. More important than exact dating is the fact that as his interest in art developed, he spent increasing time studying it.

Waldo Emerson's *Essays,* a book that, Hartley noted, "I was to carry in my pocket for the at least five ensuing years — reading it on all occasions as a priest reads his latin breviary on all occasions, it seemed so made just for me — circles, friendship, the Over-Soul, and all that."

He claimed it was "the first book I had ever read," and certainly it was the first that was important: he credited it with providing "the religious element in my experience." In it Emerson articulated ideas about which Hartley had already begun to think deeply.[15] One has only to read in the essay "Nature" such lines as "In the woods, we return to reason and faith," "Nature always wears the colors of the spirit," or "A work of art is an abstract or epitome of the world" to understand why Hartley was so taken with the American transcendentalist. He would read much during his lifetime — he was truly an intellectual, if the definition of that breed is someone in love with books and ideas — but no writer he came upon ever answered his needs better than Emerson, who struggled to explain imagination and intellect and the relationship between them. Understanding for Emerson was grounded in experience, which gave meaning to man's gropings within the realm of the mind. And it was just so, too, for Hartley; as the scholar Gail Scott has asserted about his many essays,

> There emerges from his writings an effort to forge a resolution to this conflict between the imaginative and intellectual forces of consciousness, a resolution inherent in his fundamental belief that "life itself" — experience — is the source of creative consciousness and action.[16]

When he first read Emerson's work, Hartley was not yet writing essays of his own, but by the age of twenty-one or twenty-two he had begun to puzzle about the tugs in his considerable mind between the objective reality around him and his imagination, between the fact of the natural world and his vision of it. How did one render one's experience of nature, all those things a sensitive person felt about what he or she experienced? Was there some soul in nature to which a person could become attuned? Early on, in a conventional fashion, Hartley wanted to believe there was; later he could no longer do so. But he never abandoned his fascination with the mystery of nature — hence his constant attraction to the mystics, who felt akin to the world beyond them. When in the last twelve or so years of his life Hartley painted his most forceful work, it was because he had achieved some kind of reconciliation of these dichotomies. Part of that reconciliation was his sense that there were no final answers; but there was this force called nature, and it was powerful and destroyed things and people. Still, there *were* people, and colors, and sometimes form and beauty, and all this spoke to a person and could give him or her a reason to be. In this sense Hartley was a modernist. Gail Scott again: "Hartley was caught up in a dilemma that occupied a generation of artists and thinkers who were responsible for the shift from the nineteenth-century polarity of romanticism and naturalism to twentieth-century modernism, in which a new spirit began to predominate."[17] Modernist painting has taken a number of forms, and Hartley experimented with many of them, but always he was seeking to express something of the relationship among imagination, intellect, and experience.

In 1898, however, Hartley was far from understanding these matters. Not until 1909, after he discovered the work of Albert Pinkham Ryder, did he begin to develop a style that could express what he felt, and not until the 1930s could he meld that with other styles to produce his fullest, most mature work. In Cleveland he was still learning to draw. Nina Waldeck helped him, and his work was good enough to attract the attention of one of the School of Art's trustees, Anne Walworth, who offered him a stipend of four hundred and fifty dollars a year for study, either in Cincinnati or in New York. He chose the latter, so the pattern of his life for the next thirteen years, until his departure for Europe in 1912, became New York during the winter and Lewiston or someplace nearby during the summer — which was important because it meant that as he learned his art, Maine and all it was, rather than Cleveland, poured in on him.[18]

In the fall of 1899 he moved to New York City to study at the New York School of Art, dominated by the flamboyant William Merritt Chase. Hartley did not take classes from Chase — he worked instead with competent, if less exciting, artists such as Luis Mora for drawing and Frank Vincent Dumond for composition — but what he remembered most about the School of Art was Chase's Saturday-morning performances. The man had a strong sense of himself. You *knew* when Chase was about, Hartley wrote later; he was "a kind of social spectacle" who was "always in correct morning dress, dark coat-tails and striped trousers, eyeglasses with a long silk ribbon, and the inevitable turquoise ring on a dark tie." The shy Hartley was amused by the Saturday scenes, which had Chase strutting before a room "full of well to do young ladies" and their mothers, who hoped to hear praise from the great man. He would move about, pausing dramatically whenever he found some special touch in the work of one or another student. Then "he would adjust his necktie ring once again, preen his mustaches, make a little lisping sound, flicking his fingers as if he were flicking ashes from a smoke, and [say] bravo to the innumerable little flash touches of paint on the red pepper and the copper pot, or the ever inveigling fish[,] for he was always painting them himself" — even if his had a certain "society look" about them, Hartley added sardonically. For all his amusement, he admired Chase, who spoke well about painting, understood the brushstroke, and particularly admired performance for its own sake.[19]

During the first year of his study in New York, Hartley spent a relatively fruitless "month of afternoons at the Art Students League, with eight criticisms from Kenyon Cox," a talented, if extremely conservative, artist and critic whose every instinct ran contrary to the direction in which Hartley was to turn. In fact, the instruction of that entire year seems to have had scant effect upon Hartley. He moved about during his early years in New York; in the late fall of 1900 he shifted to the National Academy of Design, partly because it was cheaper and partly because he felt he would learn more. There he continued to take classes for several years under the tutelage of several artists, including Francis C. Jones, whom Hartley called his "only influence for he showed me much about a way of painting and from him I learned how to approach a way of painting living white." Another instructor, Edgar M. Ward, insisted that Hartley try painting with crayon sauce, pastel in the form of a soft cake. "I never took his criticisms afterward," Hartley remarked. "All stipple, no body."[20] It is worth noting, however, that in Hartley's works before he discovered Ryder, there is a fair amount of stipple.

Largely unimpressed by the orthodoxy of these instructors, Hartley was nevertheless very much the student, affected by his association with other pupils at the Academy of Design — among them Abraham Walkowitz and Maurice Sterne, both of whom would become well known for their modernist work — and by the paintings of established artists such as George Inness and John Twachtman. Another instructor at the Academy, J. Scott Hartley (no relation), was Inness's son-in-law and took Hartley the student to see Inness's studio and his pallettes. "[He] was my ideal when I was in school at the Nat. Academy," Hartley wrote many years later.[21] Such moments as the studio visit were important: Hartley's awareness of Inness's Barbizon work and of Twachtman's impressionism, which was more concerned with poetic vision than with realism, helped to give form to what he experienced in the Maine countryside during the summer. He was deeply absorbed in his work; someone who knew him then recalled that after seeing her interest in art, Hartley visited her frequently in Lewiston in the summer of 1900. "He was an interesting conversationalist," Frances Holmes Everett remembered, "but so intense that he was almost bewildering."[22]

"Bewildering" was a good description. All sorts of things were bearing down on Hartley, and his intensity reflected his own bewilderment. He had traveled to Lewiston from New York in May 1900, to live in the family home, to which his father and stepmother had returned from Cleveland. His mind swirled with the crosscurrents between big city and small town, between family and independence, between orthodoxy in art and what he felt, and with his own everpresent conflict about solitude. He found his acquaintances from earlier days caught up in their own work, he told an art-student friend from New York, and he felt lonely; "but I hope before many days pass to get out to beloved Nature and there find my happiness and comfort," he added. Hartley at that time hoped to find solace in a conventional sort of religious transcendentalism. To his friend he explained, "There is nothing that sets all things at peace with me as a communion with Nature. She seems to have a balm for every pain and a cheerful song for every sorrowing heart. I can always find rest of soul when I go out to Nature." The inhibited young man was trying to articulate his urge to blend his emotions with the world beyond, though his religiosity might seem naive because he could express himself only in clichés. He continued to the friend, Richard Tweedy:

> There is nothing that will comfort me in these moments of loneliness as will a bit of verse either from the bible or from the soul of a goodly being. I always feel that the good and pure thoughts a man may utter are not wholly his, but they come from God and are given to man's soul of God, and that it is the goodness and purity of man manifesting itself to us.

The rest of this letter and others to Tweedy were in the same vein. Hartley thought himself devoutly religious; in fact his was the voice of a lonely, constricted spirit pressing hard to find an outlet for emotions and deep sensitivity: "Beauty is my one aim in life," he wrote, "beauty in character, in thought, in word, in deed, and in expression on canvas of Nature divine and the glorification of God of all who provides us with these beauties." He declared that he took pleasure in trying to live out his ideas of life. Sometimes, however, "the beauties of life" overpowered him, and then he would find himself "back in a world of selfishness and deceit, all these crowding out and taking the places of fellowship, harmony, charity, truth and Godliness." So devout did he mean to be that he apologized to Tweedy — who was to study theology the next year — for writing on a Sunday.[23]

A midsummer letter to his niece Norma Berger told of Hartley's daily activities:

> I go somewhere every day to watch and study the birds and the butterflies and insects. I have a pair of fine opera glasses that I use so when I see a bird on a tree or bush I can see him near to without disturbing him or frightening him away. Then I write down what his color is and how big he is and what his movements are. Then too, I have a nice net for catching the butterflies and bees and insects and have a bottle with poison in the bottom to kill them right away so that they won't suffer. Then I try and find out what their names are in a book and get familiar with them. Then at sunset hour I go out to sketch.

The evening of that particular day he had made what he considered to be one of his best sketches ever; it was of a hillside with pastures, a yellow-green sky, and a bluish lavender cloud with a touch of pink, and the sky pink behind it.[24] His ideas about art were conventional, like his ideas about religion, and concerned with color. Before autumn was over he would stop trying to represent nature in order to work at color, always one of his major interests.

As the summer wore on he continued his pietistic letters to Tweedy, in June complaining of having no one to study with when he walked in the countryside seeking subjects to paint: "You know it is rather lonely to go over the fields and hills and not find a heart that beats in sympathy with my work and me, that is a human heart, I mean. Of course the Master is always with me."[25] In September he wrote of his dismay at finding all the Protestant churches in Lewiston closed during the month of August and having to venture into alien territory, a

Catholic church, which he did "knowing that my God would be with me." Primly he went on to comment on the immorality of the town of Lewiston, "one of the most immoral for its size" that he had ever been in. "One finds saloons at every turn and I have seen more drunkenness since I have been here than I saw all the while I was in N.Y. which seems to me a dreadful record for so small a place."

Little wonder he was lonely; it must have been difficult for anyone to put up with the bewildering intensity that Frances Everett observed, an intensity that was heightened by Hartley's frustrations with his art. He told Tweedy that to get to the country he wanted to paint he had to travel — mostly on foot — "between four and five miles each way." Added to the problem of distance was that of finding subjects that he felt competent to paint. For a time he judged his summer a waste, but by September he came to believe that his "researches in the world of butterflies and flowers" had taught him about "the cultivation of character and mind." He had found out "how little, how little I knew of that which I was aspiring to paint." He had thought that he understood nature, but "I realize now how meagre my knowledge was, and in fact that I knew little or nothing of what I had supposed I did, but those are the experiences of one who aspires to know."[26] Years later Hartley declared that "it took me four years to develop a sense of how to go about painting [the Maine hills]" and that his release came when he saw a color print of a work by the Italian divisionist painter Giovanni Segantini.[27] Actually, it took him six years. At the beginning, in 1900, Hartley recognized only what he did not know: "I think I have a different idea of art from most people," he wrote to Tweedy in late October, referring to Chase's New York School of Art, where he thought "there is not a great deal of art ... although it goes by that name." He was sure that "technical accomplishment" was not art, which lay instead in what he had seen in the fields, in the flowers and the butterflies and insects that fed upon them. A suitable technique, which remained to be discovered, would enable him to link emotion to subject matter.

That October he backed away from sketching as he searched for technique: "These last few days I have been making a few notes of color," he told Tweedy. "I do not term them sketches, for I have disregarded accuracy of drawing and modelling wholly for the sake of my color. I find it has gone backward and it seems next to impossible for me to get my color up to nature and so I decided for a little while to try only for color."[28] Soon he would return to representing nature, but this exercise was important as he tried to render brilliant color as he saw it in nature. Inevitably he moved away from strictly representational work and toward expressionism.

As important to him that summer and early autumn as his experiments with color was meeting the artist Alice Ferrar, to whose studio on Liston Street in Lewiston he was taken by Frances Everett. Ferrar had little direct influence on Hartley, but she told him of a colony of artists under the direction of two painters, Charles Fox and Curtis Perry of Portland, Maine. Exactly when Hartley met them is not clear, but he was in contact with them during the fall of 1900 and joined their colony the next summer. When Hartley wrote his memoirs, he referred to Fox and Perry as "some sort of socialists" from wealthy families, who "adopted sack-cloth clothing, put on humility, and for years maintained a free art school in Portland with themselves as instructors."[29] In the fall of 1900, however, when Hartley wrote to Tweedy about them, he was more caught up in their utopian plans:

> These men are giving their whole time to the development of art and character in students. They have a school in Portland and they give their services to the students — they are all first class draughtsmen and painters, have studied many years abroad and have for a number of years devoted themselves to art for humanity's sake. . . . In the summer they go to Bridgton Maine which is situated at the foot of the White Mt. range I believe and there they paint and study botany, butterflies etc. etc. and it strikes me as being a truly ideal community. Their aim is to live the higher life and to apply it to their art.[30]

Fox and Perry's colony offered Hartley association with a community of like-minded artists such as he had never known before. He had friends in Cleveland and New York, but given his shyness and his interests in landscape and expression, he found no real comradeship at either Chase's school or, later, the National Academy of Design.

A visit to the New York School in the fall of 1900 confirmed his assessment of it as superficial and sent "a sort of shudder" through him. He liked the Academy more and also studied at the Artists-Artisans School on East Thirty-third Street, where he met a Mr. Jamieson, also an Episcopalian, "very devout and sincere." The church they attended together, Hartley told Tweedy, was remarkable in that the congregation was made up largely of men, so that "there is that spirit of love and fellowship among them which I am sure is so pleasing to the Master. I felt so happy when I found a home for I had always felt that my place was in the Episcopal Church." The Men's Guild of the church had recently met, and Hartley had found himself "deeply inspired in the presence of so many men old and young all with a desire to live the better life."[31]

Soon he was more deeply involved with the men's group; he, Jamieson, and another friend, Winslow, formed a society for "spiritual advancement," the purpose of which was to work for the good of others. They began serving at the mission of Saint Mary's Church, on West Fifty-second Street near Tenth Avenue, "a rather low quarter of the city," Hartley noted. The men who came to the mission were rough and tumble, likely to be loud as they played games, read books, or played the piano, but all in all they were orderly. They were also, Hartley noticed, given to watching him; he decided it was because, dressed all in black, he looked like a Catholic brother. Their attention excited him; he felt that if he could gain their respect he might be able to influence them "to a better way of living." The church was providing him with an outlet for his emotions; he told Tweedy that Jamieson, Winslow, and he spent "our Sundays in Church together and as much of our time during the week as our duties will allow."[32]

Hartley's winter in New York was a happy one. He lived, if modestly, on the money from Anne Walworth, had comfortable quarters at 23 West Sixty-fifth Street, in a house he shared with three young women and a chaperone — shades of his own home with his mother and sisters — and enjoyed the intense satisfaction of the male church community.

So important to him was the church group that the next summer, as he was about to leave for North Bridgton, he wrote to Tweedy about having "been drawn closer and closer to the Master and to my Church." He felt a strong desire to enter the ministry. The past winter had opened his eyes "to the real beauties of a spiritual life"; "in place of a wandering indifferent, restless Soul, I have become a true Churchman, trying my best to live up to the precepts of my Church, and as I go on I feel the spirit calling me to a higher and more useful position than that of an artist." He would work for a few years in art because he had already begun, he told Tweedy, and then he would see if he was still strongly attracted to the ministry.[33] His devotion to the Episcopal church lessened, in fact, probably beginning that very summer, for in Fox and Perry's small colony he discovered both the intimacy he craved and a "spirit of love and fellowship" among men that was less inhibited than that offered by the Episcopal church, a spirit that he would find even more pervasive during the next years among disciples of Walt Whitman.

2

"The Need of Comrades"

HARTLEY'S PASSION for the "Master," the church, and his particular church's male congregation was his way of channeling his sexual attraction for his friends Tweedy, Jamieson, and Winslow. Probably he was not physically intimate with them, but in their company and that of others in the Men's Guild he found a satisfaction he had rarely, if ever, felt before. The shy, introverted, naive man was unsure about accepting his homosexuality, and one of the first times he could relax his inhibitions was among the congregation, some of whom were also homosexual.

His loneliness, his peripatetic nature, his ideas, and the subjects of his paintings all stemmed in part from his homosexuality. He was a proud man who cared what society thought of him, and he even conformed to its conventional expectations by having one or two heterosexual affairs. By and large, however, he chose solitude rather than intimate physical companionship — either with females, because it was not what he wanted, or with males, because it made him uneasy. His constant travel reflected not only a restlessness about maintaining intimate relationships but also a desire for something new and better than what he had at any given moment. Above all, he was a native of Maine, brought up in the late nineteenth century and deeply aware of New England's, not to mention America's, puritanical codes. Homosexuality was forbidden, so some of the emotions that today might be vented through overt activity were in his case sublimated in painting.

One can argue about reading homosexuality into Hartley's paintings and about which reflect it: the male nudes he sketched and painted in the 1920s in Berlin and again during the last decade of his life; the powerful primitivist paintings he did in the late 1930s of the Mason family in Nova Scotia, and especially of Alty Mason, the son whom he loved most of all; the German-officer pictures he painted in 1914–1915 to honor Karl von Freyburg, a young man with whom he had fallen in love after meeting him in Paris in 1912; his myriad still lifes with their phallic imagery of flowers, trees, and fruit, and his landscapes with their male-genital imagery in rocks, boulders, and other land forms and their female, maternal imagery of breasts and genitals in mountains and ravines; and even his late portraits of small dead creatures such as birds, lobsters, sea horses, and fish. They are, as the critic Michael Lynch has pointed out, "simple, powerful, lonely, but with a dramatic sense of community in loneliness, of a shared world at the fringe." Lynch took this to be Hartley's "strongest gay testament: community at the fringe, fellowship along the deserted coast."[1] Homosexuality is not necessary in order to paint such things; still, Hartley was homosexual, and that affected him. But if one result was loneliness, another was a sensitivity revealed in his tenderness toward small, vulnerable things and in his admiration for women — who in his paintings are "androgynous, yet motherly/sisterly, full of deep mourning and caring and nurturing." He understood feminine nature in "strikingly original ways," and this gave depth and emotion not only to his figure paintings but to his landscapes.[2]

If in 1900 among his New York churchgoing friends Hartley began to make better sense of himself, he found solace as well in literature. Walt Whitman became a hero once Hartley had been introduced to the poet's work. Whitman's ideas about individualism, nature, and experience reinforced the transcendentalism Hartley had already absorbed from Emerson and Thoreau.[3] It was stirring for Hartley to read poems from Leaves of Grass, such as those of the "Calamus" section, for in them he discovered what he wanted to express, man's love and need for man, as in the first poem of the group, which speaks of rejecting the conventional — escaping "from the life that exhibits itself,/ From all the standards hitherto publish'd, from the pleasures, profits, conformities,/ Which too long I was offering to feed my soul" — and celebrates "the need of comrades."[4]

Whitman's poetic vignettes equally appealed to Hartley, fascinated as he was by someone who could write of the attraction he felt for another man:

Among the men and women the multitude,
I perceive one picking me out by secret and divine signs,
Acknowledging none else, not parent, wife, husband,
      brother, child, any nearer than I am,
Some are baffled, but that one is not — that one knows me.

Ah lover and perfect equal,
I meant that you should discover me so by faint indirections,
And I when I meet you mean to discover you by the like in you.[5]

Hartley was excited to discover an American poet who had written openly of such matters. Whitman attracted him on several levels: the physical, the social, and the spiritual. He celebrated himself even as he insisted that he was a part of the *en masse,* as he termed the populace in general:

I celebrate myself, and sing myself,
And what I assume you shall assume,
For every atom belonging to me as good belongs to you.[6]

And he celebrated love, and nature, and the amorous interplay between these in lines such as

Spontaneous me, Nature,
The loving day, the mounting sun, the friend I am happy with,
The arm of my friend hanging idly over my shoulder,
The hillside whiten'd with blossoms of the mountain ash . . .[7]

Whitman's exuberance, his sensuality, and his profound love for others were a revelation to Hartley. Whitman's poetry and Hartley's discovery of like-minded people in New York and in such places as the utopian art colonies in Maine enabled him to begin to come out of himself, though he would never feel that he could be entirely open with his affection in the United States. "I forgo much more than I want," he wrote to his friend Arnold Rönnebeck late in his life, referring to

chances to be free such as [in] small communities like this [in Nova Scotia]. . . . It doesn't do to destroy one's better side by reverse pictures — but the chances here — are on every hand & could be had for the taking & nothing would be thought — but that is the way I always have been about living intimately in such places. . . . In large cities one need care less but even there at least in our U.S. people are cheap and I found it even expedient to give up certain friendships because they were not fine & true enough.[8]

He found himself as a painter, in fact, when he began to express something of his sexual emotions in his work, specifically in the *Dark Mountain* series of 1909–1910, begun after he saw the paintings of Albert Pinkham Ryder, whose mystical, romantic scenes suggested a style that enabled Hartley to portray his deep despondency at that moment. Nearly destitute and isolated by his circumstances, Hartley painted a series of landscapes devoid of any suggestion of community or fellowship, even at the fringes. Rather, there are remote, deserted farms dwarfed by overbearing mountains, and in the foreground, dark, drooping tree trunks.

Looking back at his life in Maine, he felt he had been abandoned and made the "lone left thing" he described being as a child. His mother had died when he was only eight, and his father had seemed to offer little or no support, so the boy had transferred his affections to his much older sisters, who were preoccupied with their own affairs. To his classmates in Lewiston he had seemed strange, a loner with few if any male friends, who liked the company of women and felt unthreatened and sheltered by them. The men Hartley was most attracted to in his maturity were not the slight, feminine sort but rather handsome and virile — Whitman's comrades, capable of robust love while also being tender and compassionate. These offered the solace Hartley desired and were as well the image of what he desired to be himself. He might have said that his was a "manly" love for men, though he enjoyed using lipstick and perfumes himself.

One of the several reasons Hartley admired Germany from the moment he first visited it, in 1913, was its attitude toward homosexuality, a far more accepting one than prevailed in the United States, where "they are so damned insensitive," he declared to the writer Robert McAlmon in 1941. "Who will ever match that thing we all knew when Germany and France were still alive and not corpses as they are now," he wondered.[9] His reference was to a Europe dominated by the Nazis, who persecuted homosexuals with a vengeance. Eight years earlier, during his last visit to Germany, Hartley had noticed a change from the atmosphere he had so liked about Germany before World War I and during the early 1920s. When visiting Hamburg in 1933, he told Arnold Rönnebeck, he had had *"certain joys,"* but "there was something about it all that subconsciously made me feel one must be careful." Still, he noted, "when it comes to that angle of life — no one understands it like the Germans, and no one ever appeals to me as they did."[10] Even in 1933 the Germans had "understood these things," although "the style had changed" from before, and besides, "as for the 1920–23 period in Berlin that was too much on the surface anyhow and I can sympathize with the present regime that much."[11]

That the Berlin of the early 1920s was in retrospect "too much on the surface" for Hartley reflected his squeamishness about open displays of male love. But he had enjoyed them more than once. To one friend he had written from Berlin in 1922 to describe a "huge costume ball at the Kunstgewerbe Schule — containing 3000 people with a 'nach fest' on Saturday evening for the artists and students." The "lovely boys & lovely girls and the ensemble" had been charming, but what he dwelt on was his own costume and the responses to it:

> I myself had as fine a costume as everything — and I was often told so both evenings. I was a kind of thousand and one nights magnificent creature in a tan . . . coat with silver cloth sleeves & trousers and a turban-like hat of silver — buried in small and large spangles of silver-hemlock blue and flaming ruby — and all over the coat were glittering spangles of mirror gems — my face painted Indian-red and on my [white] mask a . . . design of small gold & blue spangles which I glued on and it gave me the pleasure of a mask without the isolation of one. . . . I was the object of much polite comment and not infrequent conscious or subconscious love-making from enamoured young men who seemed bewitched with the effect I made on them — one nice young fellow said — if I were a girl I'd make love to you at once — another said — over and over again during the evening du bist eben schon mein lieber — du bist ein huebscher mensch — another said — there is only one thing left to do with you now — put you on an altar with your legs crossed — of course the psychology of that was clear enough — he was worshipping me.

No wonder Berlin attracted him. It was titillating for someone who had been a "lone left thing" to be the object of sexual worship. The

whole matter fascinated him; in the same letter he told of a private
party where the host was dressed as a woman,

> in a champagne colored costume with a cloud of gold tulle all cov-
> ered with gold spangles — made the most beautiful lady-of-dream
> I have ever seen. Usually these [studies] of life distress me excessively
> as I dislike all or most all feminine aspects in men — but I have
> never seen a more complete adjustment of inverted psychology any-
> where.... "She" sat in a swing under palms between two doors
> under soft glowing light, for the chandeliers were covered with pink
> roses — and received her friends in this graceful picture. It is as
> complete a case of transferred psychology as is to be found prob-
> ably — and one found no embarrassment whatever. The others
> there were all somehow or other — "otherwise" [homosexual] and
> the pictures to be seen were most engaging.[12]

Hartley appreciated the sense of liberation Berlin afforded, but its
profligacy disturbed him, as it did Robert McAlmon, who wrote in his
memoir that

> At nights along the Unter den Linden it was never possible to know
> whether it was a woman or a man in woman's clothes who accosted
> one. That didn't matter, but it was sad to know that innumerable
> young and normal Germans were doing anything, from dope selling
> to every form of prostitution, to have money for themselves and their
> families, their widowed mothers and younger brothers and sisters.[13]

McAlmon also wrote a collection of short stories depicting the decadent underground night life in Berlin at the time. In one story, "Distinguished Air," a central character called Carrol Timmons is drawn
at least partly from Hartley as McAlmon remembered him. The tale,
more a sketch than a rounded story, begins with the homosexual Foster
Graham stopping to talk to the narrator on a street in Berlin. Graham
says that he has been ignored by Timmons, who has leveled his "New
England disapproval" against him. Shortly afterward the narrator encounters Timmons himself, "admiring a perfumery bottle display with
a great air of connoisseurship." He gossips about Graham before the
narrator moves on to a bar, the Germaine Polast, which was a show
hangout, mainly for men. The scene generally is one of homosexuals
at play, including "an elderly fairy ... dressed as a blond-haired doll"
and others in drag. Timmons appears and remarks that "'this place is

too erotically upsetting for me, as a steady diet.'" The narrator asks if Timmons has a companion with him; he responds that he has, and

> "such a nice boy, too; just the type that attracts me most. Such a gentle face, and so rich physically. I was quite upset about him last week, because he came home with me one night, and the experience was wonderful — wonderful.... but he disappeared the next day and I thought I had been taken in by another whore. [He stayed away] but as long as he came back.... Well perhaps he does care for me a little for myself, you know. It's so comforting to think that anyway."

But why, asks the narrator, should "these ten-mark-bought bitches" care only for him? The narrative continues:

> Carrol, to my surprise, was not offended. "I know, I know," he confessed, "so foolish of me, and how often I have been disillusioned, but after New England, and that absurd moral bugaboo pursuing me for so many years, and then the snap, and the feeling of release within myself ... but there's Foster at my table. I'll have to go back to my boy, I see. Foster doesn't seem to understand a thing about playing the game fairly."

Graham and Timmons jostle, with Graham calling the other "the countess" and dancing drunkenly with a male lover while Timmons is "sloppily affectionate with the boy at his side." The narrator announces that he is not up to the spectacle and the "wasting of emotion" that it represents, to which Timmons replies,

> "Good Christ, yes.... I get so tired of the demands of my physical nature. These boys are all right, the most they can be for what they've had a chance to know, but, my god, they must have difficulty in knowing which are their own bodies, and which limbs are their own, after all the gymnastics and promiscuity they've been through. I must admit that my nostrils and my mental will rebel against my own carnal desire, but one can't be so cowardly as never to seek release."[14]

In the sketch as a whole McAlmon makes fun of Timmons but nevertheless respects him; Timmons's last statement is to be taken straight, as that of a person of feeling, constrained by his own moral sense, both drawn to and repulsed by the raw sensuality of a promiscuous society.

The atmosphere of Berlin, both in the early 1920s and when Hartley was there in 1913–1915, encouraged sexual experimentation, and he had one or more affairs with women. In a letter of March 1915 to Alfred Stieglitz, he wrote of living "rather gayly in the Berlin fashion — with all that implies." He was referring to a heterosexual affair, which he went on to note was

> a temporary marriage of a very decent nature — without restriction whatsoever the which has interested me some of course but only emphasizes the more my determination against any fixed conditions — I think it must be so awful all this — I can't see myself into it — I know now that I shall be a wanderer taking what I can take in the way I can take it and ask nothing more — I know the masculine nature so thoroughly — I know the feminine well — and yet I still have to wonder at a woman — abstractly we all know they are lovely — intimately I don't know if anyone knows anything and I hate intimacy — I myself am too mystically composed I am certain ever to let any one person walk wholly into my domain.[15]

It was as if Hartley hoped that with a woman he might attain a degree of intimacy with less emotional turmoil than was possible for him in a relationship with a man. He discovered, however, that this particular woman wanted the same sort of intimacy he had desired with young German males, and so he retreated into mysticism.

In 1922, again in Berlin, he told Stieglitz that he had been invited to father a child but had declined. "O God the too awful responsibility with no income," he wrote with a note of panic. "Women do these things better anyhow — they proceed from passion — which is the only way after all," he added, implying that he, at least, did not act in that manner.[16] By 1922 he understood himself well enough to know that while he might feel compassion — or even love — for a woman, it would not be the stuff of which marriages are made.

Whoever invited him to father her child, it almost certainly was not the writer Djuna Barnes, about whose relationship with Hartley a very minor legend has been built up, maintaining that they were lovers. Barnes's biographer accepts it as fact;[17] William Carlos Williams, the probable source of the tale, leaves the matter open in his published autobiography, while in an unpublished version he asserts that Barnes rejected Hartley's proposal. As Hartley had a vivid imagination that tended to alter events over time, and as Williams enjoyed any good bit of gossip, one cannot be sure of the facts. Hartley, Williams claimed, told him that

> once he had made rather direct love to Djuna Barnes, whose first husband, playing with her parrot, had his nose almost bit off. I can see old Marsden now, with his practical approach, explaining to Djuna what he could offer her.
>
> "And why not?" he asked. "After all we're good friends and have known each other a long time. I'm very fond of you." — And he was.
>
> But Djuna refused.[18]

Whatever the outcome of his proposal, Hartley's attraction was not a case of a grand amour. There was something clinical about the idea: it was an experience they ought to have. More genuinely Hartley was the overture he made to Williams when the poet visited him in his small Greenwich Village apartment. Williams was exhausted after working in a medical clinic and stretched out on Hartley's couch. Hartley approached him, but Williams said no. Hartley complained that "everyone rejected him" and told the poet that he was no better than the others. "He told me I *would* have made one of the most charming whores of the city," Williams added, noting, "We were close friends until his death."[19] Perhaps, but the evidence is that the closeness was less than Williams would have had it to be. He did not entirely comprehend Hartley's desire to distance himself as a result of his natural reserve, his New England background, and his sexuality.

"Give somebody a careful look and say it's from me," Hartley wrote to Robert McAlmon late in life. "I mean to get down that way [Arizona] and do it all for myself eventually, but there will be N.Y. again in January, and that is something — my god in June and July before I left, all the navies in white duck, and the thighs and arces [asses] something to tell mother about — simply wonderful," he continued jauntily.[20] He discussed "the foolish idea" with McAlmon as much as with anyone, a month earlier having answered a remark of McAlmon's about some man's sexuality with the comment that

> I too was born that way, and still have plenty to carry, but I did get fun out of the arrangement and, well, I am still doing it and no

diminution of the foolish idea, as after all, apropos of nothing at all, a sailor sitting next me coming up from Old Orchard near Portland, Maine — "we don't live forever, you know" and so my answer was, go to it, you're absolutely right, kid.

With McAlmon as with practically no one else Hartley's tone was one of bravado, a bit as if he were strutting before an old, close friend — which McAlmon was, at least about sexual matters, since their friendship went back as far as 1919 in California. In the same letter Hartley talked about the physiques of the young servicemen he had seen in New York the previous winter, and as for homosexuals in the service, "well how in the world did they even let em in and keep em after they got it, but I guess the rigidity of the whole thing scared the piss out of the softies, and they found out that even they can act like men."[21]

His relationship with most of his longtime and intimate friends was more "old-shoe," that of a devoted companion who had no secrets: "Well, old dear," he wrote to his friend Frank Davison in 1941,

> this isn't much, but it at least shows how grateful I am that you are alive among us, and now that I have a real address, I will promise to be more regular from now on, and never believe that I don't think of you constantly and don't love you in the same old way — after all these years it would be too late to be acting funny about such ideas, and I am not that kind anyway as you must have long since surmised, so just keep thinking of me in the same old way, and you will have a plush cushion to sit on in that heaven we have heard so much of, as even the mother of pearl chairs will not have soft bottoms.[22]

This was near the end of his life; he had not always been so relaxed about his sexuality. His intimacies with people such as Rönnebeck and McAlmon may not have been frequent; he liked — loved — them, but he chose to be "common" with occasional pickups and tended not to burden his "fine & true" friendships with sexual relations. When he was living across a field from Adelaide Kuntz near Aix-en-Provence in 1929, one of the friends who stayed with her recalled, Hartley would occasionally take short trips to the port cities of Toulon and Marseilles. How was the trip? they would ask upon his return, and he would give a satisfied smile and make a circle with his thumb and forefinger to let them know he had had his pleasures. Nothing was said, nothing denied, but they understood that he had served his sexual appetites.[23]

Even being "common" had its limits, however. A good friend of his, the artist Helen Stein, told of his having burst into her house in Gloucester, Massachusetts, once when he was living nearby, probably in 1934. Perturbed, he told her that he had been walking along East Main Street and had stopped to talk to a strong, neat-looking Portuguese man whom he had nodded to several times before. The man lived in a small hut along the street and invited Hartley in. No sooner were they inside than the man handed Hartley a package of postcards, which Hartley referred to as "those lewd terrible Paris things," and opened his fly. Shocked, Hartley put down the cards and walked out. "Why did it have to happen like that?" he asked Stein. "After all this need for something. He had everything but was so indelicate. So I guess he had coarseness and that is all. I shall have to avoid East Main Street now.... It could have happened but not that way."[25]

Perhaps it was a mark of his finally having made peace with his sexuality that late in his life he could blend the fine and the true with open gestures of love. "What a pair of boys they were," he mourned to Rönnebeck in November 1936, referring to two young friends, Alty and Donny Mason of Nova Scotia, a month and a half after they drowned. He had lived with their family for two summers, idyllic times for him as he was frequently with the boys, who were "magnificent in body and the dearest things in the world." They had been "so understanding and without inhibitions about *anything* therefore terrific ... when augmented with drink — lovelier even when intoxicated than when sober — as they hadn't a mean bone in their bodies & were most demonstrative with drink whereas sober, less inclined." Now they were gone, and Hartley was "all but heartbroken." Alty, the older brother, had even planned to build a small house on the island where they resided and to live in it with Hartley, a consummation of male friendship that Hartley yearned for but that was not to be.[25] Nonetheless, by 1936 he had accepted — if not completely laid to rest — a number of his personal demons, from whose attacks he fashioned some of his most moving art.

3

A Lonely Apprenticeship
1901 – 1909

IN MID-JULY 1901, Hartley left New York for Fox and Perry's small colony in North Bridgton, Maine. *Colony* is too grandiose a term; the members lived in a "large ugly white frame house" as boarders at four dollars a week. Gertie Adams, the wife of Bill Adams, who owned the place, cooked meals of "salt pork, fried potatoes, doughnuts, soggy cake, cookies, and Saturday nights always . . . baked beans, old-fashioned New England style."[1] Fox did no painting at all, and Perry merely dabbled at sketches that were "thin in quality but quite radiant" as he concentrated on increasing his collection of butterflies and moths.[2] Hartley became reacquainted with Maine at North Bridgton, but while he admired the locale, he sought more dramatic contours and thus appreciated the suggestion of a Mrs. Broadstreet that he try Center Lovell, a small village slightly to the west, in the Stoneham Valley, at the edge of Kezar Lake. The nine-mile-long, deep-water lake was bounded to the west by steep hills and beyond them, to the northwest, the Presidential Range. The next year he moved there.

This sparsely populated region of inland Maine proved to be his training ground. As much as by the landscape, Hartley was impressed by the natives, about whom he had mixed feelings. Years later, after returning to Maine with friends, he wrote to one of them about it and its people:

What a poignant picture the wife made that day with the rosewood piano in among the soap-boxes and uncalled for spices over beyond

the wet grass, by the grey stone. Such a symbol of that country — worn to a thin edge by vulgar circumstance — Did you ever
see any of those deserted farms up in the Stoneham Valley where I
lived ten acute seasons — my God what a slant upon the stupidity
of faith & dream. I suppose the rats and the coons still have them
and the foxes are still harvesting those vestiges of grape that persist.
It's a very strange country I can tell you — and those of you who see
its surface beauty are not obliged to reap the harvest of inner distress — you will find it all in E. A. Robinson and Robert Frost —
they certainly were let in on the vicious truth. "Something there
is — that doesn't love a wall" there's the whole story — that's why
there's an ache in every understanding home. I'm sure it's the dread
of the wall that keeps all of us New Englanders on the gentle run.[3]

What few natives there were had a sense of the precariousness of
life. Hartley described the owner of the house where he stayed in 1901
as having "squeez[ed] blood out of pennies." "Short, bony, and flinty
in thought, behaviour, and speech," Bill Adams was the sort of person
who treated faith and dreams with cynicism and clung to a harsh life
in the isolated region.

Hartley admired Bill's brother, Wesley, a trapper who lived nearby
but avoided his sibling. Hartley visited Wesley often during his summer at North Bridgton and afterwards. Nearly every evening — as he
recounted it impressionistically much later — he would walk the two
miles to the village to get mail and provisions, and on his return, with
his lantern lit, he would make his way through dense pinewoods to
Wesley's cabin, where for an hour or so he would visit with the lonely
trapper, whose wife had left him ten years before. Their talk was
Maine talk, which is not infrequently silence, and when they did speak,
it was mostly about weather, mountains, and Wesley's trapping. Once
Hartley even went with him to a bear trap up in the mountains and
later tried eating some of the bear meat the trapper had given him, but
it was too strong, and he ended up feeding it to the stray dogs that
lingered near his cabin.

Adams was "one of the last of his kind, dreaming romantic of the
woods, who loved nature, hard as she was on him, for nature up that
way was certainly severe, and cruel."[4] In him Hartley saw himself, an
isolated being buffeted by life. The "ten acute seasons" that Hartley
spent in the Stoneham Valley were nearly as important in molding

him as had been his childhood in Lewiston, and formed another part of his sense of being alone, a victim of circumstances in a world that he came to see was not at all full of transcendental balm. Some years after Hartley and his fellow Maine artist John Marin came under the aegis of Alfred Stieglitz, Marin wrote to Stieglitz that "Hartley surely came out of Maine. I have run across two or three, and the likeness, a certain similarity or something, is striking. If that rainbow chaser could only have remained [in Maine] — but then, how do I know."

By 1919, the date of Marin's letter, Hartley had chased rainbows in France, Germany, Bermuda, New Mexico, California, and New York. Marin was implying that the other's best work stemmed from his native roots and from the particular slant on life that Maine instilled in a person. As Marin later wrote,

> Old mistress — Maine — she makes you to — lug — lug — lug — she makes you to — pull — pull — pull — she makes you to — haul — haul — haul — and when she's thrashed you a plenty — between those thrashings
> > she's lovely
> > she smiles
> > she's beautiful
> with an unforgettable loveliness — an unforgettable beauty
> — Turns masculine — borders big and mighty — against — the big and mighty Atlantic —
> . . . Maine — makes or breaks
> > Maine demands and rivets
> — A painter man — here — if — of — her breed or her adoption — must needs conform —[5]

Hartley understood all this, felt he had been thrashed, and did not want to conform to the demands of Maine, something he had tried to do first as a child and then as a young painter in North Bridgton and Center Lovell, where he settled for the summer of 1902. In Center Lovell he lived in a small cooper shop and then, in the summer of 1903, in a cobbler's cabin at the entrance to a farm owned by Douglas Volk.

At some point during 1902 or 1903 Hartley's dwelling was a tent in the backyard of the home of Percival Chubb, who taught English at the Ethical Culture School in Boston. Chubb and his family liked Hartley, who in turn enjoyed their company and would perch for hours on the porch steps of their house, talking eagerly about ethical culture, light and color, and many other things. Chubb's daughter remembered Hartley as something of an aesthete, lean, gangling, a bit "Greenwich Villagey," and clearly anxious to be part of their group.[6]

With his wife, Douglas Volk was attempting to restore interest in New England folk art. Hartley hoped that he might benefit from that interest, but no one was attracted to his work, so he moved away, summering next in North Lovell, at the head of Kezar Lake. It was "raw living" in those days, he recalled, as the town was remote, fifteen miles north of the hardly grand town of Fryeburg and twenty-five west of Norway. To get to North Lovell one rode up from Fryeburg on a "real Buffalo Bill coach and four" that made a single trip each day, which meant that a person had to perch wherever there was a place, usually atop some supplies, rarely on a seat.[7]

Although Hartley required solitude, he also welcomed the busyness of New York, where he returned each fall. He kept up his friendships with members of the Men's Guild of his church, but as he slowly became acclimated to the art students' world, he spent more time in it and gradually abandoned his prim religiosity. During his first years in New York he was remembered as "tall and severe, [someone who] would stride into the classes at the National Academy and dig into the other students with an eagle-like stare. He seemed combative and re-silient." Hartley was most content around the women at the Academy and tended to still-life painting or "dainty works with a Whistlerian background." His landscapes reflected his admiration for Americans such as Wyant, Homer, and Homer Martin.[8]

The writer Alfred Kreymborg recalled a somewhat altered Hartley of a few years later. Kreymborg met him in about 1903 through the poet Wallace Gould, a giant of a man whom Hartley had come to know in Lewiston and whom he admired extravagantly. In New York during the years before Hartley became part of the group at Stieglitz's 291 gallery, Kreymborg was most likely to meet the painter at Kiel's Bakery, at the corner of Eighth Avenue and Fifteenth Street. Kiel would allow impoverished patrons to eat free, which was the only thing that made his bakery attractive, Kreymborg remembered, be-cause other than that it smelled awful and the dining room was by itself in the rear, "a blunt square hole without ventilation, packed with tables and chairs." As Kreymborg portrayed Kiel's, it was a gathering place for artists and what he called a "seething mass of ponderous truck drivers." The artists were such as Ernest Roth, known as "Louis the copper-scratcher"; H. Latimer Brown, "the lachrymose portrait-painter and whilom international cricketer"; Bob Williams, "robust in physique but not so robust in landscapes"; and Albert Drefus, a sculptor who could never afford to cast his works and kept his clay models draped in wet rags so they would not crack.

Hartley, who was no better off than the others, nonetheless remained aloof from their good-natured bantering and carefully guarded the canvases he had done in Maine. These were, in Kreymborg's memory, "mysterious, bleak landscapes, with the depths of black upon black unrelieved by the solitary gray cabin or troop of gray clouds in the foreground or distance. Or stark, brooding still-lifes, in which an ivory gardenia loomed like the heroine in a tragedy of old."* Hartley, who loved music, was a fervent whistler, and amid his own inner gloom and the noise of Kiel's he would whistle away — the self-conscious defense, one imagines, of a shy man in a public place. Kreymborg continued,

> When spring came, if he could afford nothing else, Marsden managed to buy a gardenia for his buttonhole. The others thought him a snob: his ways were so superior; his devotion to William Blake and Francis Thompson seemed a little mad; and his exquisite tastes, the exotic longing he had for warm, precious stones, aggravated the impression. These predilections and starved mystical obsessions tended to give him a place apart. And he wrapped his coat like a toga about his spare form, held his extraordinary nose in the air, used his aristocratic cough as a warning not to come too close. But his friends learned to know Marsden better before many years elapsed. Among them all, he was easily the loneliest. . . . None of the young men ever froze so bitterly, or looked as frozen as the eagle from the state of Maine.[9]

Hartley was also trying his hand at poetry. He wrote a poem entitled "The Royal Love Child" in Center Lovell in June 1904 and sent it to his young niece Norma Berger. The first stanza conveys the general tone of the poem:

---

*The "mysterious, bleak landscapes" that Kreymborg remembered were probably from the *Dark Mountain* series of 1909–1910, by which time he knew Hartley well and had seen them at 291. Earlier Hartley painted more conventionally, in an academically realistic style.

"There is no life worth living"
said sad and troubled Sorrow:
"None but Poverty to lead the way,
Remorse doth follow in my step
and there is no peace of heart.
Tribulation plays her part in this
struggling strangling strife and
there is no hope in life."

Ten stanzas later glad Sorrow, from out of her bosom and with the help of Pleasure, has given birth to a "Royal Love Child."[10] Other poems from the same period, while less strictly narrative, are in the same romantic style. "To a Syrian Lute" reminds the reader of nothing so much as Keats's "Ode on a Grecian Urn." In his poetry as in his painting, Hartley had not yet found his own voice. The closest to that might be a poem entitled "Summer Evening," which Hartley sent to Norma Berger in about 1905:

Ashes of rose
Fade in the east sky

Thro the quivering poplars
Sun flashed swallows fly

Broad the blue stream flows
Under the arched bridge

Down the gleaming sun goes
Over the earth's edge

A flush in the sun's wake
A ripple — behind a swan
On the tremulous lake
And the day — Is gone![11]

The language here is less artificial than that of "The Royal Love Child," the rhymes are unforced, and the color imagery is appropriate, even if every noun is draped with an adjective and the last line is notably flat. Still, the poem is interesting because it moves toward modernism, a more natural idiom, as did Hartley's art after 1906. On the back of a small landscape painting dated 1908 he scrawled an unromantic bit of free verse — perhaps while sitting in Kiel's Bakery —

that has something of the same embittered tone about it as his *Dark Mountain* paintings:

> In the Bea[n] Shop
> The blithering drooling idiots
> Sit — sit — sit
> Lolling and sprawling
> in the green gloom of a
> soot smeared lamp —
> Sitting and sitting
> falling and crawling
> over each other
> Drooling in the spit box! —
> And they sit and sprawl
> Fall & crawl
> In and out
> Of the grey green gloom!
> Blithering idiots all —[12]

But Hartley was unsure of himself in poetry, as in other things. As late as 1909–1910 he could depart from the modern idiom and to a handsome young poet, Shaemas O'Sheel, dedicate a "Song for Eilleen" that begins

> The irish eyes of Eilleen
> Pensively dream
> The haunting smile of Eilleen
> Flits like a gleam
> On a lily nymphean
> As a white beam passes
> Over a white moonstone.[13]

The trouble was that Hartley was serious about this. After reading the poem O'Sheel had the candor to tell him, "I do not think as highly of it as I do of those few brief poems [such as "Summer Evening," one assumes], delicate and of great perfection of their sort, of which you gave me copies long ago."[14]

To earn money Hartley worked as a supernumerary in the theater. At the suggestion of two friends he found a place in *Abigail*, a play staged at the Savoy Theater, on West Thirty-fourth Street. The pay was fifty cents a performance, minus ten cents paid to George White, the manager of the "supers." Hartley's first role was as a painter, for which he wore a smock and beret. One of his friends, C. Maclean Savage, recalled an incident that illustrates Hartley's poverty then. He often visited Savage's home on East Thirty-third Street, and when he found he could have a pair of cast-off shoes that had belonged to a boarder, he eagerly accepted them. It was around this time that his friends convinced him to drop Edmund from his name and be simply Marsden Hartley — much more glamorous, they argued.[15]

Work in the theater provided Hartley with an income once the grant from Anne Walworth ended, in November 1904. He served as an extra at four dollars a week for Proctor's Theater Company in New York and toured with the company during 1905 and the summer of 1906 before returning to Lewiston in the fall to teach art.

On one of his trips to Maine aboard a ship bound for Portland, Hartley met Thomas Bird Mosher, a publisher and a member of the circle of Whitman admirers that had been formed by Horace Traubel, a close friend of the poet. Hartley was seated on deck reading Emerson's essays and planned to spend the night either there or in the ship's lounge. Mosher observed him and offered him the upper berth in his cabin. From this meeting intimacy grew: Hartley visited Mosher in Portland when he passed through, and Mosher, in turn, told Hartley of Traubel. Sometime during the fall of 1905 or the winter of 1906, while on tour with the Proctor Company, Hartley met Traubel in Philadelphia.

The meeting was particularly important to Hartley; he already knew of Whitman's work by this time, but Traubel's enthusiasm inspired him. Whitman's espousal of "adhesiveness" among men, his ideas about art and nature, and the revolutionary form of his poetry all enabled Hartley to start breaking free of the conservative forces in art that had constricted him up to that point. Hartley remained a friend until Traubel's death, in 1919, and in the years before he became part of Stieglitz's group, Traubel and friends such as Mosher were among those to whom he felt closest. Through Traubel he met Dr. Percival Wiksell, a dentist whom Traubel often visited in Boston and whom Hartley saw occasionally when he was passing through that city.

One such occasion was during the summer of 1906, when Mosher and Traubel were both in Boston. They and Hartley gathered at Wiksell's office before going to dinner. That night they were to meet Peter

Doyle, Whitman's intimate friend and now a conductor on the New York, New Haven, and Hartford Railroad. "I was all agog to see this man who figured so richly in Whitman's life — from Peter's youth as a horsecar conductor in Washington until Walt's death," Hartley recalled, adding that Doyle was "a huge man — well set up — roundish at the middle — very well dressed and wore a heavy gold watch chain across his vest — as he also wore a heavy mustache of not much character." The group went out for beer, but Doyle was not talkative, and Hartley's thrills were confined to simply being in the presence of Whitman's intimate. Little matter; Hartley wrote that he was "all Whitmanic then," and so when he could he went to New Jersey and painted two sketches of Whitman's homes.[16]

Yet another liberating experience for Hartley was his discovery of the work of the Swiss painter Giovanni Segantini in an issue of the art journal *Jugend*. He later wrote that after he saw a color print of the painting *Plowing in the Engadine*, he "produced a flock of canvases quite large with a direct sense of the topography of the scenes which I had studied intimately."[17] Hartley credited the Swiss with a perfect understanding of the "inner and outer sense of the mountain," and it was only after seeing Segantini's work that he believed he had discovered how to render the mountains of Maine. The "stitch" technique that Hartley learned from Segantini enabled him to begin to paint colors, shadows, and lights correctly. "The effects created on the body of the mountain by refractional plays of light itself" were what he was struggling to capture, he declared in an essay about Segantini.[18] He also observed that

> The idea of refraction of light is the clue to all Segantini's later expression — and he makes a very unique and original method out of it — never sacrificing the statement of nature to it however — but permeating the whole scene — either interior or exterior with the amazing exactitude of tone and half tone in this method. The combination therefore in Segantini of realism — [Hartley here crossed out the word *point(illism)*] impressionism and divisionism — suffused with very personal mysticism — gives the pictures of this very earnest man their highly original flavour. . . . The actual fact of nature in Segantini's pictures is always at hand — he never neglects the forms and the meaning of nature — and he observes meanwhile all the plays of light that take place in high mountain places.[19]

After Hartley abandoned academic realism, his painting became impressionistic. From Americans such as John Twachtman he "had assimilated an overall decorative treatment of the picture surface," the art critic Barbara Haskell has remarked, adding that by "using his muted palette, he wove together irregularly shaped areas of color with a delicate tracery of lines to create a decorative picture surface." Stitch strokes, she notes, allowed him to abandon the impressionists' technique of scumbling — laying one opaque color over another color — and the result for him was a more accurate color painting, Neo-Impressionist in style but truer to the colors of nature.[20]

Fortified by his male friendships and by a new confidence in his ability to paint, he moved to Lewiston in the fall of 1906, hoping to manage by teaching. In November he confessed that he was suffering from "the insweep of the sea of uncertainties." He told Horace Traubel that if he were the praying type he would "pray most fervently to be released from these harrowing doubts."[21] For the introverted man to establish himself was extremely difficult; "the sea of uncertainties" swept over him at such moments throughout his life. This time he found a studio to rent and at once sent out handmade announcements to drum up trade:

EDMUND MARSDEN HARTLEY
New York
Announces · classes · in
drawing · and · painting · in
all · mediums · oil · watercolor · charcoal · black · and
white · drawing · from · the
antique · (cast) · and · from · life.
A · special · all · day · class
will · be · held · on · Saturdays
in · his · studio · THE · GREELY
BUILDING · 171 · LISBON · ST
SUITE · FOUR
Arrangements · may · be · made
for · classes · on · other · days.

At the same time he was working at his own painting. He wrote to Traubel that he was doing a study of the Androscoggin "at night with a lot of buildings jutting out over the river," and another of "sunset glow through the pine woods with the first snow on the ground in patches left where the day sun has not reached there much." He was able to work quickly and so could "seize readily upon the most striking characteristics of a subject," a reference to a technique he would use for much of his career, that of catching a scene with a brief glimpse and then later sketching his impression, which he believed was the essence of the subject.[22]

Just before the turn of the year a reporter from the *Lewiston Journal* visited him and told of seeing *A Study of Speckled Mountain* in progress. (The painting was later retitled *Storm Clouds, Maine.*) Hartley showed the journalist his drawings and was quoted as saying, "Here are some sketches in oil, of the mural decorations done by Puvis de Chevannes, which, as you know, adorn the walls of the Boston public library. They are perhaps, more interesting to me than to anyone else, on account of their associations." Then Hartley opened a folio in which there were sketches of many sorts of specimens of nature, including flowers and ferns, and "prettiest of all were the water colors of rare butterflies and moths. It seemed as tho the fairy things were alive," the writer enthused. Around the studio were paintings of Lewiston scenes, *An Early Spring,* set in Dedham, Massachusetts, and the large oil of the Androscoggin, *River by Moonlight,* that Hartley had described to Traubel.[23]

He kept busy at his own work and at reading; on Christmas Day he wrote to Shaemas O'Sheel that he was enjoying the work of Pater, Ruskin, Whittier, and William Vaughn Moody.[24] With luck his teaching would pay expenses and income from selling his paintings would "relieve other pressures." In addition to local sales, he thought he might sell something through the exhibition of the National Academy in New York in March 1907. But he was soon discouraged because few students showed up at his studio, and in January he informed O'Sheel that he intended to try to "break into the field of journalistic writing of some degree or other, in New York when fall comes." Painting "as a chief occupation" was too "uncertain and precarious,"[25] he concluded. Uncertain, he felt caught — as he would always — between his need to be alone and his desire also to be part of the city and its crowds. "I know I ought to come down out of the woods," he wrote to Traubel in February 1907, "and few know how much I need the crowd and love it — God knows I want to be with it and near it always — for I loathe being apart either from my crowd or my mountains and just now I am both." His solace was that he could paint his mountains, and he was pleased with the results. He had sent five small works to Percival Wiksell in Boston but had heard nothing in response. "I am not over-expectant," he remarked, "yet I anticipate a little."[26]

Scant financial help came from these projects; by spring Hartley was frantic to find a job and wrote to Thomas Mosher for aid. He suggested that Hartley contact the Congress of Religions, a utopian community at Green Acre, Sarah Farmer's residence in Eliot, on the Piscataqua River at the southern tip of Maine. Hartley took a job there and spent the summer and fall at Green Acre, which Barbara Haskell has described as a place where "artists, theologians, and mystics could exchange spiritual and philosophical views in a pastoral setting. Farmer became increasingly involved with Eastern religion and by 1901 had converted the colony into a school of Baha'i faith."[27] Another resident was Mrs. Ole Bull, who with her wealth entertained regularly and had as guests Swamis Abedenanda and Vivekenanda, and Sister Nivedita.[28] Hartley worked as a handyman, erecting tents and doing other jobs in exchange for room and board. He enjoyed the life of the community, which broadened his artistic contacts and brought him more closely in touch with social philosophies and mysticism.

One resident, Helen Stuart Campbell, impressed him especially. She was a writer of children's books and of such studies as *Prisoners of Poverty, Women Wage Earners,* and *Household Economics;* after long discussions with Hartley she teasingly called him a philosophical anarchist. Caught up in the excitement of the community, he told O'Sheel that he could not "contain myself with the sweep of my revolutions." He was "seething with repulsion at the superficiality of art and of men — and it all boils up the blood in me and I am an uninterrupted flame of revolt these periods."[29] He felt he was on the verge of discarding art for writing because he loved life, "the dash and go of it, and where I once nursed my pain I now have violent contempt for it within myself." Aesthetics, he decided, were "most treacherous," and he wanted to abandon them.[30] For the moment he was convinced that personal art was of little value: "What once rang as deep song in my ears is now the merest tinkling of minor strains — valueless in assisting in the great aria of the human cause," he declared a month later to

O'Sheel. "We must strike our lyres with a greater purpose than mere singing — you for your Irish — I for my Universal — or in other words — American."[31]

But Hartley was not comfortable as a social thinker, and he soon returned to art. More significant for him was the interest in mysticism at Green Acre. He had previously read the likes of Emerson and Thoreau and poets such as Whitman and Blake. At the community he was among people who could discuss these writers and teach him to approach the mystics more systematically. He was less sure of his Christian faith by 1907 — the year before, he had told Horace Traubel that he was no praying man — but now the mystics, Christian and otherwise, gave him confidence about what lay beneath the surfaces of nature, and that was what he tried to convey in his painting once he got beyond impressionism.

During the summer Traubel visited Green Acre several times. Two brief notes from him in mid-August — one regarding a recent visit, the other, a visit soon to come — made Hartley rapturous, and he wrote that "the fulnesses come flooding over me like gusts of rose aroma and I am a bit overcome with the fragrances of them." He told Traubel of a visit from Charlotte Perkins Gilman, the author and suffragist, who impressed him with her intelligence. And he mentioned two men, Harlan Ober, "one of the highest of heaven born boys," and Fred Lunt, "who has the eyes of a very god and a smile of the mothers of gods upon him." Both were "lovers of mine," as Hartley referred to them in Whitmanesque fashion; together with Helen Campbell, Charlotte Gilman, Wiksell, and Traubel, they were the "golden glories of my heart's gate. How can I contain myself," he wondered. "Heavens are at my feet and gods look into my eyes and I am consumed with their glories," he exulted to Traubel.[32]

In late August and early September he had his first one-man show at the home of Mrs. Ole Bull. He remembered the interior walls as being finely paneled and lightly stained in gray, creating a restful effect. Supported by his friends from Green Acre, he felt confident and called the exhibition a "splendid success artistically." On Sunday, September 2, a small concert was given in connection with the exhibit, adding to his pleasure, and his enthusiasm was heightened even further by the fact that he earned ninety dollars from sales. With that money he planned to set himself up in Boston for the winter. He told Traubel that several important people wanted to help him establish himself; he had been offered an exhibition in Philadelphia and would have the use of a studio in the home of Mrs. Bull in Cambridge, Massachusetts.[33]

His jubilation could not last. Boston during the fall and winter was not the great success he had anticipated, and by April 1908 he was writing to Traubel that "things go badly here." A project in New York — undoubtedly the exhibition at the National Academy — had not materialized, so he lay "beached" in Boston, waiting for the tide to rise. He hoped to sell some "potboilers" at the Metaphysical Club during the latter half of April, which might provide him with the money he needed to get to Maine for the springtime. He frequently questioned his choice of painting as a career, but it could not always be so bad, he surmised, so he would continue awhile. Then, as so often happened to him, in the nick of time he had enough good fortune to carry him along. "Shout Horace Traubel — shout for Hartley's success — I'm discovered so they say and am on my way," he wrote to his friend in May. After his works were praised by the artist and critic Philip Hale, he took several to the Rowland Gallery in Boston. One painting, *Maine Blizzard,* perhaps hung as part of a group exhibition, attracted Desmond Fitzgerald, an affluent civil engineer who was a collector and also wrote about art. He lived in Brookline, a wealthy suburb of Boston. After meeting Hartley at the Rowland Gallery, he invited him to see the Monets, Sisleys, Boudins, and other impressionist works he had purchased.[34]

Fitzgerald subsequently took Hartley to Sandwich, on Cape Cod, to meet Dodge Macknight, whose watercolors he collected and who Hartley said was "as daring as Winslow Homer was direct and sober, because Macknight painted crashing sunlight in winter, a perfect deluge of orange, violent blue, and vermillion." Fitzgerald was Macknight's first patron; he bought watercolors every year and kept them in wooden folios mounted on wheels. That Hartley was so taken with the watercolors is a mark of the level of his artistic sophistication at the time. Although Macknight's paintings were lively, they were scarcely innovative and lacked the depths Hartley needed to find.

Macknight, according to an art historian familiar with his works, was a "sketchy draftsman, with a loose style and rather strident palette; New England snow scenes rendered with blue and magenta shadows constitute one of his preferred subjects."[35] No wonder, then, that Macknight congratulated Hartley on his work and called *Maine Blizzard* a *"fine picture."* A few days after their trip to Sandwich, Hartley visited Fitzgerald at his home, where the collector sat at his desk amid his Boudin paintings and wrote him a check for $400, though he had set the price for the one picture at $200.[36]

In the same letter to Traubel in which he declared that he had been discovered, Hartley repeated the praises of the critics John Joseph Ennecking, who had spoken of his "power, and tragic sense," and Philip Hale, who had offered to write about him if he had a show and urged him to send his work to the Salon des Indépendants in Paris. Subsequently he told Traubel that Hale had perceived a *"fine insanity"* in his paintings, by which he meant "a strong insistence upon the personal interpretation of the subjects chosen."[37] Fitzgerald wanted him to return to the mountains to paint, free of financial worries. Hartley reported that the collector saw in his work a "new note in art" and a unique treatment of mountains. "I am to go to California next fall for perhaps a year to paint in that vividly glowing country and to attune my senses to livelier color," Hartley concluded. "So I'm on my way Horace and I know you're glad." Later the California plan would become less certain.[38]

With Fitzgerald's $400 Hartley returned late in May 1908 to Maine, settling in North Lovell among the isolated hills of the Stoneham Valley. Buoyed by the small successes of the spring, he worked hard through the summer and fall, occasionally interrupting his solitary life with long hikes. "Walked over from N. Lovell — return this afternoon — 32 miles in all," he wrote to Traubel one day from Bridgton. In a journey that had taken him down the length of Lake Kezar, he had tramped through heavy woods, stripped to the waist, and at one point had jumped into a brook to cool off. After buying rations in Bridgton, he headed back. "Wish you could come up here but I know you love the dear crowd too well," he remarked. "So do I — but one can't have all things in the hills."[39]

He was too enthusiastic about his new work to become morose. Influenced by the impressionist paintings he had seen at Fitzgerald's and thinking himself more and more the master of the stitch stroke, he painted steadily at what he called romantic landscapes. "Like every revolutionist, I've gone through my 'periods,'" he wrote to Shaemas O'Sheel in October, "and have now come back I think to the original child within me namely the romanticist, albeit not perhaps a romance of love as of madness for the mountain madness is on me and the bizarrerie of the hills gives me stronger thoughts than ever." He assured O'Sheel that he would be interested in the new paintings, "my 'Romances Sans Paroles' I call them — my 'Autumn Impressionals' as I call them."[40] Hartley was picking up on Philip Hale's comment about the "fine insanity" in his work and was trying to interpret his subjects, to express the strong emotions they inspired in him.

The most remarkable thing about Hartley's painting at this time was that he developed his new approach "in virtual isolation," as Barbara Haskell has pointed out. The neo-impressionism he was practicing came not from his having seen what was then occurring in Europe but from his awareness of impressionism, his knowledge of Segantini's technique, and his own strong need to express color. Form followed but came more from Hartley's sense of color patterns than from a desire to emphasize the forms themselves, though he was concerned with the shapes of the mountains he drew. Haskell has noted that "discontinuing conventional perspective, Hartley united foreground and background in a single continuous plane. . . . He reduced forms to decorative, curvilinear shapes defined only by the direction and pattern of the strokes and by distinct areas of color."[41] So intent was he on conveying the patterns of color and, increasingly, the beauty but also the power of nature as he observed it during the autumn of 1908 and winter of 1909 that he began to abandon the stitch technique in some of his work in favor of what Haskell has termed "turbulent, graphic brushstrokes," creating a "gestural fluidity" typified by his nearly abstract landscapes of 1910.[42] Given his tendency toward mysticism, it is not surprising, in fact, that he was moving fast toward expressionism.

As is the case for any innovative and original artist, his progress was not plodding but rather a matter of leaps and darts. While he was still working with stitch strokes in his postimpressionist landscapes, he could on occasion paint pure abstractions, such as *Landscape No. 16 1909 (?)*, in which background and foreground merge entirely and tree limbs become curving verticals or partial horizontals in a high-color pattern that he took to the four edges of the canvas. Nothing but inspiration could have accomplished that. So caught up in the moment was Hartley that he scrawled on the back of the canvas a poem that is both impressionistic and expressive of the emotion he drew from the autumn landscape. Titled "October Dying," the poem reads:

October Lies — Dying
The dead dance frantically!
Before my eyes —
Shivering ghosts of immemorial
[illegible]
all there is is waste of
long forgotten beauty
Dead — dead — they dance!
Frantically —
Glad for the last wild dance
[illegible]
[illegible]
With bits of gold and ruby
Dangling from their [lacuna]
But they dance! dance! dance!
Frantically, divinely
Against the Turquoise.[43]

His expressionistic intent is similarly evident in a small painting dating from 1909, in which, even as he eschewed conventional Christianity, he included religious symbolism. Entitled *Resurrection,* the painting shows a shrouded figure in a postimpressionist landscape and is an early attempt to blend the meaning of religious emotion with that of emotion emanating from the physical world. The shrouded figure need not be Christ, but its religiosity is obvious and proves the point that because of his lifelong fascination with mysticism, his paintings, both early and late, tended toward expressionism.[44]

In February or early March 1909 Hartley traveled to Boston, where he met Charles and Maurice Prendergast at their home on Mount Vernon street. Maurice, in his own work nearer to neo-impressionism than to impressionism, liked Hartley's paintings, encouraged him to take them to New York, and wrote him a letter of introduction to the artists Robert Henri and William Glackens. Hartley introduced himself to Glackens at the latter's studio on Washington Square South soon after his arrival in New York. Glackens asked Hartley where his pictures were and was told they were at the American Express office. He instructed Hartley to bring them to the studio, where, once installed, they were viewed by Arthur B. Davies, John Sloan, Everett Shinn, and Ernest Lawson, all members, with Glackens, of the antiestablishment group known as The Eight. Sloan, as one might have expected given his interest in city themes and his general tendency toward realism, found the paintings somewhat affected and their mysticism a touch heavy-handed.[45] Hartley was doubtful about Lawson's interest, but Davies was enthusiastic and after seeing the pictures took Hartley to the Macklin Newcomb framers and made him a present of four frames from moldings he liked.[46] It was an auspicious start for the young artist.

4

291
1909 – 1912

IN THE SPRING OF 1909 Hartley was introduced to Alfred Stieglitz; it was one of the most important meetings of his life. Shaemas O'Sheel, talking with Hartley about prospects for showing his works, mentioned Stieglitz's Photo-Secession Gallery at 291 Fifth Avenue, which Hartley had not heard of. O'Sheel soon spoke to Stieglitz about Hartley's struggles, and Stieglitz suggested that O'Sheel bring him by the gallery. Hartley, afterward never quite able to acknowledge how desperate he had been for a showing, liked to say of their first encounter that it was Stieglitz who had wanted to see his paintings. The older man recalled it differently, and many years later, aggrieved by Hartley's rather blasé recounting of the episode in a biographical note, wrote to him that

> One evening O'Sheel brought you. And I remember the conversation as if it were yesterday. An exhibition was suggested by O'Sheel. I said: "Impossible." The season was over & I was dead tired & besides I had just turned down someone (Max Weber) who had begged for a show at 291 because it was the modern place in America. (Matisse had shown in 1908 right after Rodin) & because he had to show. He had come from Paris but a short time ago. I told him he'd have to go elsewhere. He had a small show at Haas's. When I suggested you should have a show elsewhere you remarked you'd have a show at 291 or nowhere, as you liked the spirit of the place & didn't like the spirit of the other places. I asked you a few questions & then, in

spite of myself & my great tiredness & determination not to have any
more shows, I gave you a show to <u>help you</u>. And for no other reason.
I believed in you & your work, because I felt a spirit I liked — or
rather, thought very worthwhile.

Stieglitz continued, reminding Hartley that 291 had saved him financially. A man from Brooklyn had bought a few paintings for sixty
dollars each, and from then on Hartley had "identified with 291 entirely of your own volition."[1] Still agitated a day later by the way Hartley had misrepresented, even ignored, the significance of 291 for him,
Stieglitz wrote a second time, berating Hartley for neither mentioning
291 by name nor saying anything about the "real generous spirit of
the place — a place the like of which never was nor never will be —
<u>I know that</u>." When he thought of their fourteen-year association,
which comprised 291 and all that had been involved with it — catalogues, essays in Stieglitz's journal, *Camera Work,* and Hartley's many
letters (often pleading for money, Stieglitz did not add) — he felt that
Hartley's picture of their relationship became a "grimace." "You were
given your original Show in '291' because of my reading Suffering —
Spiritual anguish — in your face," Stieglitz declared,

> and because I felt a supreme worthwhile struggle of a Soul. No other
> reason. And that is the reason why I have fought for you to this day
> and will continue to fight. "291" to me was a place where I could
> breathe freely — devoid of all commercial taint — not a business.
> I believed there could be a place where human beings could meet
> without all the dirty ugliness which the struggle for existence seems
> to bring out sooner or later in most artists.

Stieglitz was so overwrought that he wrote a third letter that same
day.[2] The bitterness he felt in 1923 was the result of personal problems
and illness, his deep resentment that 291 had never received its due,
and Hartley's mistreatment of what Stieglitz considered to be fact.
But these matters all arose after 1909. Stieglitz was correct: Hartley
had liked the spirit of the gallery and had been thrilled to have a
show there. It ran from May 8 to 18 and included thirty-three of his
paintings: *Silence of High Noon — Midsummer; Cosmos; The Hall of
the Mountain King; The Summer Camp; Proud Music of the Storm;
Winter Plumage — Blizzard; The Ice Hole;* fifteen paintings in a series
entitled *Songs of Autumn;* seven in *Songs of Winter;* and four *Blizzard
Impressions.*

The show did not create a great stir. Max Weber disliked the pictures and called Hartley an impostor.[3] But the maverick critic Sadakichi Hartmann disagreed, noting in a review for *Camera Work* that Hartley's colors were the most startling feature of his "examples of an extreme and up-to-date impressionism." Hartmann thought Hartley less an imitator of Segantini or anyone else than a self-taught artist who "amidst the scenery of his fancy . . . has learnt to reproduce nature in her most intense and luminous coloring." He liked Hartley's work and, after praising "the peculiarity and freshness of his viewpoint," went on to explain how impressionism as a method had developed.[4] The review must have pleased Hartley, though it appeared too late to attract people to his show. It identified him as part of the American avant-garde; now he belonged, and to a group whose work, if often without much support, would gradually educate other Americans to the modern.

At the center was Stieglitz; any number of artists and writers have testified to that. Mabel Dodge Luhan, for example, wrote about how much it pleased her to visit 291 and hear him talk of all sorts of things, "life and pictures and people — telling of his strange experiences, greatly magnifying them with the strong lenses of his mental vision." She met people who became her lifelong friends; "there we gathered over and over again, drawn and held together by the apparent purity of Stieglitz's intention. He was afraid of nothing, and always trusted his eyes and his heart. . . . There were always attractive people at Stieglitz's place."[5]

Hartley agreed with the others; several years after first meeting Stieglitz, in answer to the question, "What is 291?," he wrote about the gallery's uniqueness and claimed,

> It has created and fulfilled its unique and specialized function, that of bringing to view fairly and without ostent and as completely as conditions have allowed, the artistic searchings of individuals and through its generosity and faith has brought freely before a fairly curious public, the work of artists in various fields of expression who have by reason of this originality for long been excommunicated from the main body both in America and in Europe.[6]

"Generosity and faith" were among Stieglitz's qualities, his proponents believed. Detractors thought his ego too much involved with his decisions; they could not abide his long monologues or what they took to be a pose on his part of indifference toward money, which among other things lessened the chances of financial success for his circle. Stieglitz detested the commercial aspects of the art world, so much so that he would occasionally refuse to sell a painting if he did not think the buyer worthy of it. And because of his individualism — not to mention his egocentricity — he remained aloof from other groups that after the 1913 Armory Show also supported modern art in America.[7]

To Hartley, Stieglitz was an "extraordinary person" with many sides to his nature. He liked horse racing, music, and billiards and was the "world's greatest photographer," which had the effect of making members of his circle "see nature better." He was exceedingly generous, keeping a kind of open lunch table for friends at the Holland House as well as taking them to his home for meals and often to concerts in the evening. Hartley asserted that Stieglitz shared everything with his associates and never tried to impose his strong beliefs on them, but instead worked constantly to help the artists develop.[8]

As in any intimate friendship between two complex people, differences arose between Stieglitz and Hartley, as the 1923 episode reveals. Stieglitz became impatient with the other's vagaries and with his sometimes inflated sense of his own importance, while Hartley thought Stieglitz overlooked him and favored John Marin and Georgia O'Keeffe — which was in fact true, especially during the period when Hartley spent years abroad, even as Stieglitz believed American artists should be expressing their Americanness. But to Hartley Stieglitz was both confidant and father figure, a "nimbus of voluminous gray hair [under which] was a warm light and a fair understanding of all things, and anyone who entered this special place, entered it to be understood" — precisely what Hartley himself had craved when he first entered the small room on the top floor of 291 Fifth Avenue.[9]

Once Stieglitz had promised him a show in 1909, Hartley haunted 291, watching his pictures be framed and hung in the small front room and a hallway that led to a larger space in the back. For him one of the major events during the exhibition was a visit by N. E. Montross, who had his own gallery at 550 Fifth Avenue. Impressed by Hartley's work, Montross invited him to his gallery, where Hartley recalled being led into a "still room with red plush — some easels, a few chairs and pictures covered with pieces of red plush." Then or soon afterward Montross asked him how he got by and what it cost to live in Maine. Hartley said four dollars per week for room and board, and Montross offered to supply him with that amount for the next two years, expecting nothing in return.[10]

The kindly Montross, recognizing Hartley's interest in mysticism, also wanted to show him one of Albert Pinkham Ryder's marine paintings, very possibly *Moonlight Marine*. Hartley knew next to nothing of Ryder but was deeply moved by the small picture. "It had in it everything that I knew and had experienced about my own New England," he wrote later, explaining,

> It had in it the stupendous solemnity of a [William] Blake picture and it had a sense of realism besides that bore such a force of nature itself as to leave me breathless. The picture had done its work and I was a convert to the field of imagination into which I was born. I had been thrown back into the body and being of my own country as by no other influence that had come to me.[11]

When Hartley wrote this, in the early 1930s, the subject of nativeness was much on his mind. In 1909 he was already deep in the subject of his own country, as his paintings at 291 revealed, but Ryder made him aware of a style that would enable him to express more acutely his feelings about Maine and the Atlantic Ocean, their harshness and isolating power. Ryder's marine painting of "a sky and a single vessel in sail across a conquering sea" captured for Hartley "the sea's beauty, . . . its hauteurs, its supremacies," which were exactly what fascinated him about all of nature. "Ryder gave us first and last an incomparable sense of pattern and austerity of mood," Hartley wrote after Ryder's death, declaring that "he saw with an all too pitiless and pitiful eye the element of helplessness in things, the complete succumbing of things in nature to those elements greater than they that wield a fatal power."[12]

In New York in 1909 Hartley lived at 351 West Fifteenth Street, between Eighth and Ninth avenues. The place was only a short distance from Ryder's flat at 308, so, enthralled by the marine painting, Hartley introduced himself to Ryder, possibly at Kiel's Bakery, where Ryder would spend several hours over a meal. Or perhaps they met when Ryder was on one of his legendary long walks — often nocturnal to allow him to study the moon and cloud formations — which took him as far as Central Park, down to the Battery, or even to the Jersey Palisades. In any case Ryder invited Hartley to his flat to see his work. The tenement was a dismal place inside; Hartley remembered that its halls were lit by gaslight so weak that he had some difficulty making his way to the third floor, where Ryder's three rooms were. He had long since stopped discarding things, and Hartley recalled that the place was "an incredible mass of debris." Two rooms were filled to the ceiling with furniture and boxes; the third, in which Ryder lived, contained a small stove, and around it, "besides the usual overflow of chairs, broken settees, stuffed seating objects, or whatever, there were numerous piles of ashes, oatmeal boxes, tin cans of whatever sort." Weaving through this was a path, to the left of which was a roll of carpet where Ryder slept. Amid all this Hartley saw, covered with dirt from years of neglect, the paintings *Macbeth, Death on a Pale Horse,* and *The Tempest,* testimonials to the vivid imagination that so excited him.

He did not meet Ryder often, only infrequently seeing him on the street near where they both lived. Shy and distracted but kindly, the eccentric artist might have his feet "caked in straw and cold oatmeal, covered by oversize brogans," as part of his idiosyncratic treatment for rheumatism.[13] When Hartley saw him he was usually dressed in "grey wools, sweater, skull-cap to match, with a button of wool at the top. . . . This cap came down to his shaggy eyebrows which were like lichens overhanging rocks of granite, the eyes that they now tell me were brown I thought of course to be blue." He had a thick mustache and a long, full beard and was very much the odd figure that Hartley captured in his portrait of the mystical painter, executed from memory in 1939.[14]

"Ryder's spirit lived intensely in me," Hartley later wrote. He recalled that the next pictures he made after discovering Ryder's work "were solely from memory and the imagination, of which there were only four or five — those which later became known as the 'black landscapes.'" This statement might be taken to mean that Hartley's other work was less "from memory and the imagination," but that was not the case. Ryder made such a strong impression on him precisely because he saw in the artist and his work a kindred spirit. Ryder often used literary subjects for his paintings, and he wrote poems that were occasionally published. One of these appeared in the *New York Evening Sun* in May 1909; it begins,

> Oh ye beautiful trees of the forest,
> Grandest and most eloquent daughters
> Of fertile Mother Earth.[15]

In 1909, for Hartley, another would-be poet entranced with mysticism, the discovery of Ryder was as important as his association with Stieglitz. Before seeing Ryder's work, Hartley painted decoratively; after, he began to find ways to express things about the human spirit, becoming, in the words used of Ryder by the artist and teacher Hans Hofmann, a "cosmic creator."[16] Hartley knew about oceans before he saw Ryder's marines, but they made him aware that the Atlantic could be a metaphor for what he felt. Not that Hartley immediately ran to the seashore and began painting seascapes; he did not, but he understood what Ryder was doing and recognized how one could get at the things that lay beneath surfaces, beneath bright colors and pretty decorations.

Hartley was fortunate when a friend from art school, Ernest Roth, offered him space to paint in his small room on the top floor of 232 West Fourteenth Street. The place was already jammed with books, a printing press, and other possessions of Roth's, but it — and indeed the whole building, which Hartley called an "art rookery" — had a warmth that Hartley liked, so he accepted Roth's offer and during 1909 painted the pictures directly inspired by Ryder. "Somber, expressionistic canvases," Barbara Haskell has termed them, "depicting deserted farms overshadowed by mountains and dominated by broken, anthropomorphic trees."[17] On the back of one, *The Dark Mountain,* Stieglitz wrote:

> by Marsden Hartley 1909 (The Dark Mountain Period). In Hartley's opinion the finest — most expressive — example of his work of that year — never exhibited. Note: May 2 — 1917 by Alfred Steiglitz — I have had this picture before me; practically daily, for seven years — I still consider it one of the best of all Hartley's work — it always satisfies me — It is genuinely Hartley — significant — Hartley undoubtedly was on the verge of suicide during the summer which brought forth this picture.[18]

Stieglitz may have been indulging in a touch of hyperbole; Hartley, with the exposure from his 291 exhibition and a small guaranteed income from Montross, should not have been desperate. But he did brood, and Ryder's paintings showed him a way to release his feelings about Maine and his summers in the remote Stoneham Valley. Evidence suggests that he painted the *Dark Mountain* series during the late spring of 1909, before he traveled to North Lovell for the summer and fall and returned to doing less poignant, if more luminous, land-scapes, such as those he had exhibited at 291.

On the verge of suicide or not, the sensitive man had reason to be melancholy despite Montross's charity. He knew he had to go back to the isolation of Maine to paint the subjects he knew best, but he did not want to leave the exhilaration of 291. He knew also that his four-dollar-a-week stipend could not really sustain him in the city. Since 1904 he had lived a hand-to-mouth existence, with only one or two small artistic successes, and even his recent show had been a financial failure. The easy transcendentalism and firm religiosity he had earlier espoused now seemed largely irrelevant, and the poverty he saw in New York defied any simplistic view that "God's in his heaven, and all's right with the world." It was not all right for him or for many others. Moreover, he had lately had to confront his sexuality as earlier he had not, and only a vastly naive person could have failed to recog-nize the cruelty of much of society's attitude toward homosexuals. It was not only society's attitude that distressed him, however; he had also to struggle with his own New England upbringing, and through-out his days he would feel deeply constrained when it came to public gestures of intimacy.

Reluctant to depart New York, but still tied to Maine, he went north to stay through the rest of the year. Whether he returned to the city during the early months of 1910 is not clear. There were reasons for him to do so; from February 23 to March 8 Stieglitz held an exhibition of drawings and reproductions of paintings by Matisse at 291. This was the second exhibition of his work, though it was the first that Hartley could have seen. Following immediately upon Matisse was an exhibition, from March 9 to 21, of "Young American Painters," which included works by D. Putnam Brinley, Arthur B. Carles, Arthur Dove, Lawrence Fellows, Hartley, Marin, Alfred Maurer, Edward Steichen, and Max Weber.[19] Hartley may well have traveled to New York in the spring to view these exhibitions; he would have been anx-ious to see his pictures on display and excited about the European modernists. Paintings he made during the summer of 1910, such as *Red Tree* and *Sundown Kezar Lake,* a small sketch he did on July 14 for his niece Norma Berger, are fauvist; they and others from that time, Barbara Haskell has noted, "create a flattened, artificial space. In several works . . . the entire expression is conveyed through the brush-stroke itself, creating a degree of gestural abstraction that would not be surpassed in America until abstract expressionism."[20] About *Sun-down Kezar Lake* Hartley wrote to his niece from North Lovell,

> I am sending you a sketch which I made about a month ago — It is a part of our mountains here at sundown — just a half hour sketch you know — a notation merely of colors of sundown. I do not sketch much these days for I work almost wholly from the imagination — making pictures entirely from this point of view using the mountains only as backgrounds for ideas — This takes a long time and is a slow process — that is why I get so little done — as I do not allow myself to work from nature much, but from my memory of it — This is difficult art — almost anybody can paint from nature — It calls for real expert power to create an idea and produce it as one sees it in the mind. And this is what the critics call me — an imaginative colorist.[21]

Talk in the back room of 291 about the European modernists had already alerted Hartley to their work, but his painting during the summer of 1910 is so consciously fauvist that it is hard not to believe that his immediate influence was the Matisse exhibition. Of course the work of other painters was important to him as well; during the years 1909–1912, for example, after he became part of the 291 circle and before he sailed for France in April 1912, he tried various styles in rapid succession, with those of Picasso, Weber, and Cézanne affecting him to the point that he imitated their work closely even as he sought a style of his own. In the excitement of discovering modernism, he had only to see reproductions of new work before he would rush to try his own version.

Hartley's life in North Lovell during the summer and fall of 1910 was notably rustic, and sometimes that galled him. Such isolation, he told Horace Traubel in late July, was something he did not want for himself, but his work required it. If once he had found solitude "imperative," now he needed people and the warmth of male companions.[22] He was yearning to be with Traubel and Percy Wiksell when he wrote, though at other times he enjoyed his life in the woods. Of necessity he walked five or six miles a day, sometimes more. The post office serving North Lovell was two and a half miles from his cabin, he told Norma Berger, and the day before he wrote her he had walked some ten miles, hiking to a neighboring village, perhaps Center Lovell, to see a woman who taught "dramatic expression" at Smith College.

His own place was quite spacious — five rooms — and set back from the road in a field, with a mountain brook flowing through the front yard. Behind the house was a stand of large willow trees, and behind them were the mountains, "so close and brotherly." For all his isolation, he had companionship on occasion. On the Fourth of July, he reported, there had been a dance in North Lovell, from which he had not gotten home until dawn the next day.

Mentioning athletics to his niece, he hinted at his own preferences in men: "I only wish I were a great husky brute," he declared, "a prize fighter or something like it as I would love to be powerful and excel in bodily strength — It makes me terribly envious when I see men swimming or running or boxing." He was euphoric at that moment, for he was a bit in love with a young sailor named John Wilson, whom he had met recently when Wilson was home on leave. He was "so clean and well built so jovial with the most wonderful smile." They had taken to each other, Hartley confided, and were now writing once or twice a week — "and his letters are so manly and fine."

Hartley had also taken to a barber in Lewiston, but he was more attracted to Wilson,[23] whom he visited with Thomas Mosher in Boston in November after he had left North Lovell and seen his father and stepmother. The first part of that trip was laborious: it took a change of carriages and three short train rides to get the forty or so miles to Lewiston.[24]

Hartley returned to New York in late November and settled back into the house on West Fifteenth Street. He wrote to Norma Berger about his stay in Boston and sent her photographs of himself and Wilson. The best ones of Wilson he had framed and kept for himself, because the sailor was "'one grand boy' — I have never met his like — and I have met many, many people in my wanderings," he assured his niece. Wilson was a "great big strapping fellow — so tender, so large hearted — with an unconscious sense of what friendship means." Hartley told Berger that he had visited his friend on duty aboard the battleship *New Jersey* every day when he was in Boston. Wilson had wanted to see all he could of Hartley but was able to get ashore only rarely, so Hartley had gone to the Charlestown Navy Yard and boarded the *New Jersey*, where he observed "everything that pertains to war and the wilful destruction of human life and it horrified me beyond all." But after the first visit he had become accustomed to the warship and had in fact liked the atmosphere among the "many handsome sailors — strong burly fellows of all types," one of whom, a "blond fellow with soft blue eyes," had stared at Hartley for quite a while and made him feel that he was another comrade. Not that Hartley was bored with Wilson; he had simply been luxuriating in the male world of shipboard. The photos he sent Berger had been taken one day when he and Wilson were walking in Boston. Afterward they had gone to Hartley's hotel and slept for a few hours. Wilson was his "very antithesis," he declared, "so large — broad shouldered — big bodied — and I little and slender as I suppose I shall always be." He wished his niece could meet his friend, who was superbly simple and frank and pure, "big and dark with curly black hair and on board ship he looks wonderful." Hartley was more open with his niece about his attraction to men than he was with almost anyone else at that time.

Hartley hoped to see him again the following summer in Maine, but in the meantime in New York he was happy with his memories of Boston and his renewed friendships among the many men who ate at Kiel's Bakery, "chauffeurs — house-painters — young authors and artists — clerks and a medley of day laborers such strong clean wholesome men — and all so friendly too." He described to his niece an oyster-opener from Virginia and the poet Shaemas O'Sheel, and then closed,

> so you see what a variety of friendship I carry on — all so interesting and beautiful — all types of men and women — from all walks of life — artists — anarchists, poets — musicians — actors — "oyster men" — sailors, publishers — everybodies and nobodies — It is the greatest art of all — life — and friendship.[25]

His ebullience late in 1910 suggests that he would not have made the *Dark Mountain* paintings then. He was assimilating what he had learned about Matisse, and once back in New York he almost certainly studied the lithographs of Monet, Cézanne, Renoir, and Toulouse-Lautrec, the drawings of Rodin, and the paintings and drawings of Henri Rousseau, all of which were exhibited at 291 from November 18 to December 8, 1910.[26] Hartley at once did a Cézannesque still life, a creditable piece that shows he understood the French painter's ideas about form and color.*

---

*Stieglitz would later state that Hartley first saw Cézanne's work in March 1911. A letter from Hartley to Stieglitz, written during the summer of 1911, seems to suggest that Hartley had not yet seen Cézanne's oils, though it is very likely that he had viewed examples of other

By early January 1911 he was confined to the Willard Parker Hospital, on East Sixteenth Street, with a case of scarlet fever — a light one, he told Norma Berger. It kept him in the hospital until the middle of February because, he explained, his feet were slow to shed their infected skin.[27] As he was not very ill, his spirits remained good, and he enjoyed the company of the nurses and the other patients, many of them children. Once out, he immediately resumed his affairs, which involved preparing nine paintings to be hung in a show at the galleries of the Society of Beaux-Arts Architects. The invitation was "a flattering compliment indeed for the other artists are older and have reputation and so I am quite proud," he wrote to Berger in mid-March.[28] His paintings included a dark landscape from 1909, an autumn landscape from 1910, a still life, and six landscape drawings. They were exhibited along with works by Arthur B. Davies, Rockwell Kent, George Luks, John Marin, Alfred Maurer, and Maurice Prendergast, among others.[29] The show ran from March 26 to April 21. Once it was in place, Hartley took time to write to his niece, self-importantly announcing that he had been so busy that he had had "no time or thought for anything else. It is an important season in art matters in New York," he told her; there were "great changes in the development of art in America and I am among the few who are creating the change." Artists praised his work, while "the critics laugh and call it meaningless — but those who can understand it know its seriousness and call me an American individualist to [be] heard from."[30]

When he left the hospital in February he was hoping to return to Maine by the beginning of April, but his affairs kept him in New York until early May. In April he visited Horace Traubel and his wife, Anne, in Philadelphia, then traveled to Baltimore, where he tried to arrange for the sale of some pictures, and finally went to Washington, D.C.[31] Once back in New York, he gathered his possessions together and hurried to Maine to be near John Wilson, who had left the Navy and returned to the town of Norway. Hartley was correct when he told Norma Berger that the time was an important one for art; not only had his work been shown among that of older, avant-garde painters, but in January, at 291, there had been exhibitions of drawings and paintings by Max Weber, which Hartley may have seen before he went to the hospital and which included Cézannesque still lifes. In March

---

genres. As he was in New York at the time, surely he attended not only the 1911 show of watercolors but also the one in 1910 of lithographs.

there was an exhibit of twenty watercolors by Cézanne himself, and immediately afterward, one of eighty-three drawings and watercolors by Picasso.

Years later Stieglitz reminded Hartley that he had sat in front of the Picasso paintings for hours at a time and commented on their extraordinary nature, which he had come to understand through Weber's work as well. He may have undertaken his first painting based on Picasso's analytic cubism before he departed for Maine; on the back of a Hartley watercolor, *Landscape No. 32, 1911,* which resembled both Picasso's and Weber's cubist works, Stieglitz wrote, "The first painting he made after the Picasso exhibition at '291' in 1911."[32] The noted art historian William Innes Homer has observed that at the 291 show "there were enough of [Picasso's] proto-Cubist and early Analytical Cubist examples to bring about a radical change in Hartley's pictorial language." Homer adds that Picasso's 1910 style, evident in at least one work in the show, was reflected in Hartley's *Abstraction* of 1911, "a personal exercise in Analytic Cubism and probably his first nonrepresentational painting."[33] But if Picasso had a powerful, immediate effect upon him, it was Cézanne who truly captured his imagination, as one might expect, given Hartley's fascination with nature and the problems of rendering its essential forms and colors.

While he practiced his art as he understood Cézanne had, he needed to put his life in order in North Lovell. He cleaned his house and planted a garden after struggling to plow the land — "an entirely novel experience which I do not care to repeat." That completed, he traveled by coach to Norway in early June to visit John Wilson at the hotel where he worked, staying there for nearly two weeks before returning to North Lovell.[34]

To Stieglitz, who was abroad that summer, he mentioned his hope that he might change his life's routine before another year passed. "I want to strike out & get something of outer life into my blood," he insisted. "This inward life is depleting so much of it." He wanted to be a "citizen of Paris," aesthetically speaking, for a year; if he had to be poor, he mused, he might as well be so under more interesting circumstances. "It seems as though I've had nothing but denials for most of my life," he asserted. There might have been "a little caviar," but much more was "unpalatable dry crust," and one could not last forever on that. He told Stieglitz that he was working on nothing but still lifes, his aim being to render an object "with a sense of authority and artistic conviction" — on some days in order to demonstrate form, and on others, color. Expressing the impersonal was his goal: "things without mood — things existing for themselves only as shapes & forms with color — The rendering in line & form of a thought — rather than a phase, a mood."

He was already much taken with Cézanne, who seemed to have shown "how personal one can become through striving to express the impersonal."[35] He reported to Stieglitz in August on his progress and asked him to send photos of Cézanne's work as soon as he could, preferably including still lifes. On his wall he kept Cézanne's remark "When color reaches richness form attains fulness," a truth that he understood even from looking at black-and-white reproductions of Cézanne's still lifes in a book about him. "The appeal of Cézanne in color must be simply overwhelming," Hartley continued, referring to the French artist's oils. He longed to see them and hoped that in the fall, back in New York, he would have a chance to view the Havemeyer collection.[36] Stieglitz did not send photographs quickly enough for the impatient Hartley, who soon asked his friend not to forget to forward reproductions of Cézanne's and van Gogh's work, in which he detected "such strength of intellect." He was sure he would rest content if he could have several good reproductions to work from. He was doing considerably more drawing than usual, both still lifes and landscapes, in his effort to improve his treatment of form and color. "I am setting aside entirely the mood of nature and interesting myself wholly in the problem and its rendering," he told Stieglitz. "Picasso taught me much on this point — the pure beauty of the problem itself," he explained, adding that nevertheless he found Picasso's viewpoint less edifying than that of Cézanne, in whose work, even in reproductions, "there is something so satisfying so large and splendid."[37]

Shortly before Stieglitz returned to America in mid-October, Hartley received from him two reproductions of Cézanne still lifes. He was beside himself with pleasure, he told his friend, and touched them and looked at them as if they were religious objects. He planned to return to New York, and because he had received only twenty dollars of the hundred promised him the previous spring in Baltimore, he wondered if 291 would advance him forty dollars so he could pay off some small debts in North Lovell, visit his parents in Lewiston, and travel south.[38] Stieglitz obliged, and by late November Hartley was delighted to be in New York again, especially as for the first time he had a studio of his own, a room at 244 West Fourteenth Street with north light and ample space.[39] He was pleased as well when Arthur B. Davies arranged for him to see the nine Cézannes in the Havemeyer collection.[40] And then Stieglitz approached him about a second show at 291, which was held from February 7 to 26, 1912. The paintings were still lifes, "proving very interesting to the people of New York," Hartley told Norma Berger.[41] The critics praised him for his vivid colors, which, according to Joseph Edgar Chamberlin, writing in the *New York Mail,* were "deep and often spiritual."[42] When the show was over, he had sold a few pictures, and more important, his work had stimulated enough interest that Stieglitz was able to persuade benefactors to underwrite Hartley's expenses for a year's stay in Europe so that he might learn firsthand about modern European art. "Money is being raised by influential friends who believe in me and believe I should go abroad — So much for long struggles and faith in oneself," he announced proudly to Berger.[43] With the money from the sale of a painting to Agnes Meyer and additional funds that Arthur B. Davies convinced Lillie Bliss to offer, Hartley was to travel to France. He booked passage for early April and then went to Lewiston for a visit with his family — the last time he would see his father, as it turned out. Lewiston, especially in the light of his forthcoming trip, seemed to him extremely dull, a reminder of what he hoped to get away from. Short of money again, he had to ask Stieglitz for ten dollars to return to New York, where, two days before leaving, he signed over his power of attorney to his friend. On April 4, aboard the *La Savoie,* he wrote a postcard to his niece and her family:

> Au Revoir Everybody!
>
> I sail in about an hour — I am tired out getting ready and have a cold but I will be all right soon — I may be seasick — You can think of me at the rail as I shall probably be there. I will write as soon as I can from the other side.[44]

At the age of thirty-five he was finally on his way to Paris, where he would begin what was in some ways a new career, though it would be many years, and he would be back in the United States, before he completed his search for self and place.

5

Paris
1912

HARTLEY SOUNDED LIKE many a newly arrived tourist when he wrote to Norma Berger on April 12, his second day in Paris. "I've had a wondrous glimpse of perhaps the finest city in existence," he exclaimed, and he promised that he would write more as soon as he found a satisfactory place to live.[1] At that moment he was staying in a cheap hotel near the Gare Saint-Lazare while he got his bearings. Venturing over to the Boulevard Montparnasse, he discovered Alfred Maurer and another American, who helped him after several days to relocate in a small hotel on the boulevard. He wasted no time before seeking out the art he had come to France to study. "I saw 8 Van Goghs this afternoon — several fine   one ('La Berceuse') a beauty — others — landscapes — four Cézannes at Vollard's (funny place) — Tomorrow I shall go on to the Louvre — then the Salon des Indépendants," he wrote to Stieglitz on April 13.[2]

By the end of April he could tell Stieglitz that he had seen most of the "big things": the Louvre, "the most important in my esteem"; the Luxembourg, "quite ridiculous after the Louvre"; the Salon des Indépendants, "perfectly terrible"; and the Salon des Beaux Arts, "merely a National Academy of a better class." Notre Dame, Sainte-Chapelle, and the Pantheon were marvelous. He claimed that he was already familiar with most of Paris and was now ready to work, especially as it would keep him from getting too close to the "art life," which was full of "talk & gossip and no work."

Once again he was becoming caught up in the contradictory needs of intimacy and distance. He wanted to be in contact with the art scene yet also at some remove from it, and was pleased when his American friend Lee Simonson agreed to rent him his studio at 18 Rue Moulin de Beurre, in Montparnasse, "very near all things yet isolated."[3] Simonson himself planned to move south to Cassis to paint with another American, Stanton Macdonald-Wright.

Rue Moulin de Beurre no longer exists, having been obliterated by a large office complex at the Gare Montparnasse, almost in the shadow of Paris's tallest skyscraper, the Tour Montparnasse. But in 1912 Simonson's studio, in a large garden, gave Hartley the peace he needed, and still he could step outside into lively street life. "I live in a most fascinating quarter of Paris ... where the workmen live," he wrote to his niece at the end of July. His place was "just away from what is known as the art quarter," but his quarter and its people interested him more. The workmen — some very handsome, he thought — wore "baggy corduroy trousers of light blue, dark brown and some wonderful rose color — and wide sash belts of fiery red — big shoes — often sabots — and caps or hats." He saw them every day as he went to lunch and dinner, often walking along the nearby Rue de la Gaité, famous for its nightlife, which Hartley appreciated as the workers frequented the music halls there and the street was "gay and jolly." The shows at the halls were "much more intimate and amusing than anything in America though some would say shockingly vulgar, but," he added knowingly, "to the French — life is only life."

Because Hartley painted so many landscapes and still lifes, we may forget his intense interest in people. Although he almost always remained the observer, being around ordinary people offset his desire for isolation and his aloofness. Paris was the most nearly ideal place he had lived. "One may always be studying in Paris," he wrote. "Just life itself is enough — one is conscious of hobnobbing with the universe daily — for every nationality lives here — Russia is seen discussing art with Poland — and Spain talks fervently with France over poetry — while South America and India sip coffee with Persia and Greece."[4] What a person got from Paris, he told Stieglitz in July, was a sense of the "'aliveness' stirring in the air — a reverence of the people toward beauty which is truly comforting."[5] And while he liked to keep his distance from the artistic crowd, he heartily enjoyed indulging himself as he had rarely, if ever, done before. "I went to the Quatres

Arts Ball last week," he reported in late June. "Quite the most wonderful spectacle probably in existence — 2000 people in Arabian
Nights costume — myself as gorgeous as any in effect." For it he wore
white pantaloons and shoes, a dark, embroidered robe, necklaces and
a brooch, and a jeweled turban that set off his face, darkened for the
occasion. The ball remained "the last word in splendour and abandon,"
he declared, "the kind of thing one expects to come only out of books,
but that again is the French genius — It could not have happened
anywhere else on earth — the utter absence of moral code could not
be understood elsewhere."[6]

Not only did the workers around Montparnasse please him, but he
also found American artists whom he had known in New York and
made the acquaintance of others. Edward Steichen and his wife looked
him up early in May at his hotel in Montparnasse, and soon he visited
them at their home outside Paris.[7] He quickly discovered, as well, the
pleasure of café life: "No one lives at home," he informed Norma
Berger. "Everybody goes sometime during the day for coffee to some
café or other — whatever his taste may be — the poets in this side of
Paris (artists too) frequent the Café Closerie de Lilas. . . . The modern
artists go there too. It is very quiet and dignified and intellectual generally."[8] There and at other popular cafés such as the Dome and the
Rotonde he talked with the sculptor Jo Davidson; another American
modernist, Arthur Carles; and Steichen and Maurer.

Two of his most important friendships were with the young Germans Arnold Rönnebeck and his cousin Karl von Freyburg. Hartley
would walk around the corner from the Café Rotonde to have his
meals at the Restaurant Thomas, on the Boulevard Raspail. The Germans ate there, and Hartley soon met them, along with Rönnebeck's
fiancée, the American singer Alice Miriam, and a Swiss poet, Siegfried
Lang. These became Hartley's intimates. He went everywhere with
Rönnebeck, Lang, and von Freyburg after they first met. Rönnebeck
and Miriam had numerous contacts in Paris — among them Sarah
Bernhardt's leading man Lou Tellegen — and often included Hartley
in their social life.[9]

By late July Rönnebeck had sculpted a bust of Hartley, who proudly
announced that it was to be cast in bronze for the Salon d'Automme.
During the summer he was enamored of Lang. When the poet traveled to his home in Basel for a vacation, Hartley complained that his

departure had caused "a siege of melancholy." Lang was "exquisitely beautiful physically and moreso as to soul and heart — a golden blonde youth with a golden heart and a white soul — We were much together and he was so glad to learn English from me — and was I am certain fond of me for he said he loved me," Hartley confided to Rockwell and Kathleen Kent late in August.[10] Lang soon returned to Paris and was an intimate of Hartley's until he moved to Germany in 1913.[11]

As Hartley grew closer to the Germans, he began to turn not against French art but against the French, no doubt because he felt excluded from their society. Like many other expatriates, he associated with foreigners, mostly American and German. And as this continued and he realized that he would never break through the shell that separated him from French society, he became resentful. One has but to visit the fourth floor of the Pompidou Center in Paris, where the National Museum of Modern Art is housed, to see why Hartley would have felt ignored. The American art on display in the museum all dates from after World War II — paintings by the likes of Jackson Pollock, Barnett Newman, Sam Francis, Jasper Johns, Andy Warhol, and a smattering of others. There are no O'Keeffes, no Marins, no Hoppers, no Hartleys. The French were not concerned with that earlier genera-tion of American modernists. In 1912 they did not know of their exis-tence, nor would they have cared had they known.

It took little perspicacity to understand this. Hartley comprehended the situation, and stimulated by his intimacy with the Germans, he soon looked toward the new art being created in their country. The French, especially the men, were "hideous," he asserted to Stieglitz, adding, "If there was ever a more ridiculous lot of males as a class it is these French men." He wondered if someday he might see the "fine types we are accustomed to at home and in Germany"; as yet he had found "only these little china dolls horribly dressed."[12] Writing to Rockwell and Kathleen Kent, he was even more scornful. Compared to Americans, Germans, Danes, Swedes, and even the English — though mentally the British were "nearly always insufferable" — Frenchmen because of their "degeneracy" were "most pitiful to look upon." They rarely achieved "height and proportion — but look like silly tricks of nature." Even when they had attractive heads and shoul-ders, Hartley claimed, they were lacking "in legs[,] and as to carriage and physical demeanor they are dreadful." The French women, though chic, were "often ugly and tiresome."[13]

While his growing intimacy with Rönnebeck, Lang, and von Freyburg increased Hartley's feeling of "we versus they" toward the
French, a skeptical attitude toward all the world was part of what he
gained from his friendship with Charles Demuth. Hartley recalled
that one day in the Restaurant Thomas, Demuth ambled up to the
table where he, Rönnebeck, and perhaps also Alice Miriam and Lee
Simonson were eating. He joined them, and quickly Hartley discovered that he had a "quaint, incisive sort of wit with an ultra sophisticated, post-eighteen-ninety touch to it." The group enjoyed the banter
and gossip that ensued, and from that moment Demuth became one
of them and a lasting friend of Hartley's. Subsequently they would sit
together at the Thomas and take pleasure in observing the characters
who passed in front of the restaurant, such as the one with a "kind of
Fleurs du Mal silhouette," who wore black velvet, a heavily laced shirt,
and a touch of makeup that gave him a gaunt look. This man would
be accompanied by "the very manly George Banks," who looked so
much like Oscar Wilde that Hartley and his friends called her "Oscar
Wilde la Seconde." This sort of thing was "très exagéré of course,"
Hartley remarked, "but life was like that then, and it all seemed to be
part of the day's run, and brings up an amusing and funny Paris,
accentuated all the more acutely by the manner of the young cubists
who were over-dressing in the other extreme à la Londres, with white
spats on all occasions and an air of great importance whisking about
them." He had in mind particularly the French cubists Jean Metzinger
and Robert Delaunay.[14]

Hartley's friendship with the Germans and Lang mattered in several ways. Associating with these bright young men gave him confidence and shielded him from the standoffishness of the French; he was
immensely attracted physically to Lang and von Freyburg; and Rönnebeck was the one who encouraged him to visit Germany, where his
appreciation of new German art — Kandinsky, though Russian, was
painting in Germany then — led Hartley to produce a body of significantly original work. In 1912, however, yet another friendship, that
with Gertrude Stein, was nearly as important to Hartley as the others,
because her enthusiasm for his work also bolstered his confidence.

Shortly after his arrival in Paris he was taken to one of Gertrude
and her brother Leo's Saturday-evening gatherings at 27 Rue de
Fleurus. The Saturday evenings were always exciting, and the occasion afforded Hartley his first glimpse of the Steins' collection of paint-

ings by Renoir, Matisse, Cézanne, and Picasso. People talked art, and Gertrude Stein, an imposing presence, at once revealed that she understood what the modernists were about. The walls of her apartment, Hartley remembered, were "crowded with the new Picassos — many of the 'collage' epoch, with piece[s] of the daily papers stuck in, or perhaps oftener painted in, pieces of the words 'jour'nal — 'trans'igaient too perhaps — and there were still a few Cézannes and a Matisse or two."[15] On a table were several folios of Picasso's drawings; Hartley did not have the chance to study them that first evening, but Gertrude promised to invite him again in the fall, after she and Alice Toklas returned from a trip to Spain.

She was an imposing, if controversial, figure. Joseph Stella, the American artist, described her as an "immense woman carcass austerely dressed in black." During his visit to 27 Rue de Fleurus she was "enthroned on a sofa in the middle of the room where [paintings by Matisse and Picasso] were hanging." Stella, given to sarcasm, remarked that "with the forceful solemnity of a pitoness or a sibylla, she was examining pitiless all newcomers, assuming a high and distant pose."[16]

Hartley enjoyed her far more than did Stella and appreciated her generosity. "Gertrude Stein is one of the salts of the earth — she is a high power chemical value in downright human relationships," he declared much later. He was delighted when she wrote in *The Autobiography of Alice B. Toklas* that he was someone "whom we liked very much."[17] "Gertrude used to get excited with the meeting of a new person, 'a new person is an event and hinders one from sleep' sort of thing," Hartley observed. She took to him and soon did the word portrait that appeared in the catalogue for his exhibition at 291 in 1914. "Mine came out as 'A cook can see. Pointedly in uniform,'" he recalled. "And if I cared I still would have to say 'what does it mean Gertrude,' but as G. says, 'if you like a thing you understand it,' and so I liked it — perhaps — secretly a little because of the flattery."[18]

One thing that Hartley especially valued about 27 Rue de Fleurus was that he was accepted there and made to feel at home. "I was not then and am not now the type of person who gets into a room easily," he wrote:

> I always have to work my way in. I can be easy in a room when I have had time to work my way into it. I have to get settled, and see one thing at a time after I see all of it at once — and that is no small

job in a room like 27 rue de Fleurus, with walls all afire with epoch-making ideas and at least two vivid people under them. I couldn't have entertained this room any too remarkably save that it has always had space and place for all sorts and kinds of things and qualities, for Gertrude has always had a way of liking several kinds of people at once, and if they entertained her with smart talk or gossip all well and good and if they became something more homelike more carpet slipperish that was all right too — maybe Gertrude liked my disembodiedness which she says is so American — surely I was one of that kind then, for I had a tendency toward ecstasy and exaltation then — and I think that must have made me likeable — in any event I was happy I was liked.[19]

And Stein looked out for him. He told of one of the first Saturday evenings he visited her: Sonia and Robert Delaunay were present, and Robert asked Hartley what he painted. His response was "O — I don't know," at which Delaunay became irritated and insistent. "I got hectic," Hartley recounted, "and turning to Gertrude I remember saying, sotto voce, 'Will you tell this man to go to hell' — and for once smiled as I said it — to fit in with the spirit of French hypocrisy which they alone accomplish with such charm." She said she could not do that and inquired what he really did paint. He said he guessed his works were "sort of mystical abstractions." She asked if she could see them, which surprised and delighted him.

"So I decided to get a lot of canvases, and see if I could evoke patterns of images that had to do with my days," he remembered. Satisfied with his first large picture because to him it had a "real" look about it — "highly lyric and upper register in key" — he painted some twenty more and invited Stein and Toklas to tea. For the occasion he served sandwiches of whole-wheat bread, *petit suisse,* and shaved endive, which pleased the two women. Hartley set his paintings along the baseboard of his studio. Stein marveled at how good they were and before leaving announced that she wanted to see them again after thinking about them. On her next visit she declared that the paintings held up well, and proceeded to invite Hartley for lunch, asking him to bring several of his works, which they would try out among her Matisses and Picassos.[20] The eventual outcome was that she bought a painting and lent Hartley her support by writing to Stieglitz about his innovations with color.

The paintings at 27 Rue de Fleurus moved Hartley more toward modernism. They fulfilled his expectations and inspired him to range beyond his earlier emulations of Cézanne and Matisse. "His work evolved rapidly from the Cézannesque style of the previous year," Barbara Haskell has noted, citing as an example *Still Life No. 1* of 1912, "which fused Cézanne's composition and structural approach with the palette and decorative emphasis of Matisse." By the end of the summer he had shifted to a "more abstract Cubist style . . . which employed the compressed space and angular, faceted lines of Analytic Cubism."[21]

Because Hartley wrote extensively in his letters about the art he was seeing, it is tempting to study his work primarily in relation to that art. But doing so tends to diminish his own accomplishment and makes him little more than a copyist. Hartley *did* absorb deeply what he saw, and *did* work in the style of Cézanne's still lifes, for example, but he passed beyond that and other styles and achieved his own. And did so repeatedly, one might add, accepting that there was not absolute continuity in Hartley's work but rather stops and then starts in new directions. His early Maine paintings, for instance, differ radically from his "musical theme" paintings of late 1912; they, in turn, from his Berlin paintings of 1913–1915 (and they substantially from each other); they, from his New Mexico paintings of 1918–1924; and so on. Hence it is less rewarding to try to find hints of Renoir in Hartley's subsequent techniques than to see his enthusiasm as a reflection of what one young American was discovering about "the modern." He was seeing new ways to express the spiritual values he had derived from the likes of Emerson, Thoreau, and Whitman.

In the spring and summer of 1912 French art poured in on him, and he was of at least two minds about it. "Apart from Renoir & the Cézannes one may see occasionally there is absolutely nothing worth looking at," he informed Stieglitz in late June. He was "shocked of late with the mediocrity of men like Flandrin — Fries — Manguin — It is too dreadful." Compared to these artists, he maintained, "Matisse becomes one of the gods," and even Monet's paintings of Venice seemed like the real thing. French art might well be "in the descendant," and even a few great painters could not reassert its primacy. "One has a sense somehow of the more timeliness of the cubistes and the futuristes," he added. "I see them often & have met several. Have been to Delaunay's studio and seen his 'latest' — but so far it is like a demonstration for chemistry or the technical relations of color & sound. They all talk so glibly but what do they produce."[22]

Partly the art scene in Paris lacked excitement at the end of June because it was summertime, and the Parisians were about to make their annual exodus out of the city for their vacations. But Hartley's lack of enthusiasm was due to his unease with the French and, even more, to the absence of any clear sense on his part of how he might bring together his own instincts for form, color, and emotion. Several things were working on him at once, with the result that by early fall he began to make what was for him a dramatic change. Twenty years later he would write to Adelaide Kuntz that "in Paris I decided to stop painting still life and 'see what would happen' & the result was the long array of inventions which brought forth from G. Stein 'at last an original American' which I took for what it was worth then."[23]

As the months passed, Picasso's work became a major reason that Hartley's instincts about art coalesced into expressive form. He had seen Picasso's paintings at 27 Rue de Fleurus, and from that moment his letters were sprinkled with laudatory words about the Spanish artist. "After the long siege of wish-wash tableaux modernes one turns with relief and pleasure to Picasso," he wrote to Stieglitz after remarking on a "beautiful and impressive Picasso" he had seen at the Vollard Gallery, of "quite good size two standing figures two women conversing — done in 1904 — all in blue tones — very Gothic in feeling."[24] In September, after Gertrude Stein and Alice Toklas returned from their trip to Spain, Hartley visited them to see the Stein collection a second time, and the next day he wrote to Rockwell Kent that Picasso was a "wonder," unique at that moment for his profound understanding and his "insight into the inwardness of things." He was "doing very exceptional things of a most abstract psychic nature — things which are in themselves pure expression without subject matter . . . yet full of subjective realism."[25]

As soon as the Salon d'Automme opened, he went to see it and was deeply disappointed. "Nothing remarkable," he reported to Stieglitz. "The cubists say very little almost nothing — the real artists not showing — not Picasso." Steichen, Maurer, and even Matisse had work displayed, but none of it was thrilling, "& oh what a mess of awful rubbish besides," Hartley lamented, adding, "Tell [the Mexican artist Marius] de Zayas he is right — art is dead — and now expression is beginning in earnest. . . . Paris is a dead issue for art."[26] He also viewed an exhibition of cubist painters called the Section d'Or, but they too were a disappointment. "How like the Gods the others seem — Cézanne, Picasso, and even Matisse who is of all things an artist if not as great as Cézanne or Picasso," he noted. After complimenting André Derain — "a lesser man" whose paintings, if "in no sense involved," were at least "direct and noble" — Hartley continued, "But still — Picasso — I say Picasso over and over — because in my esteem he has proved himself to be the most gifted in visualizing his sensations of any man at this time. It is the pure artist's vision lofty and profound simple and with a power which produces so directly his every simple concrete or abstract sensation."

It was Picasso's gift for "visualizing his sensations" that particularly appealed to Hartley, because as he absorbed Paris and its art, he felt "certain spiritual metamorphoses taking place." To Stieglitz he confided, "I find growing in me and I think to more purpose — a recurrence of former religious aspirations — taking a finer form in personal expression."

Picasso was expressing in his work what Hartley knew he sought: "To produce my deepest sensations and organize my vision as much as possible — leaving out all reliance upon the emotional aspects of one's temperament — seeking but one object, real expression. Naturally when some see my work they will say Picasso — well I say it too — but I say it first with meaning." If later this proved to have been a mistake, it would not matter, because he would have remained faithful to himself and his ideal. He declared, "The importance of my having come here is incalculable — It has done more for clarity of ideas and sensations than I could have done at home in years. . . . I have found my place in the art scheme."[27]

Picasso's work led Hartley to the Musée de l'Homme at the Trocadero. It was in July or August that he first saw its primitive art, and soon after he took a "very sudden turn in a big direction owing to a recent visit to the Trocadero. One can no longer remain the same in the presence of these mighty children who get so close to the universal idea in their mud-baking." He already felt a power in his work that he had not known earlier.[28] Three weeks later, in the same letter to Rockwell Kent in which he praised Picasso for his uniqueness, he told of "having rather fine experiences these days. . . . They have nothing

to do with the life here — They are not a product of French experience — one has these anywhere everywhere — They are oneself
whether one be in the desert or in the mountains." He sensed as he
had not earlier the links between the expressiveness of Picasso, spiritualism, and primitive art, and now felt in his own work "a deeper
calm and . . . a majesty which it may not have known before." He often
went to the Trocadero instead of the Louvre because "among the gods
one finds art intelligence — a far closer relationship to life than among
those who merely see life and add a little by way of personality or
interpretation to it." The collections of comparative sculpture in the
Trocadero gave him "most in the way of strength and simplicity."[29]

As the fall wore on he paid more and more attention to primitive
art. Encouraged by the sculptor Jacob Epstein, he traveled in November to London to meet Augustus John and hoped that through the
Chenil Gallery, which showed the work of the John Group, he might
sell some of his still lifes. Little if anything came of that, and London
he found "oppressive," "too haughty and tragic."[30] Nonetheless he was
enthralled by the British Museum, and especially by its collections of
Egyptian, Assyrian, and African art. "In all these people there was such
a need of art — by way of glorifying the specific genius of each either
for purposes of religion or for symbolism or pure mysticism," he wrote
to Stieglitz.[31]

Mysticism — spiritualism — was fast becoming central to his work.
He was extremely aware of both the mystical and the naive, the latter
because it reflected the same subjective depths as did mysticism. He
was eager to see the work of Ferdinand Hodler, the Swiss mystical
painter, at the Salon d'Automme, but it ended by disappointing him.
Soon, however, he was raving about an exhibition of Henri Rousseau's
naive paintings at the Bernheim-Jeune Gallery in Paris. "I only wish
you could see the Rousseau Exposition," he exclaimed to Stieglitz in
early November. "It is too lovely and so timely for me as this leaves an
indelible impression upon me — If there ever was true piety in painting it is in this man." Aside from Renoir and Cézanne he found little
else to stir him other than Picasso and Rousseau. He admired the
simplicity and color of Renoir's work and the austerity and dignity of
Cézanne's, especially his watercolors, which had a "new sense of the
universe" about them. Picasso, "the first exponent of an absolutely
modern expression in art," was doing "the first thing in the way of

psychic painting." Hartley distinguished him from the cubists, whom he faulted for proceeding "mostly by intellectual processes." They were not intuitive, were guided not by the "true art vision" but by theory. Art, he asserted, could go only "a certain way with the intellectual and then it demands vision."[32]

No single aspect out of all that Hartley discovered was *the* element that brought everything together. He was simply — or complexly — finding art that expressed what he wanted to convey, as well as artists and thinkers who were articulating the ideas he held. Such was the case with Wassily Kandinsky and the Blaue Reiter group of artists in Munich. Early in the summer of 1912 Hartley read in the magazine *Rhythm* about Kandinsky, whom he understood to be a pupil of Gaugin and a "modern light in Berlin or Munich." He had also learned of the almanac *Der Blaue Reiter,* which he wanted to see, as no doubt it discussed modernism.[33] By the beginning of September he had absorbed its contents, aided by his German friends' translation of it into English. It had "turned out to be a fine thing," he told Stieglitz, because he was moving in a new direction as a result of his visit to the Trocadero. Hartley had now also studied Kandinsky's book *On the Spiritual in Art,* which was likewise in German but which he could understand with the help of Rönnebeck, Lang, and von Freyburg.[34]

The almanac, edited by Kandinsky and Franz Marc, a German artist and member of the Blaue Reiter group, was a collection of essays and illustrations that included reproductions of six works by Henri Rousseau as well as other primitive and naive art such as masks and totems from the Marquesas and Easter Islands and Alaska, a cape from Mexico, folk prints from France and Russia, and Bavarian glass paintings. The thrust of the writings was toward an understanding of the mystical: "Incomprehensible ideas express themselves in comprehensible forms," wrote Auguste Macke, another member of the group. "Form is a mystery to us for it is the expression of mysterious powers. Only through it do we sense the secret powers, the 'invisible God.' . . . Man expresses his life in forms. Each form of art is an expression of his inner life. The exterior of the form of art is its interior." Macke observed that the works of impressionists and postimpressionists such as Renoir, Cézanne, van Gogh, and Gaugin were "expressions of their inner lives, . . . the forms of these artists' interior world in the medium of painting."

It is particularly striking that Macke should have referred to "our complicated and confused era [in which] we have forms that absolutely enthrall everyone in exactly the same way as the fire dance enthralls the African." The German artists sought to hark back to essentials, exactly as did Hartley, affected as he had been by Emerson, Thoreau, and Whitman, who praised the natural in man and warned against the excesses of the present. In *Der Blaue Reiter* Hartley found the expression of what he had long felt and what in Europe he saw in the work of Cézanne and even more in that of Picasso and of the primitives at the Musée de l'Homme.[35]

Arnold Schönberg's essay "The Relationship to the Text," also included in the almanac, dealt, like Macke's, with mystical expression. Schönberg quoted the philosopher Schopenhauer:

> The composer reveals the innermost essence of the world and pronounces the most profound wisdom in a language that his reason cannot understand; he is like a mesmerized somnambulist who reveals secrets about things that he knows nothing about when he is awake.

Although Schopenhauer had failed to translate "details of musical language, *which reason cannot understand,* into the language of our concepts," noted Schönberg, the philosopher was right to strive to articulate the "essence of the world." Richard Wagner had been able to do that in his operas, where he put the essence that he sensed in music, and it stimulated a "re-creation in the material of another art."[36] Schönberg's essay must have played an important part in moving Hartley in the new direction he mentioned in his letters that fall. Even before his trip to London in November, he painted a number of abstract compositions that he called musical themes.

On the Spiritual in Art addresses many of the same questions as the almanac. Kandinsky's book influenced Hartley even more than the other, probably because it is more specifically concerned with how an artist may express inner truths — about the relationships among form, color, and emotion, for example. Perhaps it was the final ingredient that set Hartley in his new direction. In a remarkable letter that he sent to Stieglitz in December 1912, Hartley described what he considered to be the dramatic shift that had taken place in his work. He had by then abandoned his still lifes of the summer "in favor of intuitive abstraction" and was "rapidly gaining ground in this variety of expression," which was "closest to my own temperament and ideals." His new work was unlike anything else being done then, he claimed:

> It is not like Picasso — it is not like Kandinsky not like any "cubism" — It is what I call for want of a better name subliminal or cosmic cubism — It will surprise you — I did these things before I went to London as a result of spiritual illuminations and I am convinced that it is my true and real utterance — It combines a varied sense of form with my own sense of color which I believe has never needed stimulation — I am convinced of the Bergson argument in philosophy, that the intuition is the only vehicle for art expression and it is on this basis that I am proceeding — My first impulses came from the mere suggestion of Kandinsky's book [on] the spiritual in art. Naturally I cannot tell what his theories are completely but the mere title opened up the sensation for me — & from this I proceeded — In Kandinsky's own work I do not find the same convincing beauty that his theories hold — He seems to be a fine theorist first and a good painter after.[37]

Hartley's new work assimilated the "angular drawing and fragmented contours of Analytic Cubism," Barbara Haskell has written. Building on the "flat, interlocking planes and rectilinear outlines of Analytic Cubism," he "applied thin washes of pale color to his canvases to give them an inspirational, transcendent effect." Cézanne was the inspiration for Hartley's technique of "lightly coloring his canvases with dematerialized washes," which he hoped would achieve a "mystical quality," something also suggested by his "calligraphic network of lines and floating eight-pointed stars, as well as various Christian and Oriental mystical symbols such as a Buddha in a lotus position, crosses, and three upraised hands crowned by an arch."[38] As Hartley worked during the last days of 1912, his paintings "became brighter and more lyrical. Hartley continued to use a basically Cubist format of darkly outlined forms within a densely packed, shallow space, but his incorporation of circular, calligraphic images and effervescent colors differentiated his work from traditional Cubist compositions."[39]

In his letter to Stieglitz Hartley had reported that a painter from Munich who was working on the principle of music had told him that he was "probably the first to express pure mysticism in this modern tendency." He had been cultivating his mystical experiences and felt the time was ripe for them. He had been reading *Cosmic Consciousness,* by R. M. Bucke, who asserted that "varied illuminations" came to a person, especially between the ages of twenty-five and forty. Hartley assured Stieglitz, who had had these revelations himself, that he would understand: "They are apart from aesthetic vision — they are pure vision itself." Hartley related an anecdote about Picasso, in which the painter, on seeing his own work, had remarked, "You know it is strange — but I understand my own pictures best six months after I have done them — as a human being I am in no way extraordinary — I work merely from the intuition." Hartley was excited by the statement, which he saw as proof that Picasso had always "relied first upon his vision," as had El Greco. Vision came first and developed an artist's talent, rather than the other way around. And because artists such as Picasso were able to work in this way, Hartley maintained, "we are getting purer vision these days than probably ever before."

Stimulated by his own experiences, he thought of van Gogh, who with "his exceptional color sense" would have been able to do "remarkable things under later influences than the Japanese," particularly as he was "eminently a spiritual being." As he had before and would again, Hartley turned to Cézanne. "I have been thrilled of late with Cézanne water colors," he wrote. He had discovered in them a "new aspect of vision the which I am intensifying in myself in connection with what I want to do." The Bernheim-Jeune Gallery at that moment was having an exhibition of some forty watercolors, which Hartley judged to be Cézanne's "finest expression as pure vision." They were not consciously aesthetic but rather "registrations of pure sensation out of a peaceful state of mind." Cézanne's large oils had about them a "great turba" that was intriguing, but that was not the quality that Hartley admired most in the Frenchman's oeuvre. He thought Cézanne "the first cosmic painter" and predicted that his work would now be the basis for any of this sort of art. Cézanne, he was sure, "would shudder considerably at all these intellectual cataleptics" — all the buzzing, that is, about the new art on the part of the artists whom Hartley observed, "especially on Tuesday evenings at the Cafe de Lilas in the quarter where I meet my friends as it is quiet and free from prostitution and art mediocrity."

Hartley was certain that the time was one of growth for him, and to ensure that it would continue he planned to travel to Germany in January 1913, stopping in Munich to meet Kandinsky and see first-

hand the work of the Blaue Reiter group. The forces that would produce his first important paintings had already converged in him;
Germany would provide him with an even greater opportunity to
focus his concepts, stimulated as they were by his French experiences
and by his reading of such authors as Bucke, Bergson, and the German
mystic Böhme, whose work he told Stieglitz he was reading fragments
of in English translation. Böhme was "wonderful & greatest of all in
his pure mysticism," and his writings were helping Hartley to perfect
his ideas.[40]

He had already absorbed Henri Bergson's ideas before he arrived
in France. In the October 1911 and January 1912 issues of *Camera Work*
he had read extracts from Bergson's essays "Creative Evolution" and
"Laughter." "The intention of life," announced Bergson,

> the simple movement that runs through the [features of the living
> being], that binds them together and gives them significance, escapes
> [the eye]. This intention is just what the artist tries to regain, in
> placing himself back within the object by a kind of sympathy, in
> breaking down, by an effort of intuition, the barrier that space puts
> up between him and his model.

In the piece that appeared in October 1911, Bergson emphasized the
primacy of intuition. The excerpt from "Laughter," retitled "What Is
the Object of Art?," discussed much the same thing. Artists, Bergson
wrote, "contrive to make us see something of what they have seen."
Delving further than words can, "they grasp something that has nothing in common with language, certain rhythms of life and breath that
are closer to man than his inmost feelings." These rhythms, "being the
living law," are not so profound as the "secret chord" that the artist can
reach. "So art," Bergson concluded,

> whether it be painting or sculpture, poetry or music, has no other
> object than to brush aside the utilitarian symbols, the conventional
> and socially accepted generalities, in short, everything that veils re-
> ality from us, in order to bring us face to face with reality itself.[41]

At the end of 1912, Hartley wrote to Rockwell Kent that he was
"trying to express my emotions of the cosmic scene in general." His
work, he believed, represented a radical departure from cubism, and
its aim was "to present a sensation of cosmic bodies in harmony with
each other by means of color & form." He thought that he diverged

from Kandinsky; the difference was the mystical element in his work. Echoing the words of the German painter he had told Stieglitz about, he ventured that he was "probably the first to contribute this mystical element to the modern movement." He described to Kent the pictures that lay on the floor before him in his studio at that moment:

> They look like a conclave of universal elements confiding in one another — things that look like stars — birds' wings sun rays — suns themselves at the sundown time — moon shapes and star-beams all radiant together. It is a kind of cosmic dictation applied aesthetically to produce a harmony of shapes & colors — with a sense also of the color of sound as I get these feelings out of music.

He had done a painting "after a prelude of Cezar Frank's," and his work had been much assisted by his reading translations of the mystics Böhme, Eckehart, Tauler, Suso, and Ruysbroeck. These men, "wonders of inspiration" all, he could imagine inspiring van Gogh, who had a mystical nature, "this consuming fire in him," so that "all his efforts were but the desire to express his own soul."[42]

The time was an exciting and fertile one for Hartley once he put Bergson's ideas together with the art he saw in France and the writings of the mystics; added to that was his contentment with his German friends. Enthusiastically he wrote his niece, "If success compensates for anything — the respect of the artists one likes and believes in [—] then I ought to be happy for I have taken my place in the modern scheme and hope one day to produce something worthy of esteem." He explained, "It's a new theme I'm working on — did you ever hear of anyone trying to paint music — or the equivalent of sound in color — doubtless you have heard singers speak of the color of tones." Other artists had said that his work was original. Referring to Kandinsky, he asserted that "there is only one artist in Europe working on [this idea] and he is a pure theorist and his work is quite without feeling — whereas I work wholly from the intuition and the subliminal." Did he sound mad? he asked his niece. "Well never mind — I am quite sane and except that my eyes are very large and blue I look the average." His nose was large, too, he added, so that his friend Lang called him Albatross and another referred to him as The Eagle. He liked to think his appearance was "slightly unspeakable," dressed as he often was in "a lovely long black overcoat . . . a black fine velour hat and a black velvet tie somewhat of an 1830 collar and a black cane."[43]

Hartley had reason to be pleased. Not only was he receiving praise from Gertrude Stein and others in his new circle of friends, but in November the American artists Arthur B. Davies and Walt Kuhn had visited him to see what he might submit for the Armory Show, the giant exhibition that was to take place in New York, at the 69th Infantry Regiment Armory, between February 17 and March 15, 1913. It was, as Milton Brown has written, "a major event in American art history, perhaps the single most important one, if importance can be weighed at all."[44] Hartley, who would have two oils and six drawings in the show, had a sense of its importance and told Stieglitz, "It bids fair to be an electric shock to America." He was excited that Kuhn had been able to gather "Van Goghs from Germany and Holland — Cézannes & Gaugins from Vollard — and they are to have the Cubistes and I suppose Futuristes as well." He was a touch disappointed that Davies had selected two still lifes rendered before he changed the direction of his work, though he admitted that they did "show a sense of color which I have not brought out before." Davies also chose six partly abstract drawings. Hartley would have preferred to display his "direct abstract thing," but Davies assured him that the still lifes would serve best, as no American had done the other sort of work yet.[45]

Happy with his situation, Hartley could generously wish Stieglitz the best for 291. After his return from London, he made definite plans to visit Germany at the invitation of Rönnebeck. "I leave Friday evening Jan 3 on the ten o'clock train for Cologne which arrives at 8 o'clock the next morning and then the train leaves Cologne for Berlin at 10 — and arrives in B. at 5.30 PM," he wrote to his niece on December 30, spilling out details that reflected his excitement. He expected to have ten days or two weeks in Berlin before going to Munich with Rönnebeck to arrange an exhibition.[46] Paris, he knew, had been utterly important to him, but he was ready to leave. His affections were already with Berlin and the Germans, and nothing French could alter that.

6

Wunderland
1913

PRIMED FOR GERMANY, Hartley was not disappointed by Berlin, which he declared "superb" almost immediately. He was sure he wanted to live there one day, as the city was "so alive and ultra modern and so calm and quiet." Several days after his arrival he wrote to Norma Berger from the Princess Café on the Kurfürstendamm, telling her that the city was "charming" and "very gay with the handsome officers and soldiers — I have not seen the Kaiser yet but he goes about often in his auto."[1] The Germans' briskness and sense of order enthralled him. After a week he wrote to Stieglitz and again praised Berlin's "ultra-modernity" and the "calmness of its people," a refreshing change after the "unceasing gesture of the French." He marveled at the "fine types all about — a fine extravagance of physical splendour," echoing a theme he had sounded before. He wanted to believe that "nature is especially interested in her German product — the general type is so well formed and equipped with energy," in contrast to the "sickliness of the French." He was encouraged by what he saw as a German "trend toward modernity in art," having seen a show of the work of Gabriel Münter. The next week there was to be an exhibition of Robert Delaunay's painting. In the museum he had found "a wonderful lot of primitive art — much more than at either the Trocadero or the British Museum." All in all, Paris was going to seem "grey & sickly after all this 'well-keptness' and healthful system."[2]

With his artist's eyes, Hartley was extremely observant, but even someone less so would have noticed the move toward modernity in

Berlin. Before World War I there was some tendency toward modern architectural design in the city, but more apparent was the modern design of everyday objects. Hartley would have quickly discovered that the architects and designers who at the turn of the century had been working in the art nouveau style — a style known as Jugenstil, which Hartley had probably first become acquainted with when he studied reproductions of the work of Segantini and Hodler in the magazine *Jugend* in 1906 — had since turned to "new forms compatible with the forces and processes of Germany's increasingly industrial civilization." In the Keller and Reiner store on Potsdamerstrasse, for example, he would have seen integrated interior designs of the Jugenstil variety, and he would have been fascinated with the modern furnishings featured in the famous Wertheim Department Store on Leipzigerstrasse. Modernity, color, and order were in the air. Coupled with his intimate friendships with the young Germans, these forces captivated Hartley from his first moments and set him on his way toward the abstractions and collages he would paint to celebrate the color and pageantry of Berlin during his subsequent visits there in 1913 and 1914–1915.[3]

Berlin now, despite its glamour, is a pale imitation of the city Hartley found in 1913, both because of the devastation of World War II and the consequent division of the city into East and West and, of course, because of the lethal wall that separated the two for many years. While Berlin was at its most brilliant — and most decadent — during the 1920s, the city was perhaps grandest before World War I. Over time it grew up along an east-west axis at whose center still stands the Brandenburg Gate, a huge neo-Grecian structure with Doric columns and, on top, a sculpture of the goddess of Victory in a chariot drawn by four horses. To the east along Unter den Linden were the Reichschancellery, the Opera, and other official buildings leading to the Royal Palace. To the west of the gate, the Unter den Linden became Charlottenburger Chausee, passing through the Tiergarten, by the zoo and the business area of Kurfürstendamm, and then out into the wealthy suburb of Grunewald.[4]

Power, order, vitality, and pomp: what Paris, for all its culture and grace, lacked, Berlin had, in Hartley's opinion. And the year 1913 was especially splendid; parades marked twenty-five years of the kaiser's rule and one hundred years of Germany (the Völkerschlacht, the "Battle of the People," had taken place in Leipzig in 1813). It was also the year of the marriage of the kaiser's daughter, and in Berlin there was a huge exhibition of German art of earlier times. Hartley knew that for his own well-being he must return beyond this first short trip.

After nearly two weeks in Berlin, he left with Rönnebeck on January 21 for Munich. They intended to see as much art as they could, but most exciting for Hartley was the prospect of meeting Kandinsky and Gabriel Münter. Hartley was not disappointed. He found Kandinsky "a splendid man with a fine mind and a most generous and constructive attitude toward art." They agreed to exchange photographs of their work. Hartley was particularly pleased to learn that his reputation had preceded him to Munich; a German woman who had visited the 291 Gallery had brought back word of his art. One result was that the Galerie Goltz was interested in his paintings, which he hoped to send on once he returned to Paris at the end of January.[5] He wrote to Münter that he planned to ship Goltz several pictures at the beginning of March, and he wanted her and Kandinsky to see them at the gallery. "They are the expression of spiritual states of being," he told her, "just now more in the nature of composition perhaps but I am working toward more simple expression — toward improvisation." He enclosed a letter in English to Franz Marc, which he asked Münter to translate into German for him. Hartley had not met Marc in Munich, though he had very much wanted to, as he had been deeply impressed by Marc's work at the Tannhauser Galerie.[6]

Elated by his trip, Hartley wrote a long letter to Stieglitz discussing art in Germany and his own work. He asserted that during his visit he had "found my place in the art circles of Europe." He described meeting Kandinsky at his atelier in Schwabing, near Munich. Hartley sounded a theme familiar to Stieglitz: "It is with Germany I have always found myself — both in New York & in Paris." He declared that "now it is in Germany that I find my creative conditions." He was sure Stieglitz would like Kandinsky, who was "so free of convention with a hatred of all the traditions that cling to art — bohemianism — uncleanness — lack of mental order," all of these constituting the "chaos which makes Paris so charming to those who love looseness." Hartley himself was not one of these and "in no sense a bohemian," nor did he have any use for the "art cults who do little else but feed on each other." He must have sensed that he sounded ungrateful, however, for he quickly added that he did not underrate his Paris experience. Indeed, it had "freed me intellectually and spiritually — I have discovered my essential self here." But he would give credit for that to no one but himself. The sources that had led to his "newest means of experience" were "without geography"; they were "universal," and he had come to them "by way of James' pragmatism — slight touches of Bergson — and directly through the fragments of mysticism that I have found out of Boehme — Eckhardt Tauler — Suso & Ruysbroeck & the Bhagavad Gita."

Contradicting his own unwillingness to credit anything French, as Picasso and Cézanne were very much a part of France, he wrote that studying the former had taken him "into the subjective," while in Cézanne's watercolors he had discovered a "peculiar psychic revelation ... that is a purely spiritual rendering of forms in space." Inspired by these two and "out of the heat of the reading" he had begun to work and now had a "series of canvases nearly fifteen 30 × 40," which he insisted were "the first expression of mysticism in modern art." No one else had yet presented this "in the modern tendency," though Kandinsky was "theosophic," and Marc, "extremely psychic in his rendering of the soul life of animals." As if to convince himself of his imminent success, Hartley maintained that in Europe there were dealers and collectors who understood the new art, with the result that Picasso, Matisse, and Kandinsky were financially successful. Hartley was sure he would be also. Inevitably his work would travel to Russia and Holland, and he would take his place "among the European moderns."

According to Hartley, for all the painters he had come to admire — Picasso, Matisse, Cézanne, Rousseau, van Gogh — a "wondrous big sense of the cosmos" was what gave their work greatness. In the work of Kandinsky and Marc, as in his own, he saw a "perfectly logical sense of the effect of color on color," and an expression of "the desires of the spiritual." He had no use for what he called "the common egoisms" of art; his sole object was to "attend wholly to the dictations of the ideas that come to me through inner personal experience." Conditions for this were best in Germany, he declared. It was not a matter of nationality; he was positive he would "always remain the American," because the essence of what was in him was "American mysticism."

Although later in his life Hartley would believe what he told Stieglitz in this letter, it is difficult to think that he was entirely sincere when he wrote it, in 1913. He wanted to reassure Stieglitz that the European trip *was* important to him but that eventually he would return to the United States. He advised him to go and look at the paintings he had sent for the Armory Show; in them there was an "attempt to get my own rhythms," though he had now surpassed the still lifes that Arthur B. Davies had urged him to send. For him to come back to the United States now would be "destructive" because it would unsettle him, whereas Berlin offered calm and order but at the same time the excitement of an awareness of modernism.

Hartley's letter then turned into a plea for financial support. He assured Stieglitz that he was going to be successful, but this still lay in the future; in the meantime he was counting on Stieglitz's "personal co-operation" to help him out. The letter sounded self-indulgent. What Hartley took as positive signs of his impending success, and what he based his assertions about his importance on, were for the most part polite gestures on the part of the Germans. But this tone of egotism that hid deep insecurity was vintage Hartley. Stieglitz would understand.

"And now as you get this the big 'wild West' show will be on," Hartley continued, referring to the Armory Show. He was apprehensive about the methods of the organizers but had some faith that the result would be an "earthquake to the sleeping villages." He had heard that Jo Davidson was to have numerous pieces in the show, which irritated him. "This type of American artist over here is certainly a common lot," he grumbled. Although he saw such artists almost every day, he had nothing to do with them. It distressed the fastidious Hartley that Mrs. Whitney supported Davidson and others like him by giving them twenty-five dollars a week so they could "play billiards and poker . . . and do little else." They were a sorry lot and would come to nothing. If he had that income, he asserted, he "would show how one can live and work on it."[7]

Stieglitz responded quickly. "I want you to stay in Europe until autumn," he wrote. He would see to it that Hartley could have his "few months in Germany," even though he was not sure how he would raise the money, since, he admitted, "I make it very difficult for people to do anything for '291' because I feel that the thing should be done spontaneously." He recognized that this was a chronic problem for the 291 group, especially Hartley, since he was not good at self-advertisement. For now, however, "the main thing is you have had your stay," he reminded him.[8]

Hartley remained aloof in Paris, consciously distancing himself from the French as he prepared to move to Germany — and also as he convinced himself more and more that his own work was unique. "Apart from one or two friends whom I see daily, and Gertrude Stein, whom I have enjoyed of late — I have had no outer events," he wrote to Stieglitz in mid-March. "I work continually having intermittent spells of fatigue — but working always from the one point of view which I have chosen for myself — namely the mystical element." Working thus separated him from the hoi polloi of Paris art — as he saw the cubists and futurists — and placed him instead among Cézanne, Renoir, Redon, Picasso, and Matisse. "So it is sooner or later each man must go alone and in the wilderness of himself find his own depth and height," he declared dramatically. Music, art, and literature were all "going into deeper chambers of the self. Stein, for example, digs up new depths in words — Picasso makes form & color say new things — Kandinsky finds new significance in the relation of arts — Marc finds something to say for the interior nature of animals."

Torn between his nativeness and his admiration for European art and the German nation, Hartley chose to see his "interior" art as "universal because it goes into universal ideas" — just as, to cite his now constant refrain, did the painting of Picasso and Cézanne. "As for the smaller people [—] the cubistes and the futuristes — they remain minor in their essences because they prefer the exploitation of the ego instead of something larger and more impressive." Delaunay, whose showmanship grated on him, was an example of this, as was Max Weber, whose egomania was expressed even "more fanatically" than that of the Frenchman. "Delaunay spends most of his time talking about Delaunay and his gifts," Hartley insisted. Four days earlier he and Rönnebeck had visited Delaunay's home, at his request,

> and there we saw a huge canvas [one of the *Equipe de Cardiff* series] with much sky — part of the Ferris wheel — the Eiffel Tower — some foot ball players — life size — at the left a little above the center — the word "Astra" — two feet high — the name of some aero Co., and to the right over a foot high in vermilion letters on an emerald green ground — the name "Delaunay — Paris" — surely a perfect confession of ego-mania.

Delaunay had said to Rönnebeck, "Ah it's a long time since the blue sky has been painted." Both visitors were speechless after he remarked "among other things that Bergson's system was 'blague' and so on."

Hartley had a clear memory of Delaunay's painting, the third of the series. That it should annoy him, apart from its being a manifestation of the artist's own personality, is understandable. Its size and blatant nature and the busyness of the canvas — as well as the actual objects rendered — all ran counter to what Hartley the mystic was doing. "I know when he comes to see my things he will say pourquoi? But I don't care at all — I am going where the elements I seek are in their right place — There is no place for a mystic in Paris," he declared. He had confidence that the twenty canvases he now had would prove his abilities when he could get them to the friendly atmosphere of Munich.[9]

As it approached mid-April, when he was to depart for Munich and Berlin, he grew ever more excited about the prospect, and to Rockwell Kent he waxed lyrical about the Germans. He knew Kent "would be happy among them — for they are a wholesome and really warm people if one understands them rightly — the land itself is noble and dignified and nature is so wondrously interested in her product there — The result is thousands of the handsomest specimens you ever saw." Berlin itself was entirely modern, and its vehicles were quiet and smooth; consequently the city had a "unique sense of order and cleanliness and [is] as sanitary as a city can be made." Hartley acknowledged that the military system accounted for many aspects of Berlin life and that some people might not like its influence, but he confessed that "it stimulates my child's love for the public spectacle — and such wonderful specimens of health these men are — thousands all so blonde and radiant with health."

Despite his love of crowds, he was proud to remain solitary and conceived of himself as "the eagle, having raised my wings and leapt off the precipice into space and in my circlings . . . having found something which is my own and no other's." He saw himself "becoming a European gradually because of no encouragement at home." Whatever the Armory Show might do to open people's minds in the United States to modern art, he was nonetheless "resolved to take my chances in Europe after October when the little money I have will be gone."

His mysticism and his attraction to Kent as well as to the Germans made him feel Whitmanesque. Beyond creating pictures, he wrote, he spent his days

> partly in longing for the love that has been thrice denied me [a reference to his mother, father, and stepmother] and partly in giving

out my life to whoever asks for it regardless — man woman or
child — the moral and the immoral alike[,] for I know that my humanness is world humanness and that all there is in the world is in
me — that I am pure as all men are pure and that I am impure
equally.

It is revealing about what Germany meant to Hartley that he should
write this to someone who attracted him as Kent did. Eaglelike, god-
like, wrapped up in Whitmanesque sexuality and mysticism, he felt
exalted and could exclaim that he had "arrived at that state of cosmic
understanding of all things in their essences that I am free. . . . I am at
one with myself and in the spiritual sense at one with all things." Most
of those who knew him would have been surprised to hear this shy,
unsure man speak such words.

   And it is difficult not to think that it was his ideas about Germany
that made Hartley declare of Kathleen, Kent's wife, that she was not
weak but

   only frail as all pure feminine is frail in its essence — She is purely
   an intuitional feminine who is doing exactly what any real woman
   should do — be a mother as often as she can — and recreate herself
   for the good of the earth — Perhaps you will be able to replenish the
   race — with new vigor helping it to return to its native strength and
   beauty offsetting the prevailing tendency to the invasions of foreign
   blood.[10]

What seems drivel from our perspective reflects the influence of German nationalism and racism on Hartley, as well as his desire to have a
relationship that went beyond what he perceived to be the limits of a
heterosexual one.

   He never shipped the pictures to the Galerie Goltz in Munich, as
he had planned. In the midst of packing his belongings for his departure from Paris on April 19, he became daunted at the prospect of
having to pack the paintings as well. Before they were crated, Gertrude
Stein, Wilhelm Uhde, Robert Delaunay, and Patrick Henry Bruce
came to his studio to view them. Stein came twice and took four to
keep at Rue de Fleurus. She called the paintings "the most refreshing
things she has seen in a long time" and declared that Hartley had
"restored colour to its original meaning" and was "entirely new in
Paris." Stein told him that he surpassed Matisse and Picasso in making

"every part of a picture live — & not since Matisse's Femme au Chapeau has color been given its true significance."

Uhde also praised Hartley's work, saying that its supernatural quality was superior to that in Redon's paintings and that Hartley had achieved what Kandinsky sought to do. Delaunay and Bruce, no doubt, were less enthusiastic. Hartley reported to Stieglitz that they had come at the time of Stein's second visit. She had "kept them speechless" and remarked to Hartley that she was glad to have seen the paintings because it would enable her to tell later what Delaunay had taken from them.[11]

It is ironic, but not untypical, that Hartley judged it wise to move on at this moment, hoping for recognition through the Galerie Goltz in Munich even as he began to receive more attention in Paris, particularly from Uhde. But nothing could have stopped him. Germany pulled at him emotionally because he was sure that there lay the real interest in his sort of modernist art. When Stieglitz wrote in late April that the paintings and drawings of Hartley's that had been in the Armory Show had had to be returned to Paris because Hartley had not filled out his entry form properly, it hardly fazed him. Stieglitz had hoped to show them at 291 and perhaps sell them. Hartley, however, had for time being put all his eggs in the European basket.[12]

En route to Munich, he spent a few days in Sindelsdorf with Franz Marc and his wife. The village in the mountains was lovely and added to his fine spirits. Marc again encouraged him to take his work to Goltz in Munich. He also thought that Hartley could have a show afterward in Berlin at Herwarth Walden's Der Sturm, an important gallery for the modernists. When Hartley arrived in Munich, he reported all this to Stieglitz, sounding again his now common refrain — that he was unique, much appreciated by the Germans, and about to make a name for himself. Kandinsky and Marc would be coming to Munich the next week and would view his work.[13]

Hartley arranged for the Germans to see his paintings, but he warned Kandinsky and Münter that they would find him not "an art intellectual — only an art mystical — emotional spiritually striving to express high feelings — and making myself the medium of expression."[14] He was nervous about what the other artists might think of his work. Kandinsky, Münter, Marc, and a fourth artist, Albert Block, visited the Galerie Goltz with him and praised him generously. Kandinsky delivered a "discourse on the law of form — that of the individual as applied to the universal," which from Hartley's point of view was "mainly a discourse on technical indiscretions" and which he deemed unimpressive.

Although he did not say as much, he was disappointed by Kandinsky's response. Their meeting was a case of a "complete logician trying so earnestly to dispense with logic & I a simple one without logic having an implicit faith in what is higher than all intellectual solutions." He likened it to Emerson and Whitman's "discussing Leaves of Grass on the Boston Common — Whitman listening with reverence to all of Emerson's ideas — & leaving him with the firm decision to change nothing in his book." Or it was like an imagined exchange between the two mystics Swedenborg and Böhme, the former "consumed with the logic of his mysticism," the latter "the ignorant one listening with his ear to the ground & his eyes toward the light waiting for the intelligences which came to him." Hartley thought that Kandinsky had a "most logical and ordered mind" that by nature was not creative. He interpreted ideas but finally was "not very alive & not so very different." He was "by way of being an aesthetic philosoph who has a kind of power of expression."

Despite any disappointment he may have felt about Kandinsky's reaction to his work, he was pleased by the day as a whole, even if he was less sure of success than he had been. "However," he added, "my German debut is complete — I stand alone — I cannot be described as a product of any school or any system — the product is personal." And he wanted to exhibit in New York in the fall, buoyed now more by Gertrude Stein's praise than by whatever Kandinsky had had to say. Also, though several German acquaintances were urging him to stay in Munich, he found it "so village-like & domestic" that he wanted more than ever to go on to Berlin.[15]

Given what he sensed were reservations on Kandinsky's part, he was especially gratified before he left Munich to receive a note from Marc. "Dear Friend," Marc wrote in his best English, "allow me to say how much pleasure I find in your valiant pictures. I said you that in my opinion you get not out all in color and form that you could with more experience of painting — but I am sure you will do so soon or late, when you will have worked more." He declared himself "profoundly fond" of Hartley's "high sincerity" in his art, which showed a "great holiness and pureness & your ideas are always strong & absolutely personal."[16] Hartley responded at some length, writing that he was "by nature a visionary," that he had "only the attitude of the mystical nature," and that he had "only this kind of contact with life itself." He claimed that he desired an "increase of real art instinct and not art knowledge." Like William Blake, he believed it best to "put off intellect and put on imagination — The imagination is the man."[17] In Marc he hoped he had found the kindred spirit lacking in Kandinsky.

Marc's letter bolstered Hartley's fragile ego. He arrived in Berlin just after the middle of May, in good spirits. The city was in the midst of preparing both for the wedding of the kaiser's daughter the following week and for the spring military review, so he was almost at once thrust into the pageantry he admired.[18] "These few days have been filled with vivid European gaiety," he reported soon,

> for the King & Queen of England — the Czar & other celebrities are here this week for the wedding of Prinzessin Victoria Luise on Saturday — tonight Gala Opera. . . . The military life adds so much in the way of a sense of perpetual gaiety here in Berlin. It gives the stranger like myself the feeling that some great festival is being celebrated always.

In his autobiography Hartley recalled the pleasure he had taken in Berlin, with the friendship of the Rönnebeck family, "the intense flame-like quality of the life there," and the "spick-and-spanness in the order of life." A "sense of order" had pervaded everything, and he had marveled at "the pavement shining like enamel leather." He remembered the "cream white taxis lined with red leather," which conveyed order and progress. These qualities, together with his friends — "German Jewish friends who offered me home, friendliness, hospitality, bread, life, belief" — made him feel that Berlin was *his* home as few other places were. In the air there was a "voluptuous tension," he noted, a vitality that one perceived almost at once. He credited Rönnebeck with initiating him into German ways, showing him the pageantry and much else. Hartley remembered the frequent parades along the Unter den Linden, the changing of the guard in front of the Royal Palace (accompanied by a musical concert), the special spring parade for the kaiser, and the great event of the wedding of the kaiser's daughter. "It was of course the age of iron — of blood and iron," he wrote. "Every backbone in Germany was made of it. . . . The whole scene was fairly bursting with organized energy and the tension was terrific and somehow most voluptuous in the feeling of power — a sexual immensity even in it, when passion rises to the full and something must happen to quiet it."

He recalled that on the morning of the wedding the princess and the duke-to-be entered through the Brandenburg Gate and passed onto the Unter den Linden through the Pariser Platz, which was crowded with people, among them

> those huge cuirassiers of the Kaiser's special guard, all in white — white leather breeches skin tight, high plain enamel boots — those gleaming, blinding medieval breast plates of silver and brass — making the eye go black when the sun glanced like a spear as the bodies moved. There were the inspiring helmets with the imperial eagle, and the white manes hanging down. There was six foot of youth under all this garniture — everyone on a horse, and every horse white — that is how I got it, and it went into an abstract picture of soldiers riding into the sun.

The procession included most of Europe's royalty, and Hartley remembered seeing the czar and czarina, the king and queen of England, and scores of others. Soon afterward he was "hearing the best music" and seeing the new theater: "five hours of Wagner in one form, and four or five hours of two parts of Faust on wheels done by Reinhardt who had then introduced the revolving stage — and all the famous new lighting, dome ceilings and all that."[19]

He also remained excited by Marc's words of praise and to Stieglitz described at length his "desire — to make a decorative harmony of color & form as seems fitting to the subject in hand." He had a canvas that would be titled *Extase d'aeroplane,* which was his notion of "the possible ecstasy or soul state of an aeroplane if it could have one." He was painting "the nature of individual interior states," he said, of which "the forms are naturally varied." Symbologists had told him that his pictures contained forms that also appeared in early alphabets. Of that he knew nothing, he insisted. "I only know that when the thought 'golden triangle' comes into my mind — I 'see' that triangle — I have a real vision of it — and so with the other shapes." It had been suggested to him that others might not know what he meant. "Well," he responded, "I don't either & don't profess to have a lecture for every idea [a reference to Kandinsky]. While I work it is by way of being a kind of dictation from somewhere — the occults will have a definite name for it all."[20]

For a short while, before money problems set in, Hartley was happy with his lot. Kandinsky and Marc were trying to place his work in the Herbst Salon, and they also introduced him to Herwarth Walden of Der Sturm. So even as he began to doubt that Goltz in Munich would help him, he remained confident and could write to Gertrude Stein about the high colors, the abundant smiling, and the eight-pointed stars in Berlin. The stars were everywhere, on heads and over hearts. He claimed not to know their symbolic value, but he found their yellow and white color "extremely beautiful." Happy, and grateful to Stein for her friendship, he offered her her choice of the four pictures of his that she had.[21]

He quickly found a small apartment on Nassauischestrasse that suited him: two rooms, a bath, and a kitchen. Marc had put him in touch with Bernard Köhler, who had a fine collection of modern art and was the leading patron of the Blaue Reiter group. Hartley hoped the collector would buy some of his work, as he seemed to desire "new personal expression"; indeed, he came to bank entirely on this prospect and was shocked when later Köhler declined to purchase any paintings at all.[22] When he thanked Marc for the introduction to Köhler, he reported that he had also visited Herwarth Walden, but since neither man spoke the other's language, they had been able to discuss very little. Hartley therefore asked Marc to talk to Walden about having an exhibition of his paintings in Berlin and elsewhere, once the Galerie Goltz sent them on from Munich, in July.[23]

Very soon trouble arose in paradise. Goltz wrote to Hartley that the exhibition of his work that he had hoped to mount from June 2 to July 5 would have to be delayed. It was to have been a two-man show, of Hartley and another artist, but the other man's collection was so large that it took up all the exhibition space. Hartley immediately wrote to Marc, who responded that the best idea might be for him to contact Max Dietzel of the Neue Kunstsalon in Munich, to ask if there might be a chance of his having an exhibition there in August. Eventually Dietzel arranged a July exhibit, but in the meantime Hartley agonized, complaining to Stieglitz that his pictures lay unseen in a dark cellar and that he was practically out of money. Moving from Paris had cost him dearly, especially because the shippers had mistakenly sent along some of Simonson's belongings.

Now, with the pictures from the Armory Show back in Paris and lying packed at Simonson's studio, the pictures in England seemingly going unattended, and those in Munich awaiting an exhibition, Hartley was stranded, with little hope of anything happening before September, when Marc and Kandinsky would be in Berlin. Could Stieglitz forward him the remaining two months' money he had been promised? He needed it to pay advance rent, and anything additional would enable him to buy paint and canvases. He ate hardly enough and treated himself to no luxuries other than an occasional café visit. "So you see how loose all ends are with me," he wrote. "I have to keep myself very quiet to keep from nervous breakdown which I could easily have under these trying conditions — I haven't the kind of energy which thrives anyhow under adversity."

He decried his lack of cash but admitted that in any case "I am not happy interiorly and this as far as I can see cannot be changed." He had "longings which through tricks of circumstances have been left unsatisfied." The "role of spectator in life" was not a fulfilling one for him, he declared, and so he thought himself destined for an unhappy existence.[24] Not surprisingly, his life took on a different hue when he had some money, but he knew himself well enough to recognize that he was physically and emotionally fragile. It was not merely self-indulgence that prevented him from finding some work other than painting by which to support himself. He could become physically ill with worry, and his only real therapy was literally to have a room of his own to paint in, and supplies — for painting was his great passion in life, and the one thing that he had ultimate confidence about. "I am keen for a still place where no thing is," he wrote to Gertrude Stein in mid-June, "where pride is not — and ambition never will be — I think it must be fine to be a Himalayan Condor and just sit on the topmost tops and condescend occasionally to consider things beneath one's wings in the valley places."[25]

By early July matters had improved somewhat, with Dietzel having confirmed that he would show Hartley's works. Hartley dared to hope for good things also from Der Sturm, and Gertrude Stein encouraged him. He wrote to Stieglitz that there were whispers that her plays would be performed in a "new little ultra-modern theatre in New York" and that he might be asked to design the curtain. But they were only at the talking stage, and Stieglitz should say nothing. Things were very quiet now in Berlin; Rönnebeck was away, and the pageantry of May was nowhere to be seen.[26] Charles Demuth visited for two weeks, Hartley told Stein, but after that he felt flat — "conditions are so negative around me these days," he explained. His social life consisted of "chance meetings of nobodies & the round of the cafés where I see no familiar face."

His life may have been flat, but at least he was able, after a nine-week hiatus, to begin painting again. In early August he wrote to Stein that he had begun to work, with "perhaps not the same white heat at present as in the others — but still quite something of myself in it." He told her that Berlin had an "interesting source of materials . . . numbers & shapes & colors that make one wonder — and admire — It is essentially mural this German way of living — big lines & large masses — always a sense of the pageantry of living — I like it."[27] He soon wrote to Stieglitz about his new work, noting that he was completing a large piece, "a mystical presentation of the number 8 as I get it from everywhere in Berlin." He steadfastly refused to interpret the number and its representation as an eight-pointed star, however: "There is a real reason for all these signs but it remains mystical — & explanations are not necessary," he asserted.[28]

When Stein answered his letter, he immediately wrote to her again, thanking her and telling her how much he liked her word portrait of him: "It seems to have another kind of dynamic power," he claimed, "a kind of shoot to it and I feel my own color very much in what I say — my own substance." "Peaceable in the rest of the stretch," was how Stein put it, which Hartley liked because he did feel that way. His work had "a something bigger in it" then; his paintings were larger "because my emotion demands it." He was "feeling my own sensations murally." That Stein wanted to pay for the drawing he had proposed to give her pleased him as well. How would one hundred francs be as a price? Whatever she wanted to give him would be fine, and he suggested that she hold on to it until a later date.[29]

Hartley's work was taking a distinctly new turn. Inspired by the pageantry of Berlin, he began painting larger canvases, such as one entitled *The Warriors,* which presents masses of ceremonially dressed soldiers mounted on horseback and ordered in such a fashion as to imply their spiritual quality. It is a paean to the military splendor Hartley saw during the parades of May. Soon his work would become more abstract, while still celebrating what he felt for Berlin. The paintings, Barbara Haskell has commented, "represent an accomplished and genuinely personal artistic statement. By combining the pictorial energy of the Blaue Reiter Expressionists with the tightly knit, collage format of the Cubists, he achieved a remarkable synthesis of the expressive with the structured."[30] It is hard to imagine that Hartley was not aware of the synchromists Stanton Macdonald-Wright and Morgan Russell, two young Americans whose work was exhibited in Munich from June 1 to June 30, at Der Neue Kunstsalon, where Hartley's own work would be shown soon afterward. Certainly his greater use of abstract form and heightened colors is likely to have been influenced by them.[31]

Hartley had reason to be pleased with his new work, which he sensed had a power that his earlier paintings mostly lacked. And he was now accepted by artists of the stature of Kandinsky and Marc, who helped to place five of his pieces, all "mystical images," in the Herbst Salon organized by Walden, alongside 361 other paintings and sculptures by such significant European modernists as Arp, Balla, Boccioni, Chagall, Delaunay, Ernst, Kandinsky, Klee, Kokoschka, Léger, Macke, Marc, Münter, Picabia, Severini, and Henri Rousseau. The exhibition was to open on September 20; the day before, Hartley wrote to Stieglitz's wife, Emmeline, that "I have been superbly hung in a room with fine light, five of them together. In the next room right — Kandinsky — and in the left a whole room of Rousseau, very good company you see!"[32] That evening there was to be a banquet attended by a "very nice group of awfully simple people" — Hartley's criterion for the artists he liked. One who fitted this description was Paul Klee, whom Hartley later recalled as an "eery but orderly little figure . . . always off at one side of whatever speech or action there may have been." Klee was "all the more charming by [his] wilful reticence and what seemed an ardent desire to be still in the presence of so much psychic movement."[33] The Delaunays were not so reticent; Madame Delaunay came in "an orphistic dress," and her husband talked a great deal, but Hartley had to admit that Delaunay's display at the Herbst Salon was "lovely." Everyone had drinks, Hartley reported to Stieglitz, and "then we all went to a Ballhaus in another quarter & finished the night." Proudly, he wrote that he "was the only American present: Germany — Swiss — Austria — Armenia — France — Amerika — Kandinsky not there but Marc — Macke — & many I did not know." The opening the next day was a high point. Afterward, he sat in a café with Rönnebeck, enjoying the moment as the lights came on along the Leipzigerstrasse. "The show is great," he exclaimed to Stieglitz.[34]

His pleasure was short-lived. Hartley was increasingly nervous, sometimes even to the point of distraction, about his financial situation. He hoped that Marc would intervene with Bernard Köhler about the purchase of his paintings. At the opening of the Herbst Salon Köhler had seemed interested in two works in particular but had not purchased them. Marc and his wife left Berlin suddenly after the opening, so in desperation Hartley wrote to Köhler himself, explaining his dilemma. When he had not heard from him after several days, he wrote to Marc to ask for his help. Two days later Köhler replied, saying that he could not at that time add any more artists to his list.

"I had been literally sick for days with nervousness," Hartley wrote to Stieglitz after he received Köhler's answer. "I simply reeled over when I read what he said because the decision threw me into immediate chaos." He had already sent a frantic cable asking for help, which he knew would dismay Stieglitz. Hartley thrashed around in his letter, reiterating his belief in what he was doing, stressing his artistic — not financial — success in Europe, and leaping back and forth between the arguments for and against his returning to the United States to enhance the chances of selling some paintings through 291. "I am a single person fighting a fierce stream and I can't swim without help," he declared melodramatically. "Help me therefore all you can until I get my head above water again & I shall hope to make some kind of amends for all things," he closed, leaning heavily on Stieglitz's friendship, as he would numerous times more in the years ahead.[35]

Nothing reflects the complex nature of the relationship between the two men more than episodes such as this. Hartley deeply appreciated the older man's support — Stieglitz almost always came through to save the day — but because he nearly prostrated himself before him, he also resented this man whom he viewed as a father figure. And Stieglitz, naturally, could and sometimes did resent Hartley, with the result that he did not work for him to the same degree that he did for, say, Marin and O'Keeffe.

But in this instance, in 1913, he kept his patience and gently but quite firmly told Hartley that he must return to the United States if he hoped to sell his work. "I can imagine your consternation at the outcome of the Koehler matter," he wrote early in October. "I am awfully sorry. Naturally your cablegram staggered me. It was impossible for me to cable you any money. I didn't have it. . . . Prepare to come home."

Several days later he wrote again, acknowledging two letters of Hartley's and letting him know that his woes weighed heavily on his mind. "I feel that you should come over with your pictures," he declared. He understood Hartley's desire to be in Berlin, but for the moment the best thing would be for him to have all his paintings in New York. "What you are after primarily in your coming is cash. And cash must be raised. And in order to raise cash one must be able to tell those people when approaching them, that they are having the choice from all your work. They are a suspicious lot over here." In the letter he enclosed a check for $150 from his own funds, the equivalent of which he said he would take in paintings.[36]

Before he received this letter from Stieglitz, Hartley wrote to Gertrude Stein about his dilemma and, abashed, asked her for the one hundred francs they had settled on as payment for his picture. She responded quickly with a telegram that instructed him to go to American Express and pick up two hundred francs she was sending him. She followed up with a letter so effusive in its praise that Hartley immediately wrote to Stieglitz about it. "I consider you are of the important men of the present time," she told him, and she asked if there were not some benefactor in New York who might give him $100 a month. She added that she thought it better that Hartley not return to New York, as he was not the person to "explain" his work. Encouraged, Hartley again presented to Stieglitz his case for remaining in Germany. Wasn't there someone who might do what Stein had suggested? That person would not regret it. New York was a difficult place to be personal in, except with friends such as Stieglitz, Davies, and a few others. Hartley understood Stieglitz's distaste for asking for money, but it could be done.[37]

When Stieglitz received this letter, he lost his patience. What irked him most was Hartley's and Stein's blasé assumption that $1,200 a year was easy to obtain and that "some rich American should . . . be willing to let you have that amount for the coming two years. And how kind she was in sending you $40.00 for your drawing instead of $20.00," he added sarcastically. He explained that he had not conceived of Hartley's coming over to explain his pictures: "What a horrible idea to even think of that. I simply want you over here with your pictures to get you in touch with some people possibly who may, instead of holding forth hope in the future, actually, of their own accord, do something *practical* for you" — "*now,*" Stieglitz inked in, and he closed the sentence.

The letter was sensible and exactly what Hartley needed — and, ultimately, wanted — to pull himself together and find direction. "You went abroad," Stieglitz reminded him, "with one idea, and that was to study. And by study I mean work and seeing." Sales and exhibitions were not the purpose of the trip. Now he needed cash. Returning to the United States might seem a rupture to Hartley, but Stieglitz saw it differently:

> You must remember that so far, little as it may be, your European trip was made possible through American cash. Cash which was forthcoming because a few people felt you were entitled to a chance. Now I personally don't see any reason why any American should be called to give you additional cash without seeing what you have done. Gertrude Stein's appreciation is awfully fine. What Kandinsky says and what Koehler thinks, all is valuable. And what you yourself say of your work is of great value. But people who give money without seeing are very rare. The Meyers have been more kind than you realize. They are the only "rich" people who have really done anything at all for "291."

He told Hartley that he was holding the small gallery at 291 for an exhibition of his European work. "A certain responsibility towards the others rests on your shoulders," Stieglitz insisted:

> There are other poor devils here struggling just as hard as you are and who are entitled to all you are. They too must be considered. You may be the most important of all. You may be the most important painter in the world today, but that all does not make any difference to me. I look at things from a different angle. And if "291" means anything at all, and you have gotten anything out of it, it is because of this very fact that I see things from my own particular angle.

Defending 291 led Stieglitz to the subject of his own finances. Hartley had suggested that in an issue of *Camera Work* Stieglitz might publish the play of Stein's in which Hartley figured, and also reproduce several of his paintings in color. Stieglitz thought this all well and good, but he needed to see the works first. A recent issue of *Camera Work* had cost him $1,000. People had enjoyed it, but too few had bought copies. "And so it has been with me for the last thirty years," he continued:

> And still I struggle on believing in an awakening of some people. Not for me, but for the world generally. Of course it is but natural that people who conclude that because I am able to "blow in" a $1000.00 for a number of *Camera Work* that I must necessarily be well-off pecuniarily. How stupid! They may not know that it is my last cent I am spending on a mad hope. They may not know that under the dress suit, which may be twenty years old, there may be no underclothes. They may not know that instead of three meals there is only one meal and so they may not know innumerable things that they take for granted and know nothing about. It may be stupid of me not to pass around the hat and fill it with sheckles for myself and for my friends. But if I had been built that way all I have ever done would never have existed. It might have been of more "practical" value. It is too late for me to start doing anything I do not *feel*. And it is because of this very fact that I can do nothing I don't *feel*, that I can understand a lot of you fellows.

The letter was a remarkable statement of all Stieglitz was — and was not. And it did not fail to endear him to Hartley.[38]

Few imminent departures have elicited more correspondence than did Hartley's from Germany. When he received a check from Stieglitz, his mood improved vastly. He responded immediately, asserting that the crisis had "sent me spiritually onward to new expression & this last work I have done has taken on a new visionary quality as a result of it." Arnold Rönnebeck had returned to Berlin from Paris the day before and had come at once to see Hartley and report more words of praise from Gertrude Stein. She had declared that his work went beyond anyone else's. His drawing, set among works by Cézanne, Manet, and Renoir, "gave her unqualified pleasure daily & hourly." Picasso had seen the drawing and been perplexed. "Where are the eyes — & the nose," he was purported to have asked. Stein told Rönnebeck that Hartley had moved "beyond Picasso and into a sphere infinitely removed from him & them all."

Hartley went on to discuss spiritualism. His work now felt "as if it didn't belong to me in a sense — It comes from some other thing or place I can't say where." His new art was "the result of [my] having come into touch with the great mystics of the universe & [of my] having come to Berlin where for some reason which I don't know I feel myself in a 'higher' place — there is a something here struggling always toward the light." He cited R. M. Bucke's *Cosmic Consciousness* and William James's *The Varieties of Religious Experience* as two sources from which he had learned how to express his experience.[39] Stein had lent him her copy of James's book; her admiration of it was one reason Hartley was fond of her.

James's study, one suspects, was *the* centerpiece in Hartley's coming to understand what he felt. The various lectures printed as chapters in *The Varieties of Religious Experience* range widely in subject matter, from "The Reality of the Unseen" and "The Religion of Healthy-Mindedness" to "The Divided Self" and "Mysticism." In the last of these James mentions Emerson and Whitman but travels far beyond them to address Eastern religions. "Cosmic consciousness in its more striking instances," he quotes Bucke as writing, "is not simply an expansion or extension of the self-conscious mind with which we are all familiar, but the superaddition of a function as distinct from any possessed by the average man as *self*-consciousness is distinct from any function possessed by one of the higher animals." To Bucke that consciousness was a "consciousness of the cosmos, that is, of the life and order of the universe," which involved "an indescribable feeling of elevation, elation, and joyousness [and] a sense of immortality."[40]

"The East Indian mystics say that the 'senses are high — but beyond the senses is the mind — beyond the mind is the understanding & beyond the understanding is the *self*,'" Hartley wrote to Stieglitz.[41] Discussing *dhyâna,* the Buddhists' word for "higher states of contemplation," James notes the numerous states leading toward the region where "there are neither ideas nor absence of ideas," and finally the state where, "having reached the end of both idea and perception," the meditator stops, being as close to Nirvana as possible. Later in the same chapter he observes that "in mystic states we both become one with the Absolute and we become aware of our oneness. . . . In Hinduism, in Neo-platonism, in Sufism, in Christian mysticism, in Whitmanism, we find the same recurring note."[42] If anything can give us a clue to the continuity in Hartley's thinking, it is this analysis of spiritualism and the mystics. More than any worldly anchors, mysticism enabled him to grip on to life. Even when he denied imagination — as he did after World War I and through much of the 1920s — the concepts of mysticism held him, and when, in the 1930s, he came closer to the higher states of contemplation, he found the inner peace he had been seeking most of his life.

Stieglitz's annoyance could not dampen Hartley's renewed optimism about his chances for some sort of financial success in New York. He announced that he was sailing aboard the S.S. *George Washington* on November 15 and that his pictures would be shipped shortly afterward. He had asked Gertrude Stein to send the four she had, so in all there would be seventeen, a good representation, though he would be leaving five with Der Sturm at Franz Marc's request.[43]

As if his correspondence with Stieglitz were not sufficient, he also wrote frequently to Gertrude Stein, explaining his distress, thanking her for the two hundred francs, complaining about Stieglitz's unwillingness to ask for money from wealthy Americans (while acknowledging that he owed him a great deal for all he had done), proposing that she write something for the catalogue that would accompany the exhibition of his work at 291, and asking her to ship his four pictures to New York.[44] There followed another flurry of letters to Stieglitz concerning small details. One can almost hear the Berlin postal service breathing a collective sigh of relief when Hartley boarded the *George Washington* for New York in the middle of November.

7

Engulfed by War
1913 – 1915

SET AGAINST AMERICA as Hartley was, he soon began to revile New York. After two weeks he wrote to Gertrude Stein that he wanted to go home — to Europe — because the city was an "inferno — miles of hard faces and hard ambitions," few smiles and less gentleness. Still, he enjoyed the company of artistic and literary people such as Mabel Dodge, Hutchins Hapgood, Stieglitz, and several others. Sounding the theme of many American expatriates, he complained that "everything is screwed up and run to the machinery of business — the buildings get higher & the streets deeper & the people less like human things — more like vermin and creepers — then too at close range — they look like multitudes of vultures glass-eyed clutching fiendishly each at everybody."[1]

His irritation stemmed partly from nervousness over the exhibition that was to be held at 291 from January 12 to February 14, 1914. Because his paintings had to be shipped from Europe, there were worrisome delays, but in the end the show went as Stieglitz had promised, and by mid-January Hartley could write to Stein that "the days are wonderful & the nights are wonderful & life is pleasant — the show is open — four are sold — one year is secure." He had been hoping for two years of freedom but was obviously relieved at having secured the one. He reported that "the artists are all elated & enthusiastic & the people say queer & interesting things."[2]

That was about accurate. In the catalogue for the show Stieglitz had included three forewords, one each by Mabel Dodge, Gertrude

Stein, and Hartley. Critics such as Henry McBride spoofed them, especially Stein's abstract word portrait of Hartley, and took umbrage at the elitist tone of the exhibition — though McBride did seem to have a grudging admiration for its audacity. Not so J. Edgar Chamberlin, who in the *New York Evening Mail* wrote that Hartley's paintings were "past the comprehension of the ordinary mind, and must be given up as an uncrackable nut." He acknowledged that the "strange kaleidoscopic patterns, of unknown significance," undoubtedly expressed sincere artistic emotions; but neither the artist nor anyone else had made any attempt to interpret the canvases. He saw that one of the paintings from Berlin celebrating military spectacle might be "the confused impression remaining on the retina after a day spent looking at soldiers and parades," but one of the abstractions mystified him, and he dismissed it as being what the inside of one's head might look like after one drank a "bottle and a half of champagne." Chamberlin refused to call the paintings "insanity or fakery" only because Hartley *was* sincere and because "so many other people are being insane nowadays in similar ways."

Stieglitz reprinted these criticisms in the January 1914 issue of *Camera Work,* along with the comments of Charles Caffin of the *New York American,* who viewed the Paris musical-theme paintings as "the vapors from the bowels of a medieval world." Caffin did not recognize Hartley's spiritualism; rather, he saw the paintings as the expression of a "finely sensitive and serious New England spirit chafing in its inherited shackles." Although one other critic whom Stieglitz included, Adolf Wolff, praised Hartley's exuberant use of emblems and symbols, the response of the critics was generally one of skepticism or worse.

Hartley's own catalogue foreword did little to clarify matters. Quoting Whitman and then Blake, who wrote that one ought to "put off intellect and put on imagination," he explained that all the pictures stated "a personal conviction" and that his work presented "signs and symbols for ideas of the spirit or soul." He understood that "the idea of modernity is but a new attachment to things universal." Hartley did not study the theories of the modernists, and his expression took the form of spiritualism, but intuitively he comprehended the basic point of modernism — that the old ways of seeing had lost their significance, except as history, for many in the twentieth century.[3]

After the exhibition closed, in February, a number of the paintings were sent to Buffalo, where they were shown at the home of Mrs. Nina

Eliza Jane Hartley

Marsden Hartley, age seven

Self-Portrait, 1908
charcoal on cream wove paper, 12 × 9 inches
Collection of the University Art Museum,
University of Minnesota, Minneapolis
Bequest of Hudson Walker,
from the Ione and Hudson Walker Collection

Dec 25-1909

For my dear niece Norma
from her uncle Marsden Hartley

Marsden Hartley, 1908

Storm Clouds, Maine, 1906–1907
oil on canvas, 30½ × 25½ inches
Walker Art Center, Minneapolis
Gift of the T. B. Walker Foundation,
1954

Maine Snowstorm, 1908
oil on canvas, 30 × 30 inches
Collection of the University Art Museum,
University of Minnesota, Minneapolis
Gift of Ione and Hudson Walker

Landscape No. 20, Resurrection, 1909
oil on academy board, 13½ × 11½ inches
Private collection
Courtesy of Vanderwoude Tananbaum Gallery,
New York

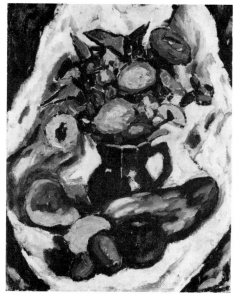

Deserted Farm, 1909
oil on composition board, 24 × 20 inches
Collection of the University Art Museum,
University of Minnesota, Minneapolis
Gift of Ione and Hudson Walker

Still Life No. 12, 1910
oil on canvas, 20 × 16 inches
Walker Art Center, Minneapolis
Gift of Bertha H. Walker, 1971

Hartley on the banks of the Androscoggin River, circa 1910

Still Life No. 1, 1913
oil on canvas, 31½ × 25⅝ inches
Columbus Museum of Art
Gift of Ferdinand Howald

Musical Theme #1, Bach Preludes, 1912
oil on canvas, 26 × 21 inches
Hirschl & Adler Galleries, New York

Portrait of Berlin, 1913
oil on canvas, 39¼ × 39⅜ inches
Beinecke Rare Book and Manuscript Library,
Yale University, New Haven, Connecticut
Gift of Mabel Dodge Luhan

Charles Demuth, 1915
platinum print by
Alfred Stieglitz (1864–1946)
National Gallery of Art,
Washington, D.C.,
Alfred Stieglitz Collection

Indian Fantasy, 1914
oil on canvas, 46¹¹⁄₁₆ × 39⁵⁄₁₆ inches
North Carolina Museum of Art, Raleigh

Provincetown, 1916
oil on composition board, 24⅛ × 20 inches
The Art Institute of Chicago,
Alfred Stieglitz Collection

Gertrude Stein, 1913

Mabel Dodge in Taos, 1917

Marsden Hartley Memorial Collection, Bates College

El Santo, 1919
oil on canvas, 36 × 32 inches
Museum of New Mexico, Santa Fe

Hartley at La Canada, California, 1918

Hartley in Santa Fe with fellow artists
Randall Davey, *center,* and John Sloan, *right,*
September 1919

Museum of New Mexico, Santa Fe

Landscape No. 3,
Cash Entry Mines, New Mexico,
1920
oil on canvas,
27¾ × 35¾ inches
The Art Institute of Chicago,
Alfred Stieglitz Collection

Hartley in Florence, 1924

Hartley with Ezra Pound, *center,*
and Fernand Léger, *right,*
Café du Dome, Paris, 1924

Landscape, Vence, 1925–1926
oil on canvas, 25½ × 31¾ inches
Collection of the University Art Gallery,
University of Minnesota, Minneapolis
Bequest of Hudson Walker,
from the Ione and Hudson Walker Collection

Hartley on the beach at Cannes, 1925

Hartley in Provence, late 1920s

Mountain No. 14, 1930
oil on canvas, 40½ × 33½ inches
Private collection
Courtesy of the Portland
Museum of Art, Portland, Maine

Mont Sainte-Victoire from just below the
Château Noir

The Whale's Jaw, Dogtown Common, Gloucester

Eight Bells Folly:
Memorial to Hart Crane, 1933
oil on canvas, 31⅝ × 39½ inches
Collection of the
University Art Museum,
University of Minnesota,
Minneapolis
Gift of Ione and Hudson Walker

Waxenstein Garmisch Partenkirchen,
1933–1934
oil on board, 29¾ × 20¾ inches
Vanderwoude Tananbaum Gallery,
New York

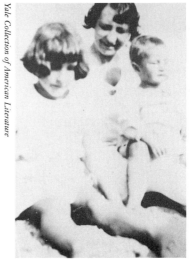

Adelaide Kuntz and her children,
Frances and John, early 1930s

Left: The Francis Mason family

Northern Seascape, off the Banks, 1936
oil on cardboard, 18³⁄₁₆ × 24 inches
Milwaukee Art Museum Collection
Bequest of Max E. Friedman

Labrador Ducks, 1936
oil on board, 17½ × 23½ inches
Private collection
Courtesy Berta Walker Gallery,
Provincetown, Massachusetts

Alfred Stieglitz and Georgia
O'Keeffe at Lake George,
circa 1938

Courtesy Sue Davidson Lowe (photograph by Josephine B. Marks)

Nova Scotia Fishermen, 1938
oil on canvas, 30 × 40 inches
IBM Corporation, Armonk,
New York

Fox Island, Maine, 1937–1938
oil on cardboard, 22 × 28 inches
Addison Gallery of American Art,
Phillips Academy, Andover, Massachusetts

Hudson Walker

Adelard the Drowned, Master of the Phantom,
1938–1939
oil on academy board, 28 × 22 inches
Collection of the University Art Museum,
University of Minnesota, Minneapolis
Bequest of Hudson Walker,
from the Ione and Hudson Walker Collection

Portrait of Albert Pinkham Ryder, 1938–1939
oil on academy board, 28½ × 22¼ inches
The Edith and Milton Lowenthal Collection
Courtesy of the Brooklyn Museum of Art

Give Us This Day, 1938
oil on canvas, 30 × 40 inches
Shaklee Corporate Art Collection,
San Francisco

The Lost Felice, 1939
oil on canvas, 40 × 30 inches
Los Angeles County Museum of Art,
Mr. and Mrs. William Preston Harrison
Collection

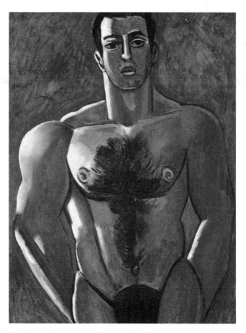

Madawaska — Acadian Light-Heavy, 1940
oil on hardboard, 40 × 30 inches
The Art Institute of Chicago
Bequest of A. James Speyer

The church in Corea, Maine, that Hartley used as
a studio in 1940

Hartley in Maine, 1941

Mount Katahdin, Maine, 1942
oil on hardboard, 30 × 40⅛ inches
National Gallery of Art, Washington
Gift of Mrs. Mellon Byers

The view from the spot where Hartley painted while staying
at Cobbs Camp in 1939, with Mount Katahdin in the
background

Marsden Hartley, 1942

The Great Good Man, 1942
oil on masonite, 40 × 30 inches
Museum of Fine Arts, Boston
Gift of the Lane Collection

Marsden Hartley, 1942

Bull. Hartley traveled there and reported to Stieglitz that he was "somewhat obsessed with the general desolateness of Buffalo," though he was pleased with the hanging and the attention the pictures received. Mabel Dodge and the painter Andrew Dasburg were there, so he had good company. He may well have seen a catalogue for the large exhibition of "Contemporary Scandinavian Art" that had been held a year earlier at the Albright Art Gallery in Buffalo. The show profoundly affected the Canadian artists J. E. H. MacDonald and Lauren Harris, whose landscape paintings (especially in the case of Harris) subsequently took on the same sort of sweep and horizontal movement that would one day become a trademark of Hartley's many paintings of New Mexico and Provence.[4]

But his mind was not on landscapes in 1914, and he found Buffalo and other such "cities of homes" oppressive. The only American place for him was New York.[5] As Mabel Dodge described him then, he would sit silently in Nina Bull's living room, "occasionally rolling his enormous diamond-shaped blue eyes and drawing down his thin lips. His long aquiline nose arched more than ever in Buffalo, and he repeated more frequently his curious gesture of running his whole thin face through his large bony fingers, crumpling it together into folds as one gathers silk."[6]

The paintings were next shipped to Chicago, where they were displayed at the home of Florence Bradley. She wanted Hartley there as well, but he announced that he was "finished with the monkey on a string business" and returned to New York, where, even with the company of the 291 group and a week's visit from Demuth, he immediately began to complain about the city's franticness, telling Gertrude Stein that he yearned for his "ain countree," Germany. Despite his grousing, however, he was momentarily confident and boasted that he was seen as a "creative American" and that his 291 show was being touted as a "big feature of the N.Y. year." He would want to show in London and Paris soon to ensure his financial security, he said, and was pushing as hard as he could to return to Europe after a visit to his family in Maine.[7] With satisfaction he left the New York scene, where in mid-March he had scoffed at some Americans: "The [Stanton Macdonald-]Wright–[Morgan] Russell trick is on now one critic calls it 'an old "ism" with tom-tom accompaniment.'" Russell had talent, he asserted, but Wright was only "fake cleverness." Hartley was put off by their publicizing themselves "as one would a mere species of vaseline or sausage — the American habit all right," he grumbled to Stein, referring to the exhibition of their synchromist paintings at the Carroll Galleries from March 2 to 16, 1914.[8]

By mid-April he was in London and soon thereafter traveled to Paris. He saw a good deal of Stein, who arranged for him to visit Picasso at his studio, "a simply huge atelier," he reported to Stieglitz, "packed with work of much the same nature — no radical & insane departures as some have suspected but all entirely logical from his standpoint." Hartley thought that "to express the objective-subjective" might be "an aesthetic obsession" on Picasso's part, but otherwise his intent was "perfectly simple and consistent." He found the artist himself a "fine simple boyish person with no ideas about his work — no discussions whatever & no way of explaining them thank heavens!"[9]

A few more days and Hartley was in Berlin, where he was warmly received with flowers and notes of welcome in his apartment.[10] While this pleased him, he felt distracted because of his experience in New York — "really an unspeakable place," he declared. He soon recognized that the sales of his work were not sufficient to support him for long; before leaving America he had become dismayed at how little was in the account that Stieglitz held for him. This and the immediate need of money to pay for his rent and living expenses in Berlin caused him to be "surfeited with negative states of mind."[11]

Stieglitz, sensing the depth of Hartley's despair, responded at once, reminding him that while New York might be unspeakable, it was also "fascinating ... like some giant machine, soulless, and without a trace of heart." Stieglitz doubted that there was any place "more truly wonderful ... just at the present." The main point of his letter, however, was to calm Hartley's fears about money. He pointed out that there was enough cash to see him through seven or eight months, during which time Hartley could create work that might ensure his security. Only time would tell. It was important that he connect in Germany, because the idea of "America supporting abstraction in the near future seems impossible." The few people who claimed to be interested were not truly so; their attention was faddish, not vital. That might come, but at the moment art was like an appendix in the body of American society; it existed but was of no use.[12]

In mid-May, before receiving Stieglitz's letter, Hartley wrote that he was feeling better generally and had begun to work "on a large scale again and it seems good and quite novel to be actually wielding pigment." He intensely desired a "long season of creative effort."[13] The paintings he began now were a series on the theme of the American Indian; by the time war broke out, in August, he had finished four. Not unmindful of what interested Europeans, he had several reasons for choosing what he later termed "the idea of America." He had just returned from there and wanted to memorialize it, or at least that part of it, Indian culture, that best reflected something of the difference between it and Europe. Like many other artists, he was interested in primitive art and had studied examples at the Trocadero Museum in Paris and the Museum für Volkerkunde in Berlin, where he had seen art by American Plains Indians. The Blaue Reiter almanac had included illustrations of native art, and Hartley was also much taken with the glass paintings of Bavarian peasants, whose style he incorporated into his own works.[14] And, too, admiring the Indians' peaceableness, he meant to commemorate it as the tension of war grew in Europe during the spring and summer of 1914.

Certainly war tensions had contributed to his malaise. Rönnebeck and von Freyburg were preoccupied with military matters, and Hartley, to some degree at least, was an outsider in Germany, as he had been in New York. By the end of May, though he thought he was working well, he still had not settled what he called "the despair of my being," which he blamed on "the oppression of isolation which is so much the part of my existence — an aloneness which is neither warranted or tolerable." He had the insight to recognize that it was "fathoms deep in my consciousness." Feeling the outsider in two countries, unable to support himself adequately, given to debilitating nervousness, he wondered if he should go on. "A life has been at stake," he announced dramatically, "& I have tried to argue for it with reason against it." The issue was being an "isolated individual . . . the alone with the alone."

The fact that he was painting marked some relief from his depression. In addition, he was working on a statement about the 291 Gallery, which Stieglitz had suggested he might want to include in a special issue of *Camera Work*.[15] Answering the question "What Is 291?" gave Hartley the opportunity to articulate the importance of the gallery — to him as to America — and in the process he was able to understand his own significance as an artist. "I am working — & very well I think," he wrote to Stieglitz at the end of May. "I hope it will matter some day to someone as much or more than to myself."[16] The gallery, he thought, was unique, "standing firm for every variety of Truth and every variety of expression of the same." For anyone interested in "progressive modern tendencies toward individual expression" it was essential.[17] He realized that, and even when he turned his back on America, 291 always served as a kind of anchor for him.

Only in June did his depression finally end, and he celebrated with a long letter to Stieglitz, whom he had not been able to write at length while what he called his sickness persisted. As usual, he fretted about money and the unfairness of any artist's having to struggle as he did in order to continue. He was pleased that Charles Daniel, of the Daniel Gallery in New York, wanted his work, but he worried about the dealer's reliability and urged Stieglitz to get some sort of written commitment from him. Three days later Hartley picked up where he had left off, now complaining less about money and instead rambling about art. He reported that Kandinsky's *On the Spiritual in Art* was being published in an English translation. It "savours too much of creeds that have nothing to do with art proper," he maintained. Trying to give a sense of the art movements abroad, he told Stieglitz that Kandinsky's book was finding favor "in England among those of the 'Rebel Art Centre[,]' an offshoot of the cubist-futurist notion in Paris." But as a result of all the attention given in London to Marinetti, "with poetic talks & now demonstrations of noise-music in vaudeville," some young artists in England had issued their own "tedious" manifesto, separating themselves from futurism and cubism and declaring themselves "Vorticists," which symbolized "the whirl and movement of our own modern tendencies." Hartley was skeptical about it all; he respected the new group "as I respect all the pages of the dictionary — but I don't think titles have ever made an art." Such was the case, too, he thought, with the Pre-Raphaelites, "these Rossettis & Watl's [?] — Millais's — Ford Madox Brown — etc. Well — they are excellent for the Pear's Soap people or the Beecham's Pills as affiches."

In London he had seen Ezra Pound, who had asked him to write a piece for the *Egoist,* along the lines of his foreword to his 291 exhibition. "If you knew Pound you would know that this is sheer flattery," Hartley explained. The essay, which was never published, was to be called "On the Decline of Vision." In it he hoped to

piec[e] out here & there the types of real visionaries — both material and spiritual — Rousseau Cezanne Picasso — Redon — Blake —

among the painters — Van Gogh of course who is one of the first since he was actually a visionary — though his was an highly organized earth vision — Gaugin in the religious sense contrasting it all to the men of the French schools of now who see actually only what the camera sees — who simply take ordinary facts out of nature & construe them ordinarily — being not artist in any distinguished sense — lacking in those qualities that set a real picture beyond nature & beyond truth — the lack of power to transpose in the truly abstract sense being realists of a mean order — whereas one like Picasso sees the material thing with an exceptional degree of power & is an artist.

Hartley wanted to make it clear that "professional eyesight" was not that which "sees as it thinks" but rather that of "the truly untroubled one like Rousseau . . . who expresses . . . the sense of vision. . . . He was beyond the help of nature." He declared that "the real visionary is beyond any help that nature can offer him — what he sees is superior to what is seen above & beyond what nature presents. It is he who actually shapes the 'soul' of nature for us & for the universe — in the arts." Such a visionary "transposes facts into their spiritual transports and arranges a harmony of them for us & the farther he sees often the less comprehensive it is."[18]

In mid-June Stieglitz wrote with the good news that Daniel had decided to purchase more paintings, so Hartley's financial situation would be improved. Now that money worries had eased, Stieglitz wanted to get something out of his system. He reminded Hartley that the day before he left for Europe he had given him a quick summary of his finances. He had dreaded doing it because Hartley was upset and nervous, but he had been drawing largish sums while in New York and had less remaining than he expected. When Stieglitz told him of his balance, Hartley had been "terrifically stunned" and apparently had not comprehended the situation. Stieglitz had said nothing more at the time but had been distressed because he knew that Hartley thought money had been withheld as a kind of commission. Stieglitz had laughed ruefully at the idea, since he had always passed on every penny he had received for any painting. In his letter he accounted for the money in detail, hoping it would settle matters.[19]

When Hartley received this, he was ashamed. Dramatically he announced that he could "only get down on the block like a man and

submit to the axe and metaphorically let any who find it diverting — watch the very blood of me drain itself upon the diffident
earth." He was mortified that Stieglitz should feel the need to recite
figures, because he did not like to let money intrude on friendships.
He did not quite acknowledge to Stieglitz — or to himself — how
frequently money had been at the center of their relationship, though
he would not have chosen for it to be that way.[20]

For Hartley there would be only a brief respite from worry before
Germany's declaration of war caused him new anxieties about friends
and money. As rumors of the impending conflict grew, Hartley described for Stieglitz the Germans' response. Amid reports of mobilization near the end of July, Berlin became not frenzied but appallingly
still, reflecting a mood of expectancy, a "psychic tension" that was "superb & awesome." A few nights earlier Hartley had watched "thousands of men & some girls marching with much dignity without police
direction — guarding & conducting themselves finely through the
main streets. With propriety and decorum they sang the national
hymn and other songs." The next day, July 30, Hartley sat in the Cafe-
Bauer on Unter den Linden and told of the crowds along the avenue.
The news was comforting — "no mobilization in Germany" — but
tensions remained high. The Hamburg-America Line office refused
to sell passage to the United States (not that Hartley wished to go), and
the Bourse was closed. Hartley immediately wrote again to recount
the situation. Friday, July 31, was a "stifling day":

> The Emperor & Empress returned to Berlin looking very sober — I
> passed closer to the Kronprinz & Princezzin later — they appearing
> gayer & less troubled looking — Unter den linden packed and after
> nine-o'clock a terrific mob hundreds of thousands passing to & fro
> from the Castle — I have just come home — the last *ausgabe* is that
> the Emperor of Germany has asked the Czar of Russia for an expla-
> nation of his mobilization & demands the reply in 12 hours.

At lunchtime the answer would be forthcoming. Meanwhile, there
was more excitement than ever and a "very strong sense of united
feeling. It is now not a romance but a real reality." The emperor had
spoken to the masses from his balcony and asked for their "blood &
money." Germany had already mobilized, in fact, and on August 1,
after Russia refused to alter its stance, Germany declared war on it. "It
is all unpleasant in a million ways," Hartley lamented. "There can be

a sudden increase in the cost of living etc." But far worse, he would see his *"best friends* off to war — perhaps not to see them again — & other thousands that will be doing likewise."[21]

On August 3 the conflict broadened as Germany declared war on France. Hartley was near despair. He had little but praise for the Germans when he next wrote to Stieglitz, a month later. Mail and cables to the United States had become uncertain, which worried him, as did the rumors he had heard that the American press was reporting that Americans in Germany were suffering and in danger. The truth, he declared, was that even the English, whose nation was now also at war, were being well treated. The Germans, he felt, had shown "the most extraordinary calmness & presence of mind" and refrained from the sort of violent reaction he would have expected from the French. The day he was writing, September 2, was a holiday, and there had been a parade in which the "First War Trophies" were displayed: "five Belgian cannons — two French — eleven Russian and three Russian machine guns."

He had also seen his first American papers since war had begun. What he read he assumed to be "incredible rubbish . . . cooked up via London — really disgustingly cheap"; this included reports that Americans were being held as spies. What was heartrending was "to see Germany's marvellous youth going off to a horrible death — this has been the dreadful vision — seeing their thousands simply walk out of homes leaving wives & children . . . & going too with a real extasy[,] for war is the only modern religious extasy." He recalled seeing three handsome men march by, "waving hands throwing kisses & shouting auf wiedersehen." Already many such had died. "It is not to conceive," he lamented. Many nations — among them England, Russia, India, and Poland — were undergoing political turmoil; "I look upon the English as the cad of the world," Hartley announced, "and upon Russia as probably the most shameful & shameless country of modern time." He wanted to believe in Germany's integrity, a quality he found every day among the people he knew; and he wanted Stieglitz to know that Americans were being treated kindly.

The only problem was that money was not getting through. Hartley was in desperate straits again, not because of price increases or any other changes due to the war, but simply because his modest funds were depleted. Collect from Simonson, Daniel, and Mabel Dodge, he implored Stieglitz.[22] When there was no response by mid-September, he became frantic and through the American embassy in Rome wired a message to Stieglitz: "CABLE TWO HUNDRED DOLLARS HELPLESS HARTLEY."[23] This was followed by pleas over the next weeks to Stieglitz, Simonson, and Mabel Dodge, until on October 27 he received $100 from Stieglitz, who wrote of the difficulties he had experienced in trying to send it. He suggested that unless Hartley could earn an income in Berlin, he ought to return to the United States, where things were hectic, no matter how calm they were in Berlin. Cables to Germany were not accepted; in fact, there seemed to be no easy way to send either money *or* letters.[24]

So overwrought was Hartley that the news of his father's death, on August 4, was accorded only the slightest mention in his letters. The death of Karl von Freyburg, on October 7, however, was another matter. When he wrote to Stieglitz shortly before the $100 arrived, Hartley described the difficulty of going on under the multiple pressures of no money, "the general gloom of continuous dark weather," and the war, which had claimed von Freyburg. Having already won an Iron Cross, he had been killed near Amiens, France, where the Germans had pushed their front lines by September. He was buried in a war grave in the region of Arras. "You know what an intense thing friendship always was & is for me," Hartley reminded Stieglitz, who could "appreciate therefore the acute pain of this experience." As if this were not painful enough, Rönnebeck had also been wounded, but at least he was alive and recuperating in Berlin. "It is the surest of miracles that he is alive and is able to walk about among the living," Hartley said. Rönnebeck had seen a great deal of death, and "a mere matter of 6 inches alteration in his position would have sent him also spinning into eternity"; as it was, he had lost the hearing in his left ear. Seeing so many young men go off, never to return, was almost more than the imagination could bear. Life just then was nothing but eternal grief for every country — for France, Russia, England, and Austria as well as Germany — "a terrible slaughter," leaving behind nothing but an unendurable agony.[25]

Hartley's despair was deep. The happiness — home — he had found in Berlin among the Germans was daily being torn from him. "I am living under conditions that destroy all attention to work," he wrote. Lack of money forced him to borrow from German friends such as the Rönnebecks, who could not afford to support him, but far worse than that was all that the war had cost him emotionally.

He mourned for von Freyburg, whose friendship was "perhaps the rarest ... in my experience," he told Gertrude Stein later that fall, intending all that his words might imply.[26] "If you knew von Freyburg you would understand what true pathos is," he declared to Stieglitz. No one was "more beloved & more necessary to the social well-being of the world — in every way a perfect being — physically — spiritually & mentally beautifully balanced — 24 years young — and of all things ---- necessary."

Von Freyburg had meant everything to Hartley. In 1938, agitated by Hitler's annexation of Austria, he would write one of his "Letters Never Sent" to the memory of von Freyburg. The annexation made him recall a walk he had taken four years earlier from Partenkirchen to Mittenwald, and then the mile or so beyond into Austria. Now, in 1938, that country was being swallowed up, and its loss made Hartley think of the loss of von Freyburg and all his bright qualities, which in turn brought to mind a dream he had had soon after the young man's death. In it he was walking in a mountain field in a thunderstorm and saw at his feet a "huge snake coiling and writhing." Lightning suddenly struck it; Hartley could remember its agonized twists, could even smell its burning flesh. Out of the charred mass came a "singular white light" that passed up Hartley's right side — a scene that he watched as a spectator in his dream. The light then became a "full length image of [von Freyburg] clad in full uniform, but the uniform, purged of all military significance, was white." He looked into von Freyburg's face; the younger man smiled, and Hartley returned the gesture. "It was the sublimation of our intended relations," he wrote, "and was without blemish." In his dream he and von Freyburg became one, consummating a relationship that arose out of the sexual attraction that Hartley, at least, had felt toward the other man.

The awfulness of war becomes real when it destroys the people we most love. "I seem to have lost all sense of victories and defeats," Hartley lamented, wondering how races could survive in the face of such atrocities. "A fearful siege of sorrow" was spreading over the land, yet things proceeded "as if war were the necessary constituent of well-being." With a certain prescience he mused, "It is said to be by some the last war — I wonder — if war will ever become unpopular. Sometimes it doesn't seem so." Twenty-four years later he would shudder as he wrote his letter to von Freyburg, fearing the consequences of Hitler's rise to power. That "house-painter" had become dictator and was, he observed, "a singularly impressive person . . . , one of strange forces, the instrument of mass idolatry." Hartley had twice heard him captivate the public with his speeches; his power was "the mystical flame of earth ecstasy with the state as the holy ideal," but it brought with it disaster.

Hartley's distress in late 1914 was amply justified. Coming to Berlin the previous year, at the age of thirty-six, he had hoped to find surcease from his loneliness and restiveness. Only in Berlin had he not complained to whoever would listen, but now, he said, "the bloom is removed for the present from what has been here for me one of the finest expressions of life impulse and universal intention anywhere in the world." The Germans had shown him what it was "to prove oneself necessary," which meant having an "instinct for life . . . a superb energy — powerful toward creation and powerful toward preservation."[27] That "instinct for life" demanded a sensitivity to emotions and a willingness to express oneself openly, but the war was destroying the people who best exemplified those qualities. "I do weep literally for I have cause," Hartley wrote to Charles Demuth that fall. "Tears are justified in these pathetic hours." He reported that with Rönnebeck he had "whatever rendezvous we can have," but despite the outward appearance of nothing's having changed in Berlin, anyone who loved it would find that "the golden leaves have fallen too pathetically these autumn days — that there is too much symbolism lying under foot upon the pavement." He had not returned to Potsdam, where Demuth, he, and almost certainly Rönnebeck and von Freyburg had gone together: "There is too much there to remember, dear old Demmy," he concluded.[28]

Later in the fall Hartley began to come out of himself, though he continued to grieve for von Freyburg and to despise what he took to be America's "blood & thunder appetite." It was "like every other adolescent — all hands feet and mouth — and always at the wrong time mostly mouth," he told Stieglitz. This particularly irritated him in the face of Germany's calm and order amidst real suffering. He found himself "wanting to be an Indian — to paint my face with the symbols of that race I adore go to the west & face the sun forever — that would seem the true expression of human dignity."

But in other ways he was finding contentment again: "I go on daily living more happily than ever in my life — with my simple joys — and sorrows too — although this might seem paradoxical," he informed Stieglitz in mid-November.[29] For the moment he was not concerned about money; Stieglitz had sent a check, and it seemed certain that he would be able to continue providing income. Hartley was satisfied, as well, with his relationship with Rönnebeck, who remained nearby, on duty in Dobritz and Berlin. Rönnebeck's friendship was "the completest thing I ever had because it has long since been realized entirely," Hartley wrote, suggesting that with the death of von Freyburg, whom they had both loved, they had become more intimate than ever. Then, too, life had "rushed in well upon me in recent times," he added, mentioning the "temporary marriage of a very decent nature" in which he was then engaged.[30] This was Life, and while events saddened him, he also felt immersed in its fulness, especially poignantly now because of his earlier sense that what Berlin had once been was being torn from him.

By the end of 1914 he had turned to painting again, without anxiety. The result was some of his most powerful work. Having finished only four pictures "on the idea of America" before his worries about money and then the death of von Freyburg had rendered him incapable of painting, he expected to return to American themes after he worked out "some war notions, which people praise highly."[31] He told Gertrude Stein that he was "working gradually & have done I think some really good things — an extreme advance over those pictures you have seen." He claimed that they were *"reine emfindung,"* or "sensation pure," which was what he had been working to achieve.[32] This purity of vision came now that he was "on the verge of real insight into the imaginative life," he informed Stieglitz. No longer was he "that terror stricken thing with a surfeit of imaginative experience undigested"; rather, he was "contained in what I feel see & hear & do & a real clarity of light pervades." Gone was the dread he had felt in New York and earlier in the autumn; now he found "vision and experience becoming one." He sensed neither struggle, alienation, nor hysteria, only "pure vision out of pure experience." At that moment his themes were "teutonic," but he would soon "return to my ideas & sensations upon the word America."[33] After his despair of only a month earlier, it is difficult to comprehend his euphoria in November. Perhaps he had by then had his powerful dream about uniting with von Freyburg. Perhaps his deeper intimacy with Rönnebeck was gratifying, or perhaps he had by then met the woman with whom he would have his temporary "Berlin marriage." Certainly everything that had happened enabled him psychologically to bring together the bitter experiences of war and his imaginative life, not as an isolated outsider but as one who shared his suffering with others. Put simply, the conflict brought him out of himself, at least for a time, and with a kind of exhilaration he began to paint from his imagination the stuff of war: uniforms, decorations, banners, and so forth. But unlike his earlier musical-theme works, or even his Indian paintings, these canvases played on the common imagination of the Germans, and they responded favorably.

"Heute habe ich wirklich etwas zu Engahlen" — "Today I really have something to tell you" — he burst out to Stieglitz early in April 1915. His excitement was over selling his four most recent paintings, "each complementary to the other," to a young German couple who planned them as the only decoration in their music room.[34]

This was the high point of his exhilaration. He still felt financially stable as a result of receiving $844.50 — "all the monies in sight" — from Stieglitz in February.[35] Also, he had read some positive reactions to a small show of his landscapes at the Daniel Gallery. These were not new works but rather paintings from the 1909–1911 period. He was, nevertheless, before those members of the public who chose to visit the gallery.

The paintings that the young couple had bought in March were based on the "war notions" Hartley had mentioned to Stieglitz in November. The pictures reflected a progression from previous work; Barbara Haskell has pointed out that something of their structure and imagery came from paintings he had completed earlier in Berlin, but these new works went beyond those. Hartley painted "arrangements of badges, German imperial flags, and military emblems like the Iron Cross and regimental insignia," and from these, "flattened out and locked together," he made "overall design[s] of overlapping and interlocking planes similar to Picasso's Synthetic Cubist compositions."[36] At first these paintings, noticeably larger than most of Hartley's other works, included symbols of von Freyburg — and of Rönnebeck, the latter would claim years later. As the series progressed in 1915, however, Hartley paid less attention to symbols of his officer friends, and the paintings, while clearly about his "war notions," became "more purely decorative combinations of abstract patterns."[37]

The officer portraits, Hartley's most famous paintings, are remarkable. Large, powerful in their colors and texture, they are more than anything else an expression of love. *Portrait of a German Officer,* for example, makes specific reference to von Freyburg and Rönnebeck. The picture includes an Iron Cross, which both men had been awarded. The initials *K v F* refer, obviously, to von Freyburg. The number 24 indicates his age at the time of his death; 4 was the number of his regiment in the kaiser's Guards, and the *E,* red on yellow, as Rönnebeck explained to the collector and art critic Duncan Phillips, represents "the initial of Queen Elizabeth of Greece." Rönnebeck wore that insignia at the time, as he was serving "as lieutenant in the reserve of Konigin Elisabeth Garde Grenadier Regiment Numer 3."[38] Hartley included these symbols in other paintings as well, sometimes varying the color schemes and incorporating the mystical numbers 8 and 9 to symbolize the regeneration, truth, and unity that he wished for in his idealized friendship with the Germans. As the paintings began to be more generalized "war notions," and less specifically about his friends, he tended to lessen such symbolism.

True to form, he did not remain content for long. By mid-May 1915 he was grumbling to Stieglitz that the difficulty of receiving monthly payments because of the war "puts a stop to existence for me.... I can do nothing."[39] Stieglitz wrote back peevishly that he was doing the best he could and that Hartley's assumptions about his due were exaggerated.[40] Worried about money, Hartley by early summer began to think of returning to the United States for a showing of his work. He would not plan to stay there, but he recognized the need to keep his work before whatever public there might be. When he wrote again in August, after a hiatus that Stieglitz must have welcomed, he apologized for his complaining.

A number of events and worries disturbed Hartley's tranquillity: money, as always; the death of his stepmother, in May; the death of a nephew; and an infected finger that required an operation. But in Berlin he had also found a gallery, Munchener Graphik-Verlag, the spirit of which he likened to that of 291. A Swiss sculptor, Friedel Huf, a friend of Hartley's, introduced him to the gallery director, a man named Haas-Haye, who invited him to exhibit his work in October. This seemed to be an opportunity for Hartley to show his paintings independent of any school or clique such as that exhibited in Der Sturm, whose director, Herwarth Walden, was not keen on him.

If Kandinsky or Marc had been around, the situation might have been different, but Kandinsky, being Russian, had left Germany, and Marc was in the German army. The exhibition would be "rather an event from many points of view," Hartley declared. He believed himself to be "the only so-called ultra-modern" American in Germany. He hoped for an artistic success. There was not much chance of his making any money; still, he had to do this, to set himself up for later. In addition, there was to be a show of forty-five of his early drawings in September, at the Schames Galerie in Frankfurt. After these two exhibitions he would ship himself and his work home, perhaps in time for a Thanksgiving dinner at the Stieglitzes'.[41]

For the exhibition at Graphik-Verlag, which opened around the middle of October and included forty-five pictures and a number of drawings from his time in Berlin as well as the drawings that had been shown in Frankfurt, Hartley wrote an introduction that was printed in German. "Pictures that I exhibit are without titles and without description," he explained. He called them "characterizations of the 'Moment,' everyday pictures, of every day, every hour." He claimed to be "free from all conventional aesthetics" — clearly making an effort to separate himself from various modernist schools. He wanted his audience to understand that he had created "according to my own conceptions of nature, of life, of aesthetics," permitting him the range to paint as he chose. "Appearance is to be imitated, reality never," he concluded, by which he meant that the reality that he, as a visionary, was painting could not be photographically imitated, only expressed in whatever way the painter might.

Baffled by Hartley's introduction, a not unfriendly reviewer for the *New York Times* described the exhibition itself. In the first of three rooms was what he thought "the most remarkable painting in the collection," probably *The Warriors,* of 1913. Also in the first room was *Indian Fantasy,* which according to the reviewer depicted a "cross between an ancient Egyptian and an ultramodern American eagle, brooding over a sultry lake on which four stolid cigar store Indians are drifting in a canoe."

The second room contained what the reviewer considered to be Hartley's "real war pictures, painted during the war." In these, "a snarl of triangles, squares, rectangles, flags of all nations, in glaring, solid, primitive colors, shuffled together, produces a picture puzzle that absolutely defies you to say that it isn't a battle." There was some disagreement as to whether or not the paintings were pro-German, the reviewer noted, and he reported the reactions of several critics, one of whom had praised Hartley's "prehistoric eye," while another had called him "A New American Misfit Genius" whose introduction "screeches" that "it's all rot, what has so far been painted — rot, rot, and again rot. . . . I, I furnish the only real painting. I Marsden Hartley from Mixed Pickles in Bluffagonia." The latter critic, offended, had had no use for any of Hartley's expressionist or abstract work.[42]

The exhibition was "very interesting from all points of view," Hartley wrote to Stieglitz in early November. "No sales of course as would be expected for reasons subtle it may be but mostly because the art viewpoint is too new." Only getting used to cubism, the Germans could not accept someone's "swinging back to caveman expression."[43] After reading Lyonel Feininger's comments about his work in a letter to a friend, Hartley wrote to thank him. "Things come into my world which is the world only of the eye," he explained, adding, "I do not trust the intellect very much for I think [it] plays sad havoc with one's real intention." He asked if he might visit him, did, and soon after faintly praised the cubist's paintings for "their earnestness — their charm — their fineness." But he wished they had more light to them. "Let yourself loose," he advised. Feininger, who had in 1913 exhibited with the Blaue Reiter group, was "mentally enslaved," Hartley decided; he told him that and conveyed his wish that Feininger might express his "spiritual conviction" fully.[44]

That he could make such comments to an established painter suggests the extent of Hartley's confidence at that moment. He considered the large exhibition to have been an artistic success, so with hopes for a quick return to Germany, where he expected his work would soon be accepted, he sailed for New York aboard the S.S. *Rotterdam* on December 11. He had little idea that he would not be back for six years, that the Berlin he would find then would hardly be like the one he was leaving, or that after all his efforts during the two years he had lived there, whatever inroads he had made into the German art world would have been obliterated by the time he returned, in November 1921.

8

"An American Discovering America"
1916 – 1919

NEW YORK had its usual effect on Hartley, who soon sounded shrill and demanding. That the pictures he had shipped from Germany did not arrive until late March exacerbated his mood, so he complained to his niece about the "crudity" of New York and of American democracy, claiming that a touch of "aristocracy of taste and expression" would suit better. He was so shut into his own egocentric world that despite the war he naively expected to sail in May for Europe, "as I have my European reputation to care for and it has begun so well," he told her.[1] His imperiousness at this instant toward others stemmed from his belief that as an experienced expatriate, he was an important part of the avant-garde art scene in America. In fact, he had almost no European reputation to care for, and little more in the United States. It was not one of his better moments.

He was, if anything, more an outsider in his own country than in Germany. Fortunately, he was able to join Mabel Dodge's salon crowd. Earlier he had hoped to visit her at her villa near Florence, Italy; now this was impossible, but she generously invited him to feel at liberty to use her apartment at 23 Fifth Avenue, a place Hartley remembered as being filled with "remarkable Italian furnishings." It was "like a jewel-box pouring out shafts of amazing light," and constantly full of people. The salon evenings were special; someone would perform or give a reading, and there would follow a great feast that the "hundreds" who attended would indulge in.[2] Dodge welcomed Hartley as well at Finney Farm, her country home in Croton-on-Hudson, where he stayed in the early spring, using the studio of her companion, Maurice Sterne, when he was not there.

While Hartley enjoyed the change from New York, he overstayed his welcome. He did not fit into the swirl that was Dodge's life wherever she was. She became annoyed with him, not because of the scraps of chiffon that he hung on the walls of his room to soften the light, but because there was "something solitary and unassimilable" in him. "It hurt me more to have him there than to write him he must go!" she recalled. Dodge's friend Nina Bull delivered her note to him on the train into the city. Acknowledging "the terrible hours of shadow" in which he had recently lived, Hartley assured Dodge that he understood her request that he not continue to use Finney Farm.[3]

He seemed to expect this rebuff and was not too dismayed by it to follow Dodge to New Mexico two years later. In the spring of 1916 two exhibitions of his work were scheduled to occur, and this lessened his consternation. The first, called the Forum Exhibition, held in March, was intended "to put before the American public in a large and complete manner the very best examples of the more modern American art."[4] Hartley was represented by six paintings and three drawings.

After the Forum Exhibition, in April, Stieglitz showed the German paintings at 291. He surprised Hartley by not telling him they had arrived from Germany and having them await him in the gallery. "He is a wonderful person," Hartley wrote to his niece, "and has actually made my success by believing in me from the first and fighting for my work when so many of his friends were against me as a painter. Suddenly now since I came back this time," Hartley insisted, "they are all discovering that I am one to be reckoned with — so it is with real individuality always." The attention the Forum Exhibition had received and the prospect of the 291 show raised his confidence as he wrote to his niece in late March. He declared that he was famous, and while he had little wealth to show for it as yet, he said, he might soon, as "there is . . . a great awakening here in New York."[5]

His expectations, as usual, were exaggerated. He and Stieglitz were taking a risk by showing the paintings amid the anti-German sentiment of the time. Hartley played down the nationalistic elements in his work, noting in the exhibition catalogue that the pictures were "but part of a series which I had contemplated of movements in various areas of war activity from which I was prevented." He asserted that the forms reflected what he had "observed casually from day to day. There is no symbolism whatsoever in them; there is no slight intention of that anywhere," he declared. Rather, these were responses to his observations, "merely consultations of the eye, . . . my notion of the purely pictural."[6] Reviewers of the show tended not to believe him; paintings such as those in the German-officer series seemed obviously to celebrate the German martial spirit. So while Hartley escaped condemnation, he was not embraced, as he had hinted to his niece he might be. His confidence jolted, he moved on to the formal studies he would continue to render during the following summer.

In July he visited Provincetown, where he was the guest of the famous journalist Jack Reed. After a week he traveled to Auburn, Maine, to see his family and have some dental work done. But the "misery of dental operation and family tedium" distressed him, and he quickly asked Stieglitz to telegraph $100 so he could pay his bills and return to Provincetown.[7]

The time after his return to Cape Cod was a memorable one for him — "The Great Provincetown Summer," he called it in a reminiscence.[8] A remarkable group of artists and writers had congregated in and around Provincetown, principally along Commercial Street, beside the harbor. Hartley enjoyed the company of the writers Mary Heaton Vorse; Susan Glaspell and her husband, George Cram Cook; Max Eastman and his wife, Ida Rauh; Neith and Hutchins Hapgood; and Jack Reed and Louise Bryant, who was living with him. Eugene O'Neill was part of the entourage, and Hartley remembered the excitement surrounding the performances of his early dramas by the newly formed Provincetown Players, who staged their productions in a small fish house on a wharf behind Mary Heaton Vorse's home. Charles Demuth was there as well, and after Reed closed up his place in August, Hartley and Demuth lived together in a house they found near the water. Hartley also met the artist Carl Sprinchorn that summer.

In all it was one of the most social times of Hartley's life, though he could still grouse to Stieglitz about Provincetown's "terrific onslaught of artistic unrest." A "siege of drama" discomfited him, carried on as it was by "minor actors suffering out major failure."[9] But if he disapproved of dramatic enthusiasms, he enjoyed the nearly constant flow of acquaintances up and down Commercial Street, from Mary Heaton Vorse's and Susan Glaspell's houses at one end to Reed's at the other.

The talk was continuous, as were the parties, and at least once Hartley entered into the spirit of things enough to get drunk. He fell down in the street, but when someone tried to assist him, he declared loudly that he could stand by himself. Doubtless he was mortified, and doubtless the people observing him were amused.[10] "What a summer," he wrote later, "in among those amazing dunes — shifting with the wind before one's eyes — burying young pine trees to their tops."[11]

Hartley was fortunate to have the companionship of his Provincetown friends, because his return to America had been traumatic. The two exhibitions in the spring had given him some sense of importance but had resulted in neither great income nor wide acceptance for his work. Moreover, during the summer he abandoned the subject matter of the German paintings — which "were among the most advanced and brilliant works produced by any American at the time" — because, as Barbara Haskell has explained, "the adverse reactions to his German iconography left him without a subject matter to which he felt committed. Hence the expressive symbolism and mystical content of his German period gave way to purely formal concerns."[12]

Earlier in 1916, in the catalogue note he wrote for the Forum Exhibition, he had encouraged viewers to seek the artist's "personal quality" in his art, by which he meant his particular style. "Objects are incidents," he concluded. "An apple does not for long remain an apple if one has the concept. Anything is therefore pictural; it remains only to be observed and considered. All expressions in illustration — of something." He felt most at ease expressing "that which exists between him and his subject," his description of Cézanne's aim. When Hartley moved away from that toward concerns about form, as he did during the summer in Provincetown, his art suffered, in the opinion of many observers. Barbara Haskell, however, disagrees, noting that Hartley "retained the tight brushwork and sharply delineated, flatly colored shapes of his simplified still lifes, but . . . reduced his elements to unified geometric shapes painted in pale, muted colors." She has called these Provincetown paintings his "most radical venture into non-objectivity" and likened them to what was being done in Europe at the time. No American artist would rival them for another ten years, but, she adds, they "proved too advanced . . . for even the more sympathetic cosmopolitan admirers of his painting to fully appreciate."[13]

When cold weather ended his stay on Cape Cod, Hartley, by now recognizing that he could not return to Europe, planned a trip to Bermuda with Demuth for the winter of 1916–17. He spent ten weeks in New York in the fall, and as always that depressed him. To Stieglitz he bemoaned his circumstances. He pleaded for help in obtaining a regular income so that he could avoid suffering "the terrific drain on my spirit which I have endured the last year." Although he did not say it outright, he was frustrated with Stieglitz's refusal to be a salesman. Hartley wrote of the "inward strife" — that is, his drive for artistic expression — that was "as tense as ever" within him, despite the indifference of others to his work. "The sheer instinct to live and express forces me toward this incessant crying against the diffidence of outward agencies," he declared, adding that he wanted "merely to find again a place where I can hide and hush myself into a respectable belief in continuity and order."[14]

He expected that Bermuda would be such a place. He arrived there at Christmastime, after a voyage that left him fatigued. But he had high hopes that the warmer weather, the thick and colorful vegetation, and the soft-spoken people would quickly revive him.[15] They did and did not. The weather was soothing, but the island itself was overly placid. The mails moved slowly, and Hartley was soon worried about money, so that by the beginning of February he was finding that Bermuda did not wear well. Had he not come there to work, he said, he would already have returned to New York, "as I find it of so little interest apart from the peculiarity of the climate. The life is so sluggish, so little to stimulate the mind with — I do not know what the natives get out of life, but I know I should perish if I remained here a year," he wrote to Stieglitz.[16]

His depression stemmed not only from mental stress; he also continued to feel extreme fatigue and at the beginning of February turned to osteopathy in hopes of finding some relief. The treatments brought temporary comfort but little more, and even Demuth's arrival early in the month did not significantly improve Hartley's spirits. When he worked hard, the nerves in his arms and legs actually tingled, and he soon felt exhausted. When he did not work, he was overcome by boredom. It was not a good time; "I am really tired out spiritually by the loss of illusions," he asserted. "I find the world a silly place and this in my sanest moments."[17]

After Demuth arrived, Hartley moved with him from Hamilton to the village of St. George, where they painted in rooms on the top floor of the Hotel St. George. For a time Eugene O'Neill joined them; he was a good foil for Demuth, who was in a pleasant mood mostly. With the benefit of his friends' companionship Hartley at last felt able to work.[18] Had he not had nagging problems with his health, he would have been in a better frame of mind; as it was, he had the satisfaction of knowing that essays of his had appeared in *Seven Arts* and the *New Republic.* Neither was a major piece — one, "The Twilight of the Acrobat," was about vaudeville acrobats, and the other an homage to Odilon Redon — but Hartley must have been pleased that his work was now being published more widely than ever before. Then, too, an exhibition of his Provincetown paintings and selected earlier work had opened at 291 in January and had been well received. Demuth praised it highly, and the reviewer for the *New York Times* complimented the exhibition's "beauty and sanity."[19] Still, such news alone could not keep up Hartley's spirits, because Bermuda simply was not stimulating enough for him. Hartley believed that he and Demuth had done "creditable" work, but he noted, "it is essentially a place for [Childe] Hassam, or for the lady painters — it is literally the colored photo."[20]

His physical ailments aside, Hartley was under considerable psychological stress. Ever since his return to the United States from Germany he had been retreating from emotional expression in his work — though to assert that he was at any time not an emotional painter would be foolish. But the effect of the war upon him, his "loss" of Germany, the too-great pastoral calm of Bermuda, and Demuth's style of realism all drew him away from tumultuous works such as his German masterpieces. In Provincetown, he had rendered paintings of a flattened, formal, cubistic sort. In Bermuda, as Barbara Haskell has observed, "Hartley's abstract style faltered."[21] For him this style had always been associated with the mystical, but now he thought he was "rapidly outliving that," and he hoped to be able "to extinguish it all together, that is from the aesthetic point of view."[22]

He also now claimed that he did not revere nature: "You know my reverence for nature is not at all keen, not nature just for itself," he wrote to Carl Sprinchorn during the winter of 1917. "Every artist is sure to outgrow that in time, and unless it symbolizes itself for him vividly in unusual images, it wearies the eye with so much of its commonness."[23] This mistrust of nature and of the mystical stemmed from the "loss of illusions" that he wrote to Stieglitz about. The paintings he did in Bermuda reflect his turn; they are still lifes of flowers, vases, and fruit, sometimes with a bit of beach, some ocean, or a few sailboats in the background. Flattened spatially even when presenting an interior-exterior view, the canvases are about form but are not stationary. Rather, the heavy application of paints as well as their strong colors and the movement of the shapes within the pictures gives them a vitality and emotion that are characteristic of Hartley's good work. He had moved less far than he thought.

Demuth left Bermuda near the end of the March, while Hartley remained behind to rest, hoping the sun and quiet would cure his lingering illness. They did not, and after he returned to New York, in May, he had his appendix removed. The result was that Hartley's depression continued. The inclusion of two of his paintings in the First Annual Exhibition of the Society of Independent Artists, from April 10 to May 6, may have been satisfying but was of no great moment. One reviewer, R. J. Coady, denigrated the exhibition and remarked about Hartley that his "attempts to invent something of real personal value are defeated, I think, by his efforts to be something he is not, and because his means is made up of borrowed material and an experimental speculation rather than feeling."[24] Coady, who was generally opposed to European modernism, lumped Hartley in with that movement.

In June he traveled by train to Lewiston, stopping in Boston for three days on the way. His hometown offered him little pleasure; it was "a vast cemetery of dead days and utterly useless memories and connections." Much of the time in Lewiston he spent with the poet Wallace Gould, a physical giant whose cause Hartley took on. He identified with Gould, whom he perceived to be buried by his existence in Maine. Gould made his living by playing the piano in movie houses around the state. Hartley championed him to Harriet Monroe, the editor of *Poetry;* in August 1918, writing to her about a manuscript of Gould's, he declared that Gould was

> locked up in the little spaces in life, and can get no rein for his magnificent talents. Experience has turned him cynical, which is but natural for he is a big man, and life has shut him in one corner, where if he had been able to get out, he would have taken a huge sweep of the world.

"He is the very voice of Maine," Hartley told Monroe.[25] To Stieglitz, in June, he lamented the poet's obscurity, citing it as yet another example of how Americans neglected the artists among them.

If this was a small inhumanity, the entry of the United States into the war in April was a large one, and it aggravated Hartley's sense of despair. He told Stieglitz that existence hardly seemed worthwhile; he was sure he would end his life "if it were not for the miracle of wanting always to create something." The fact that Stieglitz was closing 291 did not help matters. In Hartley's words of concern for his friend lay the painter's worry about his own situation, which he feared would be more precarious without the security of Stieglitz's gallery. Hartley was tired of trying to find "some little space in which to create for myself some sense of life in order to exist at all." He was "a bit weary of islands," he said, because he had lived all his life on them, with few releases — just "a flight or two" out, perhaps, but never for long.[26]

In June he was not sure what little space he might create for himself. He expected to stay at the camp of Mrs. Kate Strauss in Center Lovell but was not particularly enthusiastic about the prospect, as it would bring back "useless recollections." When Mrs. Strauss asked him to delay his arrival, he decided to move instead to a small summer art colony, the Ogunquit School of Painting and Sculpture, which the wealthy artist Hamilton Easter Field had begun several years earlier. Field offered a room to Hartley, who found the place appealing because it was at the edge of the ocean and his friends Carl Sprinchorn and Maurice Sterne were there. His stay was quiet, and he worked continuously at both writing and painting; by September he could assure Stieglitz that he had "made some beautiful discoveries in glass painting." The school exhibited ten of his paintings on glass as well as five others on other media. He reported to Stieglitz that glass was "charming as a medium though difficult."[27] As important as anything about his glass paintings is the fact that their technique and subject matter demonstrate his awareness of folk art, which was of interest, too, to Field and others at Ogunquit.[28] One thread of continuity in his works is the quality of primitiveness, which is present even in his German works, though it is not what a viewer first notices about them.

In the fall of 1917 Hartley returned to New York, where he lived in an apartment that Field owned, at 110 Columbia Heights in Brooklyn. There he painted, but he was at least as preoccupied with writing. In the spring of 1918 he submitted a number of poems to *Poetry,* edited by Harriet Monroe, and six of them were included in the July issue, marking his debut as a poet.[29]

The year 1918 was a rewarding one for him as a writer. Not only were his first poems published in a significant little magazine; several essays of his also appeared that year, in the *Dial,* the *Little Review, Poetry,* and *El Palacio,* as did two other poems in the *Little Review.* It is telling that Hartley blossomed as a writer during a less than major period for him as a painter. Not that he had spent himself as an artist; but after great passion, he was now in a relatively dormant period. With his poetry and essays he was experimenting in new media and putting a good deal of his energy into them.

In May he traveled to Maine, again visiting Wallace Gould. The state was a "hill of dullness" except for Gould, and Hartley looked forward to his next move, a trip to the Southwest, where he hoped to see "another face in nature." The only symbol he could find for the East — and for Maine especially — was the mountain, which was overwhelming. "People have done me out of my belief," he told Stieglitz; "perhaps nature will restore the proper sense, by revealing new sublimities."[30] His poems in *Poetry* give some clue to his depression. One, called "Spinsters," begins:

> October in New England:
> They are the gargoyles supporting old buttresses,
> These virgins that roam wistfully among the ruins
> Victims of an effete worship.[31]

And the three pieces of "After Battle," selected by Harriet Monroe from among the six he submitted under the title "Ironies out of St. George's," are about combatants who die at sea or on land. Their voices tell "of light, and star, and love," but who is to believe them, the poet asks, and closes,

> The earth is not the sea;
> Nor sea the earth can be;
> But death is much the same
> To them, and me —
> It is but one felicity![32]

Gargoyle spinsters and felicitous death are not elements of a contented mind.[33]

Hartley had been encouraged by Mabel Dodge and Maurice Sterne, who were now married, to visit New Mexico. A wealthy woman, a Mrs. Converse, also urged him to go so he might give her art lessons.

He boarded a train on June 9 and arrived in Santa Fe on the twelfth. The Sternes and the painter Paul Burlin met him. "Country incredibly beautiful. 7,000 ft. high here. Warm but fresh," he announced to Stieglitz the day after his arrival. It fascinated him that "the indians walk the streets here all decked & festive." The next day he was to travel to Taos. There he stayed for several days in a hotel on the town plaza as the guest of Mrs. Converse before moving into a small, three-room adobe house nearby. He was as taken with the land around Taos as he had been with Santa Fe: Taos Mountain was a "marvel," the Indian pueblo "thrilling." Most of the artists, however, he confided to Stieglitz, were "awful hackers."[34]

They were not, of course, and before long Hartley's arrogance would work against him, though for the moment all seemed well. The landscape was remarkable. Coming up from Santa Fe to Taos along the Rio Grande, he was struck by the immensity of the open spaces, by the mountains — some snowcapped even in June — that rose up sharply from the wide plain, and by the clarity of the light. The region had a singular vividness that appealed to him. Taos itself, he soon assured Stieglitz, was "a perfect place to regain one's body & soul." At that moment he was pleased with his social prospects: Leo Stein had arrived; Mabel Sterne was as pleasant to him as she had been before she asked him to leave her farm on the Hudson River; he liked Paul Burlin; and Mrs. Converse treated him well — no doubt with a touch of the deference he believed he deserved as an established artist.

He looked forward eagerly to learning the landscape. "There never was a more beautiful single mountain than Taos mountain," he enthused:

Apparently, from the external aspects it looks like any other, but from the deeper point of view it holds you through the wealth of legend & fact that attaches to it. No white man has ever been allowed to go to the top of it, and it is guarded day & night against the unwelcome evil intruder, and up on its various breasts the indians have held ceremonies to the sun these two thousand years.

The mountains had immediately made Hartley think of the Engadine of Segantini, whose paintings had first taught him how to convey the spiritual nature of landscape.[35] The land around Taos had "certain peculiarities" about it, he found, and it required some time to learn how to render it. "It is essentially blue and gold here," he explained to Stieglitz, "and not red and yellow as I had suspected in imaginative ways."

Those colors were also evident in the land further south, near Trinidad and Las Vegas, New Mexico, where, he wrote, there were "some very intense sensations." Around Taos the varieties of color were far from one another, and Hartley knew he would have to travel to get to "the chocolate coloured mountains, . . . those great isolated altar like forms that stand alone on a great mesa with the immensities of blue around & above them & that strange indian red earth making such almost unearthly foregrounds." Spaces, too, were odd. They were "huge" and "single," with "details . . . so clean that nothing seems far off and distance is like a picture for the eye." To capture it all, he would need specific paints, and he requested that Stieglitz arrange for them to be sent as quickly as possible: "two dozen tubes of zinc white, four tubes of *rose madder* [a ruby-red lake pigment] — six tubes of permanent blue, six of emerald green, 1 dozen tubes ivory black."[36] The list suggests the power of the colors that Hartley saw before him.

While he waited for the oils in late June, he did his first landscapes in pastel and in the latter part of July confided to Stieglitz that he had "several good pastels finished, and two large still-lifes on the way that I am doing in the hallway at Mabel S's." Matter-of-factly he told Stieglitz that the work he was doing was "quite interesting, in that it shows, and of course naturally, the result of so long speculating with abstractions." It had a "firmness" that was lacking in his earlier works, a directness that came from his going straight at nature, even though "distances are too great to do things out of doors complete." He was still working to get his "eye soaked with the colour and form of the place. . . . I like the country very well," he added, "for it is big and clean and true, and there is nothing dirty standing between one and the sunlight, as there is in the east."[37] In letters he wrote later in the summer and in two essays that were published in a little magazine, *El Palacio,* in December, what he was about here becomes clear. Writing to an acquaintance, W. Joseph Fulton, he urged an "honest return to nature." He insisted that cubism and futurism had "shown their limitations already by a very certain factitiousness in the result, not owing to insincerities, but to false premises."

Hartley was willing himself back to realism, in part because he thought it might elicit a greater audience for his work, but also because the avant-garde and its European associations represented the illusions he claimed to have shed. The landscape of New Mexico was native ground for Americans to celebrate, and Hartley meant to do that better than the "awful hackers" he believed he saw about him in Taos. "Any one of these beautiful arroyos and canyons is a living example of the ages," he wrote to Fulton:

> It is as classical as a Claude Lorrain, and I am bewitched with their magnificence and their austerity; as for the color it is of course the only place in America where true color exists, excepting the short autumnal season in New England, which is a classic by itself. I made myself famous among painters with the hills of Maine, and I often think I shall go back to them and do them once again.[38]

"I am an American discovering America," he declared in the second of the two essays in *El Palacio*. American landscape was "untouched," he believed, and he cited the example of the landscape around Santa Fe. What had been painted heretofore was "paper painting," not the real thing, which would catch the "stark simplicity, and . . . solidity" of the region. He asserted that there would be an "art in America only when there are artists big enough and really interested enough to comprehend the American scene." New Englanders knew themselves and had adequately rendered their landscapes, but, he concluded, Americans "are not New Englanders now. . . . America is calling for radical interpretation, her earth voices are being spoke for."

In the earlier essay in *El Palacio* Hartley called for "aesthetic sincerity" and in effect claimed that to date there had been little "authenticity of emotion" in the painting done of the region around Taos and Santa Fe. Painters had to understand that "the country of the southwest is essentially a sculptural country. . . . The sense of form in New Mexico is for me one of the profoundest, most original, and most beautiful I have personally experienced." He pointed out the need for painters to learn to combine a "consistent relation of colour to the form that is visible here" with their own emotional reactions. Taken together, the two essays reflect remarkably well what Hartley did with landscape for the rest of his life. He might vacillate about how much he was the American, but form and essence guided him always, no matter how varied his styles might seem.[39]

At the beginning of August he wrote to Stieglitz that he was "doing large pastels these days, to get my hand in, copying nature as faithfully as possible." He was satisfied with them, as they had the same qualities as his landscapes of earlier years, "plus a certain something that has come to me out of six years devotion to abstraction." He continued to be moved by the country, by its "bigness" and "dignity," and by settings such as Arroyo Hondo, fourteen miles from Taos, where there was a canyon "full of classical grandeur" that had something of the form of Claude Lorrain's painting, as well as the feeling of Courbet's work. "I am getting back to my old richness of colour again," he wrote, assuring Stieglitz that he would see this in the pastels. All he needed, he was confident, was "to get warmed up to life again, and I feel it coming on." He meant to "give up all worthless intellectual and philosphical deductions." After "three solid years of introspection, esthetic as well as spiritual," he wished to rid himself of that and to start "with a new influx of sensibility."[40]

His choice of pastel for his first New Mexican landscapes was wise; he was not immediately prepared to work with oils to represent the qualities of a countryside that was completely new to him. With pastels, moreover, he could picture the landscape naturalistically, as he might not have with oils. "It is the only way I can get a line on the qualities [of the landscape]," he wrote in September, "and it is a very important and typical medium for this country which has such wonderful dry quality of colour, and such hardness and brilliancy."[41]

It was easier for him, also, to capture form and the essence of the subject with pastels. Hartley could do that masterfully in oil when he was in full control of both subject and medium, and in 1918 he was working toward such mastery. But if the pastels he made that summer lack the grandeur of his best oils or of the New Mexico landscapes he did from memory in the early 1920s, it is not because he was flat, but because of the medium he selected and his decision to concentrate on foreground rather than on spaces, distances, and the striking quality of the sky. With the pastels he was getting his hand in, as he told Stieglitz. The best of these have the qualities of his fine work; the intriguing form, the fundamental aspects of the subject, the regard for nature of an Emerson or a Cézanne — all these are there.

If Hartley found satisfaction in the countryside, he was soon disappointed with the people whom he met in Taos, excepting the Sternes, Mrs. Converse, Leo Stein, and a few others. The rest were "simply impossible, dreadful painters, who are just nasty tongued." He found Taos a mean place, where there was "immense jealousy toward

any outside artist." The other artists, no doubt, were put off by Hartley's affectations, his penchant for solitude, and the arrogance he displayed about both his painting and his writing.[42] Then, too, most of
the other male artists liked to display their manliness. There was a
macho quality about them, and this set Hartley off. So he avoided that
company, kept to himself, and occasionally took trips into the countryside, such as a week-long camping expedition near Arroyo Hondo
with a hermitlike man named Jack Bidwell, who guarded the abandoned machinery of a mining company in the deserted village of
Twinning.[43] Hartley enjoyed the trip, but health problems arose. The
altitude and the dryness of the air affected him, and then in August he
got dysentery.[44]

By October he had decided to move to Santa Fe for the winter,
especially since he had been offered a studio at the School of American
Research, in the museum. He would be pleased to be out of Taos,
which he found boring and without character, "nothing but a little
town just eaten up by a group of artists whose minds are as big as
peanuts."[45] Even his friends provided little comfort: Leo Stein was
planning to stay in the mountains until the weather got bad, and Mabel
Dodge Sterne, Hartley reported in September, was "building a house
with great frenzy, . . . living the life of the indians all she can. . . . It is
just another of her acting episodes," he surmised, "and has its worth to
her as something to take up the time with, having no life of her own
to live in reality." Hartley thought she had "turned savage in her attitudes" and was "barbarically simple now, which for a cultivated person
is of course an excrescence, a something acquired."[46] When in the latter
part of October her son came down with the flu, Hartley hastened to
Sante Fe to escape.[47]

He was pleased to find that Santa Fe was less a village with its closed
society than Taos, but this did nothing to relieve his constant worry
about money. By November he was beside himself; Mrs. Converse had
not helped as much as he had hoped she would, and back in New York
the dealers Daniel and Montross were not producing results. Melodramatically Hartley told Stieglitz that he must have sustenance: "A diet
of dry crusts is not sustaining to the soul of any human. Pity is not
enough," he moaned, asserting that he wanted "a man's muscle and a
man's assurance."

He heaped up similes that all equated to "futility," having heard
from Stieglitz that there was no guarantee of adequate funds for any

length of time. Now he was faced with the necessity of paying forty-five dollars for dental work, and he was distraught. Not only did he need money to live in Santa Fe, which was not cheap, but he also had to be able to travel out into the countryside. "I sit in my two rooms alone," he told Stieglitz, "and these are my complexities." He perceived himself as a "classical unfit," "really a sick man for no well person can have complaint."[48]

Stieglitz wrote back about two weeks later to assure Hartley that the situation was not as bleak as he made it out to be. Both Daniel and Montross would try to sell his work. In the meantime, Mrs. Converse had made the third payment on the pastel she had bought, and Hartley suggested that she might help Stieglitz convince another dealer to try to sell some of his simpler pastels, since the dealer had not understood his more extreme work, presumably the abstractions of previous years. "You see I am copying nature for the present as closely as I can in my way," he explained again to Stieglitz. This was the only avenue to stronger things — "to combine the earlier approach with the later, and make them unify in the things I want to do now." Hartley was in good spirits, too, because he had just begun to work in the studio that the Santa Fe Museum was providing for him. He had two pieces under way. "You will see a little Courbet," he warned Stieglitz, "and a little Renoir, and a little Cézanne, and you will also see myself." The country was "sculptural," the landscape was "strong, sober, starkly simple, and the light is hard and clear, not at all an impressionistic country as these small men are trying to show."[49]

Amid his worries, Hartley carried on a lively correspondence with Harriet Monroe about his own and others' poetry. He continued to champion Wallace Gould and sent her two manuscript versions of Gould's collection "The Drift of the Year." She was not enthusiastic. "Sorry you & Gould did not get on," Hartley wrote to her in December. "Odd boy but a real one. Weighs 280 lbs. 6ft. one. very huge but petulant. Should like to have seen it come off amicably, but there must be enemies I suppose. Gould is one now for sure. You will get an attack now & then, but you are brave." Hartley called him "a superb fellow but a red flame."[50] Neither did Monroe want the essay that Hartley sent her about Gould's work; eventually it appeared in the *Little Review*.[51] He submitted other pieces as well, among them a tribute to the poet Joyce Kilmer, who had died in the war, and, in January 1919, two more poems — an advance, he believed, over what had appeared in

Poetry the previous summer. He told Monroe that in these he was working mostly "for the quality of sound." She did not accept them, but Hartley was unfazed and continued to submit both prose and poetry.[52]

The trouble with writing poetry is that it does not pay. Hartley had reason to be proud of his second career as a poet, but he could not live on print alone. That frustrated him, as it would anyone. Beginning in 1918 he was being published in important little magazines, but the recompense was hardly enough to finance a trip to one of the splendid sites where he wanted to paint outside Santa Fe. Nevertheless, the poetry — whatever its quality as we judge it now — was important to him because it was an outlet for his modernist views. In his correspondence with Harriet Monroe he decried the "modern struggle for intellectualism both in poetry and music" and hoped that there might develop a "more natural type of expression in the field of poetry, and in the field of painting, . . . a simpler type of painting through a fusion of the modern extravagance and an honest return to nature."[53] But Hartley's own poetry, like his painting, tended toward intellectualism, much as he might like to believe otherwise. Two poems that appeared in the *Little Review* in December 1918 were merely studied, though he meant them to be erotic. One begins, "Upon the etagere of her quaint mind she was fond/ of arranging the bijouteries of her queer fancies/ Like gems sheathed with glass." It goes on to describe a woman who is titillated by male and female voices. In the other poem, "Sunbather," the narrator is taken with the sensuousness of a rock saurian, a lizard, and imagines himself to be the sun and the sea caressing the reptile. Hartley intended the poem to touch upon basic emotions, but most readers will doubtless have a difficult time responding to the lizard's "hairy flank."[54]

Two poems that appeared in Alfred Kreymborg's *Others* in February and March 1919 — perhaps the poems that Monroe rejected — seem precious rather than notable for their "quality of sound." In one of these Scaramouche, or "little Mouchie," asks the narrator about a woman whose "secrets of many a luscious moment/ Clambered up the still traceries of her cool throat/ And plunged like slim frogs into the autumn pools/ For their winter's hiding, into the very wells of her eyes." Even if Hartley's aim was to be sardonic, the poem fails. The other poem, slightly less studied, describes swallows, "swift points of beetle-blue" that "dot the pale vowels on the pages of the sun."[55]

For an anthology, *Others for 1919*, Kreymborg selected six of Hartley's poems and placed them immediately after six of Gould's. The two poets were in good company; the anthology included poems by, among others, Conrad Aiken, Robert Frost, Vachel Lindsay, Marianne Moore, Wallace Stevens, and William Carlos Williams. Again Hartley's poems are brittle; lines such as "Prometheus fire/ Never can worship/ The smell of hams and hocks/ Issuing from the smoke house" do not work well, no matter what Hartley's intentions were.[56]

His winter stay in Santa Fe began depressingly. No sooner had he arrived than a record cold spell — "sixteen below at New Year's" — settled on the region. The cold did nothing for his health, nor was his mood improved when the museum asked him to move from the studio he had been given. A month later he felt so ill that all he could do was type a short note conveying to Stieglitz a notarized copy of a will he had made the previous spring, listing as his relatives his five sisters, and as his intimates Stieglitz, Wallace Gould, and Kate Strauss, another friend from Maine.[57] But within two weeks his condition had improved, and he apologized to Stieglitz for his "melodramatic haste." He had been frightened, he wrote, but had since learned that he merely had symptoms of the flu. He needed someone to hold his hand, he observed wryly, and while his woman neighbor might be in love with him, she would not suffice. Not only was he feeling better since the flu had subsided, but his financial distress had eased somewhat: the director of the museum had offered him $200 from a patron for one of his oils, "a rather large still life of New Mexican objects."[58]

He accepted the money immediately, as it would enable him to travel to California, where he planned to stay with Carl Sprinchorn in La Canada, near Pasadena. By mid-March he had arrived there, and Sprinchorn quickly brought him into his circle of friends. Sprinchorn had come to know and admire a young rancher and painter, Rex Slinkard, who had died of the flu in 1918 while in the East. Sprinchorn and Hartley visited Gladys Williams, Slinkard's fiancée; Hartley was taken with her and also much impressed by the paintings and drawings she showed him by Slinkard. He wrote an appreciative essay about the young painter, which became the introduction to a catalogue for an exhibition of his works in Los Angeles and, later, in San Francisco and New York.

Through Alfred Kreymborg Hartley met a woman in Los Angeles who invited him to give a reading of modern poetry to her poetry society. It was enough of a success that he was asked to give a second one. At the first he met Robert McAlmon, with whom he quickly became friends. "McAlmon is the real thing, though I won't say as poet," Hartley wrote to Harriet Monroe in July. "He is extremely intelligent and radical in his viewpoints about art, which is very good for a young artist. He knows what he thinks and why he thinks it." Hartley added that he had read McAlmon's poems at his second reading in Los Angeles, "and even though some of them have a stiffness and are therefore unnatural, they have the advantage of having a fresh flavor of subject [aviation]."

While staying with Sprinchorn, Hartley had visited San Diego, where he watched the airplanes that were attached to the Naval Air Station. "I became a fierce enthusiast for aviation while at San Diego," he told Monroe. "It is simply too beautiful as a theme. To watch these planes cavort about like lambkins on a green at such vastitudes in height, is nothing short of thrilling," he concluded. Trite though his effusion about airplanes might seem, it reflected a romantic attitude toward technology that was typical of the era. Equally it reflected the fascination Hartley had felt for the machinery of war in Berlin, which he now felt as well for southern California. The place seemed to him a "stage set," an "eccentric" country, but also one filled with beautiful people — "luscious," he called them, understanding how different a land it was from the East.[59]

He returned to Santa Fe toward the end of June, determined to paint New Mexico as he had not before. While still in Los Angeles he had written to Stieglitz, asking for half a ream of a particular sort of paper, which produced excellent texture and color in pastels. The only problem was its shape, he reported. He was going to have to figure out how to make a longer sheet so that he could paint the skies as he wanted to in larger pictures. The paper was fine as to length, "for the country is all mural out in the west," he explained, making quick drawings in his letter to show how the landscape tended toward "long lines with triangles out of them or quadrangles."[60]

This second summer was important for his work. He began to have a feeling for the countryside, which meant he understood its shapes and its meanings. "I have kept rather well on the side of realities for I have such realities before & around me," he wrote to Stieglitz at the end of September. There was a "Courbet intention" in his work, he observed; the war had done that to him, which was to say that it had rid him of the illusions that had earlier produced the sorts of obscure, "spiritual" paintings he had made in Europe. Living "by the intellect" rather than "by anything so deceptive as spirit": this was how he described his new stance in July.[61] "The work I am doing now anyone can see if perhaps not wholly understand," he wrote shortly thereafter. "It has the abstraction underneath it all now & that is what I was working toward & what I deliberately set out to do down here." He reported that the painter B. J. O. Nordfeldt had visited him recently to see what he had accomplished that summer. Nordfeldt thought Hartley had "really achieved" and told him the paintings were "fine, dignified, and authentic picture-making," Hartley quoted the other painter as saying. "You'll see," Hartley told Stieglitz. "They don't get me here. Say I am too terrific in my feelings."[62]

Amid intermittent bouts of intestinal trouble he worked into November, on the nineteenth departing Santa Fe for New York, planning a stopover in Chicago to meet Harriet Monroe and, he hoped, others such as Carl Sandburg and Sherwood Anderson.[63] During the summer Stieglitz had sent on to him a letter he had received from Arnold Rönnebeck, asking about Hartley, from whom Rönnebeck had heard nothing since 1915, when he left Berlin. Hartley's room there had been rented out, Rönnebeck said, but he kept an attic space where he had stored Hartley's pictures and other possessions. Rönnebeck wanted news of Hartley, who he thought might be afraid to write for fear of hearing bad news about how the war had left the Rönnebeck family. Everyone had survived, he reported. "Please let me know what has become of him who for so long has been my dearest friend & with [whom] I share the finest & most beautiful memories."[64] Rönnebeck's letter immediately stirred Hartley's interest in returning to Europe; that became his goal.

His time in the Southwest was bittersweet. He admired the landscape but never felt accepted by the artistic community in Taos or, to a lesser extent, in Santa Fe. He enjoyed his visit to California, yet the country did not impress him as a subject for painting. Still, he knew that during the nearly year and a half he had been in the West, he had worked through a fallow period toward something substantially new, and by the time of his departure for the East in November 1919 he was beginning, in a seemingly new style, to paint powerful landscapes that conveyed his sense of what he called the "mural" country of the Southwest. Then, too, he learned about the ceremonies of the Indians and wrote repeatedly about them, publishing a long essay entitled "Red Man Ceremonials" in 1920 and a two-part piece in 1922 entitled "The Scientific Esthetic of the Redman," about "The Great Corn Ceremony at Santo Domingo" and "The Fiesta of San Geronimo at Taos." He drew from these essays for his piece "The Red Man," included in his collection of essays, *Adventures in the Arts,* and in addition published a long poem in *Poetry* about the ceremony at Santo Domingo.

Although the Indian ceremonies provided Hartley with a fertile subject for writing, more significant to him was their symbolic value, both as native American rituals and as expressions of mankind's relationship to the earth. At a time when Hartley was espousing realism as opposed to imagination, he discovered once again in the various Indian ceremonies the basic human impulse to symbolize. Through their dances and songs the Indians created symbols; Hartley understood again that he must make them in his art, whether he was painting naturalistically or abstractly. And by studying the ceremonies and the cultural artifacts of the Indians, he developed an even greater appreciation of the folk art he had first discovered in France and Germany. New Mexico was American soil, and being among the Indians whose culture produced the objects and rituals he admired was a more powerful, more direct experience for Hartley than his initial exposure to folk art in Europe. His artistic career was renewed by his experiences in the West; his art weakened only when he forgot the lessons he had learned about people and the land from observing the Indians.

He studied them hard. The writer Paul Horgan has told of meeting Hartley in early August 1919 at the pueblo of Santo Domingo, where both had gone to see the Corn Dance. The young Horgan was fascinated with Hartley, who was in "lively good spirits" and kind to him. Horgan recalled Hartley's "intensely light blue eyes like half-moons with the flat sides down. Their color made me think of the stones worked into silver and worn by the Indians." When the ceremony began with a single, loud drumbeat, the watchers were enthralled by the rhythms, color, and motion of the dance, and none more so than Hartley, who "leaned forward, his knees crossed, his elbow on his knee, his fingers curled against his rather sunken mouth, his *turquoise* eyes transfixed by the wonder of what we watched."[65]

"In the esthetic sense alone," Hartley wrote in his essay "The Red Man," "we have the redman as a gift. As Americans we should accept the one American genius we possess. . . . [The redman] has at least two contributions to confer, a very aristocratic notion of religion, and a superb gift for stylistic expression." He concluded:

> To "impose" something — that is the modern culture. . . . The primitives created a complete cosmos for themselves, an entire principle. I want merely, then, esthetic recognition in full of the contribution of the redman as artist, as one of the finest artists of time; the poetic redman ceremonialist, celebrant of the universe as he sees it, and master among masters of the art of symbolic gesture.[66]

It is tempting to insist that through the landscape and the Indians of the Southwest Hartley had found himself, and that from them until the end of his life a certain consistency marked his painting. This is partly true, but he would also have to control his own emotions, to be able to distance himself from them while not denying them, before he could paint inevitably with the power we associate with his finest work.

9

"I Hunger to Be All Artist"
1920 – 1924

FOR HARTLEY the 1920s roared intermittently at best; they were
not a time for the big money. He began them in poverty and ended
them still impoverished and compelled to return to the United States
from abroad because he was less in touch than ever with the American
scene. Moreover, to many observers his art seemed to have suffered.
Gail Scott has summarized the general opinion about Hartley's career
then, noting that for him the period "is usually considered a 'lost decade,' and the work issuing from it often dismissed as eclectic, unreal-
ized, and unfocused."[1] Such a view is convenient, for it makes more
dramatic Hartley's emergence in the 1930s as a powerful expressionistic painter of North American scenes. That Hartley became this is
true, but it is equally true that during the 1920s he painted with great
force a series of recollections of New Mexico and Texas, some landscapes of Provence, and many still lifes. The finest of these are the
equal of his best work and demonstrate a continuity in his painting;
they are hardly the thrashings of an artist who has lost his way.

Hartley did not think he was floundering artistically in 1920, but
he desired the sort of consistent support that would enable him to
continue his career with less worry than before. That support was not
forthcoming, however, and neither the fact that his work was shown
in several exhibitions during the spring of 1920 nor the appearance of
seven of his poems in *Poetry* in May was able to cheer him. Neither
was a summer spent in Gloucester, which, despite the friendships of
the artists Elie Nadelman and Stuart Davis, Hartley deemed "the cess-

pool of American vulgarity and cheapness." With but a few exceptions the painters were "execrable"; they deserved to be hung at dawn. He was at his most sarcastic about art in Gloucester, which according to him was symbolized by a "gallery for the degradation of Art... run by a rich woman and her jellyfish husband who suffers with loss of words to repress the absence of intelligence."[2]

Little wonder that Hartley disparaged the art scene. In his own work he was pursuing something far different than were the artists who flocked to Cape Ann to paint scenes of its quaint harbors and shorelines. Preying on his mind were his modernist ideas and his memories of the vast horizontal spaces of the Southwest. The cramped landscape around Gloucester did not inspire him, especially as it reminded him of Maine and the pinched, puritanical mind-set that he wanted no part of. Eleven years later, finally understanding what it meant to commit oneself emotionally but also to step outside one's personality, he would return to Cape Ann and find in the woods behind Gloucester, in Dogtown, a landscape exactly suited to his purposes.

That was in 1931, though; in 1920 he chafed at American conventions and yearned to return to Europe. He must get back there, he declared to Stieglitz in midsummer, for he could not starve intellectually and artistically when he was at the height of his powers. He needed at least a year abroad, where he might "float and write and get the flavor of the sublime joke" now that the war had ended. "I have achieved great mastery to my own thinking," he announced grandly. "I have brought up the inevitable smile of satire on my cheek after the years of hope and faith and love." Now he had discarded hope and faith, and love had become a "kind of devilish tenacity to keep from letting the whole thing die on one's hands like a sick lizard."[3]

He claimed he was happy to be a satirist — a puzzling stance, for his best art is rarely satiric. He was, of course, describing his feelings at the time, which did not necessarily translate into satirical scenes on his canvases, though the poetry he was writing then has about it a brittleness, a forced quality that one often associates with satire. To satirize is to distance oneself from one's subject, to feign an aloofness and objectivity that is intended to mask the pain that produced the satire in the first place. Hartley wanted to distance himself because he had been deeply aggrieved by World War I and by the world's neglect of him. And so he tried to be a satirist, with the result that his work seemed to others to lack fire, even though in January he had written to Georgia O'Keeffe that painting was a "medium for passion." At that moment he meant "passion for an idea."[4] Driven to satire by disaffection with his life, and thinking that the only worthwhile thing, the only thing to be trusted, was intellect, he could produce art that was self-conscious and studied. Years later, in the catalogue for an exhibition of his and Stuart Davis's work in Cincinnati, he made a statement that reflects the basic Hartley:

> Theoretical painting has little or no meaning for me, because it takes place above the eyebrows — I want the whole body, the whole flesh, in painting. Renoir said that he painted with all his manhood, and is that not evident?
> It is the "blood" of good painting, that makes it all right, with me.[5]

When in August 1920 he wrote to Stieglitz that he felt he had never painted so well, his claim sounded mechanical, as if he was trying to convince himself that his work suited his intellectual position, which was that "to be thoroughly supreme is to laugh at everything — because human attitudes are the joke of existence — one must 'do' nothing — only look and laugh and be exquisitely impressed."[6] Easier said than done. He could never laugh at uncertainty for long, and three weeks later he was worried about the coming fall with its hill of decisions. All he had before him was "potentiality," and that was where life might end. He fretted about storage for his paintings; as usual he could find no solution, and Stieglitz had to help.[7]

His first reaction to being back in New York in early October was to see his situation as bleak — Stieglitz was away from New York at that moment and had no gallery then in any case, and Hartley had no money. "Something is putting an end to my life and my hopes — in spite of myself," he wrote to Stieglitz in a panic. Existence had become "one long drawn out tension of pain" for him, so that he had lost what strength he had gained during his summer in Gloucester. He suggested that there was little reason for him to continue living, to endure the chains that now held him. He pleaded for Stieglitz's help, closing his letter, "I can't make a go of it alone."[8]

Two weeks later matters had improved; having moved into the 550 East Eighty-fifth Street apartment of the actor George de Winter, whose wife had returned to Belgium for a year with their child, he found life pleasant again. He was able to cook for himself, the apartment was in a comfortable, quiet area near the East River, and his share of the rent was less than half of what he would have had to pay for a furnished room. De Winter was kind to him, and companionship, as much as anything, was what he desired. In addition, Katherine Dreier, who with Marcel Duchamp and Man Ray had recently founded the Société Anonyme, met Hartley immediately after he arrived in New York and asked him to exhibit with the Société and to be its secretary and chairman of publicity. Hartley hoped these tasks would prove his ability with "executive ideas" — a touching notion for one as dependent on others as he — and was excited by the possibility that the Société might send him abroad as its foreign correspondent.

Depression behind him for the moment, he boasted that those who had seen his new painting admired it, and claimed he was "the new genuine personality in poetry in America & someone for once essentially American in poetic quality." The first issue of *Contact,* to be edited by William Carlos Williams, would include two of his poems.[9] A week later he announced that he intended to begin a group of paintings "of a very high whitish key to represent the renaissance of myself."[10]

That winter in New York was a lively time for Hartley. He felt very much a part of the art scene; his paintings were among those exhibited at the Société Anonyme in November and December, and at the end of November he gave a lecture about modern art in the Société's rooms. The art critic Henry McBride quoted Hartley as saying, "The business of the artist is to present his experience directly without too much interpretation." What the artist painted was "his personal appreciation of his object," but his effort should not be "purely personal"; rather, it should be a "penetrating understanding of the object itself." Hartley's most telling remark was that the artist's mood "should be controlled by his intellectual interest in the thing[,] for painting is essentially intellectual." According to McBride, the lecture stimulated heated discussion.[11]

It is difficult to believe that in terms of advancing his career, Hartley did not make a mistake by returning to Europe in 1921. He thought it absolutely essential for his artistic development and personal wellbeing, but the fact remains that in 1920 and the first part of 1921, in an atmosphere of new excitement about American art, he had at last begun to receive the attention he craved. He was a part of the Société Anonyme; his works were exhibited among those of other notable modernists; and he was being published more than ever before, with poems appearing in *Poetry,* the *Dial, Contact,* and elsewhere, and essays in several journals, culminating with the publication in 1921 of *Adventures in the Arts: Informal Chapters on Painters, Vaudeville, and Poets.*

His piece "The Importance of Being 'Dada,'" which appeared as the afterword to the book, demonstrates Hartley's understanding of that significant, if short-lived, avant-garde movement, and reflects how much a part of it he was then. Though never a Dadaist himself, he nonetheless recognized the movement's "exhilarating quality of nihilism," its provocative thesis that "nothing is greater than anything else."[12] He stood to gain from the attitude toward and growing acceptance of "the new" in the arts in the United States during the 1920s, but the idea that American artists had to remain home to be bought annoyed him. Having drawn attention to himself through his writing as well as his art, he refused to stay put to capitalize on any hard-earned fame. Had he spent more time in the United States, he surely would have benefited from "the big money"; as it was, from 1921 until the end of the decade he practically disappeared from view, except for the rare exhibition or piece in a little magazine. This is not to suggest that aesthetically the time was wasted; as Gail Scott has remarked, the 1920s "provided him with proving ground upon which to test and assimilate the forces of modernism, and from which his unmistakable individuality as artist and writer would emerge in the 1930s."[13]

Nothing could have changed his mind about returning to Europe. During the spring of 1921 he became more and more determined to go abroad and kept after Stieglitz to devise some plan that would enable him to depart. Specifically, he needed at least $1,500 to $2,000 for a year's stay. Stieglitz later told Hudson Walker that it was Hartley's stated intention, once the money had been raised, to go to Europe, "write a book of hate, and then commit suicide." Stieglitz understood the hyperbole but did not have the money himself, so he approached the dealers Daniel and Montross about buying Hartley's works — roughly two hundred of them — for $1,200. Neither man was willing. After warning Hartley about the financial dangers of selling all of his work at once, leaving nothing to fall back on, Stieglitz spoke to their mutual friend Mitchell Kennerly, then at the Anderson Galleries. Kennerly told Stieglitz that the last exhibition date of the season had been given to a wealthy amateur painter, James Rosenberg. He did not need the money, Stieglitz responded, so why not exhibit both artists together and hold an evening auction? This was agreed to, and Stieglitz and O'Keeffe hung 117 of Hartley's paintings from floor to ceiling in one room in the galleries, where they were exhibited from May 10 to 17.[14]

In a piece he wrote for the catalogue Stieglitz explained that Hartley was being forced to hold an auction to free himself from want. Henry McBride, reporting on the exhibition, was intrigued by the idea, more so than the writer for the *New York Times,* who commented not on the novelty of the auction but on the "lack of maturity" in some of Hartley's canvases, and, in others, "a tendency that comes generally with old age and the change in the eyeball." But some showed "handsome arrangements of color," he admitted, and the New Mexico landscapes exhibited "breadth and distinction of form." Often, the critic felt, Hartley's art was literary, telling a story that the viewer had to puzzle out.[15]

More important to Hartley than what the critics thought was the attention that the exhibition and auction received. Hundreds of people came to the show, he later recalled — all of them anticipating bargains, he supposed. By the evening of the sale he was a nervous wreck. He had coffee beforehand with Alice Miriam and her sister across the street from the galleries, then thought — as he told the story — to slip in at the back of the crowded auction room. After another attack of nerves he did so, watching with fascination as his pictures went fast, some for as little as $10 and others for considerably more, such as a Bermuda painting to Dr. Albert C. Barnes for $100 and two 1908 Maine scenes to another collector for $200 each. When it was over, Hartley's works had grossed $4,913.50, from which Stieglitz took $1,000 for the Anderson Galleries.

Stieglitz's account of Hartley's presence at the auction was somewhat different. He told Hudson Walker that Hartley, after declaring that he would not attend the sale, had marched into the room where the crowd was seated and sat down near the front, next to Albert Barnes. After the sale people had crowded around him, and Hartley, Stieglitz remembered, had theatrically announced that he wished his mother were alive so he could telegraph her. Walker, who disapproved of Stieglitz's contradictory attitudes toward Hartley, doubted this account. Whatever the facts, the occasion was momentous for Hartley, who earned three times what he had expected to and could now plan on an extended stay in Europe.[16]

The success of the auction no doubt convinced him that he was sufficiently established to live in Europe without diminishing his prestige in the United States. His generally euphoric mood was further enhanced by enthusiastic words from the likes of Albert Barnes, who wrote in early June to tell him that he was elated by the effect created when in his private office he placed two of Hartley's 1916 cubist boat paintings on either side of a Charles Prendergast panel he had bought at that year's Independent show. "Demuth was here while I hung them," Barnes wrote, "and he agreed with me that outside of a few spots in my house there is probably nothing in America that can touch the wall in sheer, potent, exquisite, meaningful beauty." Barnes added that a flower piece he had also bought at the sale now had an important place in his collection.[17]

Savoring such praise, Hartley wasted little time before arranging to depart for Europe. Early in June he wrote to ask Stieglitz to manage his affairs and, in the event of his death, to divide whatever property he might have among his five sisters. He turned over on consignment various jewelry he had collected, chiefly Indian necklaces, as well as a valuable antique ship model.[18]

His departure represented as complete a break as he could make. In July he sailed for France, and once there, he immersed himself in the life of Paris, taking little time to look back at the America he had left. Stieglitz received few if any letters over the next several months; it was late October when a mutual friend, Lillian Baer, conveyed to him a letter that Hartley had written to her. In it he reported that he had been suffering from a lingering illness, and on another note, he asked her to tell Stieglitz that the moment was ripe for "the American idea in Europe." If Stieglitz could put together a show of the new American paintings, it would be well received.[19]

Hartley may well have been correct, but nothing came of the plan, and he was soon on to other things, still taking pleasure in the idea that he was at the forefront of American art. In November the editor of *Art in America,* Frederic Fairchild Sherman, having read and admired *Adventures in the Arts,* encouraged him to write something for the magazine, perhaps some essays about the art of North American Indians. And in October Herbert Seligmann published "The Elegance of Marsden Hartley — Craftsman," a touching appreciation that attempted to summarize Hartley's career and lauded him for his eloquent, varied work, which was on occasion lacking only in completion, in Seligmann's view. The piece was high praise indeed, and Seligmann followed up with another essay early in 1922 that acclaimed *Adventures in the Arts*. In August 1922 Paul Rosenfeld would exclaim "Marvelous Hartley!" in *Vanity Fair* and celebrate the "exquisite distinguishedness" of his paintings.[20] In the atmosphere of the early 1920s, Hartley's reputation in America had grown. Unfortunately for him, he did not understand that it had to be cultivated, not benignly neglected.

During his first months in Europe, Hartley took a vacation from painting and enjoyed Paris, reestablishing old contacts and making new friends, such as the young American Matilde Rice and Charles Kuntz, the husband of Adelaide, who would later become his confidante. In 1921, with money in his pocket, Hartley must have felt that the world was his. He was in no rush to abandon Paris, but Berlin awaited, and in November he returned there, to what he told Stieglitz was an "almost royal welcome."[21] The Rönnebecks greeted him warmly, and other expatriates whom Hartley knew from New York and Paris drew him into their small society. The poet Robert McAlmon was in Berlin at the time and in his memoir recalled that among the group were Thelma Wood, a sculptor; Djuna Barnes; the photographer Berenice Abbott; the dancers Harriet Marsden and Isadora Duncan; and a number of others who either passed through briefly or stayed to enjoy the high life. "No one knew from one day to the next what the dollar would bring in marks," McAlmon remembered, "but everybody knew that, whatever happened, the dollar bought in Berlin as much as ten or twenty dollars would buy elsewhere. It made for wildness."[22]

Hartley lived with the Rönnebecks until late December, when he found a place at 150 Kantstrasse, two rooms with a view out over "two of the best old mansions in Berlin with huge private gardens." Here he expected to have the privacy that the last months had lacked — the only drawback to staying with the Rönnebecks, whose familial ways were a major reason Berlin was so appealing to him. He adored Arnold Rönnebeck's mother, who reminded him of his own. He spent literally hundreds of evenings with the family, flirting with Mrs. Rönnebeck, passing her cigarettes, and listening to her husband play Beethoven or Chopin on their piano. Hartley had his own "cozy corner" on the living-room sofa, Rönnebeck remembered, where he would curl up, smoking a cigarette in a long holder, and savor the Rönnebecks' life. Whenever Arnold's father rang for the maid and requested that a fine wine be served, Hartley, reveling in the pleasures of domesticity, would exclaim *"Wunderbar, wunderbar!"*[23]

Berlin, perhaps even more now than during his earlier stay, offered Hartley everything: a sense of family with the Rönnebecks such as he had rarely if ever had in America; intimate, relaxed friendship with Arnold, among others; inexpensive living, so that he could make his precious money go far; an artistic community that gave him recognition; and a hedonistic element into which he could plunge as he chose but from which he could also draw back as he saw fit.

Hartley's rooms on Kantstrasse were brightened by a "charming collection of plants and cacti on his window sill," Rönnebeck recalled, "and he painted — in the drab grey atmosphere of that town[—] the sunny hills of New Mexico!" Another acquaintance of Hartley's, Rogers Bordley, remembered no "charming" flora, only "a lot of very broken down cactus plants" that Hartley claimed served as inspiration.[24] In any event Hartley's rooms were comfortable for him, a "home" such as he had seldom had.

With the German mark severely devalued, he could indulge himself. One afternoon he invited Rönnebeck to tea at the Hotel Adlon, but what he really wanted was to have his friend see a ring in the window of Cartier's jewelry store. Together they gazed at the ring that Hartley yearned for, and three days later he was wearing it, a large blue sapphire and two diamonds set in platinum. "I couldn't stand it always just *looking* at the damned thing any longer," he told Rönnebeck. "Well, I guess I'll just call it an 'investment.'"[25] And he could afford to play the role of social lion — or at least he was no longer the impoverished loner. Robert McAlmon recollected Hartley's appearing in evening dress at a nightclub, wearing in his lapel a large orchid he had purchased at a flower shop adjacent to the Hotel Adlon. He "certainly did luxuriate in orchidean emotions for a time," McAlmon observed, noting that Hartley also enjoyed being able to give marks to the young Germans who liked to sit with him in the nightclubs and tell him their woes.[26]

With Stieglitz he tended to adopt the pose of a serious, quiet soul: "I write & paint," Hartley told him late in February 1922. "There is little to tell." He likened Berlin to a "good old comfortable shoe"; it was less radiant than before because the royalty had disappeared, but it retained "its fatherly-motherly character" and still provided the simple pleasures of a good bed and enough to eat.[27] The hedonistic side of Berlin was equally important to him, however, as it provided a release from his New England inhibitions. He went to immense costume balls where in exotic dress he was worshipped by young men; transvestite parties such as those he described to Matilde Rice; and homosexual bars where he might fawn over a young male pickup such as Robert McAlmon told of in his short stories. "Life in Berlin then was at the height of heights — that is to the highest pitch of sophistication and abandon," Hartley wrote in his memoir. "None of us had seen anything quite like the spectacle. The psychological themes were incredible.... It was a vast jury of life and had to be gone through in that way."[28]

Hartley's indulgence in that abandon could lead to distress, not only from guilt over his extravagances or jealousy over the attentions of a young male prostitute, but also from the pain of disease. During the early months of 1922 he was confined to bed most mornings, feeling miserable from the arsenic-strychnine shots he received three times a week as a treatment for syphilis. But while he felt weak, he was not entirely dispirited because he was constantly with friends such as Rönnebeck and Frank Davison, the Canadian novelist he had recently met.[29]

He had picked up on the new atmosphere of postwar Berlin immediately after his arrival. The city was "in many ways more extraordinary than ever," he wrote to Stieglitz in late November. Politically the republic was "unformed" as yet, but this led to remarkable freedoms. And with a polyglot population — "300,000 Russians — not to speak of Japs — Spaniards and a multitude of people who do not have countries owing to the changing of the borders" — Berlin was more cosmopolitan than it had ever been.[30] The theater, while not as lively as that in New York, was nonetheless diverting, as was the art, even if he himself found it overladen with cubism.[31] Newness in art, architecture, and film — in high culture as well as in the mundane — made Berlin extraordinary, and all that the city was played on Hartley's imagination.

As early as the end of February 1922 he was writing that he saw New Mexico often in his mind.[32] Although Berlin provided many diversions from his art, he began working once he was settled in his own place, doing still lifes first and then some lithographs on stone.

The initial pieces were modest — "I have a group of good drawings & perhaps 20 paintings in all — mostly small," he reported in September — but he thought them some of the best work he had ever done, "true expression ... devoid of all that extraneous passion which comes to the surface and must of necessity be no other than aspects of one's private life."[33] He was moving toward what he would call his New Mexico recollections. In May he had acknowledged to Stieglitz that he could not work fast because there was "a lot stewing in my mind."[34]

What was "stewing" was memories of the Southwest, bittersweet thoughts about America, a recognition of his complex relationship with Stieglitz, and his responses to what Berlin meant to him. Late in 1922 and on into the next years he worked at the recollections, an extended series of extremely stylized New Mexico landscapes, which were "not pictures thank god — but paintings," he insisted.[35] Mass, horizontal movement, upheaval, undulation, and sensuality characterize these works. "The artist's sense of irony reversed the notion of tranquility [as in Wordsworth's idea of "emotion recollected in tranquility"] since these recollections evolved from and partially reflected the turmoil of postwar Berlin, with its social and sexual decadence," Gail Scott has observed.[36] The recollections are, in fact, some of Hartley's most forceful paintings. They are larger than most of his other work, with a monumental quality that reflects the space and power of the Western landscape, and an absence of human form that suggests Hartley's nagging sense of isolation — though in Berlin in 1922 and 1923 he suffered from no lack of friendships among other expatriates.

In this important series of paintings Hartley picked up on the powerful impressions the New Mexico and Texas landscapes had made on him during his stay in the Southwest, impressions that had not surfaced in his earlier pastels, still lifes, and relatively placid landscapes. Now he was a respected American artist living in Germany, where America was admired, at least among his crowd of artists and expatriates. It represented power, newness, and even the exotic to Europeans, who were still recoiling from the Great War and were aware as never before that the conventions of old cultures and the relative smallness of their spaces hemmed them in.

Hartley perceived all of this and began his recollections, painting in a style that was new to him in order to convey the spaciousness of the American Southwest and link it to the fascinating sensuality of 1920s Berlin. They show roundness, motion, crevasses, and projections. He was expressing through paintings of his homeland what he felt about a Berlin bristling with sensuality and with "the new." These are celebrations of landscape; in contrast to Berlin, with its flat, closed-in, forested terrain, New Mexico offered plateaus, canyons, mountains, and distant vistas.

Then, too, Hartley was painting partly for Stieglitz, because he knew that his friend, not to mention American art critics, had doubts about the merit of American painters' working abroad. And he also knew that Stieglitz favored O'Keeffe among the painters he championed. So Hartley took as his own and painted the region that most attracted his rival, not entirely coincidentally rendering it in a style that bears some resemblance to that of the earliest works of hers that he and Stieglitz saw — and for that matter, to that of the work of Arthur Dove, another of Stieglitz's entourage. Resemblances should not be pushed too far, but some of O'Keeffe's art from 1916, such as the charcoal *Special No. 15* and the similar oil, *Special No. 21,* with their round shapes and rolling motion, are suggestive of Hartley's recollection paintings.

He worked steadily on, saddened near the end of 1922 to learn of the death of Alice Miriam. Earlier he had enjoyed trips to Dresden for its art and to Hamburg for its nightlife — "I have never seen such a handsome rough-neck quarter anywhere," he exclaimed.[37] By the end of January 1923 he could report to Stieglitz that he had sixty canvases, which with the addition of some good landscapes would be enough for a show to mark his return to the United States after two years in Europe.

When in 1923 Germany announced the suspension of its war-reparations payments, France occupied the Ruhr, and tensions rose. Hotels in Berlin would not serve the French, and Hartley nervously considered moving up a trip he was planning to Italy, where he wanted to see not only art but the landscape, something he missed in Berlin. He had been working long enough from "indoor emotions," he observed.[38] But the political crisis soon subsided, so despite a drastic devaluation of the mark — which cost Hartley money because he had purchased marks at 550 to a dollar, while now they were at 21,500 to one — he remained in Berlin, excited about his new work. In February he secretively showed his paintings for the first time to Rönnebeck, Rita Matthias, an American friend, and Frank Davison. There was some chance that the publisher Albert Boni might do a portfolio of his work, so Hartley had asked Stieglitz to mail photos of his earlier paintings; they reached him just before his friends were due to arrive at his apartment. He was pleased with his new art, which, viewed in the context of his previous work, seemed to him to cap his career. Now he was ready to move outside and travel south for a "true landscape experience." He had, he believed, "worked out the aspects of period experiences & sensation" — the tendency to jump from one style to another — and hoped now "to achieve a kind of solid continuity." No more "art novelty" for him; he sought "art directness," which he thought he had achieved with the "plastic simplicity" of his new paintings.[39]

He was sure that this simplicity marked a "certain coming toward repose and ... at last, no intervention of private states of personal existence." There was little of "me" in the new work, he asserted, which excited him because his goal was "just good old fashioned honest painting" such as Renoir, Cézanne, and Courbet cared about, "the idea for its own sake." Hartley hungered "to be all artist & nothing else ... just pure sensibility & nothing else." The world, it seemed to him, was "a hopeless place to put one's faith in." The photographs that Stieglitz had sent of his earlier paintings made him see that he had done "some pioneering and stone blasting." "I realize how much I was those deserted farms myself," he remarked. Unhappy that the people he knew in Maine were departing, leaving him "to rattle in the wind," he had "like a fool ... put my faith in something more than there was to touch or see — for in reality what one can touch & see is the damned thing anyway without all that superfluous spiritual 'gas on the stomach.'" He wanted to "go into the idea that nothing is left of me other than the idea itself — that is of painting." But the special qualities of his painting always came from the imposition of his imagination upon what he touched and saw. He could no more make his work pure idea than he could make himself such, appealing though the concept was to him as a protection against the ravages of emotion.

Thinking to ready himself for the trip to Italy, he was painting his recollections with intensity; they were "more vivid in the sense of nature than they were when I worked from the same thoughts in N.Y.," he claimed.[40] The prospect of his trip inspired him, and rather than slowing down, he continued to paint what he termed a month later a "series of New Mexican & Texas landscape inventions ... the best landscapes I've done ... taking merely just the natural wave rhythms which are so predominant in that southwestern scene." He was working in no more than "three or four tones — predominant black & white," and it amused him that only now, after five years, and in Berlin, could he imagine the Southwest as it really was, "especially the Texas aspects on the train from El Paso to Los Angeles."[41]

Hartley's creative outburst in the series of recollections was a reflection of his general sense of artistic achievement at that time. Not only was he painting in a new way, but he was about to have his first volume of poetry published, in Paris, by Robert McAlmon's Contact Press. In December 1922 Albert Boni, the American publisher, then living near him in Berlin, had proposed publishing two volumes of Hartley's work, a collection of poetry and another of "little satirical episodes" he had written in Santa Fe. Moreover, Boni wanted also to print a portfolio of Hartley's paintings, to be accompanied by a foreword about him.[42] By April, however, Boni's plans to publish these works in Berlin had evaporated, though he still hoped to bring them out in the United States. Hartley was not particularly disheartened by all of this, as McAlmon had already offered to publish the poems, and did so during the summer of 1923.

Twenty-five Poems, "written in Gloucester, New York, Santa Fe, and Berlin, during 1917–1922," is a collection of poetry ranging from straightforward free verse such as the autobiographical piece "World — Passport Visa" to a poem written for a "DADA evening meeting" of the Société Anonyme in New York in 1920. "DIABOLO," it begins,

> I have many playmates —
> POPOCATAPETL, ORIZABA, VESUVIUS — MATTERHORN —
> one check gone.

Other poems convey something of what Hartley felt about the oppressiveness of life in Maine, but the most intriguing pieces may be two written in a freewheeling, avant-garde style that captures the pace and excitement of Manhattan and of *saltimbanques,* or tumblers. None has the depth, the genuineness, of his later poetry, but these poems are entertaining and less supercilious than his earlier work. Hartley had a right to be pleased; the poems were an accomplishment and demonstrated his ability to work in contemporary modes if he chose.[43]

In August Hartley took a short trip to Salzburg, where he had been invited by the theater producer Max Reinhardt to attend a performance of *Le Malade Imaginaire* at Reinhardt's magnificent Schloss Leopoldskron, the famous eighteenth-century castle that stands just outside the old city. Hartley loved the entire affair; he liked to think he had been invited because he was a well-known American whose presence could add to the publicity Reinhardt sought. "Was photo-d with Reinhardt & Claire Ames — then alone by Hoppe for American-Reinhardt publicity," he announced to Stieglitz from Salzburg.[44] Back in Berlin, he wrote that the audience for the play had been "more than exceptional and in nearly all ways handsome — people from London-Paris-Rome-Venice-Vienna-Munich, Berlin, New York." He again reported having been photographed with celebrities, then joked that he hoped sometime during his two and a half years away from New York to be free of Greenwich Village — a reference to the many Americans who, like himself, were more or less residing in postwar Germany.

Hartley's intention was to sail directly for the United States after his Italian trip. During the summer he expected to be home before the end of the year; in fact, he would not arrive until mid-March 1924. In the late summer of 1923 he was painting well and rapidly, regretting as October neared that he was about to have to cease in order to pack his materials and paintings for shipment back to the United States. He was particularly sorry to stop because he had just begun what he called his "first attempt at sculpture": five pictures of nudes, the first figure paintings he had ever undertaken. He was typically enthusiastic about these new efforts, believing that he had never before achieved such force in his work. The nudes represented an "actual return to life itself," he claimed.[45] The observer is likely to be less ecstatic; the pictures, pastels in sanguine and pencil drawings, are neither large nor compelling. The figures, especially one woman's, are stolid and muscular rather than graceful, with genitalia almost awkwardly blurred. What is most interesting about them is simply the fact that Hartley *did* them. His newfound assurance about himself and the sensual experiences of Berlin enabled him to approach the human form as previously he had not. Before his death Hartley would feel rebuffed by humankind many times, but these initial, tentative pictures marked a new willingness on his part to embrace others.

He was trying to express in the nude drawings something of what he felt about the people he had found in Hamburg, where he traveled for a short visit in mid-October. Writing in a café on the back of three ten-million-mark notes, which he insisted were cheaper than the paper he would otherwise have to buy, he told Stieglitz he had come to Hamburg for a last look at the Saturday-night life in this, "the nicest of all the German cities." He took great comfort in being among the natural people of the tough Reeperbahn St. Pauli quarter, who were "so hard looking outside & so gentle inside — the hard men up from the sea and the hard women waiting for them."[46]

The end of an important period in his life was imminent, he knew, though he would not have guessed that it would be ten years before he returned to Germany, or that he would never again be in Berlin for more than a brief visit. But Rönnebeck was about to leave for the United States, where he would remain, and Hartley sensed that in the present climate of political and economic unrest, and especially with the rise of nazism, the Germany he loved was disappearing. Then, too, other parts of Europe, particularly France, attracted him. Back in Berlin five days before he was to leave for Italy, he went to Nassau-ischestrasse 4, where he had lived before the war and where various belongings of his had been stored ever since. He pulled all sorts of things out of boxes — "pictures in books old hats rubbers every kind of odd and end that can attach to one... several copies of *Camera Work* — Van Gogh letters — November Boughs prose of Whitman" — and either threw them out or packed them for shipment. It was like shedding his seven years' skin, he thought, and he "felt fresh again."[47]

On the evening of October 31 he left Berlin for Vienna, where he remained for eight days, investigating forgettable small museums, seeing a flat revue called *Vienna Laughs Again,* and enjoying the city. From there he headed to Florence, changing trains at Innsbruck and admiring the Alps, which were freshly covered with snow. The scenery was beautiful and the ride comfortable, but Hartley got a hint of the new Germany that was just then arising when in his train compartment an elderly woman told of her horror at Adolf Hitler's attempt to overthrow the government. This was the Munich Beer Hall putsch of November 8, which failed after some violence; Hitler would return.

The wintry pall of fear dropped behind him when the train arrived early the next morning in Florence, allowing him to immediately start viewing what he had traveled south to see. First it was the Ponte Vecchio and the initially disappointing yellowish water of the Arno River, though he quickly realized that its muddy color blended well with the golden hue of the buildings. He called on Leo Stein and his wife, who were living in Florence. Their friendship was pleasantly relaxed, and Mrs. Stein soon took him to the Pensione Balestri, located on the Arno, with the Ponte Vecchio on one side and the Uffizi Gallery two blocks away on the other. The residents of the pensione were an international lot; among them was Scott Moncrieff, the masterful translator of Proust. As if this were not enough of a treat, Hartley had a room with a view of picturesque roofs and the parapets and tower of the Palazzo Vecchio, from which on at least one occasion he could see torches flaming at night.

The presence of Mussolini's fascist soldiers scarcely detracted from the excitement, or more nearly the awe, Hartley felt about Florence. He would never have believed that so much could be in one place, he wrote to Stieglitz after spending two weeks there. The days had been "arduous," he said, because the art was overwhelming, and he needed time to go back and absorb what he had as yet merely dipped into. His first visit was to the Uffizi; he was enthralled by its holdings, though less inspired by the "saccharine" quality of Raphael, Michelangelo, and some others than he might have been. The next day he visited the Pitti Palace, which he found "not so great a story."

On the third day "the vision rose — & I was going to say ascended into Heaven," he exclaimed, because he had discovered the Brancacci Chapel in the Church of Santa Maria del Carmine. He was swept away by what he declared was "the greatest work of art ever rendered in all the entire range": Masaccio's *Adam and Eve Banished from Paradise*. For Hartley the fresco fulfilled "all the laws of expression of vision — it is the very life of life made real in art." He asserted that if he had never seen a painting before and were never to see one again, still he would have seen "all the art there is." Masaccio's work stood out, and put together with the primitive qualities of Angelico, Lippi, and Masolino, it was what art was meant to be. He had viewed religion as it should "seem and be and feel." In these works, he continued, "the essentials are there for what anyone needs in any time or state of culture." When he wrote to Stieglitz late in November, he knew that more discoveries lay ahead for him, but he doubted that any would displace Masaccio as the footing for all else. His work and that of Angelico in fresco had an unparalleled "unity and simplicity & superb tonal grandeur." The trouble with oil paintings was that they became "so elaborate and so endless in the glorification of the idea"; frescoes, in contrast, were "so far brought forward with simplicity as to seem just like they were breathed on — called forth — 'spoken' and thereby realized."[48]

Coupled with his experiences in Berlin, Hartley's discovery of the primitives in Florence had the profoundest of influences upon him. Masaccio's fresco of Adam and Eve was remarkably simple in comparison to most of what Hartley saw in Florence, but to him the work's clear and direct form and color, as well as the emotion expressed in the looks and gestures of the figures, caught what he wanted to convey in his art, be it landscape or figure painting.

Late in his life Hartley wrote an essay, which he never published, about the work of Masaccio in the Brancacci Chapel and that of Piero della Francesca in the church of San Francesco in Arezzo, where he stopped on his way to Rome for Christmas 1923. "What living humanism pulsated in the heart and mind of this gifted young man," he wrote of Masaccio, "such plausible sense of reality." He could imagine no more "humanistic interpretation of Christ" than the artist's *The Tribute Money,* in which Christ was less a god than a man deeply desiring to free the world of "its troubles and its agonies." Masaccio was so nearly supreme because somehow he had an "advanced notion of life in its entirety and the meaning of art in its relation to life — life in relation to art — life in relation, best of all, to itself, for life is first and last a human experience." Not Raphael nor Botticelli nor Rubens could approach Masaccio; only Piero della Francesca could, with his "high regard for simplicity and the last reduction of emotion, glorious tact, [and] superb rendering of the pause in rhythm." Piero allowed no outburst of sentiment "to over-ride his sense of measure, order, proportion and reality."[49]

Hartley was feeling his way toward the art that would emerge most conspicuously in the 1930s, but in 1923, especially after viewing the paintings in Florence, he began to develop a consistency that made his work more of a piece than it had been before. The figure paintings and portraits Hartley did in the 1930s, like his landscapes of that period, bear certain similarities to his 1920s work from the Berlin series onward. It is as if the very real, if sometimes tawdry, sense of humanity he gained in that city, combined with the simplicity and directness of the Italian primitives, led him to understand better what his idol Cézanne had been driving at when he pared things down and down, to their basic elements.[50]

Despite the pleasures of life in Florence, which included friendships with people such as the Leo Steins and a visit to the home of the Bernard Berensons, Hartley wished to be in Rome for Christmas. He left Florence, spent some days in Arezzo enjoying a small inn, the Albergo Stella d'Italia, and repeatedly studying the work of Piero della Francesca, and then arrived in Rome for Christmas week.[51] He visited Maurice Sterne, who had a studio there, and saw various sights with him. But for Hartley Rome was not a place to see art; he was more content with the grandeur of the Colosseum. He was not impressed with Saint Peter's, which he thought had a "tone of interior extravagance and tastelessness," and found even the Sistine Chapel a disappointment because of its "gloom" and "spiritual ponderousness."[52] From Rome he traveled north again, running into the journalist Walter Lippmann in the station in Florence. Lippmann talked him into visiting Pisa with him and his wife, and then Hartley was off to Cannes with the idea of locating a place where he might settle after he returned from the United States. He was bemused by the Riviera, calling that part of the Mediterranean "the mills of pleasure" and thinking it a "wonderful playground for elephants and clowns."[53]

In late February 1924, with some reluctance because he knew he had come to the end of one of the most enjoyable periods of his life, he boarded the S.S. *Patria* in Marseilles, expecting to arrive in New York about ten days later, after an easy, uncrowded trip along a southern route. But in Naples, where the ship laid over for two days, some 340 Italian emigrants were taken aboard, to Hartley's eventual dismay. During the voyage the weather was stormy, and the passengers, overcrowded, were constantly sick on deck and in the cabins, which soon smelled of sewage. In the end the trip took almost three weeks, with the result that the ship nearly ran out of food and water. What food there was was terrible, and Hartley's left leg swelled up so badly that he could walk only with great difficulty. "Better ships have been blown up for lesser reasons," he lamented. Eventually the *Patria* reached harbor, not in New York but in Providence, Rhode Island, where, Hartley surmised, the emigrants might have a better chance of being allowed into the United States. Before traveling on to New York, he rested his leg at the Providence home of a friend, Stewart Macdonald. Despite the trip and his discomfort, he was anxious to get on with things: "My eye is full of wonder & my mind full of determination," he announced, referring to his recent experiences in Italy, for him "the El Dorado of the creative sense," where he planned to return soon.[54]

10

Cézanne Country
1924 – 1928

HARTLEY'S STAY in the United States in 1924 was only three months long, hardly enough for him to settle down. He visited relatives in Cleveland, made arrangements about the paintings he had shipped back from Berlin, and completed two informal essays that he submitted to *Vanity Fair*. The magazine's editor, Frank Crowninshield, rejected one, about the French Riviera, but accepted the other, "The Greatest Show on Earth: An Appreciation of the Circus from One of Its Grown-up Admirers."[1] In mid-June Hartley sailed for England, where he went immediately to London after landing at Plymouth. He delighted in the life-style of Britain — its leisurely pace, its manners, and its dress. He was, in fact, thoroughly pleased to be back in Europe.[2]

After spending several weeks in London he crossed the Channel to Rotterdam and from there visited The Hague, where he was impressed by a large collection of van Goghs and several fine post-impressionist works by van Rysselberghe, Signac, and Seurat, especially the latter's large canvas of a music hall, *Le Chahut*. Hartley next traveled south to Antwerp, where he met a sailor friend stationed aboard the battleship *New York*. The two of them visited Brussels, and then Hartley continued on to Paris, arriving near the end of July and at once encountering "the entire world so it seemed — Duchamp — Varèse — Man Ray — Leo Stein — and many less conspicuous playmates."[3] Instead of settling down to paint right away, he took the time to journey out of Paris to visit such places as Rouen and Chartres —

"such grace dignity-power-repose-splendour-and simply not to believe — the glass," he remarked about the cathedral at Chartres. And he spent some time looking about Paris as well, getting a sense of it as never before.

He expected to move to the South of France during the autumn, but Paris life was too stimulating, and he was offered exhibition opportunities, so that it would be the following July before he would actually take up residence in Vence. Meanwhile he enjoyed the city, its cafés, and the splendid variety of people with whom he could be close or not so close, as he chose. Hartley recalled the character Fougita, a Japanese artist who was the most flamboyant foreigner among the "terrace life" — except perhaps for "the debonair pink and white Bosshard, who might be superficially called the Swiss Modigliani, since he then painted thin female nudes usually lying down with a faint lyrical mountain landscape in the distance of the same hue as his own skin." Hartley saw something of Gertrude Stein and Sherwood Anderson, who was close to her then, and of Ernest Hemingway and Edna Saint Vincent Millay at the Rotonde, one of the "literary" cafés. At the Café Royal he chatted with an English group, among whom were Augustus John, sporting an earring or two, Wyndham Lewis, and Jacob Epstein, and more than once he drank with James Joyce at the Café des Deux Magots. And though he had little use for surrealism, he enjoyed the company of André Breton, Louis Aragon, Philippe Soupault, and "the irrepressible Tristan Tzara."[4]

But it was not only the café life that diverted him from traveling south; more important, he believed, was the chance to exhibit in Paris with several other Americans. The artists George Biddle and John Storrs approached him during the summer about exhibiting at a new gallery, the Briant-Robert, in November. Hartley agreed, and on that basis Biddle offered him his studio for most of August. Within three weeks Hartley had fifteen canvases that were either finished or prepared, of which six — five landscapes and one still life — would go into the show, whose opening was delayed until January 1925. So Hartley remained in Paris, using Biddle's studio daily while thriving on the city's busy life, of which he felt very much a part.

Two days after the show of American painting opened, he sat in the Café de l'Univers, across from the Comédie Française, and wrote Stieglitz a long letter about the exhibition and about French art in general. In a good mood because of the show and because he was to meet some American friends and see the Comédie, he discussed the exhibition, which was interesting "in the novelty of its precedent — it being the first time the French have actually invited Americans to show." He was critical of the other artists selected, who were "quite hopeless in view of what might have been accomplished," but felt that it had gone as well as it could under the circumstances. Jules Pascin, whose inclusion was "a bit far-fetched as there is nothing whatsoever American in his sensations and methods of expression," was represented by three paintings of nudes, which had an Oriental flair about them. Hartley found Maurice Sterne's works "far too saccharine to appeal for longer than a moment," while those of John Barber mattered little and had "no American feeling" about them. Paul Burlin's suffered from not being "passionately endowed" and lacked an "undying conviction." His work and that of George Biddle and John Storrs seemed to him the most essentially American.

His was being called the best, he claimed, and he cited the critic in the European edition of the *Chicago Tribune,* who had written that "for sheer, sincere modernism... the prize at the exhibit is carried off by Marsden Hartley, whose vigorous, sweeping strokes — devoted to the depicting of abstract ideas — have almost terrifying power, though sometimes reminding one rather more of a bad dream than a picture."[5] His six paintings had the best wall, and they drew responses such as "apocalyptic — inevitable — unquestionably personal." He described the paintings as being an almost monochromatic "black white umber or venetian red and green — the first time in my life I've ever done what I've always aspired to — a black & white painting." Of the four of this sort, two were "large rearrangements of the Maine landscapes of former years." He called them an "attempt to attain true dramatic scale in subject with a sculptural method of treatment."

John Storrs had complimented Hartley's ability as a sculptor, which pleased him because in fashioning these paintings he had had in mind "the Courbet sense of truth and reality — and the Maillol sense of form and sensibility." Hartley's concept was interesting, but few would judge these somber paintings among his better works. Most intriguing about them, perhaps, is the fact that Hartley, as content as ever he could be with his life, chose that moment to confront Maine, translating the rolling curves and expanses of his New Mexico reminiscences into dark — even nightmarish — form and a near absence of color. As he approached his fiftieth year, a milestone he did not take lightly, he was in some ways beginning to come to terms with his birthplace, though the process would take a decade more to complete.

While most of the viewers at the show's "vernissage" were American, several French artists also appeared, among them Chagall and Mondzain, whose opinion Hartley did not hear, and Fauconnier, a cubist, who declared that Hartley's paintings showed a "fine temperament but 'confused orchestration,'" a term Hartley chose to dismiss. He did not feel overwhelmed by the French and thought the new interest in American art promising. He had been invited to exhibit in another show in May, this one to include artists such as Elizabeth Nourse, Alexander Harrison, Mary Cassatt, and Frederick Carl Frieseke, among others. Although he was slightly scornful of the group and eventually decided not to show with them, at that point he wanted to and as a result planned to remain in Paris at least until May. He had been given an atelier all to himself near Montmartre and knew he ought to take advantage of it.

Whatever the importance of the projected exhibition in May, the time generally was a propitious one for art. There were numerous small shows displaying the major artists, though none of them, in Hartley's opinion, was doing striking new work: "Utrillo — Chagall, Pascin... Utrillo attractive in its way — Chagall most distressing to me — a kind of expression of altogether bad judgement in painting — Pascin well — it's Pascin better but no deeper." Paul Rosenberg's gallery was having a show of the "great" moderns, in which Matisse was "tamed to propriety," Braque was "quietly returning to the figure," and Picasso had "nobly returned to cubism." At the Grand Maison de Blanc — "Shades of John Wanamaker," Hartley scoffed, referring to the mass-market quality of that exhibition — Utrillo, Vlaminck, and a subdued Morgan Russell were on display, while elsewhere was a retrospective of the Section d'Or group of 1912–13, so "caviar" then and "so sort of calm rice pudding now." The *fauves,* Hartley thought, domesticated themselves by repeating their work; now they were "painting flat patterns," but these were inane. French art, in other words, had lost its momentum.[6]

Unfortunately, Hartley's work would not seem to many to be the sort of dramatic innovation he had hoped it would. His paintings did not draw great attention in France, and in a show of seven American artists organized by Stieglitz at the Anderson Galleries in New York, his twenty-five canvases were received lukewarmly. Although his friends praised the works, the critics were less than enthusiastic. One wrote of Hartley's New Mexico reminiscences that many of them had little color and a "great deal of pose." The paintings that failed might collectively have been called "Studies in Liver," he declared, but half a dozen worked, and this made up for the rest. Deogh Fulton, the critic, was more taken by the paintings of Arthur Dove and John Marin.[7] Georgia O'Keeffe, who was never fond of Hartley's work for long — she had been able to live with one of his early Maine landscapes for only three or four days — and always ambivalent in her feelings toward him, wrote to the critic Henry McBride that she had found his review of the show amusing and was going to send a copy of it to Hartley so that he might see what McBride thought of American painters living abroad. Describing Hartley's work as "old world, old souled, and awfully fatigued," McBride sounded a criticism that he would continue until after Hartley returned to America in 1930.[8]

But in 1925 Hartley was not ready to be discouraged; Europe still seemed to hold promise. In addition, for the moment he felt reasonably secure financially, due to an arrangement that had come about through a visit with Louise Bryant the previous fall in Paris. He had known and liked Bryant since his summer in Provincetown, in 1916. Jack Reed, her first husband, had died in Russia after World War I, and she was now married to the wealthy American diplomat William Bullitt. They were living in the ornate home of Elinor Glyn, a British novelist, in Boulogne-sur-Seine, near Paris, where Hartley went to see them. During the course of their time together Bullitt asked him about his financial situation. Hartley explained his wish for a steady income over the next years, and Bullitt told him of William V. Griffin, a friend who he believed might be interested in arranging a regular income for Hartley. The result was an agreement whereby Griffin and three friends would pay Hartley $2,000 per year in exchange for ten paintings, the agreement to last four years. In November 1924 Hartley received his first check, for $500.[9] Although he would come to feel burdened by the need to produce ten paintings on others' terms, in early 1925 he was happy with the arrangement.

A siege of carbuncles during the spring lessened the pleasure of Paris for Hartley. They required daily dressings for three weeks, as well as serum injections, and even though he was later able to work comfortably at the Bullitts' in Boulogne-sur-Seine, he yearned to move to the South of France.[10] In July he traveled to Cannes, where he remained for five weeks, sunning himself and enjoying the relative quiet after Paris. He was convinced that he needed a home, warmth, and isolation for his well-being, and the small town of Vence, in the hills behind Nice, seemed an ideal place for him to settle for the next few years. He had the good fortune to find a suitable house almost immediately upon his arrival, taking possession of it on September 15. The idea of domesticity appealed to him, and with a cocker spaniel puppy completing his ménage, he thought for a short while that he had achieved an ideal existence. La Petite Maison, with its living room, dining room, and bedroom as well as its kitchen, bath, W.C., and garage, was more of a home than he had lived in since Maine. And though a lot of retired English people and several artists resided in Vence, there was almost none of the hubbub of Paris, or even of art colonies such as nearby Cagnes.

Provence was also important to Hartley because he felt he needed the stimulation of new landscapes, and he had responded enthusiastically to the region when he visited it in early 1924. For him Provence contained "every aspect of landscape," and it had an austerity that he considered essential to painting. Vence, in the hills, seemed a good spot to work from, with easy access both to the ocean and to the mountains, though Hartley later would deem these hills less interesting than those to the east, between Marseilles and Cassis; than stretches of the land between Avignon and Nîmes; or than the "strange and bizarre" outcroppings of hills and stone around the medieval ruins of Les Baux. (The latter shapes would have much the same effect on him as the rocks he eventually discovered in Dogtown, behind Gloucester, and as the formations he observed along the coastlines of Maine and, later, Nova Scotia.)[11] When he was first in Vence he hoped to begin working directly from nature, in an environment that was new to him. He thought there would be "less danger of losing sight of the essentials" that way than if he merely repeated "the experiences of the past." It would take time for the Provençal landscape to seep into his imagination, but eventually it would give him a "new space to explore in the imagination," he told Stieglitz in early October.[12]

Vence seemed well suited to Hartley's need alternately to socialize and withdraw into himself. He was visited by his nephew Clifton Newell, from Cleveland, and for a while he enjoyed acting as an informal tutor about art and France to the young man. The two took long walks together, and on one of these, between Vence and St. Paul

de Vence, they met Charles and Adelaide Kuntz, who were staying in
a hotel in Villefranche, on the coast next to Nice. Charles, whom Hartley described as a "magnificent big thing, big Germanic football type,"
had met Hartley before, in Paris in 1921, but Adelaide had not, and
she was pleased when Hartley, not reticent at all, invited them to have
lunch with him and his nephew.[13] They discussed the Kuntzes' plan
to live in Aix-en-Provence after they returned from a trip to Italy.
Hartley was intrigued, as he already had some reservations about remaining in Vence because of its plethora of English tourists. The
Kuntzes would not see Hartley again until 1927, by which time he had
settled outside Aix, but the meeting in Vence was the beginning of one
of Hartley's great friendships, that with Adelaide.[14]

Other artistic friends passed through the area as well. The novelist
Glenway Wescott and the art historian Monroe Wheeler stayed during
October at the Hotel Welcome in Villefranche, where Hartley saw
them several times, on two occasions along with the singer and actor
Paul Robeson and his wife.[15] But as the fall progressed there were
fewer friends to visit, and the English tourists became more and more
intolerable — "so like a constant diet of liver and suet pudding with
their constipated mentalities and the British wish to make everything
British they step on — Ugh!!" Hartley wrote that winter.[16] Also, the
weather was neither sunny nor warm, and he fretted that he would
not be able to meet the terms of his contract with William Griffin.
Despite such woes, he had a pleasant Christmas Eve with four Americans who lived nearby, Ada Gilmore, Ethel Mears, Oliver Chaffee,
and Maud Squire; they had a fine buffet supper and then lit a beautifully decorated tree. His mood worsened by the end of December,
when he found that the pictures he had painted to send to New York
were not yet dry, and that three of them had gone dead on him, as he
put it. In a panic he asked Stieglitz to give Griffin ten from those he
had on hand, "20 × 24 in size . . . not of the very best of course — at
least those less abstract better say."[17]

Hartley was despondent in part because he thought his tardiness in
delivering the works was the reason he had not received payments on
schedule. From talking with Bullitt, Hartley had gained the impression that Griffin was a hard-driving businessman, when in fact he was
rather lax and had merely been casual about forwarding Hartley's
money. Matters were straightened out in January 1926; Griffin sent
the money and was willing to wait for the paintings from France.

Hartley, however, was not able to relax. His habitual fretting, combined with lingering bronchitis and his concerns about Vence, drove him into a deep depression. He was not satisfied with painting directly from nature, as he had hoped to be, and this discouraged him. French artists, the Matisses and Picassos, he noted bitterly, seemed to be able to grind out their wares anywhere, "with their enviable gift for labour & that French self confidence that always can knock a thing off in the 'manicure'"; and then the dealers sold their work, and the artists enjoyed their success. Not so the Americans. Although his situation was certainly not as dire as it had sometimes been, Hartley let himself despair, feeling that he had lost control.

As much as anything, his moroseness came from being too isolated after the excitement of Paris. He needed companionship, which he would find more of once he moved to Aix the following September. And as he himself knew, he needed time to assimilate the landscape in his mind. Even though after touring some of the countryside with his nephew he found it "marvelous — and so amazingly like New Mexico . . . never just that rich romantic color — but a nobility of design that is exciting really," still he had difficulty in painting it at first. Before leaving Vence for Aix he spent three weeks in a small village along the Gorge du Loup, where from high on a promontory he could overlook the valleys and the mountains beyond; the large, more nearly realistic landscapes he rendered of the views he saw there suggest what a hard time he had been having of it. A viaduct near the base of a gorge, a sliver of road cut along a steep hillside, or a distant, indistinct château is the only sign of humanity among mountains that loom above but lack the expressiveness of those in his New Mexico recollections or his later paintings of Mont Sainte-Victoire or Mount Katahdin. The hills and mountains seem merely *there,* so that while the colors in the paintings are more vivid than those in the near monochromes of 1924, the effect is flatter, one of distance, objectivity, and uninvolvement, no matter how much Hartley professed to admire the mountains and valleys around Vence, "with their austere simplicity and refined grandeur."[18] In his best work he was always fiercely involved with his subject matter, whatever he felt toward it.

Not all of his paintings from this period are flat; smaller, less ambitious landscapes, probably painted from memory, engage the subject, as does *The Cagnes Road, Vence,* which captures the various hues of the earth, its shapes and those of the trees, and the lights and shadows created by the clear atmosphere. Strong gesture and impasto convey Hartley's feelings about the country. And once Hartley set his mind on Aix and on learning the region around it that Cézanne had painted, his work began to reflect his deepening involvement with the land, strive as he might for realism and objectivity.

After nearly a year of floundering in Vence, Hartley in June 1926 thought he might at last have found what he had come to Provence for. On his way to Paris to see a Cézanne show and six of his own pictures from 1924 on exhibit at the Salon des Tuileries, he spent a day in Aix, liked it, and then stopped for three more days on his return. He took two long walks out into the country — far enough from the center of Aix to visit Cézanne's studio on the Chemin des Lauves in one direction, and in another to be a good way toward the Château Noir, along the Route du Tholonet, where Cézanne had lived for a time.

Looming always in the distance was Mont Sainte-Victoire. "I couldn't believe my eyes for what I saw in the way of dignified beauty," he wrote afterward, "and one mountain — which in one time or another would have brought worshippers for the sense of grandeur & majesty it possesses." Seen from Aix, the mountain is perfectly angled to give the greatest visual effect; viewed from elsewhere, it can appear little more than a ledge. The earth around it, like that in New Mexico, had the redness that Hartley had been hoping to find, along with shapely trees and a certain "general opulence of nature" that accounted for the qualities of Cézanne's work. When Hartley first wrote to Stieglitz to describe Aix and Mont Sainte-Victoire, he had just arrived in the small village overlooking the Gorge du Loup, where during his stay he literally painted his way out of the depression occasioned by his year in Vence. While his pictures of the environs of the Gorge lack the conviction of his best work, they were nonetheless a start toward his fine late art. Knowing now that he would live in Aix after the lease on La Petite Maison expired in September, he began to feel rejuvenated, particularly as he came more and more to comprehend what Cézanne had been working toward. From the hill village Hartley wrote about the land around Aix that "such color exists nowhere outside of the windows of Chartres & St. Chapelle — the earth itself seems as if it were naturally incandescent & seems fired from underneath somehow — yet withal so restrained & dignified. & How remarkable that Cézanne should have found it to be so complete."

Perhaps thinking of his own complex feelings toward Maine, Hartley remarked that Cézanne had known the country around Aix from his infancy, making it all the more surprising that he could discover the special qualities of the region. The blossoming to fullness of Hartley's late style began at that moment, when, in the context of what he felt about the landscape, he partly perceived Cézanne's intentions in his own late work. Hartley would never quite achieve his best art in Provence, but his years in Vence and Aix would set the stage. He would have to return to the United States and learn again to trust his imagination when it was fired by the harshness of Dogtown, Nova Scotia, and, most fully, Maine. In France, excited by the Gorge du Loup and the country around Aix after months of feeling hemmed in, he distrusted his imagination and went where he believed he should have in the first place: "directly to nature." Life, he declared, had taught him that a little imagination was dangerous. "What therefore must a huge imagination do to one like me?" he asked rhetorically. One must turn toward the light of the world, but the light "as it is — uncoloured by dreams and interpretations."[19]

In Vence in early September, packing for his move to Aix, Hartley tried to explain why he had been so depressed, and why he had cared so little about anything. Life had seemed utterly stupid, he said, and he had felt "the victim of an unimportant and valueless idealism" that had denied him power over anything. His imaginative painting had been judged wanting, and now that he had "revolted" against imagination, he hoped he might "pass out as a possible realist." Through his art he reached others, and when it did not succeed, he experienced an intolerable loneliness. Realistic art might enable him to make contact; he would see.[20]

He moved to Aix in mid-September and stayed for more than two weeks at a pleasant, small place, the Hotel du Palais, before deciding to find more permanent quarters. That was accomplished quickly, and in October he moved into Canto Grihet, a house located two kilometers from town, on the Petite Route du Tholonet. From it he could look over a garden plot and see Mont Sainte-Victoire. Following an absolutely consistent pattern, he became ebullient about the promise of his new locale. At Canto Grihet he would have privacy without isolation, charming Provençal peasants as neighbors, and a generally pleasant atmosphere that would permit him "colour application and richer observation than ever in my life."[21] Only later would he admit that life there had been a strain because he had had to walk into Aix three times a week for food and supplies, which meant that he lost a lot of working time.[22]

After spending a week at Canto Grihet, he wrote to Stieglitz about the mountain, which was "full of hypnotic attraction," and about Cézanne's paintings of it. Hartley could not yet understand why the older painter had "ignored the actual truth in nearly every picture he did"; all the paintings of his that Hartley had seen were "reduced to an excessive abstraction," which puzzled him as he clung to his desire to be a realist. Already he himself had made almost thirty large drawings of the mountain, but he was not satisfied that he was getting down what he saw. Resisting his imagination, he could not yet achieve the fundamentals as had Cézanne. Hartley turned to an imaginative use of color, but that alone could not result in entirely successful landscapes of a terrain whose particular beauty lay in the forms of trees, rocks, and Mont Sainte-Victoire.[23]

"I am painting colour once more," he announced to Stieglitz in November. He felt he had come to a dead halt in Vence, and had recognized that "something had to be done about this 'imagination' business." His first efforts were three canvases he painted at the Gorge du Loup, "three good size pictures of the same thing at different hours." He worked on each piece during the same hours each day, and "almost had them pulled through in the presence of nature," though he did find it necessary to assume a bit in order to finish them. He regretted this because he had sworn "never to do another picture away from nature." Since moving to Aix, he reported, he had been hampered by rain, so after starting on one large canvas of Mont Sainte-Victoire he had had to set it aside to work on brightly colored still lifes. "I might one day become a colourist," he suggested, noting that his work was also calm. "Can you imagine me doing a colour painting?" he asked Stieglitz, and he confessed that such was his "new aspiration."[24]

He was convinced that these new directions were saving him from destruction. "Imagination is in her grave," he declared shortly before Christmas and his fiftieth birthday in early January — a prospect that distressed him considerably. By December he had started "five largish portraits of the mountain" and was cautiously optimistic. They had a sense of discovery in them, he thought, and an "absence of personal life." Impersonality nearly obsessed him, and he struggled to correlate it with what he understood Cézanne to have been doing. Writing to Stieglitz on December 8, Hartley remarked on the death of Claude Monet the day before, adding that "half a mile or a mile away the ashes of Cézanne powder themselves into infinity." He was struck by the manner in which the two painters had turned "nature into a kind of esthetic relic in a high beholden monstrance." Their work was "so easy of approach & so difficult of comprehension," he commented, intrigued because he recognized that they had melded a sort of impersonality with the sensibility that lent meaning to a work. In the case of Cézanne, Hartley noted the painter's kinship with the mystic Jacob Böhme, whose "Franciscan purity" was akin to Cézanne's experience of what he called the *sensation coloré* — his particular sensibility, through which were poured "the principles of impressionism."[25]

Hartley was straining to absorb what he perceived about the French painters. The problem was, how did one combine form, color, and the balance between caring and not caring in such a way as to be able to paint and yet not be swept away by the imagination? Hartley's first efforts in Aix, completed in 1927, were intensely colored renderings of Mont Sainte-Victoire, as seen from where he lived. Barbara Haskell has pointed out that he "appropriated not only Cézanne's subject matter, but his style as well, although the parallel brush strokes in Hartley's paintings and their raw primary hues were clearly post-Cézannean."[26] In his eagerness to leave imagination behind, Hartley adopted a formal, architectonic style in which color is clearly articulated in order to say, in effect, These are the elements in their shapes, primary colors, and overall form — with no subjectivity, no symbolism. But there was more to it than that. As a friend of Hartley's observed in a piece intended to be an introduction to his paintings when they were shown in America in 1928, the works "are not cold, but their warmth is not of the surface. It lies in depth and in density." The author, Mrs. John Storrs, understood Hartley's intense imaginative sense and felt the colors to be not "of the exterior; they come, it seems, from behind the canvas." She was more perceptive than most of the early viewers of these works, which were not well received. She could see that Hartley had "the religion of life" and that his piety was "a little mystic but infinitely moved by things themselves."[27]

After fretting about turning fifty because he felt it marked a significant moment in his life, at which he still had not accomplished what he had set out to in art, Hartley passed his actual birthday pleasantly, in the company of Frank Davison, who drove him to Toulon, Cassis, and Marseilles, where they had a fine dinner together. Being with his friend, who remained briefly in Aix, dissipated the loneliness Hartley felt living in Canto Grihet. And so he began 1927, he declared, with a "new comprehension of colour — a deeper sense of form & orderly rhythms etc.," which he said would be apparent in his pictures when his friends viewed them in the United States. He was now able to work slowly, and this gave the paintings nobility; "a calm of the inner life" pervaded them, he thought.[28]

As usual, however, his euphoria lasted only a short while, and when he wrote to Stieglitz in May, he reported that the first months of 1927 had been disastrous. "Numbed with cold" and "paralyzed with the feeling of horrible isolation," he had been devastated and indeed had become fearful of what might happen to him, or what he might do to himself. The event that had precipitated this "illness . . . of the mind or what they call the soul" was a request from the owner of Canto Grihet that he move. Even though the owner offered to locate Hartley in a house nearby, the Maison Maria on the estate of the Château Noir, and to put in a stove and return Hartley's rent, he was crushed. His sense of his own transiency grew overwhelming, and even a winter trip to Paris, Berlin, and Hamburg did not cheer him much. He saw himself as a drifter who had gone off in the wrong direction in his painting, so that at fifty he was essentially right back where he had begun years before: isolated in the woods, cooking, washing, and carrying wood, coal, and water for himself. Not even the diversion of seeing friends during his trip helped much. Artists and writers unnerved him, especially Leo Stein, who when Hartley met him in Paris was so hysterically fixated on his own small work, *ABC of Aesthetics,* that Hartley could not stand to be in his presence for long.[29]

If Hartley felt alone, it was partly because he loved Davison but saw him only at infrequent intervals. His spirits rose during the summer of 1927 when they were able to be together, touring Provence and spending two weeks at a house Davison had bought in Banyuls-sur-Mer, almost at the Spanish border on the Mediterranean. Such companionship, along with the warm weather of the South, the ease of being in Aix after the time in Banyuls, and having a regular routine of living that included a monthly visit to Marseilles, calmed Hartley. When he wrote to Stieglitz about all of this in October, it was as if he had not anguished repeatedly about his woes the previous winter.

Once again he was sure he was a "new & more plausible being," who having been "born to the imagination & almost doomed by it" could now work out ideas logically, believing that "all personal expression is rubbish." Hartley was drawing more than he ever had before, and he thought it was improving the "sureness of structure" in his work. That and the high colors of Provence gave him renewed confidence, and he could understand how Cézanne had been able to achieve "the greatest realization of colour."

Hartley's output was "oils — a few water-colour colour arrangements — many pencil drawings — silver points — lithographs all from nature." He was anxious for his American friends to see these works, which he planned to ship to the United States for a show at the Chicago Arts Club in late January or early February 1928.[30]

The prospect of returning to America excited him. He had missed the company of Stieglitz, O'Keeffe, Marin, Paul and Rebecca Strand, and numerous other friends in New York. He had heard from Arnold Rönnebeck, now married and serving as the director of the Denver Art Museum, who proposed that Hartley take his show there after Chicago. And he understood that he needed to reconfirm his reputation in the United States, though he planned to hasten back to Provence after his visit. Full of expectations, he worked happily during the late fall, satisfied for the moment that he was achieving the equilibrium he needed to paint his best. He recalled Cézanne's words, as he had long before, and translated them loosely for Stieglitz as "When the colour is at its richest, the form reaches its plenitude." Having been bathed in the colors of Provence, Hartley at last felt that he understood Cézanne, and that he had progressed in his own work to the point where his landscapes captured the form and color he desired without an excessive imposition of his imagination.[31] He completed his paintings, then took all his work to Paris for framing. After a cheerful Christmas spent at the Bullitts' and with friends, he sailed for New York aboard the *Rochambeau* on January 18, 1928.

The show at the Arts Club of Chicago, "Paintings and Watercolors by Marsden Hartley," which ran from February 28 through March 13, pleased him. It was well hung and attracted attention, though it resulted in few sales. For it he wrote a prose poem entitled "The MOUNTAIN and the RECONSTRUCTION," about how Provence and Cézanne had changed him. At "the end of a botched pattern," unable to "see the fabric for the tatters," he had told himself to "Change all ... everything — EVERYTHING!/ change the moyen, the form, the substance, even." In the countryside around Mont Sainte-Victoire he had had a vision of Cézanne and had come to comprehend his artistic principles. "To ANNIHILATE MYSELF IN THE SUBJECT/ — to become ONE/ with it" — this had been Cézanne's purpose, Hartley wrote, clearly signaling his desire to do the same.[32]

To proclaim his new stance Hartley also wrote a piece called "Art — and the Personal Life," which appeared in *Creative Art* in June. In it he announced that he had joined "the ranks of the intellectual experimentalists" for good. Such words as *expressionism, emotionalism,* and *personalism* were anathema to him because they implied "the wish to express personal life," which he preferred to have none of.[33] The critic Edward Jewell challenged the piece, saying that he doubted any painting could be purely intellectual. One glance would prove that Hartley's works were not, Jewell observed.[34]

Hartley understood Jewell's objection and was pleased with the attention, which mattered more to him than everyone's accepting his work as being devoid of emotional expression. Attention was important to him as he tried to readapt to America, and to New England in particular, which, as he wrote to Adelaide Kuntz, was "like a first wife that one cannot help revering — & yet cannot possibly live with." At that moment he was staying with the Bullitts in Conway, Massachusetts.[35] Although he knew he needed an American base for his art and assiduously denied being a thorough expatriate, he was anxious to return to Provence. He might accomplish some writing and complete a painting or two while at the Bullitts', but he did not feel inspired by the "green reminiscent landscape" of Massachusetts.

Even a visit to Gaston and Isabel Lachaise in Georgetown, Maine, did not change his mind about New England. While he appreciated the Lachaises' hospitality, he still recoiled against the land. "Pity nature should be so affable in appearance here & so inherently cruel in character," he wrote to Stieglitz from Georgetown. The first time he heard a New England accent again, he reported, "a sad recollection rushed into my very flesh like sharpened knives." Five years' absence had not softened his reactions; New England only made him yearn for the gentleness of Provence.[36] If by the end of a two-week stay in Maine he could claim that he had established a "fresh & vital contact with my native soil," he was nonetheless eager after seven months to return to Europe for "one more of these almost strange interludes," as he referred to his sojourn abroad when he bade farewell to Stieglitz and O'Keeffe, who he knew were critical of the move. His life again seemed uncertain because his reputation — and hence his income — was firm neither in America nor in Europe, and William Griffin had declined to continue the financial arrangement he had maintained with Hartley over the previous four years.

11

Looking Homeward
1928 – 1930

HARTLEY was of at least two minds about America in 1928. He understood that Stieglitz and others wanted him to settle there; it was to satisfy them and a part of himself that he referred to his stay in Europe as a "strange interlude" and, once back in Paris, wrote to thank Isabel Lachaise for a "perfect reintroduction to my native land."[1] But Europe still attracted him more, despite his usual complaints about its art, weather, and people. He arrived in Paris near the end of August, intending at first to remain there for only two weeks before traveling south to Aix-en-Provence. It did not take him long to change his mind, however, settled as he was in a small, comfortable hotel facing onto the Luxembourg Gardens, a situation he thought much preferable to spending the rainy fall in the remote Maison Maria near Aix. Further, the new art season in Paris was "extraordinary"; it had "opened with a real fanfare of autumnal trumpets," he told Stieglitz late in September.[2]

Hartley was not painting then and would not begin to paint again until December. He was revitalizing himself in Paris, writing some and absorbing the fall exhibitions, which he considered to be "extremely good" because the artists were "discarding theory and trying to reveal — well — nature — or the effect of nature, or the 'selflessness' of her." The intellectual artists Picabia, Max Jacob, and Jean Crotti, he wrote to Rebecca Strand, were "denying modern art or any other [while] asserting nothing but a hope for release" — like himself, he might have added.[3] When he started painting again, the subject was still life, a safe way for a person who was unsure of his work to keep some distance from the emotions generated by landscapes.

During the fall of 1928 circumstances were conspiring to make Hartley nervous. Excited by the Paris season, he grew increasingly anxious to be painting again. In December he managed to find a hotel room on the Boulevard Jourdan that suited his needs better than the place he had been staying. Large and airy, the new room enabled him to paint during the best winter light, at midday. This relieved him once he started, but nothing could calm his nervousness about the show of his work that Stieglitz was putting together at his new venue, the Intimate Gallery, for January 1929. A great deal hinged on it, Hartley believed. Intending no humor, he wrote to Stieglitz that he was praying "to all the deities of kindliness to make a decent affair of it — for everything depends on this particular show as far as I am concerned." A success would justify his and Stieglitz's efforts of the past years, as well as his lengthy stays abroad. He hoped to net a minimum of $10,000 in sales, enough to sustain him for a good while, even without William Griffin's support.[4] It was a bad sign — and a touch sad — that Hartley's list of guests to be invited included no more than a few people from New York and elsewhere who would be likely to attend the exhibition. Hartley's artist friends, such as Eugene Speicher and Rockwell Kent, were unlikely to buy his work, much as they might admire it; members of his family would not travel from Maine or Ohio for the show, nor would friends in Germany or France. Stieglitz did all he could to make the exhibition a success, even cabling Hartley as it opened to wish him the best and a happy birthday.[5] The show, as the brochure for it claimed, consisted of "one hundred paintings in oil, water-color, silver-point, and pencil: still-life, landscape — mountains — trees — etc — by Marsden Hartley, painted in Paris and Aix-en-Provence — France — 1924–1927." Hartley's old friend Lee Simonson applauded him in the foreword for realizing a "direct intensification of his inner sensibility that blazed forth 20 years ago" and called him "one of the three or four important painters of our generation — the generation which began to work about 1900 and will have had its say about 1950."[6] Unhappily for Hartley, most critical responses were lukewarm at best. Murdock Pemberton, for instance, wrote that though he admired the artist, he felt "ignorant of what he is doing and how he is doing it." Pemberton offered faint praise when he remarked that Hartley had "intellectualized his life to the point where he can go over to Europe and worship Cézanne at the foot of his own shrine and not be ashamed of it." The review concluded with the observation that the painter needed "some 'imaginative wisdom' or 'emotional richness'" to distinguish his work from that of Cézanne, Segonzac, Derain, and Braque; otherwise he would continue to be no more than "the usual American boy copying the usual French."[7]

A day or so after the exhibition closed, at the end of January, Stieglitz wrote Hartley a lengthy, thoughtful letter. The show had gone on for thirty-four days, he noted, and the Intimate Gallery had "looked rich and full." When Stieglitz was ill with the flu, Georgia O'Keeffe, his assistant Emil Zoler, and Paul and Rebecca Strand had tended the gallery. Stieglitz sent Hartley clippings of the critics' comments, which were "both kindly disposed and some decidedly the reverse." Henry McBride, for one, had not liked the new work, deeming Hartley's paintings "reminiscent of too many others." McBride thought that "Americans should not flee their country but should work in America even though the conditions for the artist be impossible here." Stieglitz had hoped that the show might overcome McBride's prejudice against expatriate painters; nevertheless — and here he went to the heart of the matter — he had to confess that he felt much as McBride did. Various of Hartley's old friends, both collectors and artists, had visited the exhibition, and some had been impressed at how far Hartley had come with these paintings. They had admired his still lifes but by and large not so the new mountain scenes, with the result that no matter what price Stieglitz quoted for the oils — $2,000, $1,000, or $500 — nothing happened. What was worse, when he told people "that this exhibition stood between [the artist] and starvation, they looked blank — the general American expression," Stieglitz noted wryly. There was some income, but hardly "the much-hoped-for $10,000."

He tried to present the situation realistically:

Eventually, unless a miracle happens, and I am not a great believer in miracles, you will have to face a reality which I fear you never tried to understand. You have really made no "practical" contact in Europe and you are really without contact in your own country. Spiritually you undoubtedly are achieving what you must achieve, but the so-called economic problem, which after all is one that none of us can escape, is quite as difficult, if not more so, than it was when you originally came to 291. Of course one can always hope if one is so inclined but unless that hope is actually rooted in one's spirit and is not self-deception, it is bound to end in disaster.

His assessment was accurate. As always he offered whatever help he could through the Intimate Gallery and advised, "it may not give you what you desire but it is most likely a means of keeping you from actually dire need." And Stieglitz had his own struggles: "I cannot possibly become an art dealer. And I cannot possibly become a rich man," he told the painter, for he despised "the idea [of richness] or dealing in art more than ever." He hated to equate pictures with money, and would use whatever funds he could get to make things better for artists such as Hartley, but there was little likelihood of that, he realized. "The whole situation is ghastly," he concluded.

Although Stieglitz wrote from the heart, he was also trying to soften what he knew would be a severe blow. He held the letter for five days, then added a note. In it he told Hartley that he could count on $2,800 — money from friends, really, as the Strands had promised $800 for one painting, and Stieglitz and O'Keeffe were to pay $2,000 for others — and possibly another $1,000 if the collector Duncan Phillips purchased a work, as he had intimated he might. If Hartley felt neglected, he should remember that he was not the only one of Stieglitz's group whose paintings lay in storage: "There are vaults and vaults full of O'Keeffes and Marins and Doves, not to say that practically all my own work is there. So you are not alone," Stieglitz pointed out, and remarked that "as a matter of fact, you are in very good company, a true aristocrat and aristocracy comes high in the U.S.A."[8]

Hartley the aristocrat received Stieglitz's long letter on February 24; the next day he sat down in his hotel room and wrote his friend an even lengthier letter than usual. "Yesterday was an eventful day of singular and I am willing to say very special significance to me," he began, "and I was obliged to bring together all the forces there are in me to appreciate them at their true value, and I do not mean by any means to imply that any sense of struggle was involved, merely a need of adjustment." He had that day completed the last of his obligation to the Griffin syndicate. While he would miss the guaranteed income, he was relieved to be released from the arrangement, the only time in his life that he had such obligations placed on him: "I am now free to perish or survive and in view again of all that I have experienced I seem to feel that a way is still possible to be found, to survive." He claimed that much more on his mind was Stieglitz's letter, "an achievement in spiritual beauty" for which he had "only words of unqualified praise."

Throughout the letter, Hartley kept returning to Henry McBride's criticism, which was in fact less harsh than he perceived it to be. The critic simply had not admired Hartley's French mountains, finding them "disappointingly academic" while praising the works' colors and the still lifes.[9] "That the exhibition from the stranger's point of view may be considered a failure is easy to surmise," Hartley wrote, because it was not "à la mode from the New York point of view." He had expected McBride not to be pleased, and it did not matter, "excepting to a very few individuals." "I read something of his to the effect that the landscapes were academically disappointing," he continued, observing not quite logically that "he is logically not the one to be disappointed[;] it is I who have that right and it is I who am most legitimately disappointed, because I couldn't pull off pure realism, which I would give one eye to be able to do."

Hartley argued that expatriatism should not be an issue; American artists who traveled abroad did so to find an atmosphere more compatible with their interests. What did it matter where they painted? Except that it did, of course — not only because of the essential bond between the artist and his subject but because of his audience's expectations. Chauvinistic or not, Americans looked for native subjects in landscapes by American artists, and paintings of Vence would only be compared — usually unfavorably — to those by French artists.

He defended at length "the privilege of experimentation" and praised Stieglitz, O'Keeffe, and the Strands for their fineness and goodness in standing by him. They might understand his search for place, something that had plagued him for many years. He was sure there was an answer to his predicament, but the question was, "if and when I return as the punished and penitent prodigal, just where I would have to go to find the inevitable and final way out?" It could not be New England; he had learned that when visiting Maine the previous summer. Maine was "the country that taught me how to endure pain, and it is the country that has spiritually denied me thrice so to speak" — a reference to his distant relationships with his parents and his general disaffection with New England.

Despite any assertions to the contrary, Hartley was deeply wounded by McBride's review. He rapidly became convinced that this was a critical moment in his career. Soon he was writing to Rebecca Strand that the review was a "vicious and vulgar article . . . as cheap a piece of journalism as has been pulled off in years." He could not believe McBride had descended so low.[10] To Adelaide Kuntz he commented that the critic had "now seen fit to spew forth vicious publicity on the expatriates," which was "simply too filthy for words." No sooner had he swallowed McBride's opinions than he heard "from the very curb-stones of Paris" — in the person of a woman recently back from the United States — that the talk was that he had slipped terribly in his painting over the last four years.[11] He complained bitterly about this statement, which was rumored to have come straight from the Inti-mate, even from Stieglitz's own lips. Hartley wanted to believe that Stieglitz had only repeated, not begun, the insult. But even that judg-ment soon became, in his mind, "an after all not so important truth," because, he wrote, "modern history is witness to the fact that nearly everyone is up and down. Picasso has just added the worst exposition of stupidity in all his variable and not so brilliant career as it would now seem by his last summer's work at Dinard." André Derain like-wise was contributing daily to his own "magnificent downfall," and almost every other artist "had signed his death warrant some time ago." Hartley claimed that Emily Dickinson's axiom "After great pain, a formal feeling comes" helped to calm him in the face of what he termed "the treacherous spirit of New York that all of us have to encounter."

He was hardly calm, but he was beginning to work his way through the dilemmas he faced: whether to return to the United States or not; develop some plan to finance himself or not; care about French art or not; move toward realism and intellectualism in his art or not. The process would take him several years, and the questions would not really be resolved until the mid-1930s, when he visited Nova Scotia. Meanwhile, in the spring of 1929, he reached a conclusion that had to have been partly a rationalization: French art was dead, and there was little value in his being around it any longer, so he would return to America by choice and work at nativist painting, which might have more appeal to the art-buying public.

He was riddled with conflicting emotions, but soon he was deter-mined to overcome what he told Rebecca Strand were "exceedingly sour trials" and "simple stinking fish on the shores of a foul sea."[12] It is easy to imagine him seated either in his hotel room in Paris or, by

midspring, in the Maison Maria, dashing off a poem that helped to
sustain him:

> The eagle wants no friends,
> employs his thoughts to other ends —
> he has his circles to inscribe
> twelve thousand feet from where
> the fishes comb the sea,
> he finds his solace in unscathed
> immensity,
> where eagles think, there is no need
> of being lonesome —
> In isolation
> is a deep revealing sense
> of home.[13]

Isolation had always been a sort of home for him, and now he would
take advantage of it to try to find order and some kind of peace.

Disappointed at the results of the exhibition, he was nonetheless not
entirely surprised, as resistance to his work was hardly new. Even
before he heard from Stieglitz about the show, he wrote to Rebecca
Strand that he must change things if he wanted ever to sell his pictures.
No more large canvases; small paintings were "more to the point," he
acknowledged, particularly if he was going to have to store many of
them. And he announced that he was working with a new technique,
one similar to that used for glass painting. The effect, he claimed, made
it seem "almost as if the objects are seen through windows or by mirror
reflection." Continuing a theme he had been expressing for some time
now, he told Strand that he used "no blacks — no violent contrasts,"
with the result that he was achieving "almost selfless painting." His
consuming ambition was "to remove all trace of 'inwardness'" and to
"have the image revealed as an immediate experience & not by thought
or reflective processes." Paris was "so over run with personal painters"
that it was sickening. Nature should be the clue, and life the inspiration, as with the Chinese, or Pissarro and Maillol. Surrealist painting
was "*somnambuliste,*" he asserted; it was now no more than a worn-
out movement whose aims had already been attained by Kandinsky
and Klee.[14]

Hartley was buoyed to hear from Stieglitz in March that Duncan

Phillips had in fact bought a still life for $1,000, and, soon after, that a Mr. Hunt Henderson of New Orleans had purchased a small Vence painting for $500.[15] Now he could believe that a few Americans appreciated his work after all, which made it easier for him to announce that he would return to the United States at the end of the year.[16] Once back, he would begin a campaign for himself. No more French landscapes would be shown; he did not want to give the likes of Henry McBride ammunition to use against him. He looked forward to the challenge of reestablishing himself, he declared to Rebecca Strand, and of creating a "sense of organization." William Carlos Williams had once called him a "painter who writes," Hartley noted; perhaps now he would be published "as the writer who paints." He maintained that he would do "whatever the thing calls for — teach — lecture — write — or metaphysically speaking, dance in the prevailing dervish in whatever form it may take."[17]

On the same day that he wrote Strand, he composed a letter to Stieglitz defending his stay in Paris. It had taught him much, he said, about contemporary French art — which was uninspired at best — and about the art market and how to use it to one's advantage. In Paris there was "nothing but money talk"; artists turned out works as fast as they could, dead though the results were. He had learned from all this and now would "put on whatever league boots are necessary & see what kind of a magic stride I can make for myself."[18] These brave words promised more than the introverted artist could possibly accomplish, but they were enough to sustain him during the summer of 1929, before he sailed for the United States.

Having made the decision to return to America, Hartley seemed remarkably relaxed once he returned to Provence early in May. He painted no more landscapes, restricting himself instead to still lifes and to writing and reading, his aim being to develop a new style of existence that would permit him to get free of himself. "How hard it is to escape the feeling that anything is important — that oneself is important — that expression is important," he remarked to Rebecca Strand that summer. He puzzled over why people felt compelled to achieve and observed that "the trouble with artists is . . . they are so willfully oblique and trust implicitly in their ego-eccentricity to get them through." In Paris the previous winter he had got a stomachful of their self-centeredness, to the point where he believed that the expression of self was useless. In an effort to comprehend all this he had begun reading philosophers and mystics such as Santayana, Miguel Una-muno, and Sainte Thérèse of Lisieux, "the 23 yr. old girl who died and literally went to heaven." He enjoyed "the radiant shine of the mystics" such as Sainte Thérèse, Böhme, Ruysbroeck, and Eckhardt, who seemed to him to "take on the light they believe in just as . . . Fra Angelico did in his painting."[19]

As the summer progressed he read more and more of Santayana. After he finished *Platonism and the Spiritual Life,* he asked Adelaide Kuntz to send him others of the philosopher's essays. "Santayana seems made for the artist's requirements," he told her,[20] and in November, in a letter that was a kind of retrospection of his time in Provence, written just before he left for America, he praised a line of Santayana's about "'distinguish[ing] the edge of truth from the might of the imagination.'" This, Hartley thought, was "one of the finest appreciations" he had ever read; Santayana's work had helped him immensely. He was coming closer to being able to hold to "the edge of truth" by separating himself from his self-centered, if powerful, imagination: "I value myself less & less.... There are ideas far more important than oneself," he wrote elsewhere in the same letter.

He believed he had risen above "the worst defects of the [artistic] psychology" and was working toward a calm that came through accepting life as it was. "After all what is visible is all we can seem to know and the rest is left to romanticism & to ecstasy," he observed. He delighted in the mystics because of "their sense of certainty," though he himself was not specifically religious. What they wrote was "at least a romantic excursion into the souls of other beings" who had "found the living truth" for themselves — or so he remarked at about that time in an essay on Sainte Thérèse, whose mystical experience spoke "for the perfect sense of the relation of artistry to the religious function."[21]

In Hartley's view, reading the mystics enabled him to draw off his romantic imagination from what he perceived, allowing him to render the "edge of truth" about it without succumbing to the demands of "ego-eccentricity." Later, in 1931, he would move closer to religious belief and to an acceptance of the idea that the personal, if it was not merely self-centered, could become a valid part of "the edge of truth."

His reading and friendships consoled him during his last months in Provence: "I had an excellent summer — spiritually speaking," he told Stieglitz.[22] Knowing that he was about to depart a region he loved and relinquish a style of life whose relative calm pleased him as much as any life's could, he savored the time. He had become extremely close to Adelaide Kuntz, whose husband, Charles, had died after a motorcycle accident in 1927. She lived near the Maison Maria, and Hartley saw her frequently. She understood him, admired his work, even looked after him from time to time. Among other friends he saw Glenway Wescott and Monroe Wheeler, who were visiting in Aix, and Frank Davison, whom he stayed with in Villeneuve les Avignon. In May he ran across the American poet Hart Crane in Marseilles. Crane, who was prone to aggressively stalk sailors, was a "nice boy but a little flagrant in his methods," Hartley informed Kuntz. He was lonely and sought out Hartley after their first chance meeting, but the latter "couldn't cope with [Crane's] private hysteria for long." They discussed Crane's poem "The Bridge" when they first met and the next time watched a water carnival in the Marseilles harbor, but Crane's impulsive, frantic nature made Hartley uncomfortable, even though he liked the man.[23]

He willed himself to be pleased about returning to the United States, even declaring that he had "never once stepped off my own soil" because "you don't transpose a New Englander." Nevertheless, it was a wrench to leave Provence. "I have lived perfect days here — because they have been the most reasonable days I have experienced," he told Stieglitz in November. Nothing defied him, nothing forbade him, nothing commanded him. He had been allowed to live, and it was "the sun & the incredible force of the light" that had permitted it. If he were to make a pilgrimage, it would be to Provence, "because my very tissues feel good here — it has nothing to do with Europe."[24] During the summer and autumn he wrote poems about Provence, their tone suggesting his calm and his love for the region, where when summer was done the mistral carried it out over the Mediterranean and transformed the land. With the advent of fall, no more did "the perdreaux skim above / the pungent gorse, / the newts and lizards seek / a lingering warmth of wall, / the junipers a multiplying blue, / [or] the cigales sing." In the hills around Aix solitude could be beautiful, and one could at least be "within" oneself and cease to be like "perishable blooms / of fruits and leaves —/ the thing upon the surface/ giving only shine/ from other superficial things" — which, variously shaped, filled up the mold of existence but were less than all it was.[25]

After packing up his belongings in November, storing some, and taking others and his dog to Frank Davison in Avignon, Hartley headed north by way of Toulouse, taking trips from there to the smaller towns of Albi and Montauban to see the work of Toulouse-Lautrec and Ingres. He spent Christmas and the first weeks of 1930 in London visiting Adelaide Kuntz, who had rented a place there for the winter. By late January he was in Paris, having his pictures framed, seeing a lot of Leo Stein, and renewing his friendship with Gertrude during a visit to 27 Rue de Fleurus. Then he traveled to Berlin and Hamburg before arriving at Bremen, whence he sailed on March 5, 1930, for the United States.[26]

12

Return of the Native
1930–1931

BEING IN NEW YORK exhilarated Hartley for a short while, despite his inclination to let the city discourage him. He basked in the memory of his "superb" visit to Germany, which had been "so full of love and warmth — I still feel all blanketed with it," he told Adelaide Kuntz, adding that he doubted that any other race understood so well "the value of the quality of love and affection in life."

He wanted to believe that it would be easy for him to reestablish himself, and announced that "New York has received me very graciously — and my return seems to be accepted on all sides with satisfaction." Two galleries had approached him about showing his work, while the editors of the *American Caravan* had asked for poems for possible inclusion in their next edition. After a short stay in a hotel, Hartley took rooms in a house in Brooklyn that belonged to a married sister of Alice Miriam, the fiancée of Arnold Rönnebeck's whom Hartley had known in Germany before her death. The situation was a good one; he was among friends and could feel relaxed living at 42 Livingston Street. Karl Dworak, the son of the owner, recalled that Hartley occasionally brought home sailors, men with whom he had a brief intimacy but little more. Dworak, intrigued by this man with unusual habits, went into his room once and got a surprise when what he thought was a cigarette lighter turned out to be a perfume bottle that sprayed him when he gave it a squeeze.

Hartley was extremely fond of Esther Pinch, another of Alice's sisters who also lived at the house. Like him, she was both an artist and a poet, and at one point he proposed to her, but she declined his offer.[1] It is hard not to see his proposal as an attempt to allay the basic loneliness he felt. Whatever bravado he displayed to Adelaide Kuntz was only skin deep; he understood that he would have to work hard to establish himself on the American art scene, and he had no great record of success.

He told Kuntz that there would be no showing of his work in 1930, as he knew he would have to produce new paintings before he could have a "big coming out ... the prima donna kind," such as he hoped for. But there were possibilities; he reported to Kuntz that John Marin had done well, receiving "$6000 for one water-colour and several others." He was aware that he was in competition with other painters. Not with relish exactly, but with assurance, he declared that Georgia O'Keeffe had had a "poor year & for obvious reasons because she must have a re-birth in order to live in the world's eye. Her introvert's story is told." He added that "when she attempts extraversion she is as feeble as a child of premature birth. All that is good for her," he remarked with a touch of condenscension.[2]

It galled him that Marin and O'Keeffe could have more success than he, the more cosmopolitan, international figure, in his estimation. He could put on a brave front even for someone like Adelaide Kuntz but at the same time fret terribly and let an offhand remark of Rebecca Strand's undo him. "I am ill," he proclaimed dramatically to Stieglitz in mid-April, several days after she said something that wounded him. Although he continually insisted that he did not want to burden anyone with his emotional distress, he would do exactly that. He told Stieglitz that he believed he had "built up a spiritual and philosophical defense" against the things that might disturb him, but said that he now found his life more complex than usual: "someone has come into my life & wants to stay," he announced, referring to Esther Pinch, whose desire for permanency may have been less than he chose to think. Seeing this as a "new responsibility" that created problems was a way for Hartley to deflect his basic emotional fragility, as well as his grave uncertainty about being able to establish his Americanness.

"I feel so single handed and in reality so feeble minded with what surrounds and confronts me," he declared, recognizing that New York, American art, and the rush of friends were overwhelming him, as always.[3] Soon, however, he felt well enough to write to Stieglitz that he would "live and have being again." His doctors, "Descartes, Spinoza, Unamuno," had proved to him that where there was faith, there was hope. He was struggling for equanimity, but as usual it was difficult to find. He made his peace with Rebecca Strand, who probably never sensed the depth of his hurt and cheerily continued to type manuscripts for him. "O star of my precarious East!/ Thou shalt have a wreath of hummingbirds' fancies for thy hair," he wrote to her in hyperbolic thanks for her work.[4]

He undertook to write about artists and America after learning of the suicide of Jules Pascin on June 20, a death that had particular meaning for him both because Pascin was a fellow artist who had despaired of life and because while he was referred to as American, he was really a man of two countries, France and the United States. After viewing an exhibition of American art at the Museum of Modern Art, Hartley took the occasion of Pascin's death to consider the Americanness of the work of Thomas Eakins, Winslow Homer, and Albert Pinkham Ryder. At issue was the "integral quality that is supposed to constitute a basis for a real and vital American art." Reflecting his own concern, he asserted that the prejudice of the moment was that to be an American artist, "one must live, move, and have one's entire being in the strictly American atmosphere." Was this a valid criterion? Not precisely, he argued, citing the example of these three artists, who, while having something in common, were distinctly different. There was no one *American* quality to their work. What made art important was the concept of truth that emerged from a work — or Cézanne's essences, to put it another way. For Hartley, the documentary quality that made a painting "American" mattered little; what counted was the expression of "the qualities of life as it is and the essential truths of experience — experience unembellished and unadorned."[5]

Hartley's volatile moods continued, fueled by the general uncertainty of his situation. He wrote to Norma Berger in late May that things were very bad for him, both financially and psychologically. Slights, imagined and real, were much on his mind, and in that state he discussed getting his affairs in order, which included making arrangements for what would happen after his death. When Berger immediately wrote back, in some distress, Hartley replied adamantly, "I wish to be cremated and I want the dusty residue scattered to the winds wherever convenient and in *no case whatever* to be deposited in the family plot in Riverside Cemetery at Lewiston Maine." He strictly forbade his burial there, explaining that he had "nothing but the unhappiest memories of that place and all it means." He did not want one atom of himself left in an environment where he never had had nor could have repose.[6]

More than anything else, Hartley was distressed by what he perceived to be Stieglitz's lukewarmness toward his work. He simply did not care for it, Hartley told the Lachaises in June.[7] His explanation was that Stieglitz was not well and felt "much antagonism from the outer world." Stieglitz thought, Hartley went on, that the work done in France was "too foreign" for An American Place, his new gallery.

Hartley's response was to return to New England for the summer of 1930 — not to Maine this time, but rather to New Hampshire, where friends had suggested he might find a good area for painting west of the White Mountains, near Franconia. Hartley hired a young Polish man to drive him and serve as a kind of assistant for the summer, and the two set off for Franconia. The wealthy man with whom they first stayed after they arrived in town sent them out with his superintendent to find a house. They soon located one; its windows were broken and it was full of debris and much in need of repair, but it was satisfactory once they cleaned it up. The place was near such famous spots as Crawford Notch and Echo Lake, and the country was beautiful, but Hartley immediately chafed against his memories of New England, and almost as immediately against the summer tourists who flooded into the region. Wild animals ate out of refuse baskets or were killed by the automobiles that crowded the roads; hotels and boardinghouses filled the little town nearby, and nature was so domesticated that one had to pay to see it. Still, he could hope for September and October, when the landscape would be splendid and free of tourists, who during the summer would sometimes literally peer over his shoulder as he tried to paint a mountain scene.[8]

He was anxious to paint enough canvases so that Stieglitz could have an impressive exhibition the following winter. His work from this period, in which he meant to carry through with the effects he had created in the paintings he did around Aix, is for the most part lacking in inspiration. There was no Mont Sainte-Victoire for him to paint; the New Hampshire mountains had none of its dramatic flair, or even that of the Bavarian Alps or Mount Katahdin in Maine. This, along with the commercialism of the region, Hartley's inability to get along well with his Polish assistant, and a drought that dulled the fall colors, contributed to making his painting workmanlike, often pleasantly colorful, but less striking than he wished. He seemed to be cautious, unsure of himself, and searching for, rather than asserting, what he felt about nature. His paintings of rocks in a river, backed by trees, though invested with deep color, lack the focal point of a monumental rock or some other compelling shape. Even the mountain paintings, such as *Mountain Number 14*, consist largely of blockish shapes of small trees and bushes in primary colors in the foreground, with horizontal bands of color behind them and, as background, the deep purple shape of a mountain that is high but less dramatically contoured than Mont Sainte-Victoire. The foreground, not the mountain, dominates the picture, which has none of the intriguing form — or the two-dimensionality — of the work he would do the following year. He had not yet found his new mountains, nor a landscape that would draw out his distinctive — and American — vision.

Even so, he created some strong art during this period, most often when he sought out-of-the-way locales. He would hike along difficult trails to find the scene he wanted to paint, almost as if the effort assuaged some puritanical sense that good things could come only after hard work. Certainly the difficulty of the hike was a reminder of nature's ruggedness. A painting such as the one he did of Kinsman Falls, near Franconia, conveys the force of nature in its rendition of rocks and rushing water against a dark background of trees, while his somber green and black picture of a mountain behind Beaver Lake does away with nearly all horizontals in the foreground, so that the mountain fills the canvas as an icon, an object in itself rather than merely part of a larger landscape. When Hartley moved on to paint in Dogtown, behind Gloucester, and in the Bavarian Alps during the next years, he would use this technique again and again, and as a result emphasize the iconographic qualities of natural objects.

Little about New Hampshire pleased him as the summer wore on, and even a trip to Montreal was no help. By October, when it was apparent that the fall would not be a spectacular one in terms of foliage, he was moping to Stieglitz about his condition and the difficulty of living with someone else. The Polish man lacked the sensibility that Hartley wished for; only Carl Sprinchorn, in fact, had been a suitable companion, when he and Hartley had lived together fifteen years earlier. All this weighed on Hartley as he tried to finish his paintings, some of which he would not be able to complete until he was back in Brooklyn.[9]

By mid-November he was more depressed than he had been earlier in the fall. He did not return to the Dworak residence, but instead settled into a room at the Hotel Pierrepont in Brooklyn, after another place proved unsatisfactory. "I don't know how I am going to get through this," he wrote to Stieglitz as he worried anew about finances and his artistic reputation. He despaired because he continued to be a millstone around Stieglitz's neck and at that moment wondered why he should go on. "It would be so easy to settle it all," he declared dramatically, "loathing and despising" himself for the troubles he had caused his friend, who was also suffering from depression. Hartley was spending much of his time in bed right then, hoping that he might restore his energies but knowing that his illness was as much psychological as it was physical.[10]

Doubts about his New Hampshire paintings added to his moroseness, much of which stemmed from the "American" issue and also, quite apart from that, his awareness that critics felt he had achieved nothing of a high order in recent years. One of these, Samuel M. Kootz, writing in 1930, chose to include as examples of Hartley's work a pair of New Mexico landscapes of 1923 and 1925 and two still lifes from the twenties. Apparently on the basis of these works, Kootz asserted that Hartley had "never developed into the high levels his early work promised. Informed with taste, a certain daintiness and acceptable coloring, his work never flares with genius." Damning Hartley with faint praise, the critic allowed that he "steadily maintains a decent level." Citing Hartley's 1928 piece "Art — and the Personal Life," Kootz faulted him for having renounced "personal art" and the "life of the imagination." In his opinion, Hartley had never dared to let go, to paint anything other than "acceptable" pictures. "A Hartley who could conceivably be spiritually indelicate would be highly welcome in America's painting ranks," he concluded.[11]

No matter that Hartley would seem to have painted a great many unacceptable pictures; judgments such as Kootz's stood. Hartley believed, therefore, that his next show would have to demonstrate that he had not lost his ability. The inclusion of three of his paintings in a large exhibition of living American painters and sculptors at the Museum of Modern Art, in December 1930 and January 1931, would not suffice, especially because one of these was a German-officer painting from years before and the other two were still lifes from the twenties, not major works.

More significant was the show Stieglitz mounted at An American Place in mid-December, which consisted of still lifes Hartley had done in France in the twenties and his New Hampshire landscapes. "Marsden Hartley's Comeback," Henry McBride entitled his review of the show, which he declared represented "the return of a prodigal son." Typically, McBride emphasized the American quality of the better work, assuring his readers that "Americans can go to see the show without any sense of incongruity.... [Although there are still some European pictures,] the American pictures decidedly overtop them. It is distinctly of a case of America uber alles." So pleased was he that he even credited the New Hampshire paintings with having in them the emotion of "the rock-bound shores and austere hills of Maine."[12] Edward Alden Jewell based his review for the *New York Times* on Hartley's 1928 statement about art and the personal life, and seemed relieved that the artist's work reflected a more personal sense than the essay espoused. Nonetheless, he was ambivalent about the new work.[13] The reviewer for *Art News* celebrated Hartley's return to color after the alternating gloom and too-bright tones of his twenties landscapes. The still lifes Stieglitz had chosen to show were "neat and vigorous," he reported, while the landscapes reminded him of much earlier work of Hartley's, such as the German-officer painting at MOMA.[14]

Hartley's relative success with this exhibition served to cheer him early in 1931 during an attack of bronchitis that was so severe as to be life-threatening. Adelaide Kuntz came to his small apartment every day to nurse him, giving him medicine and feeding him until he began to recuperate. When he could, he wrote to Stieglitz that he had heard from the Downtown Gallery that they had received eleven pictures from him, which they planned to exhibit later. Several of the best from the exhibition he was wary about releasing: two waterfalls, a black landscape, and a large still life with two fish in it. Clearly he sensed which were the best of this lot. The Newark Museum had also asked for several paintings from which to make a selection, a request that pleased him.[15]

If Hartley had not exactly burst back onto the art scene in America, he had at least been recognized sufficiently that he felt encouraged to go on, albeit with a sense of life's vicissitudes. Before being taken so ill in January he had written to Harriet Monroe, the editor of *Poetry,* to inform her that he was composing a "series of poetic tabloids of New York city," which he thought might be appropriate for an announced

objectivist number of *Poetry* — "as all art is for obvious reasons swinging back to reality," he explained, adding that he himself had "returned
to objective nature in painting during the past four years." He reported
that "much ado has been made about the 'return of the prodigal.'"
Paintings of his had been taken by the Cleveland, Whitney, and Columbus museums. He did not send the poems on then. When Monroe
answered, in March, he responded immediately, again mentioning the
poems he wanted to show her and announcing that he had received a
Guggenheim Fellowship for the following year. He noted that four of
his poems had just appeared in *American Caravan*. Three were collected under the title "From a Paris Window — High," and a fourth
was called "Corniche — Marseilles"; all were gentle odes to the two
French cities he most admired. "How certain," he wrote in the last
one, "that the morning is a myth/ to [islands off the shore], and night,/
a casual theorem of conceit/ where thoughtlessness of thought/ can
never intervene/ within the geodetic scene," echoing what he believed
then about the relationship between man's imagination and objective
nature.[16] Things such as islands are geodetic forms, he meant, and
human concepts such as time — morning and night — hold no meaning for them. They endure beyond our imaginings, without thought,
without dreams. But still the poet — or artist — can render them, and
though they are fictions, the renderings have meaning for the human
eye and mind.

Encouraged by these small successes, Hartley soon mailed Monroe
eight poems, six of which he grouped together under the title "Tomp-
kins Square Tabloids." Two of these would be published the following
spring.[17] Heartened, he began to gather new strength; he read even
more voraciously than usual and in what he read found new definition
for himself. The French author Paul Valéry wrote, in his *Treatise on
Leonardo,* "There is no act of genius that is not less than an act of
being"; this was what he lived for, Hartley told Stieglitz. Without such
a philosophic equation, a painting could have nothing but "emotional
and technical vapidities." "To attain to a state of being is the work of a
man," he continued, "and no artist need flatter himself he has arrived
or will arrive until he has projected some degree or other of this condition.... The complete annihilation of personality is the only hope of
a human being, certainly of any artist," he concluded.[18] Valéry and
Santayana were Hartley's staples at that moment, as he strove for spiritual certainty as a way of coping with what seemed to him a very

uncertain existence, filled with continuing worry inspired by what he called "the up & down pattern of N.Y. life — the only city without horizon in the world."[19] But things were good enough now that he could think it humorous when a member of the Guggenheim family came over to him at a cocktail party for the fellowship recipients and congratulated him on the beautiful and interesting novel he had recently written.[20]

His worries would not be solved anytime soon, but he was about to find an answer to his search for landscapes that were appropriate to what he wanted to express in his painting. His Guggenheim award carried with it the stipulation that he must spend it out of the country. He decided to go to Mexico, but before doing so he wanted to visit Gloucester, where he had spent much of a summer eleven years earlier. He had not admired the scenery of the harbor or the town's "arty" crowd, but he remembered an area in the hills behind it, called Dogtown, which he thought might help prepare him for Mexico. Still weak from and somewhat unnerved by his illness of the spring and the worries of city life, he traveled by boat from New York to Gloucester in the latter part of June and immediately took rooms in the same boardinghouse where he had stayed in 1920, located at 1 Eastern Point Road.

Perhaps it was the new friendships he made in Gloucester, or his pleasure at receiving a warmly affectionate postcard from Gertrude Stein, and certainly it had something to do with the relief he felt when his hearing, which had worsened badly during the winter, began to come back — whatever it was, the place was as satisfying as New Hampshire the previous summer had been disappointing. The result was an outpouring of painting and poetry that marked the beginning of Hartley's greatest sustained period of creativity.

At the center of it in 1931 was Dogtown: "I go every day to 'Dogtown' which is one of the most ancient settlements in the U.S.," Hartley wrote to Adelaide Kuntz in mid-July, and "a very strange stretch of landscape it is." He likened it to the landscape of the Yorkshire moors he had once visited as a child with his father, the mood of which was like that of Emily Brontë's *Wuthering Heights*. The place was "full of magnificent boulders driven & left there by the glacial pressure ages ago."[21] Almost no one went there, so "a sense of eeriness pervades all the place ... and the white ghosts of those huge boulders — mostly granite — stand like sentinels guarding nothing but space," he wrote in his memoir. "Sea gulls fly over it on their way from the marshes to the sea. Otherwise the place is forsaken and majestically lovely as if nature had at last formed one spot where she can live for herself alone." He called it a "cross between Easter Island and Stonehenge"; to appreciate it required "someone to be obsessed by nature for its own sake, one with a feeling for the austerities and the intellectual aloofness which lost lonesome areas can persist in."[22]

He knew this was a spot from which he could draw sustenance and artistic inspiration, even if he had "to return to memory painting as in former years." It was a long way from his boardinghouse to Dogtown, and he did not have the strength to carry his painting materials that distance. He would either ride a bus and get as close to the area as he could or else walk the entire way; then, often as not, he would sit for hours absorbing one scene or another and sketching it on a board in the briefest of fashions. He would indicate the primary colors in the sketch, but the scene would later take shape chiefly from his memory, after he had digested the essences of the landscape.[23]

Those whom Hartley scoffingly referred to as the "artists" of Gloucester never trudged back into Dogtown "because it is so unrelated to cults and tricks and monuments," he wrote to Stieglitz. Although it offered "the fake modernists nothing," he said, it would have stirred the likes of Courbet or Ryder. By mid-August Hartley had five paintings under way, small but intense works, he was sure, which would establish him as "the" painter of Dogtown — granted that few enough people strove for that title. Once again he believed that he was experiencing a rebirth: "It may prove this summer to be general resurrection-revelation — evolution out of revolution I am wanting to phrase it," he declared. It was "emotion contained — 'art condensed not diluted' as Degas puts it," he told Stieglitz.[24]

Stimulated by Dogtown, he read widely: memoirs, the short stories of the New England author Sarah Orne Jewett, T. S. Eliot's poetry and that of Gerard Manley Hopkins, as well as his by then usual quotient of mystics and philosophers. Jewett in particular helped him to set his own New England experiences in the context of nature. Her poignant tales about the harsh and isolated life in Maine moved him deeply, and he began to see more and more clearly that the land and its people could be the subject of art as well as of scorn. Eliot's poem "Ash Wednesday," published in 1930, struck a central chord in him. He understood the other poet's search for meaning in faith:

> This is the time of tension between dying and birth
> The place of solitude where three dreams cross
> Between blue rocks

So wrote Eliot in the last section of the poem, which Hartley may have read as he sat among the boulders of Dogtown. Soon he would pick up on other lines from the section and write them on the back of one of his memory paintings of Dogtown, which he titled *In the Moraine, Dogtown Common:*

> Teach us to care and not to care
> Teach us to sit still
> [Even] among these rocks

"I paint rocks & rocks only," he wrote to his friend the artist Florine Stettheimer, adding that he had put the lines from Eliot's poem on the back of a painting. The poem served him "as a kind of biblical motto," he observed, "for it is what I am trying to practice in my life just now. To care magnificently — & equally not to care — in the same [manner] — Precept enough don't you think for one [tame] life."[25]

Dogtown and the poetry of others inspired him to write as well as paint. On the back of another painting done that fall, *Flaming Pool, Dogtown, 1931,* he inscribed a poem that he called "Beethoven (in Dogtown)":

> Deep chested trills arise —
> from organ pipes of juniper
> Oboe's throat expands — mezzo cries
> of blueberry and sage and ferns prefer
> to die among the rocks, nobly perish
> mire of torrid green —
> Summer's strident blades of damascene
> hot tone or here is garish
> the vox human swells and dwells
> Persistently mid nuances of lapis grey
> So much more wonderful this way
> than summer in a trance
> of chlorophyll or other circumstance.[26]

Later he would expand the poem and call it "Soliloquy in Dogtown, Cape Ann." While that version is longer and its images are perhaps more powerful, the first version conveys the grand sense of calm and closeness to nature that Hartley strove for. Other places and things around Gloucester also moved him: he wrote about brown gulls and Wingaersheek Beach to the west of Dogtown. The observer described in the poem about the gulls realizes that "the work of his mind was made/ of seeing mostly, believing that what there is/ to see is so much more than what there is/ to hear."[27] New England was taking on new meaning for Hartley, becoming the subject of art rather than of anger.

It was a slow process, though, because he had to sort out his memories of Maine and his family and resolve the enduring struggle between his need for solitude and his enjoyment of people — on his own terms. Solitude had become less attractive to him; it had been forced on him when he was young, and he had imagined that he could stand it, he wrote to Adelaide Kuntz from Gloucester, but now he did not seem to be able to stand it at all. Earlier there had been "faith & hope and a certain desire . . . all that has been gone through — registered & duly placed. . . . I am much more humanized than I was in those earlier times and I need the warmth of someone I care for near me."[28]

The necessity of being American grated on him also. He wrote to Gertrude Stein that he had been "home" for more than a year, "and for the life of me with all the will in the world I can only say *pour quoi* save that you know there was a movement against the American artists living out of the U.S. and they would have starved me out otherwise." He felt like a political prisoner because he was not supposed to leave, even though American life was uninteresting to him. The result was that he went around with blinders on, looking neither left nor right. The psychology of this situation was curious: he was a "natural *paysagiste* and the only thing I'll ever know is this landscape — whereas humanly my sense of diversions is patterned in the European style."[29]

As the summer wore on he found good companionship in Gloucester. He moved from the boardinghouse to a place on Rocky Neck, a small peninsula jutting out into Gloucester Harbor, on which there was an artists' colony. Soon he met the painter Helen Stein and some of her artist friends and so began to have the human contact he craved. Stein understood and liked him and was willing to put up with his moods and his distaste for anyone he did not find interesting. They were together constantly; they walked on Wingaersheek Beach, saw movies together and with friends of hers, and often had meals at her place, gossiping about others among the Gloucester art colony, most of whom Hartley disapproved of. She enjoyed his banter and appreciated his loyalty to her, even if frequently it took the form of jealousy when she paid attention to other Gloucester artists whom he did not like for one reason or another.[30]

"It has been a curious summer, indeed, the interval between the past and some sort of future," Hartley wrote to Carl Sprinchorn at the beginning of September. He talked of having to "practice peace" as often as he could because he was so tired, especially from the tensions created by his having returned from Europe. He felt driven in on himself — which meant being private — but he could tolerate that if he must, and he would learn to make a work of art out of it. "I am clearing my mind of all art nonsense, trying to accomplish simplicity and purity of vision for Life itself," he asserted. It is apparent from this letter that Hartley was consciously trying to structure his life in ways he had not done before. More than ever, he had a sense of his own mortality; he was, after all, fifty-four, and his illness of the previous winter had been extremely severe. Also, his return from Europe demanded that he take stock of his situation, and then the particular effect of Dogtown, in conjunction with his readings in mystical and religious literature, seemed to be moving him toward a clearer "vision for Life itself": "I am trying to return to the earlier conditions of my inner life — and take out of experience as it has come to me in the intervening years that which has enriched it — and make something of it more than just intellectual diversion," he explained. What he was trying to do was "the equivalent of what the religious minded do when they enter a monastery or a convent and give up all the strain and ugliness of Life itself." Not that he would actually retire from life, but he wanted to get some distance between himself and it, to learn, as Eliot wrote, "to care and not to care."[31]

During the summer and fall he worked at defining some sort of understanding, if not faith, that would enable him to achieve the equanimity he tried to describe to Sprinchorn. "I have no recourse to superimposed faiths or beliefs to fool myself with into thinking that what is is all right," he wrote to his niece in late July. "What [an awful] thing it is — this indomitable will to live," he declared, "and it is the body that persists when the mind sees through it all too acutely. Faith does not increase with experience if experience comes through thought."[32] He was continuing his readings in religious literature, telling Adelaide Kuntz in November that he needed to become better informed about

the Bible, "unfortunately not for religious expansion as I could wish —
for I'd really love to have a consuming faith in something — but alas,
I guess I am a typical skeptic of the epoch. I just don't know and
therefore can't say." He also ventured beyond the Bible; when he wrote
to Kuntz he had just finished reading about Saint Thérese of Lisieux.[33]

Things were coming together for Hartley under the influence of
Dogtown. In another letter to Kuntz that fall he informed her that he
wanted to dedicate a book of his poetry to her. As with his painting,
the poems were "to have the emotions *beneath the pattern* as sharply as
possible."[34] It was a matter of reconstruction, he told Rebecca Strand
at the end of September. "I have laid new principles of life for myself,"
he claimed, "and have given up old forms and concepts." He hoped to
rid himself of "all aesthetic baggage [in favor of] something richer and
deeper." He believed that this would show in his new paintings; he
wanted them to be "painted sculpture & no ordinary painting and I
think they mostly are. I feel as if I am casting off a wearisome chrysalis
& hope to emerge a clearer and more logical and consequent being,"
he announced, noting that he had "read deeply this summer — felt &
thought deeply — & written deeply."[35]

As the beautiful fall colors poured over him, he felt he was being
baptized into a new faith. Dogtown offered him "psychic liberty," as
had Provence and the Southwest, so he went back into the lonely
terrain every afternoon, making drawings for further paintings. The
colors were unique, he reported to Kuntz. They were "the closest to
the analogy of music" that he had ever seen, and he was relieved that
nature was "at last being thoroughly original again." He was sure he
was the only painter to give all his attention to "this extraordinary
stretch of almost metaphysical landscape — it cannot appeal to dull
painters because it calls for deep contact and study and I am capable of
both, and while my pictures are small — they are more intense than
ever before, and I have for once (again) immersed myself in the mysticism of nature."[36]

That he had, and he would continue to do so for the rest of his life,
with noteworthy success as he came to discover a kind of faith that
enabled him to make art from adversity and from the harshness and
stolidness that he felt to be inherent in nature. Place, after all, was
intensely important, but not in a superficial way. Rather, what mattered was what he told Kuntz he was striving for: "the emotions *beneath the pattern*." Both early and late in his career Hartley tried to

The Warriors, 1913
oil on canvas, 47¾ × 47½ inches
The Regis Collection, Minneapolis

Landscape No. 16, 1909
oil on academy board,
11⅞ × 8⅞ inches
Private collection
Courtesy of Salander-O'Reilly
Galleries, Inc., New York

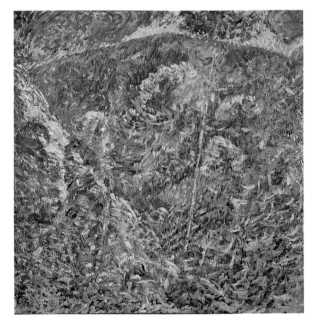

Winter Chaos, Blizzard, 1909
oil on canvas, 34 × 34 inches
Philadelphia Museum of Art,
Alfred Stieglitz Collection

Right:
Portrait of a German Officer, 1914
oil on canvas, 68¼ × 41⅛ inches
The Metropolitan Museum of Art,
New York, Alfred Stieglitz
Collection, 1949

New Mexico Recollection, No. 13, 1922–1923
oil on canvas, 30 × 40 inches
Sid Deutsch Gallery, New York

Above right:
Flaming Pool, Dogtown, 1931
oil on academy board, 18 × 24 inches
Yale Collection of American Literature,
Beinecke Rare Book and Manuscript Library,
Yale University, New Haven, Connecticut

Right:
Mountains in Stone, Dogtown, 1931
oil on board, 18 × 24 inches
Harvey and Françoise Rambach

Fishermen's Last Supper, 1940–1941
oil on board, 29⅞ × 41 inches
Roy R. Neuberger
Courtesy of Salander-O'Reilly Galleries,
Inc., New York

Above left:
Morgenrot, Mexico, 1932
oil on board, 25 × 23 inches
Babcock Galleries, New York

Left:
Alspitz-Mittenwald Road, circa winter 1933–34
oil on paper board, 17⅝ × 29¾ inches
Collection of the Santa Barbara Museum of Art,
Mrs. Sterling Morton for the
Preston Morton Collection

Summer, Sea, Window, Red Curtain, 1942
oil on fiberboard, 40 × 30 inches
Addison Gallery of American Art, Phillips Academy, Andover, Massachusetts

paint "not ideas about the thing but the thing itself," as the poet Wallace Stevens put it in a poem describing what he, like Hartley, was trying to achieve in his work. Dogtown had brought Hartley back to where he had earlier been. He was using locale to express broader issues, and the power of form and color to convey his sense of man's place in this world and the need for endurance. In one magnificent small painting, *Mountains in Stone, Dogtown,* the reds and yellows of bushes in autumn play against the light and dark grays of large boulders, while a cross-shaped tree, bare of branches and leaves, reaches into the sky and in the plane of the painting actually touches one of the two white clouds that stretch across a deep-blue sky. The scene transmits a sense of solitude and tranquillity but also of vitality and even of pleasure, because the colors pulsate, the heavy texture of the paint gives the picture a tactile quality, and the design of the forms has movement. The painting is full, not at all vacant, and just as the work of the abstract expressionists later would — Jackson Pollock's action paintings and the blocks of color filling Mark Rothko's canvases come immediately to mind — this substantially abstract work evokes a response more on its own terms than as a representation of literal nature.

For Hartley, nothing conveyed the impermanency of man more than the Whale's Jaw, an outcropping of rock at the north end of Dogtown Common. Split apart thousands of years before, the two parts of a boulder looked like the head of a whale as it broke from the water. The rock loomed over anyone who approached it, its shape a reminder of nature's power and age. Hartley knew his Melville; the Whale's Jaw was a keen reminder of Moby Dick's endurance — and of Ahab's finitude and futile egotism. The feebleness of man's assertions of self seemed especially poignant to Hartley when he came upon workers who at the behest of a local industrialist, Roger Babson, were chipping away at boulders in the Common in order to carve out words and phrases such as *Integrity, Study,* and *If Work Stops Values Decay.* Hartley knew his Shelley also, and these carvings, as well as the initials sculpted into the Whale's Jaw, dating back to 1891, reminded him of Ozymandias, the King of Kings, whose boastful words remained sculpted in the ruins of an immense statue long after his voice had been stilled.[37]

"It was a fine example of intuitive truth the coming here," Hartley wrote to Stieglitz as the fall wore on. He had done many things inwardly for himself, he knew, and had written enough poetry to fill a volume, all the while steeping himself in literature, especially about Mexico, where he was soon to go. He singled out a book, *Mexican Maze,* by Carleton Beals — long a resident of Mexico and writer about the country — which was full of "spiritual documentation" that interested him deeply in his present mood.[38] Near the middle of December he finally stopped painting, telling Rebecca Strand on the twelfth that he had cleaned his palette for the last time in 1931. "Finished the last picture thereby closing another epoch," he remarked, adding that he wished he could stay on in Gloucester because it took him so long to hit his stride in writing and painting. In any event he hoped to return in two years, as he wanted to do more Dogtown pictures; while he might paint from memory as he had in the past, he would prefer to be close to the place he now called his, the place he had "put . . . on the esthetic map."[39]

Having made arrangements to journey to Mexico with his nephew Clifton Newell, he returned to New York, where he spent Christmas and New Year's with Adelaide Kuntz. Sick part of the time with grippe and neuritis, he remained in the city until the end of February 1932, when he traveled to Cleveland to visit with family. Shortly after that, he and his nephew returned to the East Coast and boarded a ship for Vera Cruz. The trip was uneventful except for a violent storm that struck just as the ship was attempting to anchor in Progreso.

13

A Last Venture Out
Mexico and Germany
1932 – 1934

HAVING ARRIVED by train from Vera Cruz, Hartley was immediately enthusiastic about Mexico City: he felt "the excitement of the new beauty" as well as the effect of the high altitude, which would soon become a problem for him. In mid-March he could exclaim to Adelaide Kuntz, "What a lovely city and such people — so captivating — so winsome — so genteel — so polite and so full of character — every face is a copy of aztec sculpture." The first reaction was typical Hartley — excited, sure that he had found an ideal setting, and tending to romanticize his surroundings. Soon enough, however, he would change his mind, because Mexico — its landscape, its color, and its people, who had a mysticism quite different from that which he felt akin to — would come to seem overpowering, and he would feel alienated from the land, even though the painting he did there was powerfully symbolic and continuous with the rush of new inspiration that had begun in Dogtown. But unlike Dogtown (and his New England aesthetic), Mexico City was Latin, full of primary color, and loud. It was "all russet — silverish goldish stained with pale prime — and ascetic blue," he told Kuntz. There was great strength in the first art he saw, the Diego Rivera frescoes, and beyond the city, looming over it, were "the [two] volcanoes . . . superb in their perpetual whiteness." He planned to remain in the city for a few weeks and then find a place nearby.[1]

During his first weeks in Mexico City he visited the National

Museum frequently, studying sculptures from the Mayan and Aztec periods and even buying a Toltec mask made of jade and some Aztec fragments of terra cotta with the thought of painting them. They were, he reminded Kuntz, symbols of the people he saw on the streets, a vivid way of linking the land with its people. Soon he saw the paintings of José Orozco, which he found to be full of "beautiful dark brooding . . . a great return to the fullness of the inner world." He romanticized the Mexican peasants, claiming that they "will not be torn from their earth & there is something superb about it." Recounting a scene he observed from his hotel window, in which a peasant lay down on some papers at four in the morning and went to sleep, he declared that "the earth feeds him — warms him." During his first few weeks in Mexico, before he came to realize that such proximity of man to earth was too much for his New England sensibility to bear, he was temporarily transported by what he saw: "O these pyramids of Teotihuacan & the Temple of Quetzalcoatl," he exclaimed, "such nobility — really I am larger myself than I was for having caressed them with hand and eye" — referring to the ancient ruins he had visited, about thirty miles from Mexico City.[2]

Being in Mexico kept him from worrying too much about the reception of his work in New York. The Downtown Gallery had an exhibition of twenty of his Dogtown landscapes in April and May, titling the show "Pictures of New England by a New Englander." Edward Alden Jewell was quite complimentary in his short review of it in the *New York Times,* describing the pictures as "fragments fitted together, not with excessive neatness, the effect of the whole being curiously staccato and sometimes full of a kind of harsh, strange power."[3] When a friend sent him a copy of the review, Hartley at once responded that he thought Jewell had gotten "the key of the idea — and I am happy to register myself once again as a New England artist."[4] The show was a failure financially, but distance kept him from being distraught about that. He had, as he remarked, registered himself as a New England artist again, and that was at least as important to him as sales, given that his Guggenheim grant was keeping him solvent for the moment. As a foreword to the exhibition catalogue he had included a poem, "Return of the Native," which he had undoubtedly written in the euphoria of his time in Gloucester:

Rock, juniper, and wind,
and a sea gull sitting still —
all these of one mind.
He who finds will
to come home
will surely find old faith
made new again,
and lavish welcome.
Old things breaketh
new, when heart and soul
lose no whit of old refrain;
it is a smiling festival
when rock, juniper, and wind
are of one mind;
a sea gull signs the bond
makes what was broken, whole.[5]

If Hartley's return to the United States had not really been a "smiling festival," there was something of that about his first weeks in Mexico. A number of Americans, some of them Guggenheim grantees like himself, congregated frequently, and for a while he found the company stimulating. "There is a small group of quite interesting compatriots here which gathers occasionally at one or another of our houses," the poet Hart Crane wrote to a friend in late March from Mexico City. He named several other people as well as "Marsden Hartley, the painter, who has just arrived and who is wildly enthusiastic." In another letter Crane mentioned that Andrew Dasburg was also present, which meant Hartley had the chance to be among painters, writers, and academics with whom he felt comfortable.[6]

Chief among these was Crane himself. Having known him in France several years earlier — and liked him, though Crane's boisterous ways could distress the quieter man — Hartley quickly renewed their friendship, which involved long talks, strolls, and much listening and advising on Hartley's part as Crane tried to work through the depression that would surge up in him after his frequent drinking binges, which often as not landed him in a jail cell.

Despite the friendship of Hartley and others, Crane was on what his biographer has described as a "long downhill descent."[7] All sorts of things weighed on him: his drinking, his inability to finish the poetry he was writing, a convoluted relationship with his family, and, ultimately, his own erratic behavior in Mexico. Amid personal chaos he departed on April 24 for the United States aboard the S.S. *Orizaba,* accompanied by Peggy Cowley, who was his companion during his last months in Mexico and whom he intended to marry. Three days later, after further bizarre behavior, Crane stepped to the ship's railing at two minutes before noon. Clad in pajamas and an overcoat, which he threw off, he climbed over the railing and leapt into the ocean. Life preservers were immediately thrown to him, but he did not grab any of them, and no one in the four lifeboats that were lowered to search for him was able to find his body. Several people aboard ship claimed to have seen his hand above the waves for an instant; there was some debate as to whether he was clutching for a life preserver or waving goodbye.[8]

For Hartley, Crane's suicide was a severe blow, and it marked the beginning of his ambivalence toward Mexico. Not that he blamed it for Crane's death, exactly — but the poet's struggles and eventual demise were vivid reminders of his own depressions and his mortality, regardless of the fact that he clung to life, finally, as Crane had not. In the months that followed Hartley would write repeatedly about his friend, expressing his grief and attempting to analyze the reasons for Crane's suicide in three essays, a long poem, and finally a painting, *Eight Bells Folly.*

For Crane, "life was a dynamic thing," Hartley wrote in a memorial piece. He was "no cloistered intellectual," but rather a vital personality who was also a "blustering boisterous playmate." Finally, Hartley could not say what had driven Crane to kill himself. It was not his skirmishes with the police, which had usually ended up with everyone's drinking and singing together; and Crane was so talented that Hartley could not believe he had really killed himself because he thought he had no more to say. Hartley insisted that "he should have respected life, and the surging life in himself, [enough not to] destroy it" — a statement that reflected Hartley's own powerful drive to carry on, as well as his unwillingness to acknowledge the explanations others had suggested for Crane's despair, which came too close to his own fears. "It was the crazed decision of a moment," he concluded, adding that Mexico might have been "too terrific and stimulating for him." Hartley may have had a point, but he was speaking as much for himself as for Crane when he noted that Mexico was a "breath-taking country and literally takes the breath and demands new apparatus and new energy to cope with it." He had come quickly to understand that in that country there was a "constant flowing of strange and powerful energy from terribly powerful sources unhindered for centuries. . . . The people still believe in the majesty of the earth."[9]

"Un Recuerdo — Hermano — Hart Crane R.I.P." is a fine poem, and one of Hartley's longest. He knew Crane's work, including the major poem "The Bridge" and such beautiful lyrics as "Voyages," whose language, even more than is usual with poetry, is used in such an original way that it takes on new meanings.

> And yet this great wink of eternity,
> Of rimless floods, unfettered leewardings,
> Samite sheeted and processioned where
> Her undinal vast belly moonward bends,
> Laughing the wrapt inflections of our love

Crane wrote, describing the ocean in which he would one day drown.[10] For his memorial poem, Hartley adopted Crane's lyric style and used rhyme, as generally he did not. Moreover, the poem is consciously Whitmanesque in scope, tone, and theme, thus linking Crane — and Hartley — to the American poetic tradition of transcendental romanticism, as well as to the sweeping grandeur that Whitman achieved in such poems as his magnificent elegy to Abraham Lincoln, "When Lilacs Last in the Dooryard Bloom'd." Hartley's lamentation begins:

> And, should it be left like this,
> dear Hart, like this,
> too much of fulfillment, no more promise,
> given over petulantly, fevered,
> you the severing, we the severed,
> to wind-wash,
> wave-flow, wave-toss and thrash.

The poem gradually works its way through grief to a grudging acceptance of death. "Well so it is, and the bridge-end broken,/ creaked from its moorings," it concludes, drawing on the central image in Crane's greatest poem. Crane had "gone to the end of the bridge and over/ worn with roving the bridge, bridge rover,/ done with all the walking and the stalking,/ and all the cheap talking." In a short "Afterlude" a voice announces, "IT IS DEATH,/ IT IS DEATH, DEATH TO STAY, DEATH TO STAY,/ DEATH TO STAY, OR GO AWAY,/ IT IS DEATH ANYWAY," marking Hartley's acceptance of the inevitable.[11]

He did not write the essays and the poem, or paint the picture, immediately after Crane's drowning, but just as had the death of Karl von Freyburg, his friend's suicide stimulated Hartley's creativity. He began several symbolic paintings during the summer, and by the late fall of 1932 he could inform Adelaide Kuntz that he had six paintings under way, four small still lifes and two large works, one illustrating an Aztec legend about a great white bird, pierced with an arrow, that flew over the now-defunct city of Tollan, the other a "marine fantasy symbolic of Hart Crane's death by drowning." The latter canvas had a "very mad look" about it, he remarked, explaining that

> there is a ship foundering — a sun, a moon, two triangles, clouds — a shark pushing up out of the mad waters — and at the right corner — a bell with "8" on it — symbolizing 8 bells — or noon when he jumped off — and around the bell are a lot of men's eyes — that look up from below to see who the new lodger is to be — on one cloud will be the number 33 — Hart's age — and according to some occult beliefs [that] is the dangerous age of a man — for if he survives 33 he lives on — Christ was supposed to be 33 — on the other cloud will be 2 — the sum of his poetic product.

The painting, which is extremely powerful, is quite the way he described it, with the addition on the left cloud of two six-pointed stars, not the number 2, 6 being associated with ambivalence, equilibrium, and also hermaphroditism, all matters that were relevant to Crane himself as well as to his poetry. Hartley moved the number 33 to the ship's sail, added another 8 to a cloud, and placed the number 9 — the tripling of the triple, and thus a complete image of the body, mind, and spirit — in front of the shark.[12]

Mexico, as Hartley thought it might have done for Crane, took his breath away, and delighted though he had been with it when he first arrived, he became increasingly disenchanted as time passed. The land and the people had an effect on him that he had not expected. Dogtown had inspired him to paint directly from the landscape; Mexico did not, as he felt too removed from its culture. But as he read deeply in the mystics, he was brought closer to a sense of the "thing itself" that lay beneath surfaces — call it God, soul, essence, or what you will. In Mexico he painted symbolically, out of his readings; later, in what was to him the more amicable atmosphere of Austria and then of Nova Scotia and the United States, he could paint with a new serenity — a real sense of faith — taking as his subject mountains, birds, fish, islands, or even the human figure, which had been notably absent from almost all of his earlier work.

This is not to say that his Mexican paintings are weak. He did several forceful landscapes, and the Crane piece is dramatic, as are the other symbolic works. The colors are vivid, and the symbols, if obscure in meaning to most viewers, are nonetheless aesthetically pleasing — though understanding them adds to one's enjoyment. *Morgenrot, Mexico* (or "Red Morning, Mexico"), which was probably begun during the summer of 1932, is a painting of a large red hand framed in whitish light and backed by six gold spheres, with a seventh on a gold wristband. All of this is set against a deep-blue background. As a design it is striking; if one knows that Hartley was representing what he had read among the mystics — in this case Paracelsus and his follower the German mystic Jakob Böhme — it becomes fascinating.

For Böhme, the seventh realm of divine corporeality — or the materialized word — was where the sounds of individual things contributed to the divine harmony of the spheres. In Hartley's painting the seventh sphere is on the divine hand made corporeal, 7 being a symbol of perfect order and completeness. The colors remind one of the strong tones Hartley found everywhere in Mexico. Why *Morgenrot,* then? His use of German for the title reflects his love of Germany, as well as the simple fact that he was among Germans in Mexico. The red hand is a reminder of the Indians, the land, the brilliant sun, and even the blood of man, all of which are parts of God made corporeal in the bright-red morning of the seventh day, when all was in harmony. The point, finally, is not to insist that this is *the* way Hartley's painting must be read; it is simply *a* way, and it shows how his mind was working in Mexico, when, steeping himself in mysticism but overwhelmed by the country, he painted out of the inspiration that he had first discovered in Dogtown and that he then integrated with elements of the native Latin culture. Mexico marked a transition for him, a time when he came to a fuller understanding of faith, something he craved but admittedly did not possess.[13]

In late May 1932 Hartley moved to Cuernavaca to get away from city life and the altitude and to cut down on his expenses. His nephew had returned to the United States, so he took a room by himself in a pension run by a German couple, the Harmsens, whom he found compatible. The place was near town and had good food, a swimming pool, a terrace on the roof, clean rooms, and a large, sloping garden, so he had no complaints, he told Adelaide Kuntz. Besides, he felt at home with his German hosts, who were "obviously ex-royalists," and even with the other guests, Germans who "eat-eat, eat and spread about in typical German fashion." None of them broke the mold of "blondness — and no one comes who is not rather sodden with domesticity, but it is somehow wholesome — and they do not yodel or sing Tristan and Isolde — which they might do if the spirit of Mexico permitted."

That spirit would dominate Hartley for as long as he remained in the country. "It was a place that devitalized my energies," he wrote in a memoir after he left. He found "all the colours and the forms . . . at variance with each other — nothing becomes precise — neither form, design, or colour." Because the Spaniards had invaded the country, it had never had "the privilege of completing its mystical significance through its own people," he surmised. Indians, Spaniards, and mixed breeds made for what he termed a "novel, powerful, dramatic Mexico — full of irrelevant bravadoes, extravagant notions of power, animalistic impulses ruling everything — to hate, to kill, [is] any man's diversion and bothers no one — take what you want, kill whatever stands in the way."

The Puritan from Maine could not adapt to the mélange of life and terrain he encountered, however much it fascinated him: "Grandeur of scene, splendour of race, smoldering volcanoes, fire coloured birds, the most amazing light eye has ever encountered, which few Mexicans seek — either pure or mestizo [mixed] — pestilence, miasmas, crocodiles, aigrettes, lizards, flame consuming the whole aspect of life." He had never seen anything like Mexico, nor would he ever again seek out such a land. "Strange country — Mexico," he mused. "Melodrama in big doses affects different people differently. I found it too incessantly picturesque, incessantly handsome human beings — the Indians, not the mestizos," he concluded in his memoir, likening the country to an "enormous antediluvian animal that no one can quite manage the hugeness of, and so they all bite into its flanks and take off what they can get."[14]

His was a bittersweet bite, but it stimulated him, and he wrote about it repeatedly. In a piece entitled "Mexican Vignette," he remarked on "the magic of nature," something that he believed an artist could not learn about but must somehow intuit. The magic — "the mystical sense of earth" — existed "beneath the surface of what the eye sees," he claimed, noting that Cézanne had striven for it, for that thing that lay between the artist and the object. "It is not a deity but a presence," Hartley asserted, hinting at his difficulty with Mexico by adding that "primitive peoples made everything into a deity because everything natural contained the presence of the supernatural." In order to represent nature properly, the artist needed to find out what it was. Its essence was in mountains, lakes, rivers, and seas. It was what religious cults and mythologies were made from; in Mexico, he observed, "among the Aztec ruins, you get a terrific sense of the belief in the supernatural.... Everyone here in Mexico is an earth-cultist." He went on to describe seeing an infant creep along the earth, very much like a four-legged animal. His aim was not to disparage the child but rather to point out its closeness to the earth, its "sustenance of life ... [its] medium of expression ... [and] the metier of [its] body and spirit."[15]

In such a context, religion became a totally personal, physical matter, Hartley believed, and in an essay entitled "The Bleeding Christs of Mexico" he wrote about "the significance of blood to the Spanish soul and mind" and how that significance was reflected in Mexican churches. Blood and suffering were important to the Spanish nature, he thought, and again and again in the ornately decorated Mexican churches one could discover representations of them. The churches, such as a small chapel in the village of Acatapec, were ablaze with color, from jewels and glazes of azure, lapis, primrose, and pomegranate and from layers of the richest gold leaf. "Gold on gold on gold," he marveled, "no matter where you look, no escape from gold, all the varieties of monochrome painting joined with it to give it variety and still more splendour, fabrics of the richest sort, the illusion magnificently achieved of the visit of the holy spirit among the yearning."

In such settings one found statues of Christ on the cross, as in a church in Taxco, where the figure was uncannily lifelike, invested with human hair and flesh that seemed remarkably real, even to the gaping knife wounds that moved an observer to recoil. "What an orgy of penitence must have been furnished to the image-maker alone," Hartley wrote, "once for Christ and once for himself, the seemingly still living streams of blood flowing down over the pale body."[16] Little wonder, then, that the sensitive, reserved Northerner felt himself out-side the native culture, and little wonder, too, that when he did paint he turned to vivid, basic colors in an effort to convey something of what he saw all about him.

Amid what he called "this strange life and climate" he lived out his year in Mexico, reading and painting.[17] Soon after moving to Cuer-navaca he wrote to Adelaide Kuntz that he had finished reading Mabel Dodge Luhan's book about D. H. Lawrence, *Lorenzo in Taos.* "What a revelation of a woman," he exclaimed. "She lives all in her abdomen. . . . Such a messing 'messes of mortals.' Not a really nice human in the book save Tony [Luhan] who was always going off & leaving the men when it wearied him." Hartley admitted that he shrank from Lawrence "as a 'man' — with his 'livid coloured' flesh — it is the colour of his creation as well." In the end Lawrence left him "with the feeling of something cold and clammy in the hand one wants to shake off. . . . I was not repulsed by Mabel's book as I thought I might be," he concluded. "It is a very clear picture of her last great defeat."[18]

In Cuernavaca he became friendly with Mary and Eric Ostlund, who had a large collection of books on mysticism. Almost immediately he delved deeply into these works. The lyrics of Richard Rolle excited him; they "fairly burn with fervor," he told Kuntz, and his only regret was that he could not "join with them in belief." Rolle was especially attractive to him because he was not "hysterical or neurotic." He noted that "the mystical contact with life itself is anyone's privilege and one doesn't have to be a Christian to feel the glow and the glory of being, and life should be that."[19] By the end of July he had read much of two volumes of Paracelsus's work and had run through the two volumes of *Isis Unveiled,* a study of mysticism by Helena Blavatsky, one of the founders of Theosophy. Hartley thought the mystics "the great writers of romance because the highest love is the basis of all their themes." Rolle, for instance, would have had nothing to do with theorists or dogmatists, he was confident, because the one truth for him "was the love of Christ."

By this time Hartley had begun what he termed "two pictures of mystical import." This was "the first time I have come so close to these things [i.e., mystical matters]," he believed, and he hoped that it would create new interest in his work. There was little point in copying "the common facts of life," he asserted. Cubism, "hollow as it was and is," had represented a great release from fact, as had for Hartley the numerous canvases based on mysticism that he had done in 1912–1915. The two new pictures were "*The Heimkehr* [or *Return,* which he later changed to *Transference*] *of Richard Rolle*" and the "*Breath of Iliaster,*" he wrote. He had discarded all blacks and browns and returned to primary colors, so that at least his pictures would be "gayer and more exciting to the eyes — if not to the average mind."

He knew he was moving in a new direction, that of the imagination. "I have wanted ever since 1915 to go back to these ideas," he claimed, "but through the perverse belief that I could be a realist — I have neglected them — so I am swinging off into the field of the imagination again." He told Kuntz that he felt a "curious sense of release in having done these two pictures whether they are important or not."[20] They were important to *him* because they represented another step toward the paintings of his last decade, which would combine the qualities of his Dogtown and his Mexican work.

He remained at the Harmsens' Casa Aleman in Cuernavaca until November, when he returned to Mexico City for the rest of his stay. There were things about Mexico that he continued to like — in a letter to his niece he called it "one of the oblique countries of the world."[21] He had a fine Christmas Day, for instance, walking in Chapultepec Park near his apartment, listening to an orchestra play, and then having dinner with the photographer Paul Strand and friends of his. Several days later, on his birthday, Hartley was feted by other friends, who bought him presents and took him out for cocktails and supper — exactly the sort of social moment he thrived on. Paul Strand kept up with him and frequently complimented him on his work; he particularly liked the new "semi-mystical" paintings and told Hartley that it was good to see him returning to his "more real self." When Strand's wife, Rebecca, arrived in Mexico City, the three of them spent time together and took short trips into the country. Once Hartley traveled by auto to Acapulco and afterward claimed that he was almost killed when the car skidded toward the edge of a high precipice.[22]

In February Harriet Monroe, the editor of *Poetry,* was also there, so he did what for him was a tremendous amount of socializing. And he was pleased, even if he grumbled about the preparations, to be asked to give an exhibition of his work. "Exposición Marsden Hartley," a show of twenty paintings, was held for one week in late February and early March 1933 at the Galería de la Escuela Central de Artes Plásticas. Paul Strand and two Mexican friends helped Hartley mount the show. He was afraid that some of the pictures would confuse his Mexican audience, "as they [are] outspokenly mystical," and he guessed that few people would have heard of Richard Rolle and Paracelsus, or of the legend of the white bird Iztac Quixtli. Nonetheless he was momentarily exhilarated by the prospect of the exhibition, telling Kuntz that he was "happy that I have risen to [the] field of sensation and experience, and that I have realized the desire of years to really enter the field of true fancy and imagination, and that I don't think that even Blake would laugh at my *fantasías* if he were to see them."

"So this is what Mexico has done for me," he concluded, "and for that I feel it was worth coming — for it is such a land of romance, far too much so for its own practical good, but also to the credit of the indians that they should be so intelligent and gifted in imaginative matters.... It has been a rich year intellectually and spiritually," he admitted, "and the physical side will I think readjust itself when I get down out of this trying altitude [to a place] where I can feel a little less like being hung up by the heels all the time."[23] Constant nosebleeds from the altitude did not improve his mood. Shortly before he left Mexico he had one so violent that a Mexican first-aid worker, seeing his plight, ministered to him and ended up taking him home in a taxi.[24]

As March approached he began to worry intensely about the renewal of his Guggenheim Fellowship. He had earlier felt confident that he would win a second year, which he planned to spend in Germany, but as the time grew close for the decision, he feared that he would be left without a source of income. When in the middle of the month he was informed that his fellowship would not be renewed, his reaction was predictable: "well — I've done [Mexico]," he wrote to a friend, the artist Donald Greason, "& now I get the kick in the balls I was more or less looking for — no renewal of 2nd year Guggenheim — well — I'm shoving off for Hamburg in April with to live on $50 — a month — all I can count on — ... can get to Hamburg cheaper than N.Y. & I love that city full of flares & shots — as all ports are."

He took his frustration out on Mexico. He knew it had provided him with many things, but he had never been able to approach it frontally, only "obliquely," as he said. "Don't like no kind of Mexis nohow am so tired of looking at black & dark green people — don't know that I'm sorry I came — but a year is far too long," he railed.

He had had "too many difficulties," and the place was "too 'pictur-esque' — all like cigar box labels of 1880": it wore out the eye and dulled the mind. "Maybe," he conceded, "I'm too New England any-how I've lived a life of scope too long to be taking this seriously — big hats and sallow skins — and much pistols on hips — thousands of blind people or one eye white — small pox skins — menace of food & water & all that." He claimed that the volcanoes were the only things there that really interested him, "and they don't talk enough — shoot fire & flames only twice a century & this is not the year — historically very grand wondrous pyramids & temples out of Aztec times — but they are speechless too."[25]

By mid-April, as he was about to sail for Hamburg, he had calmed down somewhat, for he was assured of receiving seventy-five dollars a month from payments that Adelaide Kuntz and his nephew Clifton Newell intended to make to him for paintings they had bought. But still he fulminated about the art world, which seemed entirely unap-preciative of him, as evidenced by the lack of commercial success of his show in New York in the spring of 1932, the failure of the Whitney Museum to purchase a single painting of his, and the nonrenewal of his Guggenheim Fellowship. "I am sick of the importance of art," he announced to Greason. He declared that henceforth he would paint only when he felt the urge — "no more horse-piss in a puddle — all through — I want to live my way as Ryder did his. He lived in his world of fancy, and stayed out of the rest. Well I want to get into a world of thought & stay in it." Like a celebrated prima donna, he would "put on a swell evening wrap ... & say, fuck the art & all the arties." He was going home to "the outer world of rational being," and if he had had "another trade or trick" he would have said "shit on all of it" — on the art world, that is.[26] The trouble was, as he had written a bit earlier to Adelaide Kuntz, he had a tremendous amount of energy that he wanted to pour into his art. He had "richer feelings & emotions" now than he had had in years, and he could not limit himself to paint-ing a small number of pictures each year to save costs.[27]

On April 20 he sailed for Hamburg aboard the *Orinoco*. His third-class accommodations were less than comfortable, with four people to a room and a full complement of "spitting, vomiting Spaniards leaving Havana & Cuba because of bad times & revolution there." None of this discouraged him as much as it might have, however, because he was on his way "home," Germany being as much that as anywhere. "The

sense of one's own North   heaps of snow to cool the eyes and the
senses — back to the Anglos and the Aryans who have light in their
faces, enough of the dark face and the dark concept": this was what he
anticipated. On the European side of the Atlantic the ship stopped at
Gijón, Santander, Boulogne, Southampton, and Amsterdam before
docking in Hamburg near mid-May.

Having "insulted my finer senses for so long a stay in Mexico," he
exulted in northern Europe. He went ashore in Amsterdam and luxu-
riated in the rain, the lushness of spring, green, wet fields, and a riot of
flowers. Rich coffee and the Dutch sense of order pervaded his being,
and everything he esteemed seemed to come together around Rem-
brandt's *The Night Watch,* which he went to see. "All that music can
bring to the mind this picture brings to the eye," he concluded, "paci-
fying all the rest of one's emotions, of one's interpretations — it will
cure the 'sick soul' for it contains the complete hypnosis of well-being
in completed degree."[28] He could hardly have been in a more perfect
mood for his return to Germany and Hamburg, which he judged "all
in all — the most beautiful city in the world."[29]

After spending several days in a hotel, resting because he had bronchitis, he moved into a two-room apartment in a private house. He
ventured out happily to see what he could of "the new Germany,"
that of the National Socialist Party of Chancellor Hitler, who had
come to power several months earlier, in January 1933. The Aryan
faces pleased him, though he was uneasy about the Nazi regime,
which was now thoroughly in control, imposing its ever more repres-
sive measures on the country as a whole and on the Jewish people in
particular, who were already suffering beatings and attacks on their
stores. Hartley liked the excitement of the banners, posters, rallies, and
torchlight parades that were common in Hamburg and elsewhere, but
Germanophile though he was, he was bothered by the persecution of
the Jews.

He would have called himself apolitical, touched by others' plights
yet intent on remaining uninvolved. He observed the increasingly
troubled situation, remarked on it, and tried to go about his affairs.
His acquiescence mirrored that of millions of others. He did not agree
with the Nazis' policies toward the Jews, but he thought they had some
right to want to purify their nation, and he half sympathized with
their charge that the Jews had overstepped their privileges. "If [the

Nazis] must have them out of politics, out of art, out of banking, that is their business," he declared late in his stay in Germany. He thought the result was "pretty bad"; nevertheless, he could accept the notion that "the modern playwrights, to name only one sort, are all jews and all of a decidedly revolutionist basis, and so they have to be put out." He believed there was some sort of basic logic behind this, though he admitted that it produced "human tragedies." And he argued that it was "just as rational and sensible to want to purify a race physically and mentally as not to do it."[30]

Murderously dangerous opinions, we would say, and ones that smacked of lethal prejudices. Yet during the summer Hartley could assert to the owner of the Downtown Gallery, Edith Halpert, "Heaven knows if love for those [Jews] I know and understanding them racially, emotionally, and spiritually — would make me a Jew, I would be one surely by now." He claimed that "years ago once when I raved over gefilte fish done by a Viennese cook in the family who were closest to me for 25 years [the Rönnebecks] — the father of the house said — that settles it now we know you're Jewish. I said alright fine." In 1933 he did not recognize that the argument that "some of my best friends are Jewish" was not an adequate response to the oppression that was rapidly mounting.

He was more aware of that oppression than he cared to admit. In the same letter to Edith Halpert, he wrote, "As for the Jewish question I don't get much of that either because as I say I know no one here in Hamburg of either 'party.'" He thought it "pretty terrible" that Jews were forbidden to teach either in schools or in universities and were not allowed to practice law or medicine. Further, any Jew who had come to Germany after 1914 was automatically considered an alien, unless he had fought in World War I. It was "all awful really," Hartley concluded, adding that "the prejudice has always been fiercely strong in Germany and especially in Berlin — even in 1914 I remember."[31]

Enamored as always of Germany and relieved to be back in his beloved north, Hartley was willing to tolerate the Nazi position as he understood it. "I can't talk of political realities," he wrote to Adelaide Kuntz soon after arriving in Hamburg. "I know little or nothing of them — only that Hitlerism does nothing to the surface of life as far as I can make out." He had heard of many good things that Hitler had accomplished: the lower classes admired him because he was feeding them, and the upper classes felt he had saved them from bolshevism. Now there was only the National Socialist party in control, but Hartley did not yet have any sense of "the real truth" about things.[32]

Days later, comfortably situated in his new apartment, he went out to the Polizei Stadium to "see what the new Germany would show of its knowledge of athletics." He was pleased with what he found: a fine stadium and handsome young gymnasts who looked well in their Hitlerite uniforms. Hitler, he maintained, represented a "fresh feeling of idealism and national piety." Hartley had seen him in the movies and heard him on a radio wagon in the street. His Austrian accent was ingratiating, his voice magnificent. Hartley still had to learn about the doctrine. "Of course," he remarked, "all states have to be built or rebuilt out of the youth of a race and youth is a terrifying thing often for youth has no respect for anything but itself."[33] The Germans, he explained to Edith Halpert,

> all believe in Hitler for natural reasons — he is their only savior. He saved them from internal revolution less than six months ago whatever his faults are, and heroes always are full of faults. So they can only believe in him. The outcome seems promising then for everyone but Jews and it must be sad for them, for to be a member of the new party is to be anti semitic instantly.

But aside from being banned from many forms of livelihood, the Jews were not being abused, he thought.[34]

One reason for Hartley's acceptance of Hitlerism was the contrast between its order and cleanliness — which he admitted could be excessive — and what he remembered of Mexico, "a living cauldron of deceits & hatreds of murder and no respect at all for human life."[35] The monstrous irony of that comparison was not apparent at the time, but even in his enthusiasm Hartley understood that there was an underside to "the new Germany" that went beyond its treatment of the Jews. He told Kuntz of meeting a destitute seaman one night in the streets of Hamburg and giving him thirty pfennigs, for which the man had been extravagantly thankful. He could not find work, he said — one had to be a member of the National Socialist party to be assured of a job — but like hundreds of others he would be arrested if he were caught begging, as the Nazis had outlawed it. Hartley did not generally dare to talk to such people, particularly because as a foreigner he might get in trouble, so any real knowledge of actual conditions eluded him, he insisted. "I go about my business which is minding my own," he declared, even as he fretted that the regime might be reading his mail to check for seditious remarks.[36]

The longer Hartley remained in Germany, the more eager he was to meet Hitler. It became almost an obsession, and he hoped that he might fulfill his wish through his acquaintance with Ernst Hanfstängl, a Harvard-educated German whom he had known in Berlin in the early 1920s and who in 1933 was Hitler's foreign press chief. Whatever reservations Hartley had about the Nazis were effectively muted by his eagerness to meet the führer. Stopping in Munich on his way to the Bavarian mountains in August, he tried to get in touch with Hanfstängl, who had a friend call him and offer to give him information about the regime. Hartley was convinced that Hanfstängl himself "would all but get out the band for me for he is one mass of fire and devotion if he cares at all."

Despite his persistence, he would be disappointed in his quest. He never met with Hanfstängl, much less with Hitler, and in the end had to settle for talking with Hanfstängl's sister Erna, in November, in the shop she ran in Munich. During that same visit to the city he heard a speech of Hitler's over the radio; he assured Adelaide Kuntz that the chancellor had an "incredibly fine voice and fine style, with all the rapture and ecstasy in it of an imbued person, mounting at times to nothing less of course than religious fervor." Hartley insisted that there was "no bluff about him no matter what his faults are," nor any "cheap rhetoric whatever, for he is of course a plain person himself, and having but one object in heart and mind, the restoration of the people to their rightful place."

Hartley observed, rightly, that the people were with Hitler. In Garmisch-Partenkirchen, where he lived from September 1933 until his departure for America in March 1934 via Munich, Berlin, and finally Hamburg, he noted an "air of satisfaction all round," as well as a "sense of prosperity, new houses being built, and in general the sights and sounds of renewal."[37] All this made him readier to accept the German leader. Still trying to meet him, he ventured to Munich once more in January 1934 to celebrate his fifty-seventh birthday. He went to see Erna Hanfstängl again, hoping that it might result in an introduction to Hitler. It did not, but Hartley nonetheless enjoyed the occasion of lunch with her, reporting afterward that she was "the real thing," a German who understood her nation well. Hartley asked her about Hitler, as she had known and supported him since his attempted putsch in Munich in 1923. She informed Hartley that the Jews were not hated but had "misused their privileges." She claimed to have argued with Hitler over this matter, telling him that "it was wrong socially and humanly to have this present point of view." Hitler had asserted that it was "not a human question," that he did not hate the Jews, that the "best" Jews had not left Germany, and that their human rights were not being abused. Hanfstängl maintained that she had no adverse feelings toward them, nor did she boycott their shops. They would, she predicted, return to Germany "because it is the only place they have lived and prospered," and she was scornful when Hartley mentioned the Jews' going into exile — such a thing was unnecessary, she protested, and only a "part of their emotionalism."[38]

Hartley had sympathy for the Jews, but in a letter to his niece in which he described his luncheon with Erna Hanfstängl, he reflected the prejudice that allowed the Nazis to forge ahead with their murderous plans. Hanfstängl had assured him that she had many Jewish friends, but she condemned "their faults as to money passions," and that, Hartley added, was "the root of the Jewish defect, that they cannot get above the spirit of usury, which is, I too must say, their great defect." With such an attitude, he saw nothing wrong in wanting to meet Hitler, who was "from all accounts personally a most nice person, and of course having wanted to be an artist, he likes artists, and I would like to be in the presence of the man if only for a few minutes."[39]

If Hartley's political perceptions were singularly unimpressive, his artistic ones were much more acute. Two months in Hamburg restored his "pleasure in existence" after the rigors of Mexican life; happy to be in a north much like his native New England, he geared up to paint again. The writings of the likes of Plotinus and Santayana sustained him.[40] Plotinus was his "idea of a true thinker," he wrote to Adelaide Kuntz in June. "Modified mysticism through mind processes suits me perfectly," he told her. "I give up all else. I read the Christian mystics as novels — but they all end by being vague." Then, too, a number of the figures seemed to be "all hysterics who I'm sure were physical neurotics."[41]

Such things as films about German alpinists — he saw one four or five times — brought him into needed contact with "mystical nature." One film was about climbing the Matterhorn, and the mountaineers, he claimed, gave "the world the personalities of the mountains as never before." He recalled his admiration for Giovanni Segantini — "the only artist who has ever put a mountain spirit on canvas" and the man to whom he owed his "first start," in 1905. He must, he decided, "live with a few Alps [for] a time"; he needed to see them, face them, and "have them enlarge my spirit."

In a good mood, in Hamburg, he felt sure that he had "established my means of escape into a new life now — Mexico began it — and it is only the soul of the north that will complete it for me." He knew that he had "come back to nature pure & simple again" and hoped never to leave it. He had in effect returned to his native land "symbolically & mystically," he believed. Now he heard "the voices of Emerson, Thoreau, Emily Dickinson and they are true voices — they belong to my space — my innate areas." At that moment he was trying to distance himself from the ugly side of nazism, trying to explain to his close friend how Germany was working for him both artistically and spiritually.[42] The Alps were beckoning; he declared that he was a "mountain person and a snow person," and he wanted "to get all that back into my consciousness for good and all." He had never gotten over his feeling for mountains after spending three days in the Alps with Franz Marc, many years earlier.[43] One of the mountain films affected him particularly; "it brought about a conversion to nature," he said, which was "the religion that I began my life with up in Maine, and I feel all aquiver with the new conversion as a result."[44]

All this steered him toward the Alps. He thought about living in Berchtesgaden, on the Austrian border near Salzburg, but determined that it would be too costly. He settled on Partenkirchen, a bit west and also near the border. There, in early September, he found a comfortable room for one mark a day — cause for celebration — with modern fixtures, running water, and steam heat. He immediately began to look about — "alpining," he called it — and was nearly ecstatic about being "next to rocks & earth again." To the south he could see the Waxenstein peaks, about which he exclaimed, "there can be no single form more glorious in all the Alps than these are." The central peak alone, he thought, "would start another school of Chinese painting." Reflecting his own interests, he praised the Chinese for their understanding of mountains, "the meaning of space the significance of rhythm and the quality of time in appearances." Right away he began making sketches — from the very simplest penciled sort to more stylized silverpoint drawings — from which he expected to build other work, and he kept up this practice whenever the weather permitted, until he left, in February 1934. He noted the nearness of the mountains, and the similarity of one, the Eckbauer, to Mont Sainte-Victoire. He thought of the mountains he had painted in New Hampshire, and of what he knew of Mount Katahdin, in Maine, and considered his painting of the Alps to be a "proud preparation for recovering the 'eye' for the native scene" — that is, the New England landscape, which was excatly like the Alps "in structure & repetition."[45]

It is interesting that he picked up at once on the closeness of the mountains. Anyone would have noticed in it the literal sense, of course, but what fascinated Hartley was that there was "almost no intervening atmosphere, as nothing is more than a mile from the eye, and as it is all shut in here, the play of light is very small or limited, so they just stand like monuments, a cross between Blake and the Chinese." As monuments, the mountains became the subject of his paintings in ways they usually did not. Just as he had done with his paintings of Dogtown, Hartley now lessened the distance between object and viewer, so that one has a greater sense of the painter's having achieved the poet Wallace Stevens's ideal of "not ideas about the thing but the thing itself." In some of his paintings of the Alps he included only the barest of foregrounds while others have no foreground at all, so that while the mountain is still clearly recognizable as such, it is foregrounded and flattened out and thus more than merely a part of the world beyond. The painting becomes the total object and comes to have "a quality of stature and *presence*," as Gail Scott has observed.[46] Object, canvas, and viewer merge — which is exactly how the modernists would have had it be as they struggled through their art to capture the world directly, without the intervention of conventional dogmas. Could philosophy intervene? Yes, but only insofar as it brought things into direct apprehension, which is one reason the mystics became so fascinating to Hartley and other modern artists. "I think it must be Plotinus has refined my sense of essence so much that I am able to see right down to the last detail," Hartley told Adelaide Kuntz late in December 1933.[47]

Not long after his stay in the Alps, in a collection of poems that he would call *Tangent Decisions*, Hartley included two translations he had made from the work of Gérard de Nerval:

> How is it — I said to myself,
> that I can possibly have lived
> so long outside nature, without
> identifying myself with her?
> All things live, all things have
> motion, all things correspond.
> The majestic rays emanating from
> myself to others, traverse without
> obstacle, the infinite chain of
> created things. . . .
>
> I want to govern my dreams, instead
> of endure them.[48]

Man, that is to say, is close to nature, entirely a part of it, and to express that, to govern his dreams rather than merely to suffer them, he has to come directly up to it, as in Hartley's new mountain paintings. If dreams emerge from the imagination, which takes whatever form it does from the relationship among the self, the unconscious, and the world beyond, then a person gains control by mastering the essences of nature, by rendering close up and precisely the monumental objects that represent it.

Once Hartley understood the mountains, he began to work well. "I have never painted like I am doing now," he declared to Adelaide Kuntz on Christmas Day, and five days later he boasted to his niece that he had "nearly finished 15 paintings and walked over 100 miles to make the drawings and observations."[49] A particularly solitary time in many ways, his stay in the Alps was nonetheless busy. He knew he could not remain there for long, and he fully sensed that he was experiencing a creative burst, one that would result in a remarkable number of drawings, pastels, and oils. The walking was good for him, he ate well, and he was able to read extensively, not only the writings of his beloved mystics but also the works of Shakespeare and *The Autobiography of Alice B. Toklas.*

He had heard from a friend in New York that the book was out and mentioned him; he was anxious to read what Stein had said, and he wrote to her to ask if she would lend him a copy. She obliged, sending him a copy of his own, which he read immediately and with immense relish. "Well, Gertrude," he reported to her after he read it a second time,

I read and I read and I read, and it got lunch time, I washed and
dressed for I usually sit around negligee until noon when there are
bushels of steam heat to make it possible — then I went and ate and
went and walked and came home and went to reading again, and
read until I had finished it once, and then I began the next day and
started it all over again.

He gushed on in Steinlike long sentences, complimenting her on the
pure pleasure the book had given him and remarking specifically on
some of the portraits she had rendered of various figures whom he had
known or not known. He had laughed at the portrait of Ezra Pound,
and again at that of Ernest Hemingway. There was only a brief reference to Hartley himself — "whom we liked very much," wrote
Stein — but he could confidently testify that "it is all told so well so
directly and so flowingly."[50] Only to other friends did he grouse a little
about her having paid more attention to Arnold Rönnebeck than she
had to him.

Inspired by the book, Hartley at once began what he termed an
"exercise in memory," taking the precaution of calling it "a 'Little
Past,'" he noted, because he had had "only average moments and average experience." He told his niece that "there has been no trace of
drama in my life save the inner one, the spirit piercing through stone
walls kind of thing, for I have had to do everything by spirit since my
hands would do nothing of themselves. A story of desire, faith and
despair, but I am keeping out the despair as it is not of the heroic
variety."[51] He wrote rapidly and within three weeks had brought the
narrative up to his arrival in Hamburg the previous April. There he
stopped, unfortunately never to finish the manuscript, which he now
called "Somehow a Past."[52]

As content as he had ever been in his life, situated among mountains
and enjoying a surge of creativity, he believed that he understood the
mystics better than he had before. Ruysbroeck's dictum "perfect stillness — perfect fecundity" precisely conveyed his state of mind at this
moment, or at least expressed what he strove for and now felt close to.
And the divine for him was Plotinus's "supreme intellect," which
seemed to represent that which was "more than ourselves," the "fourth
dimension" that Cézanne had tried to paint. "I wish to paint that thing
which exists between me and the object," Hartley quoted Cézanne as
having said. That was what he himself was trying to do in his paintings

of the Alps, and in the context of his comfortable, if solitary, life in Partenkirchen, it gave him as much pleasure and confidence as he had ever had. "My problem has been fears," he told Norma Berger, "but I think I can surmount them and I have taken new courage since the morning of last week when it seemed as if I had had a 'visitation' as mystics say they had a vision of God — I seemed to get a vision of certainty."

He told of a recurrent dream he had had, first in 1912, before he went to Europe; then the previous August in Hamburg, prior to his departure for the Alps; and most recently the week before. Each time the dream had involved a boat heading for safety, and each time, after the dream, his life had taken the direction he needed. And now he was satisfied, painting well, at ease with himself, and even anxious to return to the United States, having found his way again in his new painting.[53] He worked rapidly on through New Year's, and then on his fifty-seventh birthday treated himself to a trip to Munich, where he registered in a comfortable small hotel, met an American acquaintance, fed himself well for lunch, had a steam bath and a rubdown, went to the Alpine and Lenbach museums, ate goose for dinner, and saw several boxing matches. Over the next few days he fitted in visits to several more museums, some movies houses, and at least one circus before having lunch with Erna Hanfstängl and returning to Partenkirchen.

Full of energy, he drew and worked on his paintings right up to the time he left for Berlin, spending a few weeks there before traveling to Hamburg, where he boarded a ship for the United States. So wrapped up in his plans for himself was he that he gave little thought to the fact that Hitler was rapidly molding "the new Germany" into a place he would never be able to visit again. The country had served him well: his stay in the Alps had been one of the most invigorating periods of his life, and he felt ready to face New York once more, even venturing to declare that he saw "no great obstacles ahead." He was out of touch with Depression America.[54]

14

Beyond Intellect
1934 – 1939

I

Gloucester, New York as Usual, and Nova Scotia, 1934–1936

HARTLEY'S LAST TRIP across the Atlantic Ocean was uneventful, except for some heavy weather the first four days. During the voyage he tried to clarify what Germany had meant to him. It was best represented by the "life and vitality" of Hamburg, he thought; he had found Berlin to be "utterly changed," and he no longer cared for it. He looked forward to returning to the United States, which he expected to be alive, while Europe as a whole, he declared, was "down at the heel with all its political and national absurdities." He was cynical about it: people talked of peace but were afraid of it and instead supported war, which would be paid for with taxes and blood. He arrived in New York at the end of March and a month later was still relieved to be free of "everlasting flags and soldiers marching." Among his acquaintances he found a great deal of hatred for Germany, which distressed him, but he did not try to defend the nation because "the only Germany I can defend anyhow is that one of the heart which has nothing to do with external purposes."[1]

He enjoyed seeing friends, and it gave him an opportunity to get out of his small room at 38 West Twelfth Street. An acquaintance loaned him a loft that he could use during the day, and in the spring friends helped him to find work with the Public Works of Art Project;

the job paid $38.25 a week but lasted only a month.[2] Despite the security, he did not like being captive to any program and was relieved when it ended. He felt "sort of between this world and the next," he told his niece in June. After talking with a woman who was an officer in the "Society for Psychical Research," he toyed with the idea of starting a class in psychic painting, but he was no organizer, and nothing came of the scheme. Several of his paintings were sold, albeit at low prices, so he remained confident that he could earn some sort of income; still, he had no clear sense of direction.[3]

Hoping to find one, he returned to Gloucester in early July, renting a room in the same place he had stayed three years earlier. He found that Gloucester had the same shortcomings as before: tourists and, to him, phony artists. He indulged himself during the summer by going to numerous films and taking trips such as one to Hanover, New Hampshire, to see the Orosco mural paintings that had recently been installed at Dartmouth College.[4] And he had friends, none closer than Helen Stein, whom he knew from his time in Gloucester in 1931. She was part of a group of painters with whom he was more or less friendly — and, when not friendly, of whom he was jealous.

One of these was Ernest Thurn, who had an artists' school in East Gloucester and who in 1936 married Stein, to Hartley's great consternation. He tried to be nice to Hartley, but the two had nothing in common. Hartley tolerated him but could be meanspirited, as he was on one occasion when Thurn drove him around in his car for a while and finally asked, "What shall we do now?" Hartley responded, "Little I care what you are going to do. I'm going to see Helen." Thurn, scarcely fond of Hartley, more than once dismissed him to Stein with a twitter and the announcement, "He's a fairy." Hartley's cheapness irritated Thurn, who told Stein that when the two men went to buy groceries for Thanksgiving, Hartley did not even offer to pay for the onions. "The S.O.B.," Thurn remarked angrily, "can't he at least help me carry the bundles in?" Stein usually served as a go-between, while Hartley, jealous of Thurn's attention to Stein, would become absolutely silent whenever Thurn showed up. When another of the Gloucester group appeared just as Hartley and Stein were finishing lunch and preparing to go to Dogtown, Hartley tried to dismiss him by saying that he and Stein were going off to paint. The visitor, Monsur Karem, laughed unpleasantly and asked Hartley to repeat what he had said.

Hartley responded, "I said we are going off to paint — I don't know which language you speak but I speak English." Turning to Stein, he declared that he could never be in Karem's presence again. She asked Karem to leave, and the incident ended.

Stein also recalled that one day Hartley stormed into her house, complaining about a local restaurant, the Blacksmith Shop, and about a particular waiter there. Hartley would not say what the matter was, but from the waiter Stein found out that Hartley was furious at not being granted the same discount as students at Thurn's art school. The difference, Stein noted, was ten cents.

Despite such petty animosities, Hartley needed what Stein and Gloucester offered. He was, loosely, part of a group there, and he had Stein's genuine affection, which he returned. Once, when some of her friends were cooking at her house, Hartley called to Stein from her studio, and she went in to find him standing in front of one of her paintings, weeping. He put his arm around her and asked, "Child, do you know what kind of a painter you are?" Extending his hand toward the picture, he asked, "May I touch it?"[5]

The autumn of 1934 was splendid for painting. Hartley did a second series of Dogtown works as well as several still lifes set in front of telescoped seascapes, paintings that he hoped might catch the eye of what few buyers there were in the depths of the Depression. But no buyers appeared, and by November he was becoming desperate about money. His dealer, Edith Halpert, at the Downtown Gallery, forwarded a letter from the Lincoln Storage Company, informing him that he owed $184 for the storage of his paintings, which were housed in three vaults. Hartley immediately appealed to Stieglitz for help, but Stieglitz declined, explaining that he had little money himself, and implying that Hartley's problems were Edith Halpert's business now. Stieglitz, who had always paid the storage costs when he was handling Hartley's work, did not see why Halpert could not negotiate some arrangement, perhaps taking a certain number of paintings for herself in return. But she did not have the necessary cash to pay the storage bill, and only after much agonizing was Hartley able to raise $50 from his nephew Clifton Newell and eventually $50 from Adelaide Kuntz and $100 from a man in Boston who admired his work, Louis Shapiro. This stayed the storage company from emptying the vaults of Hartley's paintings, but Hartley knew he must do something about the situation by the start of the new year.

He talked about setting up an art class in Gloucester the following summer — an idea, he confided to several friends, that made good sense because the students who were studying with the artist Hans Hofmann in Gloucester were tired of his abstraction and would welcome someone like Hartley. He knew he could not count on Stieglitz any longer. While Hartley was friendly in his letters to the older man, he told his niece that "Stieglitz in spite of himself goes on with the injured papa attitude whose son went out and married a woman beneath him — woman being the art market [—] and is silently saying — well son — you would have her — knowing what a slut she is." Hartley went on, "I'm just novelizing. In the name of heaven, why must the Hartley crew make such a mess of things." He took much of the blame on himself, but he also faulted the American art market for ignoring its own artists. He had at last come face to face with the Depression.[6]

With the storage crisis alleviated for the moment, he wrote Stieglitz a meandering letter to assure him that he had passed "the worst aspect of the catastrophe as to storage at least." Stung by the episode, he tried to make sense of his troubles; how tiresome they all were, he felt. He would lose the paintings unless he could devise some plan to pay for storing them; he had already lost his furniture and those belongings of his that had been stored in Provence. But what did it matter? he asked. What was anything at all "but self-possession & a faith in something more than oneself whatever it be — but there is something and Plotinus makes it easy to believe it is 'superior intellect' 'the principle of good' etc." He recounted two visions he had had while in the Alps: he was being pursued "by a kind of courier of the realities who had a message for me and caught up in time. I thanked the courier & he went speeding on his horse." From this Hartley came to believe that

> there *is* something that protects us — or how could [a] simple one like me have proceeded. I can't give it a personal name for I have never seen a person — but I certainly can think of it as the element of good in my life — and I must believe it from now on — I love life with all my heart more than ever because I know now what it really is — and it has little or nothing to do with human beings.

It had to do, rather, with nature; he had driven the day before to southern Maine with some acquaintances and had seen "the deep flow-

ing solemn Piscataqua River at Eliot & Kittery," he explained to
Stieglitz,

> and it came to me again — a river of my own earth & country —
> deep flowing sure going — unquestioning — nothing like a river
> to show one just that — the mountain will give you the lesson of
> sobriety and moral purpose — and aristocratic imperturbability —
> the rock such as I have here in Dogtown delivers sermons of integ-
> rity piety wholesome continuity — and so you see one can go to
> church anywhere & pray standing up at all times — because simple
> true desire is profound prayer.[7]

Frequently he could not remain calm and removed, but he had
achieved a new vision in the last three years, and it gave him something
to cling to through the next months, which were extremely taxing.

Back in New York in December, he could take a certain wry pleasure in seeing paintings of his displayed at the Museum of Modern Art
and the Whitney Museum, but it also frustrated him. How could a
well-known artist be faced with such poverty? He made plans to reduce the number of his paintings in storage. In a dramatic gesture, on
his birthday, January 4, 1935, and with a letter in his hand telling of
one of his sisters' having died penniless in California, he went to the
vaults with Adelaide Kuntz and her friend Lydia Allison, who had
volunteered to help him with his publicity. When the paintings were
spread out before them, they inventoried what was there. "I nearly
went blind at the sight of the quantity alone," Hartley wrote to his
niece. "It was like a rodeo almost." He let his nephew Clifton Newell
take something in payment for the money he had advanced on the
storage bill, and then he began the process of destroying more than
one hundred paintings and drawings. He called it a holocaust, and it
drove him to despair. For four days he continued the business, on the
second accompanied by Carl Sprinchorn, who prevented him from
slashing some paintings. "We waded there up to our ankles in cut up
paintings," Sprinchorn later wrote to Norma Berger. "He did not really want to destroy any but he was full of revenge on a hard-fated
life."[8] By the time he was finished, Hartley had reduced his holdings
to what could be stored in a single vault.

The experience was as shattering as any he had ever had. While he
could recognize that it was frugal to reduce his inventory of unsold
paintings, he knew that had the public acknowledged his work, he

would not have had to destroy anything. A bit of him was torn away, and it resulted in a difficult time for him, with his psychological wounding and his poverty both contributing to a case of bronchitis that left him confined to his hotel room for much of the winter.

When he was able to get out, he was discouraged by what he found: the exhibitions, with one or two exceptions, were "tiresome and very common," consisting largely of "that 'American scene' stuff" that was then filling the galleries, and against which Hartley felt himself to be pitted.[9] New York was a "hell-hole, really," he told Rebecca Strand, where foolish games were being played in the art world. Thomas Hart Benton had attacked Stieglitz and his group in *Time* magazine, saying that he thought Stieglitz was dead. Benton and the other "American scene" painters were having good success; while their works sold, Hartley was reduced during the spring of 1935 to eating on sixty cents a day and once a week having a good meal at the Hotel Shelton, thanks to Stieglitz.

One artist whom Hartley could respect was the Frenchman Dunoyer de Segonzac, whose show at the Brummer Gallery that winter excited him. Hartley wrote de Segonzac one of his "Letters Never Sent," praising him for his ability to present nature as "seen through the mirror of herself, and not through a temperament alone." At a time when in America there was a "passionate assertion of our native American scene," it was good to have the French artist's paintings as a reminder of what true passion was. "When the artist is in rapport with nature as the image of himself," Hartley went on, "there may come, and this does come in your case, the complete sense of the reality of nature as idea, of thought, of sustenance, of benefaction."[10] Hartley understood that the spareness of his own canvases set them against the work of Benton and other "American scene" painters such as Grant Wood and John Steuart Curry, and he took some satisfaction in finding another painter who had what he considered to be a "fine sense of earth and the solid meanings of experiences in such," unlike the other Americans, or the surrealists, for that matter, whose work Hartley could not abide.[11]

He was acutely aware of friendships and hurt when an old friend, the writer Ettie Stettheimer, refused to see him because he had been in Hitler's Germany. Word got back to him that Gertrude Stein, whom he had attempted to make contact with when she was in Boston on a tour in the fall of 1934, thought he had fallen short of his potential. He reported to Adelaide Kuntz, "The voluminous Gertrude Stein told someone in Boston that I had 'missed my cue somewhere along the line' which of course means she was hoping I would be 'at last an original American' as she said in 1913 — to me personally."[12] Even Stieglitz seemed strange — "a funny boy," Hartley called him. He acknowledged that Stieglitz had been kind to him socially, but he was "too queer for words about prices & me — and I don't wish to play cymbals to the 'first violins.'"[13]

By May 1935 he was utterly fatigued. He was plagued by what he had come to recognize was a congenital case of frail nerves, and his doctor instructed him not to go north during the summer. Buoyed slightly by some money he had received from selling a painting to a relative and by a fifty-dollar-a-month stipend from "an angel," Hartley planned a trip with Mark Tobey to Bermuda, where he expected to remain throughout the summer instead of returning to Gloucester. "I had a very bad time... before I left," he wrote to Adelaide Kuntz shortly after he arrived in Bermuda, in late June. He referred to what he called "those psychic sinking spells — double dose of old E[ngland] and N[ew] E[ngland] isn't any too good to get by on — if one could only change one's personality & be something else for awhile." He acknowledged that his depression had a lot to do with

> basic aloneness — no channels to pour one's natural qualities into — and it's a long time since I was eight yrs. old — half a century — think of it — of the same frights & fears — at 8 however a child has faith & how does one get it & hold it a half century later — family complaint — no one really has "gone off" — no one died of anything dramatic — but the nerves go frazzle at a certain time — and it's hard to pick up nerves.

Although in the end Mark Tobey had not accompanied him, Hartley was nonetheless pleased to have made the trip and to be in Bermuda, which "is what it is — nothing whatever but sunlight — soft air — & the water like thermal baths & they have soothed me quite a bit." He swam and sunbathed constantly. After spending a short while in a rented room in the town of Hamilton, he found lodging on the North Shore, in the home of Elmo Petty, a plumber whose wife was away and who, eager for companionship, was happy to let Hartley have part of the house for fifteen dollars a month.[14]

Just as he had on his first visit to Bermuda, many years earlier, he found the island bland, calm and soothing but hardly inspiring. It was a place for a watercolorist, he announced, but no good at all for someone working in oil. He was painting small pictures of what he termed "pure spirit," as well as some flower pieces and fish arrangements. Perhaps his most interesting paintings from this trip were the ones he did of the bright fish Elmo Petty caught in the traps he set out over the ocean reef that lay six miles off Bermuda. Each Sunday Hartley would go out with Petty and observe the fish, which seemed "more like birds & flowers than fish — one mottled green one with vermillion wings (or fins) others pure blue — one a parrot fish all parrot colours — other mystical white or pink." His paintings were not "accurate scientifically," he told Adelaide Kuntz, "but they represent this mystical appearance — and you can't go wrong in paint because they run the whole chromatic scale themselves."

Satisfied enough with the peacefulness of Bermuda, and appreciative of Elmo Petty's friendship, Hartley nevertheless by mid-August became restless and decided to travel north to visit his intimate friend Frank Davison in Nova Scotia.[15] Late in September, after returning to the United States from Bermuda, he took a ship from Boston to Yarmouth, on the southern tip of Nova Scotia, and from there an eight-hour train ride to Lunenberg, on the eastern coast, where he expected to meet Davison. When he discovered that Davison had departed for Halifax the day before, Hartley resolved to stay on without him, and he rented a room in a tourist home. Finding that unsatisfactory, after a week he took the advice of a taxi driver and walked four miles to the small village of Blue Rocks, where he arranged for lodging at a dollar a day in the home of Libby and Leander Knickle. He was immediately entranced: "such a sweet family far more cultivated than average — you'd love them — especially the mother — I fell for her at once — a pretty shy little thing — mother of four grown sons and daughters," Hartley wrote to Adelaide Kuntz soon after he settled in Blue Rocks.

The Knickles took Hartley in as one of the family, and he responded warmly, sensing that he had at last found the companionship he sought. It enabled him to embrace the north as a whole as well; instead of damning it, he delighted in the small village, with its neat white houses clustered fifty feet from the ocean, amid the rocks and little coves that marked the shoreline. Inside the Knickles' house were furnishings and bric-a-brac that charmed him: "and O the crayon portraits — the seashell frames — hooked rugs & braided ones — and a reed organ on which Leander Knickle — (papa) played & sang me 'Beautiful Isle of Somewhere' first evening," Hartley reported.

"It is a salt of the earth country & so good to get down to earth and its true values again," he declared. The life was primitive:

> The well up in one corner of the field & the 'comfort station' in another — bowl & pitcher in room of course — but O — so honest to God — all of it — they have a marvelous cow who all but churns her own butter — cream is so thick — all bread cake & cookies so good and the dearest woman who makes them — and love rules this home — & tho they are pious they are not boring about it — but no scandal or malign talk.[16]

It seemed to Hartley to be almost everything he had been missing, and he continued to rave about it, in his letters remarking on the simple beauty of the Knickle boys and on the abundance of food. Leander Knickle one night drew him four lobsters from one of his traps; another time Hartley bought an eight-pound cod fresh off a boat for ten cents and brought it home to cook.[17]

As if life with the Knickles were not good enough, Hartley soon found an even more completely satisfying arrangement. At the Knickles' he had met Martha Mason, an elderly woman who came to spin wool with Libby and several others. She and her family lived on East Point Island, a quarter of a mile across an inlet from Blue Rocks. In the village Hartley met her two sons, Alton (or Alty), age thirty-one, and Donald (Donny), slightly younger, whom he found immensely attractive. They invited him to the island to see their new speedboat, and soon after that Hartley asked the Masons if he could live with them. Early in November he moved over; as he explained to Adelaide Kuntz,

> I came up last night in the moonlight to Eastern Points [the postal designation for the island] — to stay the rest of the time or three weeks more — because I fell in love with a most amazing family of men & women the like of which I have never in my life seen — veritable rocks of Gibraltar in appearance the very salt of salt — how I would love to paint a series of them all.

The boys, he said, had "nearly devoured me with affectionate devotion" from the start. They were drinkers, and Alty had asked Hartley to have a good drink with him when they met in Blue Rocks.

Hartley had waited until the day he spent on the island looking at the speedboat, and drinking there with the Mason boys and several other men had captivated him. The bonding, the high spirits, the ease with which he was accepted into the group — all of it nearly overwhelmed him. This was as full an expression of male love as he had experienced. "The boys build their own boats," he reported to Arnold Rönnebeck the next spring, "and just finished a speed boat before I left & and I was first passenger — they get wildly drunk every now & then — & my God — well you know — simply wild."[18]

He recognized that things were coming together for him now as they had all too rarely done before, in Berlin, in Provence, in Gloucester in 1931, and once or twice elsewhere. The setting was important: "It is an island here — only a mile & a half from Blue Rocks and is gorgeously wild with deep forests & the trees all hanging with grizzly moss etc. and all still more secluded than Blue Rocks & really what I have been looking for & I see my next summer here very easily." He enjoyed being the center of attention, "the mystery wonder — the magical personage in places like this," but he did not mean to take undue advantage of that. The Masons "are so humble," he noted, "& they are so grateful for attention from the outside world of which they get very little naturally." They were "O so true & real like the sea & the rocks." The father, Francis Mason, and the boys were "dark and rugged... all of them look like cinnamon bears & are terrifically powerful — and so gentle and childlike." He felt as if he had found his "chosen people"; among them, for once, his "social style" was correct. "My whole summer has been so rich in the human sense," he told Adelaide Kuntz. In Bermuda people had been "affectionate and endearing," and now he had discovered even more of that sort of humanity. "I see Francis Mason with his majestic face lean over the table & say grace — 'O God we thank thee etc.,'" Hartley wrote, "[and] I feel so honoured to be among them."

Two days later he wrote to Adelaide Kuntz again, reaffirming his happiness. He knew that he would return in the spring of 1936; "all this vital energy & force is too good to miss," he said. He felt, moreover, that he had "never been so near the real thing before — for a fisherman is more of a 'thing' than a shut in farmer — that is a N[ew] E[ngland] one — & it's all so new to me and enveloping." He described once again the rugged beauty of the Masons, their "sweet characters & their good brains." He had not liked himself for some time, he admitted to

Kuntz, "because I don't like to hate for it is bad for the soul & unhealthy for the body — and I'm capable of loving hard & strong so I must become violently in love again. . . . I don't want escapes via intellectual ruses — I want affirmations via passionate embraces — & you can't have life unless you give it." Already he envisioned painting the Masons: "if I did murals," he wrote, "I'd do one of the family at supper or noon meal — the table is long & narrow — I in the center — Donny right — Alty left — & sister [Alice] on the other side — walls blue furniture black — mama always in black with white apron — boys & papa in overalls — all dark & mystic looking — already I even think of doing studies of the men next year."[19]

Having made plans to return to the Mason's home in 1936, Hartley could face New York for the winter, though he dreaded another season of small hotel rooms, cafeteria food, and the intrigues of the little world of art. He arrived in early December and quickly looked into the possibility of working in an arts project. The process took several weeks but was worth it, because he was offered $95.44 a month and had five weeks to complete his first work. Nonetheless, he chafed at the arrangement, which called for him to sign in at the project office four days a week at 9:00 A.M.; pleading illness, he convinced the administrators to instead send someone around to verify that he was working. By early February he was on the job but already complaining about the bureaucratic way the project was handled, writing out his version of it in long letters.[20] He was being unfair; the project was providing him with much-needed cash, and its administrators had bent over backwards to accommodate his wishes. Participating in the project made him feel important because other prominent artists were also involved; he considered himself a major American painter, and this was a validation of his opinion. Perhaps his touch of arrogance came from the sense of security he had gained from living with the Masons and from knowing he could return there, which caused him to feel particularly removed from the New York scene, a milieu that irritated him in any case.

Then, too, his confidence was further bolstered when Stieglitz asked him to write the introduction to a catalogue for a show of Georgia O'Keeffe's work, held at An American Place in January and early February 1936. After his disappointing time with the Downtown Gallery, Hartley was pleased to be invited back into Stieglitz's fold. In his essay he meant to be generous toward O'Keeffe, and to a degree he succeeded. He thought he was making a fine gesture toward her, but the circumstances enabled him to condescend, just as he had done when he wrote about her in the early 1920s. He acknowledged the mystic qualities of her work, but he went on to assert that O'Keeffe herself laid "no claim to intellectualism" and "fret[ted] herself in no way with philosophical or esthetic theories — it is hardly likely she knows one premise from another." Hartley called her a "highly developed intuitive," and ended his piece by declaring that she remained, as always, "a woman, having woman's interests, a woman's ardours in pursuit of the sense of beauty — a woman's need of getting at her own notion of truths — she is never struggling for man-power or man quality — she has no need of such irrelevant ambitions . . . she is a woman, utterly free."[21] One can imagine an indignant O'Keeffe replying that Hartley had no idea of who she really was. He did not know her that well, had never seen her on her own turf, the Southwest, and could not get beyond his jealousy over her intimacy with Stieglitz.

O'Keeffe was vexed enough with Hartley to let him know that she disagreed with his word-portrait of the recently dead Charles Demuth, which he did at about the same time as the one of her. She told Hartley that his Demuth was "not a Demuth I know." He countered that she could not have known the person he knew, who was "impressed by 'celebrities' etc." O'Keeffe would have drawn forth Demuth's "'lamb-like aspect,'" Hartley wrote to Rebecca Strand, "and so she never knew how naughty-nasty he could be."[22]

Emboldened by writing the O'Keeffe piece, Hartley at the beginning of February asked Stieglitz for an exhibition. He asserted that he needed it now more than ever before, and he assured his old friend that "all the blackness is gone out of my pictures and this is victory enough for it typifies a comforting state of progression." He told Stieglitz that he had at least forty pictures that had never been seen publicly, and that he had already written a preface for the catalogue.[23] Stieglitz agreed to the idea, and Hartley had his next-to-last exhibition with Stieglitz from March 22 to April 14, 1936.

Things were going well for him. Despite the saddening death of his dearest sister in Cleveland late in February, he was soon buoyed by a series of successes. The *New Caravan* accepted his essay on Demuth and one about Albert Pinkham Ryder; he had income from his project work and attention from his O'Keeffe piece; his show of twenty-nine paintings at An American Place would be well received when it opened; and he was invited to deliver a paper at the Museum of Modern Art in conjunction with their major show "Cubism and Modern Art."

"Cubistic show french of course at Modern Museum," he reported to Rebecca Strand shortly after the opening, on March 2. "Historical from 1908 on — and how sleepy & tired they all look now — too much celebration — no human warmth — without which nothing can last — I say & so I have written the first draft of an essay called — 'and the Nude has descended the Staircase.'"[24] His paper was appreciated, he reported later to Adelaide Kuntz. He declared that he did not like the museum but had thought the publicity would be good, and indeed it was.[25] His talk was an excellent consideration of cubism and a criticism of surrealism, "a strange field for painting," he thought. Although he perhaps spent too much time letting his audience know what a good friend of Gertrude Stein's he was, he nonetheless provided them with an entertaining overview of the cubist movement in Paris. Revolutionary when they were created, the paintings now seemed somehow quaint, more of historical interest than anything else. While a surrealist painting could never be much more than a "pathological chart," Hartley maintained, Duchamp's *Nude,* the painting that had been the scandal of the 1913 Armory Show and that was symbolic of the best of cubism, had "descended the staircase and most gracefully, and she may now parade the halls and foyers of common experience without the least fear of insolent interference."[26]

Two weeks before his own show opened on March 22, he was still having difficulty building up the paintings that he had begun in Bermuda and intended to include. These were "'fantasies' and 'romantic intervals' . . . many of them fish and roses as seen and sensed in Bermuda," he told Rebecca Strand.[27] There were also scenes from Garmisch-Partenkirchen. His introduction in the catalogue took the form of a "Letter Never Sent" to Aurelie Cheronne, a Frenchwoman he had met before World War I. In it Hartley spoke of the place of art — "in the feelings more than in the thought" — of the "conflict between fact and the imagination, of intellect and intuition," and of sentimentality. He remarked that he had thought a lot about these matters and a few years earlier had begun

to think of the White Horse Legend of Yorkshire, or was it more precisely Cheshire, that was tossed over to me on the saltstrewn rocks of New England, and of the same geographic heritage of Richard Rolle and his undying song-fervours to his beloved Yhesu, and the much too living Brontës, binding awful truths together with their herbaceous sentiments and frozen ecstasies, and at my child's elbow, the warm diffidences of Emerson and Thoreau nudging me to consciousness.

His new work came out of these influences, he said, as well as a "more or less sudden vision accepting experience, made cautious with need of reasonableness, denying the importance of anything at all but the quality and principle of life itself." Somewhat obtusely, he was acknowledging that many things in his life had converged. He concluded by adding a mystical anagram, "Own, Won, ONE," to suggest what he felt his paintings represented. Finally, he included a poem, "This Portrait of a Sea Dove, Dead":

> Sea dove in a shroud
> of sand, all shiny with
> thick clips of sun —
> sea dove in a shroud
> of sand, and the last word
> spoken — alone.
> I did not carry messages
> for love or war to end their ways,
> I only bore flicked wave caresses
> and took them to a timely place.
> I gave them to my brood to drink —
> a draft of silence on the brink
> of death I gave, telling them also
> to be brave,
> have grace
> to face
> the loneness of their days.
> I shut my eye on a kiss
> of sun,
> and this I give to
> everyone.[28]

"My show gave me great cause for rejoicing as I received so many compliments from knowns and unknowns," Hartley wrote to Adelaide Kuntz after it was over. He sold six paintings at low prices, which annoyed him, but he was delighted with the "superb treatment" Henry McBride had given him in a review, in which he praised the exhibition and called Hartley "one of the last of the New England Puritans," noting that "the half-dozen paintings in the New England series quite overtop all the other things in the collection."[29] Other reviews were likewise complimentary, even if the reviewers did not appreciate one or another set of paintings.

Hartley had a right to be pleased, and he was, though he understood that one reason for his critical success was his acquiescence to the demand for *American* scenes. "I propose a 100% Yankee show next year — to ram that idea down their throat till it chokes them even," he declared to Kuntz.[30] Still embittered and frustrated by the knowledge that even now, when he was recognized as a significant American painter, he could not sell his work effectively, he played the martyr. Despite the help that Stieglitz and others had given him, he saw himself as being alone against the world. He told his niece that he had faced the crisis of reducing the paintings in the storage vaults "utterly alone," when in fact friends had provided him with what money and assistance they could; and he asserted that "*never* have I asked anyone for an exhibition or a write-up," when that was precisely what he had done to get his exhibition at An American Place.[31] Despite whatever success he was having, the New York scene dismayed him, and he took his displeasure out on Stieglitz and O'Keeffe, who he felt were less than totally enthusiastic about him. It was probably that summer, during a brief visit to Gloucester, that he talked to Helen Stein about O'Keeffe, describing one of her paintings of a long barn and making a sketch of it on an envelope. "That's the sort of thing she does," he remarked. "No one knows what the attraction is — turned on its side." And he turned the envelope upright so that the sketch suggested female genitals.[32] Only once more would he have an exhibition with Stieglitz.

After stopping in Gloucester in late June, he made the lengthy train trip to Nova Scotia, enjoying the scenery as he passed through New Brunswick and on to Halifax. Once he was settled at the Masons' again, he began what he expected would be another idyllic stay. For two months it was, and he reveled in being among the Mason men when they worked on the island. He was included as much as he wanted and even accompanied them on a fishing trip in August, catching several mackerel and feeling very much a part of the crew as he hauled lines and bunked in the cramped quarters of the ship. On the island he would poke around inside the Masons' house, often stepping into the kitchen and peering into the pots on the stove to see what "Aunt Martha" Mason was cooking. He walked about the island with his hands clasped behind his back, as if staring into — or studying — the nature he would then draw. He did many drawings that summer — "should like to achieve something like myopic observation if not exactly vision — The power to see minutely and exactly is a rare gift and not all even good or great painters had it," he told Adelaide Kuntz in July.[33]

His contentment fostered his writing. He inscribed fragments about life on the island in a journal, once noting the great variety of books he had brought with him and another time recounting a conversation he had had with "Cleophas," the name he had given to Francis Mason to disguise his identity when he wrote about him. Yet another piece was entitled "Our Island," a loving account of the community of which Hartley now felt entirely a part:

> This is the only island I ever knew. There are countless like it doubtless, but was ever an island of its size wilder, more terrific, more untamed and untamable than this one.
>
> There are people living on our side of it, the inner side, the shore side. They intertwine, raise families & go to their death on the inner side, from which years of fishing have accomplished all they know of success.
>
> There is no hunger — no one is idle — no one will ever need assistance & fail of receiving it — the pulse of the community is full and responsive — no one is surprised — they know each other for generations — no one deceives.

Not infrequently he would head toward the center of the island or to the shore to sunbathe naked, enjoying the absolute solitude, and then walk along somewhere and notice the tiny things — "urchins, clam shells & mussels in the deepest of the woods" — that crows and seagulls had carried there. He observed both the abundance and the cruelty of nature, and imagined himself the "self-appointed spiritual owner of the island."[34]

He did his painting, he reported to Stieglitz in late August, in what was called a "fish store," a small shed in which fishing nets and coils of rope, stone anchors, lobster buoys, and other equipment were stored. The odors of salted mackerel and cod-liver oil were powerful reminders of his environment. He had one-fourth of the small room, "with a door that swings to the north where I can see the indications of Labrador or almost." It provided a "clear view of horizontal immensity," which he incorporated into the seascapes that were soon to come. "I can shut the east door & am not seen," he noted, "& my corner is full of sea shells bleached crabs — cork floats — coils of rope that the sun has bleached white — & these then are the new subject matter which I try to make portraits of, and if there is a hint of the abstract in the result it is the quality of nature itself that rules for I want to have no emotion of my own."

He told Stieglitz that he was "all but imbedded" in the Mason family, and went on to describe the characters of Francis and Martha, the two boys, and Alice. He must have begun to record his experiences with them by this time, for in a letter he sent to Adelaide Kuntz in early September he again spoke glowingly of the family, referring to Francis as Cleophas. If he had not already given the others fictitious names also, he would soon do so: Martha would be Marie Sainte Esprit; Alty, Adelard; Donny, Etienne; Alice, Madeleine (later changed to Marguerite) Felice, and Ruby, a daughter who worked in Halifax, Jeanne Marthe.[35]

"It had been such a long lyrical summer," Hartley observed in "Cleophas and His Own," the piece he wrote about his Nova Scotia experience before he departed in late November. "And then it came September, September crashing down upon our hearts and souls like earthquake upon ruin." On the twenty-third he wrote to Adelaide Kuntz, "I don't want to tell what I have to tell — but a terrific tragedy has fallen on our house here & the two big lovely boys of the family & their pretty young cousin were drowned Saturday night in the teeth of the gale that swept up from Florida all along the Atlantic seaboard." Donny, Alty, and their cousin Allen had been in Lunenburg on Saturday night, the nineteenth, and had drunk a lot, as they often did. But instead of remaining ashore they had decided to cross over from Blue Rocks to the island at night, during the violent storm, when high winds had whipped up giant waves. Fine seamen though they were, the attempt was utterly foolhardy. The waves were ferocious, as was the current running between the mainland and the small islands located between Blue Rocks and East Point Island; the coastline was lined with jagged rocks; and Alty's punt, in which they tried to cross, was hardly large enough for two people, let alone three, in addition to being round-bottomed and hence unstable. Even so, they made it across to Miller Island, between Blue Rocks and their own place. They portaged Miller, got back into the punt, and then were drowned when either it overturned or they lost their oars as they struggled toward home, which lay no more than five minutes away from where they died.

Sunday morning, after the storm, the weather was clear and the sun bright. But when the boys did not appear, the rest of the family began to worry. All the evidence pointed to their having been lost. A few days later the punt was found washed ashore twenty miles away, and six days after the drowning the bodies of Alty and Allen were found on the beach of one of the little nearby islands. That of Donny, mutilated, surfaced three days later.[36]

Hartley was so distraught that during the first days after the boys were lost he went to visit neighbors nearby and talked with them; he could not bear the Masons' sadness. "O the wrench even to me who had grown to love them dearly & been so proud to know them," he wrote to Adelaide Kuntz.

Fool-hardy Alty — so lovable & so terrific — so affectionate — so theatric — dear sweet gentle lyrical Donny who never had a dark thought or an exaggerated one about anything has left his little gold-finch girl in misery as they were heading strong toward marriage & another life. . . . The sea outside the door now might be a quiet little pool in a green meadow it is so calm.

Hartley understood full well the pathos of the situation, and beyond that, the fierce contrariness of man's relation to the harsh but beautiful north sea and to the rugged land behind it.[37]

Hartley thought he ought to leave so as not to burden the Masons further, but Ruby urged him to stay to comfort her parents. This was, in fact, a comfort to him as well, because he grieved as rarely he had before. Not only had men he loved died, but the family he had finally found had been broken apart, and he sensed, accurately, that he would never return to what remained of it. "It has been the hardest two weeks I have ever encountered," he confessed to Adelaide Kuntz, "for I had to show my powers to help these dear people support their bur-den — and I had my own love to support." A month later he could begin to distance himself from the episode, but he felt no less sad. "They are *gone*," he cried out to Arnold Rönnebeck, "and I am all but heartbroken — and I doubt if I can ever come here again — because the place is nothing without them. . . . I haven't felt anything like it since the death of Karl von F[reyburg,] who as you well know became an image in my spiritual experience." He asserted that "one must love what one loves to the end & so I shall love these boys as long as I have memory of them . . . and the biggest one [Alty] wanted to build a little shack with me & live in it with me — as he was 'off' women he said because the one girl he thought he wanted jilted him." [38]

The strength of the Masons and others helped him. When early in October the annual Memorial Day was held for fishermen lost at sea during the year, he was moved by the dignity and simple devotion of the large crowd that gathered around the bandstand in Lunenburg to sing and pray and then march in procession to the docks, where a wreath and an anchor of flowers were cast onto the ocean. [39]

His painting and writing helped as well. While the island itself did not provide him with spectacular landscapes or seascapes in the literal sense, his imagination was fueled by his associations and, of course, by the terrible intensity of his experiences. "This is a wondrous place for a writer — though for painting not offering very much," he asserted, recognizing that "the life has enriched me greatly — and I have lived so logically and well." [40] He underestimated the effect on his painting; when he departed, he had made more than twenty pictures and numerous drawings. One of his first responses to the death of the boys was *Northern Seascape, off the Banks,* a somber, Ryderesque scene of jagged, toothlike rocks with surf smashing against them, and on the dark sea beyond, two wave-tossed sailing ships driving toward a black-lined horizon above which loom lowering clouds and a threatening sky. Hartley would paint the scene again, a reminder of the side of nature that swallowed lives violently.

At the same time he also did a delicate, detailed study of two dead Labrador ducks that emphasizes the pathos of life for all creatures — and its beauty. He worked in the blacksmith shop where Donny and Alty had made their tools and boats, "now pathetically so quiet — no hammer — no anvil tones — no blustering boys — no rich thick flavour of manly energy in labour there which made last year such a social delight and privilege." After trying himself alone in the shop, he had decided that he could "make everything now so silent have life through associations of memory." From all the silent tools there emanated "a kind of almost companionship," which gave poignancy to his work. Painting the two ducks was, he told Adelaide Kuntz, "a test of observation — and what [John] Marin calls the 'piercing seeing of the object.'"[41]

He worked equally hard at his writing, so by the time he left Nova Scotia he had "two sets of poetics ... 'Cleophas and His Own' — and 'Between Point and Point' — the latter completed as I get to New York for I want a few touches of Quebec to give Canadian flavours — the other is all but settled in place but needs re-arrangement probably — ending of course in the tone of deep threnody for obvious reasons."[42] Not until 1940, inspired by finding Corea, Maine, a fishing village southeast of Ellsworth that reminded him of Blue Rocks, would he make his final revisions to "Cleophas and His Own," but the manuscript was essentially complete when he left Canada in 1936. A complex piece, it consists of a long threnody that describes Hartley's life among the Masons, the death of the boys, and eventually his departure. It concludes with a poem, "Fishermen's Last Supper." To this he added "Postludes," a series of prose and poetic pieces about life after the death of the boys, including scenes of Hartley's time on the island and laments for Alty, Donny, and Allen. "*Si tu n'avais pas connu* ["If I hadn't known you," a line from a French sailor song] — / So long, my five beauties, whose lives enlarged my own," he ended the entire work, referring to the Mason family.[43]

His departure was poignant. As they stood together on the Masons' dock, Martha threw herself into his arms, weeping. He promised her that he would return, then shook hands with Francis and assured him of the same thing. With rain and snow falling, Hartley climbed down into a dory manned by two boys from Blue Rocks, and the three of them crossed the gut to the mainland. "Five magnificent chapters out of an amazing human book, these beautiful human beings, loving, tender, strong, courageous, dutiful, kind, so like the salt of the sea, the grit of the earth, the sheer face of the cliff," he wrote in "Cleophas." He had gone to the cemetery on the island before he left, with seagulls swirling above him, a soft breeze blowing, a white fence marking the Masons' land nearby, and said aloud, "Adelard and Etienne, I loved you more than myself, I love you because I was equal with you in every way but the strength, and it was the strength that fortified me — I truly loved you." The only response was the wind "rustling among the

paper flowers, twisting their worn petals east to west." "Fishermen's
Last Supper" serves as a sort of epigraph for the boys, reading, in its
revised and final form,

> For wine, they drank the ocean —
> for bread, they ate their own despairs;
> counsel from the moon was theirs
> for the foolish contention.
>
> Murder is not a pretty thing
> yet seas do raucous everything
> to make it pretty —
> for the foolish or the brave,
> a way seas have.[44]

Even at that, Hartley had not yet written through his emotions, and
then or later wrote other poems about the Masons, with titles such as
"Two Drowned at the Gateway," "O Bitter Madrigal," and "Encompassed," the last a passionate poem about his physical longing for Alty.
Hartley dreamed of the moments when Alty had encompassed him in
his arms — "hair stood on end like fury-fire/ mouth blowing steam of
thick desire." "I will be love/ you never heard of," Hartley cried out,
then ended, "I walked along/ beaten with the song."[45]

Hartley sensed as poignantly as ever he would that in Nova Scotia
everything had come together to make emphatic what he had called
in his introduction to his recent show at An American Place "the quality and principle of life itself." This "everything" consisted of a "life
spent in plain beliefs, in despairs, understanding, and with more or
less sudden vision accepting experience." At Dogtown in 1931 he had
begun to accept the form of life; Nova Scotia — the human community, the island, and the ocean — had then made his vision more lucid,
and finally the deaths of the Mason boys and the responses of the other
members of the family had made that vision crystal-clear, so that it
allowed him to accept life itself as before he could not.

We tend to believe that we can't go home again. For Hartley, and
for the rest of us, that was and is mostly true. Home for him, as much
as anywhere, was Nova Scotia; and after November 1936 he never
went back, except in his imagination. There he returned many times,
producing rich memory portraits, landscapes and seascapes, still lifes,
and studies of small, delicate animals and fish until his death nearly

seven years later. Shortly before he died he bought a copy of W. B. Yeats's *Collected Poems*. He loved the poetry and noted especially several poems, among them "The White Birds," in which the narrator, "haunted by numberless islands, and many a Danaän shore," wishes he and his beloved were birds far out to sea on "the wandering foam," where time might forget them and sorrow never come.[46]

For Hartley Nova Scotia came to encompass the idyllic and the ideal that could never remain: the Masons, particularly Alty, were his beloved, like the imagined "white birds on the foam of the sea," while East Point Island and the islands around it were Yeats's "numberless islands, and many a Danaän shore." Alas, even the white birds perish, as Hartley realized. But art gives them a certain immortality, and for Hartley Nova Scotia, probably more than any other place, made him understand this and enabled him to paint about his new sense of life.

II

Maine, 1937–1939

While he was in Nova Scotia, Hartley wrote some "New England Notations" in his journal. He quoted someone he had known in 1916 in Provincetown, who had observed that New Englanders were wonderful when they went the other way—meaning, Hartley explained, "when they go out to get there—and they usually do." He was thinking of himself, of course, for he had gone a long way out to get to Maine, but now he felt it could be home because it had the qualities and the sort of people he had come to admire in Nova Scotia.[47]

He would work toward spending much of the next summer and fall in Maine, but before that he would have to contend with New York. During the winter of 1936 he suffered from ill health: his hearing got worse, and he had severe dental problems, resulting in the loss of many teeth. He took to putting his hand in front of his mouth when he spoke, out of embarrassment.

The most important event for him in the spring of 1937 was his last show with Stieglitz, from April 20 to May 17. It consisted of twenty-one paintings from Dogtown and Nova Scotia, and for it he wrote an introduction entitled "On the Subject of Nativeness — a Tribute to Maine," even though not one of the paintings was literally of Maine. To him the state was a "strong, simple, stately, and perhaps brutal country." He listed artists and writers who had come from there, conspicuously including himself, because his entire purpose was to identify himself with the state after many years away. "If there are no pictures of Maine in this present exhibition," he claimed, "it is due entirely to forward circumstance and never in any sense to lack of interest." He asserted that his education had begun in Maine's hills and had stayed with him wherever he was, be it Paris, Berlin, or Provence. Dogtown and Nova Scotia were "as much my native land as if I had been born in them, for they are of the same stout substance and texture, and bear the same steely integrity. . . . This quality of nativeness is coloured by heritage, birth, and environment, and it is therefore for this reason that I wish to declare myself the painter from Maine."[48] Although he did not indicate it, he very much meant to emphasize that last *the*.

Shortly before the exhibition opened, he wrote to Adelaide Kuntz that "it will be my best show in years — and I am all agog about it myself." It was "all straight nature" and so should not confuse potential buyers. He was as excited as always before a show and told Kuntz that Madame Gaston Lachaise had invited him to visit her in Georgetown, Maine, for part of the coming summer. He meant "to be known as *the* painter of Maine," he confessed, adding that he had "already accomplished something on that point." In Maine, he was sure, he would be happier than he could be in New York or elsewhere.[49]

Despite his high hopes, the show was not a success. While friends came and praised the work, the critics were nonplussed. He sold nothing, so that he was constrained to write to, among others, Lloyd Goodrich, curator of the Whitney Museum, and practically implore him to purchase a painting for the museum. Hartley believed he needed to disassociate himself from Stieglitz because An American Place was widely disliked. He rambled on about this to Goodrich, and about possible sales and his own ill health and lack of decent food — the result, he insisted, of his not having been able to get back his job with the artists' project. "I am not a book of the month painter," he closed his entreaty, "and I have no gift for the tricks of the game, all I can do is be sincere with myself and therefore the world." The Whitney eventually did purchase one painting, *The Old Bars — Dogtown,* for eight hundred dollars.[50]

Hartley held Stieglitz partly responsible for the failure, as his letter to Goodrich indicated. Stieglitz bore the costs of the exhibition but was unenthusiastic, at one point accompanying the art critic Elizabeth

McCausland as she viewed it and telling her that Hartley was not a major artist. The others in Stieglitz's group, Stieglitz believed, were more truly American in their work — O'Keeffe, Marin, Dove, and Paul Strand.[51]

Too many resentments had built up between Hartley and the man who had been his mentor for much of the time since their first meeting, in 1909. When a young dealer, Hudson Walker, visited the 1937 exhibition and told Stieglitz that he was interested in Hartley's work, the other was happy to turn everything over to him. Hartley knew that Stieglitz disapproved of him, which grated on him deeply. "I once saw a bill of consignment on the table in the office of the American Place," he wrote to Walker after the break with Stieglitz had been finalized. The bill was

> to the Downtown Gallery and it was for three O'Keeffe's and the prices ran $3000 — for the smallest, $4800, for the next size, and — $10,000.00 for the largest which would doubtless have been a petunia or an ox-skull, all that without batting an eyelash and yet he seems to think that nothing at all is a lot for me, and I never could make out his psychology in the matter, save that he is just hyped about O'Keeffe and Marin and he gets a racetrack quiver when he mentions these names or hears them mentioned.[52]

After the exhibition Walker took nine paintings from An American Place and in addition asked if he might have Hartley's next show. "Delightful, Walker & Mrs. W.," Hartley wrote to Adelaide Kuntz, "both handsome — young — simple. . . . They are fresh & hopeful & will work hard to promote this 'prima donna' as they need strong names — so I feel as if I were out of the old cul-de-sac." Soon he was visiting the Walkers frequently at their New York apartment and enjoying the family atmosphere.

He was pleased with his new prospects. The sale of a small painting for $225 was a relief, and glad to have ended another difficult New York season, he arrived in Georgetown in June with high expectations, after spending a week with relatives and friends in Auburn and Lewiston. He liked being near Madame Lachaise and liked getting into a routine of reading in the morning and then painting when the light was best. The problem for him in Georgetown was that he had to walk several miles to find his seascapes, so while his house was quite suitable and initially his neighbors seemed pleasant enough, presently the situation became tedious. The people, while nice, lacked the intellectual vitality he sought, and he felt lonely, realizing that he could not re-create anything of what he had had in Nova Scotia, despite the friendship of Madame Lachaise.[53]

His work that summer was fine; in paintings such as *Fox Island, Georgetown, Maine* he achieved the power of his best seascapes. He called this his first "'laureate' picture . . . a really accurate portrait of the off-shore seascape from Indian Point," near Georgetown. Rocks, waves, a low, spare island, and, in the far background, a lighthouse all convey the sense of a hard yet beautiful Maine seacoast. Hartley was restless, however, and in September he took the ferry from Rockland to the island of Vinalhaven, some twelve miles out to sea, where he visited an acquaintance, the poet Harold Vinal, and investigated the possibility of making that his home for the following summer.[54] Ten days later he returned to the mainland, excited by the prospect of living on the island. He had found the people friendly and the place "as near like N. S. as anything out of it can be, and so perfectly to my liking." "New subject matter of all sea kinds" would be right at his doorstep, and living on Vinalhaven would enhance his intention to establish himself as "the painter of Maine from Maine," for, as he kept asserting, "there is no one else so qualified."[55]

By November he was preparing to leave Georgetown and move to Portland. Typically, he dismissed the place where he was, now judging the people in Georgetown "a dull lot — mostly Boston suburbanites — and I think the name Dedham — changed to Dead 'em would cover them all." But he remained pleased with his work, which he thought would "thrill — for I have a whole row of forceful sea pieces — two of them crashing seas on the rocks and I am delighted with myself to come so near to the real thing — and all so alive and spontaneous." Despite any misgivings he might have about Georgetown, he was satisfied with his choice to return to Maine: "It has been such a joy to come home to my native heath & feel so content here & now I am completely in the thing." Indefatigable, he was sure that "these are my big years. . . . Life not only begins but doubles at 60 — and such an onrush of fresh energy fairly surrounds me."[56]

He had planned to spend some time in Brunswick, Maine, before returning to New York, but he ended up going to Portland instead, early in December. He took a room in an old mansion that was comfortable and quiet, where he could work steadily on his writing and painting. People whom years before he would have shunned because they were too representative of Maine he now took to for that very reason, and before he left he gave two lectures. He thoroughly enjoyed being something of a luminary. Late in January 1938 he returned to New York to prepare for his first exhibition with Hudson Walker, which was held from February 28 to April 2. As had happened so often before, friends were kind about it but no sales resulted, though Hartley reported that the directors of the Addison Gallery of American Art, at Phillips Academy in Andover, Massachusetts, had taken *Fox Island* for consideration. Eventually they purchased it.

The days were, he remarked, "vacuity itself," and he yearned to return to Maine, not only to cut down on the cost of living but also so he could get on with his painting.[57] Vinalhaven seemed ideal to him when he arrived there in midspring. He had a comfortable room that looked out over a harbor, and he ate many meals at a good restaurant nearby, where he could watch the other patrons, "all fishermen up from the sea — picturesque men of course — quiet, gentle — and all say 'hi' or hello here — so you can't escape a friendly recognition." He painted with tremendous energy, noting, when he had been on the island for only a short while, that he already had seven pictures under way. One that he remarked on particularly was a memory portrait of Albert Pinkham Ryder, which was, he said, "remarkable as a feat of memory since I have nothing else to go by. . . . It will take a time to 'fill out' but — I got a good start." He also mentioned his wish to do "a large 'Fishermen's Last Supper' of the beloved family up in N.S. as I see the whole five of them so clearly."[58]

By midsummer he had accomplished a lot: "I have nearly finished one of the 30 × 40 canvases," he wrote to Adelaide Kuntz. "It looks very well. Two fishermen mending nets in the rain — Father & Son of Nova Scotia." It needed only the finishing touches, and then he would send it to the Whitney Museum for a fall exhibition. Another large canvas was "of seagulls on the rocks with fish in the foreground — and I am glad to be working on large sizes again," he added. He reiterated his intention to do a big painting of "the N. S. family at table — never have I seen such an epic sight as it was three times a day — such a sense of unity — as they all loved and admired each other & were so gracious to each other at all times & that is what love & harmony can bring forth when two parents are perfectly joined." He was working on three sets of paintings: highly symbolic ones such as the Nova Scotia fishermen and the seagulls (he would also do a first version of the Masons at their table); memory portraits of Ryder and of the Masons; and powerful seascapes — coastal scapes, really — which were also symbolic, of course, picking up images of a rugged, rocky shoreline pounded by waves, very much like his *Northern Seascape,* painted immediately after the death of the Mason sons.

Nova Scotia Fishermen depicts two figures, meant to be Francis and Donny Mason, attired in rain gear, working at their nets on a dock, the entire foreground set against a deep-blue backdrop of sea and sky. Their upper bodies are surrounded by a sort of halo, highlighting them and suggesting some sacred quality. The visual effect of the painting is powerful; moreover, as Gail Scott has suggested,

> The large size of the canvas [30 × 40 inches], plus its handmade, hand-rubbed mahogany frame [made by a Vinalhaven boatbuilder for Hartley, who rubbed it himself], and his stated intention to send it to the Whitney Annual that fall indicate that [he] had calculated the stir it would cause in New York because of the sudden reappearance of the figure and descriptive subject matter in his work.[59]

Give Us This Day is a more obviously symbolic piece about community and communion, in which five gulls (the Masons), with a sixth somewhat further back and off to one side (Hartley), are poised behind three fish in the foreground. The background is the familiar rocky coastline, ocean, and sky, with a single schooner outbound. The harmony of the painting's forms and colors and the stillness of the gulls themselves convey the sense of calm that Hartley most admired about the Mason household.

While it is in itself an important painting, it was also in some ways a warm-up for Hartley's first version of the family at their table, completed later during his stay on Vinalhaven. In *Fishermen's Last Supper* the five Masons are seated at a dining table. On the wall behind Francis, at the center, is a picture of a schooner; seated at either end of the group are the two boys, with eight-pointed stars above their heads, symbolizing regeneration. In the immediate foreground are three empty chairs, the two outer ones wrapped at the top with wreaths to mark the drowned boys, the center chair being symbolic either of Hartley himself or of Allen, the third boy who drowned. On the front edge of the tablecloth between the chairs is written *"mene, mene,"* a reference to the Old Testament tale of the proud and defiant King Belshazzar, whose doom God warned of by His handwriting on the wall, which said, in effect, "You have been judged and found wanting." Alty's proud defiance of the elements was, of course, believed to have been the cause of the three boys' deaths. In 1940 Hartley would begin another version of the same scene. Larger and more brilliantly colored — a deep-blue wall instead of a pale-blue one serves as the background — the painting is more forceful not only because of that but also because it is less overtly symbolic. Hartley removed the eight-pointed stars and the "*mene, mene,*" and the figures of the family, while still primitivist in style — Hartley called them archaic — are more fully rendered and dominate the picture as they do not in the earlier version.

Memory portraits that Hartley began in 1938 of Alty, Francis, and Martha Mason, like the figures in *Fishermen's Last Supper,* are "archaic." Barbara Haskell has noted that "although individualized, these portraits are not intended to be naturalistic. Rather, as with other artists, like Georges Rouault and Gaugin, who attempted to depict religious faith and renewal in contemporary terms, Hartley was inspired by pre-Renaissance sources." The figures were meant to be icons, and in these paintings Hartley picked up on the "abstract rigidity and [the] mannered, stylized effect [of] his Mexican paintings."[60]

His newfound interest in the human figure marked his deepening involvement in the idea of community, which had culminated for him in his two stays at the Masons' home. Life itself had become no easier for him — indeed, economically and emotionally it may have grown even harsher — but through the family he had discovered new meaning and, certainly, new faith. The primitive, archaic quality of his portraits did not spring from an inability on his part to paint the human figure well; rather, he was making a conscious effort to render the figures as direct, simple icons. He loved Ryder and the Masons for their elemental natures; sophisticated, naturalistic portraits would have conveyed his emotion less well.

He worked hard to finish his major paintings by the beginning of September, when he wanted to start smaller works and to paint landscapes and seascapes, for "then the colour is much more remarkable as when the sun lowers — there is a hard brilliance comes over it all — & makes it very distinguished and unusual." In the Vinalhaven harbor ships came and went frequently, giving it life; and in the town he saw handsome "middle aged men . . . so strong and muscular so normal & healthy looking—and it is nice to be where there are no 'over-wrought' types—no hyper sophisticates no city neurotics." Toward the end of the summer, too much normality had made life seem "peculiarly two-dimensional"; still, its gentleness and the natural beauty of the island kept him working, and he was remarkably prolific. Not only did he complete the symbolic paintings and begin the memory portraits, but he also did some seascapes that were almost—if not entirely—as significant as the other works.

It is no wonder that he became restless during the summer; he was that by nature. Hard work produced an emotional "high" that eventually resulted in a letdown; and, too, life on an island that lacked the intellectual sophistication he craved, no matter how scenic the views, led him to feel the need to get away. A new radio offered some solace, but it also whetted his appetite. "I do want so much to swing out a little in August & go down to Old Orchard for a few days as it seems too bad not to enjoy so lovely a spectacle as that five mile beach [in southern Maine] covered with handsome humanity," he wrote in July. "What fun it would be to be going again out into the world & having a fresh look at it—one gets rusty in some ways sitting still even though life is around me at all times."[61]

A month later what he called a "psychic fatigue" was dragging him down. It was "mental strain" from the difficulty of his artistic situation that brought on his depression, he was sure; there was "nothing obviously organic" in his fatigue, and his body was "stronger than ever."[62] His intense work and "island fever" contributed to the problem, no doubt, but more important was his weakening heart. At sixty-one, he was not in good condition, due to poor eating habits as well as an almost constant case of nervousness, not to mention nearly annual bronchitis and other sicknesses that plagued him during his winters in New York.

It was time for him to move again. Tired of Vinalhaven by the fall, he had applied for a Guggenheim Fellowship in creative writing, which would enable him to return the following year—not to Maine this time, but rather to the Southwest. "Perhaps I shall be obliged to change my idea of returning to native soil as I have done this past year—and as I would have a rousing welcome in the Southwest—& am asked so often why I don't go there again," he wrote to a young friend from California, Nick Brigante. Fatigued, Hartley believed that he was

> learning by degrees that [in] Maine though excitingly beautiful & profound in its solemnity, the human life seems sort of desiccated — washed out of its former stylism — and so one feels little related to anything these people think or do. The scope is small intellectually & spiritually & my two seasons in my native country have not proven that I shall get any more out of it than I now have — because life is not experience here.

He remarked, as he had before, that he was the most important artist in Maine, there being few others of note, not excepting Waldo Pierce, "who treats of his native subjects most casually — painting himself [and] his babies chiefly."[63]

In early November he moved to Portland, which, in contrast to his regard of the year before, he now judged to be "down at the heel & you feel it everywhere and the atmosphere is too circumscribed." He remained there until February, when he returned to New York, buoyed slightly by having given two lectures in Ohio in January, and by the knowledge that his severe dental problems were soon to be alleviated, thanks to Hudson Walker's having sold his mother a painting for $125, the proceeds to be used specifically for the needed dentistry.[64] Hartley put great stock in the possibility of the Guggenheim Fellowship, which would provide him with money and hence the chance to travel. He toyed with the idea of going to Finland as well as the Southwest, imagining that he might paint its northern landscapes to good effect.

But in the end he was not awarded the grant, and to add to that, he had sales of only a hundred dollars at his second exhibition with the Walker Gallery. He was distraught.[65] He considered trying to obtain another arts-project assignment but soon decided against it, even though he heard of another artist who had gotten a job painting a mural in the Portland Post Office: "two panels — just two waves — with cellophane water & paper rocks . . . for which he got $6000 — & did them in six weeks."[66] It was then that Helen Stein, in New York and attending an Easter Sunday service at Saint John's Church on Fifth Avenue, saw Hartley "walking slowly like a lost soul in front of the altar." Knowing of his plight, she assumed he was in great distress. She rushed over to him, seized him by the arm, and led him back to where she was sitting with two friends. He may have been distracted, but he still had fire about him, for as they walked up the aisle, he said to her in a rage, "'That bleached blond curly headed marcelled rouged whore' (referring apparently to the organist) 'what is he doing to that music? Take a look at him and you will see why.'"[67]

Hartley's dilemma was alleviated somewhat when Mabel Dodge's son, John Evans, and his wife, Claire Spencer Evans, invited him to spend the summer with them in the coastal village of West Brooksville, Maine. And he was pleased with his show, despite the minimal sales. He told Adelaide Kuntz that there had been many people there, "three times as many as ever before." Several dealers had appeared, and a number of young painters, "who now call me the greatest American painter — etc."[68] The art critic Elizabeth McCausland visited the show and wrote enthusiastically about it for the *Springfield* (Massachusetts) *Republican*. When he read her review, he contacted her at once, telling her that he was impressed by her going "into the 'new pieces' with such sympathetic understanding. It is quite my purpose to get out of the scale of 'cliche' which a lot of good painting sometimes displays — even in far greater artists than myself." He noted that "simplification is not easy — but I felt I had accomplished it to a respectable degree," explaining that "the people with whom I lived in the north taught me that to an encouraging degree by their profoundly simple & humble behaviour concerning all things."[69]

He enjoyed New York more than he had in the past. During the spring he visited Coney Island and liked it, and before departing for West Brooksville he saw the 1939 World's Fair, where he had a painting in the Contemporary American Art Show. At the fair he met the painter Max Weber, who was full of praise for his work and invited him to have dinner with him and his wife in Great Neck, Long Island. Weber, whom Hartley had not particularly liked years before when they saw each other at 291, now struck him as a "unique person . . . so full of the qualities of genius — and the finest artist in America without question," he told Helen Stein later, "tho," he added with no modesty whatsoever, "the new generation are giving that laurel to me now, quite touching and gratifying really."[70] Hartley was being noticed; he even had an old friend from Berlin in the twenties, Rogers Bordley, visit him in New York, and he preened a bit, something he could do more easily now that he had a new set of dentures.[71]

A short stopover in Portland was dispiriting. It had become, for him,

> dead — and full of corpses of past wealth and glory — The hotels in P. are full of old girls and boys hobbling on canes and crutches — ear trumpets and white hair and all that — they have cheap rooms and eat at the Y.W.C.A. which by the way has the best food in P. and at lunch there are the ladies and the men are fagged out married men who have settled into their own flesh and forgotten that of their spouses.[72]

He was pleased to get to the Evanses' place in West Brooksville in early July, but he soon found that he had "too much comfort really — spacious room — spacious work room — all privacy when I want it — wonderful food — books plenty — marvelous records." Tranquillity abounded, and he had as much privacy outdoors as in: "I ought not to be writing like this in the glare of the sun," he told Rogers Bordley early in August as he lay naked, sunning himself, "but I feel so free out here with the little waves making lovely music and the wind sort of pushing at me, even my [genitals — Bordley cut the word out] are taking it gracefully."[73]

Across the Bagaduce River from where he was staying was Castine, a lovely town but "messed up with huge summer houses and a golf course." Life was "synthesized," too homogenous and too full of the same sorts of people he had found in Georgetown two years earlier. Even the Evanses, charming and generous as they were, had a social style that could grate a bit. And as he could find nothing to paint — "no landscape — it is all scenery — not a single thing 'compares' pictorially" — he was restless and took to inventing his own scenes, "a series of created sea windows looking out to sea with flowers and books on a table as motive." He also painted figures: "a large one of a champ swimmer of Yale — Claire's nephew & my God! is he handsome — wonderful body — & so clean and nice."[74]

Too much tranquillity soon began to vex him: "I can't be happy away from crowds," he complained. "I need them as one needs drinks, and oftener than that."[75] Although his finances were still a great worry, he appreciated the touches of attention that were increasingly coming his way, and solitude was becoming less attractive to him. After the middle of September he moved to Bangor, "one of the most engaging

towns I ever came across. It is fairly reeking with magnificent history."
He made that home until well into the spring of 1940, enjoying it partly
because he was a celebrity there.

The state of Maine made a fuss over him, asking for his signature,
to which he added photos of a dozen of his Maine paintings and a copy
of the information given about him in the *Index of Twentieth-Century
American Artists*. The state librarian sent him an "official letter giving
me full State recognition." He delighted in the gesture and told Helen
Stein that "there is only Waldo Pierce and myself as outstanding painters from Maine and I really paint Maine and Waldo does not — poor
Waldo — such a nice person but not a good artist — one of the best of
the not so good ones, or he wouldn't be a feature of the Midtown
Gallery in N.Y. would he? No he wouldn't."[76] Given Hartley's lifelong
difficulty in making ends meet, his confidence in his plan to "market"
himself was more touching than irritating. He frequently railed
against artists who had succeeded publicly; speaking of Kansas, for
example, he told Rogers Bordley, "Now they've got Thomas Benton
stuffing his disguised modern art in the name of pure Americanism
up their arses and down their throats."[77]

Part of Hartley's scheme to publicize himself as a Maine artist was
his plan to paint Mount Katahdin, located in Baxter State Park in
north-central Maine, one of the highest peaks on the East Coast. With
the help of Carl Sprinchorn he found someone who would take him
to the park and guide him to the vicinity of the mountain. Near mid-
October Caleb Scribner, chief fish and game warden of the district and
only four years younger than Hartley himself, picked the painter up
from his room in Bangor and drove him the several hours to his home
in Patten. The next afternoon they drove thirty miles into the park,
left their automobile at a site called Avalanche Field, and began the
four-mile hike into Cobbs Camp, the spot Scribner had chosen for
Hartley to do his painting in.

The hike was over difficult terrain; in places they could walk on an
old corduroy road made of logs, but most of the way was on a trail full
of rocks, bushes, and wet bogs. Hartley and Scribner set out just before
five in the afternoon, so for most of the way they were walking in the
dark. Hartley's flashlight gave out, it rained, and the trip became a
"terrific ordeal" during which he twice fell headlong over boulders
into the brush. At sixty-two and in generally poor condition, he found

the walk a tremendous effort, but achieving it made the entire experience all the more monumental for him.

Once at Cobbs Camp, Hartley had a log cabin to himself that looked out over Katahdin Lake. He could eat his meals in a somewhat larger main lodge. The camp was run by Bud and Della Cobb, hearty, direct people of the sort that Hartley admired. They were fiercely independent and endured stern conditions in the wilderness, regularly having to trek the same path Hartley had taken to haul in supplies. Animals had to be fed, and during the harsh winters, with up to five feet of snow on the ground and temperatures to minus forty degrees, wood stoves had to be kept going at all times. Snow fell there as late as May.[78]

He remained at the camp for eight days, six of which were clear enough to allow him to study the mountain, draw, and paint. Near the end of his stay "nature even staged a beauteous snow storm covering everything with velvety & soothing white." From the beach at the edge of the lake below his cabin he could look toward Baxter Peak, the highest part of the mountain, and make quick sketches as well as swift, gestural paintings from which he would later do a series of rich oils.

The experience filled him with remarkable energy. "My work is getting stronger & stronger and more intense all the time which is most heartening at 63," he wrote to Adelaide Kuntz early in February 1940. "I have such a rush of new energy & motives coming into my head — over my horizon, like chariots of fire [—] that all I want is freedom to step aside and execute them." Back in Bangor, he immediately began to paint the mountain; by the time he wrote to Kuntz, he had finished a series of six works.[79] When he completed his memory paintings of the mountain three years later, he had nearly twenty canvases in all. None of the paintings is literal; the main peak, for example, is moved to the center of the canvas, as if viewed from an angle different from the one he actually had, and the colors he saw — vivid in the late autumn — are simplified down to two or three in each painting. But he captured the mountain as he had long hoped to. "All the tentativeness and overt symbolism of [Hartley's] other mountains — Mont Sainte-Victoire, Popocatepetl, the Alps — have given way to the moment of mastery when the experiential meaning of *mountain* has been thoroughly internalized," Gail Scott has observed. "Only the perfectly expressed image remains." He made portraits of Mount

Katahdin, and "the metaphor of man as mountain/mountain as man achieved a fluid interchangeability."[80]

The trip was the last great adventure of his life. In the nearly four years that remained to him he would have the satisfaction of real success and of discovering a living situation that approached the idyllic quality of East Point Island, but never again would he feel the elation he did during his days with Caleb Scribner and at Cobbs Camp. The warden became one of his male heroes on the dimensions of Walt Whitman or even Karl von Freyburg and Alty Mason, while the arduous hikes in and out made Hartley feel a part of a life and a natural world that he had rarely known and certainly not experienced for many years. After the trip he wrote a poem, "The Pilgrimage, and the Game Warden," which speaks in reverential terms of Scribner:

> he that had Ktaadn [Hartley used the Indian spelling] in his flesh and bone,
> and the look of windbeaten eyries in his eyes —
> wings that have battered many a thunder-
> ridden cliff —
> sweeping his priest-like nostrils
> and the pale wash of many a proud
> interval of rain, upon his hyper-
> weathered cheek.

The poem catches Hartley's sense of man's relation to nature, ending,

> The moment of a man clawing at a cliff
> is nothing to a cliff.
> It is the man that bursts with enmity
> toward something bigger than himself —
> the whisper of a mountain floors him
> suspending his ankles to a laughing
> wind.[81]

"I know I have seen God now," he wrote to a friend soon after returning to Bangor. "The occult connection that is established when one loves nature was complete — and so I felt transported to a visible fourth dimension — and since heaven is inviolably a state of mind I have been there these past ten days." He felt "lifted ... out of a long siege of psychic languor and emotional lassitude," and planned to "paint many Ktaadn's from all sides of it." His enthusiasm for Maine was renewed, and he settled happily back into life in Bangor, where he could use the public library every morning for two hours, paint in the afternoon, and then return to the library in the evening. In addition he began to give painting classes that eventually brought in $12.50 a week, so he was both earning something and getting the public attention he craved. He worked on the paintings he had begun earlier and added another, *The Lost Felice,* a large one of Alice Mason "sitting staring out of the picture and dark visions of the two brothers in the background offering her blue fish at either side." Now he felt "more full of victory than defeat" for the first time since his departure from New York the previous June.[82]

The fine Bangor library and the energy generated by the Katahdin trip set him to reading the many volumes of Thoreau's journals. Caleb Scribner reminded him of Thoreau: "he has that something — the same that Thoreau has — that limpidness of spirit & the further down you look the more life you find growing there," Hartley wrote to Adelaide Kuntz in November. "After I came back [from Katahdin] I plunged headlong into Concord Man — my long nose in the 20 vols of Thoreau's notes."[83] "What a man [Thoreau] was — what a true spirit," he wrote to another friend. "He was overshadowed in his time by Emerson Hawthorne etc — just as Ryder was by Inness & Co — all of them successful & Ryder & Thoreau living on nut shells. Ryder on 13 cents a day he said. It costs me 75 cents a day for food and I can't afford that."[84] Hartley's identification with Thoreau as a great but neglected and impoverished figure is obvious, but more important for his art was his recognition of heroic figures who represented to him the essence of life. Thoreau was one; Whitman, Ryder, and Cézanne were others; and before long he would add the poet John Donne and Abraham Lincoln to his panoply of great men by painting "archaic" portraits of them. Equally important were living people such as Francis and Martha Mason and Caleb Scribner, whose qualities he celebrated both in portraits and in poetry. His feeling for them — his understanding of who and what they were — led him to draw and paint the human figure abundantly during the last years of his life.

The result was a group of paintings that glorified the physical, including *Madawaska — Acadian Light-Heavy,* a frontal view of a nearly naked man with a striking physique; others that honor fishermen or young men on a beach; and still others that treat religious themes and relate them to the death of the Mason boys, such as *Christ Held by*

Half-Naked Men, which shows the figure of Christ, dead, in the lap of a seated man, behind whom stand seven more men. These were hardly the only works he did in these years, but they signaled his acceptance of, even reverence for, humanity — not its foolishnesses but rather what was best about it, those attributes that he found in its heroic figures.

15

"A High Position as a Painter"
1940–1943

SHORTLY BEFORE CHRISTMAS 1942, Hartley wrote to his niece,

> I have a high position as a painter — as high as anyone — but I never did get hold of much money and probably never will — I am not a "book of the month" artist — and do not paint pretty pictures — but when I am no longer here my name will register forever in the history of American art and so that's something too. But O the difficulties — all monetary, of course because the rest is pure satisfaction — joy — and a feeling of having gone to where one was heading for.[1]

His judgment was accurate; during the last three and a half years of his life his reputation grew, and he even prospered some, though so accustomed was he to poverty that he hoarded what money he earned and even did such petty things as helping himself to small tips left by others on restaurant tables. When he died, his niece recalled, he had "between fifteen and sixteen thousand dollars in one bank and several hundred in another and I think about two hundred dollars in his wallet."[2]

The 1940s began happily for him. A show of his work at Symphony Hall in Boston in December 1939 was well received. "I seem to have made an impression on the B[oston] reviewers," he wrote to Helen Stein late the next month. The reviews "were all long and good generally." While "the old crowd" still favored the gentle work of impres-

sionists such as Frank Benson and Edmund Tarbell, a new crowd
went in "for other things apparently like myself and of course the great
men like Matisse — and the once so great Picasso — poor man, such
a painter and now foisting on us hydra-headed ladies and roos-
ters — all escapism I find." Hartley told Stein that later in the winter,
when he passed through Boston on his way to New York, he was going
to invite the reviewers to meet him so that he might thank them. He
wanted to tell one of them never to call him an expatriate again. "I
never was and never will be because the true ex p's are such as T. S.
Eliot — Ezra Pound — the earlier H. James. . . . I never was 'Ex' anything but exhausted with the general wear and tear of arts, — etc."[3]

At the end of January 1940 he received a telegram from Hudson
Walker, informing him that his painting *End of the Hurricane,* on
exhibit at the Pennsylvania Academy of Fine Arts, had been awarded
a prize of three hundred dollars. "I sure am glad of it," he told Stein,
"and have now enough to run the most of a year careful figuring and
maybe now the damn wagon won't creak so or lose its tires for a while,
but I must get three years ahead of me as I have had before — that is
the only way to get really important work done and I have so many
ideas to express." In Bangor until the beginning of March, he worked
hard to finish new paintings for his next show, "Recent Paintings of
Maine," at the Walker Gallery. He gave up his plan to stop in Boston
because the winter weather was daunting and, as he explained to Stein,
he was too tired after completing his four painting classes and seeing
to it that the pictures to be shipped to Walker were properly packed.[4]

Hartley was gratified to receive an invitation to serve on the Advi-
sory Council of Cooper Union, especially because it might involve an
occasional lecture and some teaching, but his stay in New York was
otherwise uneventful. The show at the Walker Gallery was accorded
no particular notice, and after spending part of the summer in the city
he was glad to depart for Maine toward the end of July. The summer
before, Waldo Pierce had driven him up the coast from West Brooksville. They had first visited Mount Desert Island, a large and strikingly
beautiful island with cliffs, deep-water harbors, and almost majestic
small mountains just off the coast near Ellsworth; from there they had
continued eastward some forty miles to the fishing village of Corea.
"Pretty name — and God! was it a beauty," he wrote to Adelaide
Kuntz after seeing it. He described it to Rogers Bordley as a "*wonderful*
fishing village, a real one, and so like my beloved Nova Scotia, dear

old boys sitting in their fish house doorways, quantities of lobster-pots lying around, a P.O. and grocery, and a fish-shop."[5]

So it was to Corea that he went this summer, and after five weeks he wrote to Adelaide Kuntz that he had made no mistake in choosing it. Across the street from where he was living was a Baptist church, the upper floor of which he was allowed to use as his studio. It provided him with good north light, though the other end of the room had "nothing but lecherous light" because of the "fake" stained glass in the windows. He could look out a small window toward the town harbor or, in the other direction, over an expanse of brush-covered land stretching inland. "I am well fed & well slept & well-liked apparently I have such calm & have started ten pictures & several drawings of the coast," he told his friend.[6]

Much of the pleasure he took in Corea had to do with the people in whose house he lived. Forrest and Katie Young had many of the same qualities Hartley had admired in the Masons. Forrest was a lobster fisherman, and Katie ran a small restaurant where Hartley ate his meals. She was patient, would listen to him talk, and did not mind when he poked around in her kitchen. The Youngs had two children, Joe and Louise, both of college age, who were also pleasant to Hartley when they were around. Joe supplied him with mussels and "wrinkles" (sea snails) that the artist enjoyed eating, and even found him dead birds to paint; Louise would do errands for him and later helped him when he was living in Bangor during the winter of 1941, despite the fact that he was occasionally quite short with her. What mattered most to Hartley was the Youngs' values; much later Joe would answer, when asked about what he thought worthwhile, "I guess just the simple values you get from everyday contact with people and living as close as you can to nature."[7] All the Youngs were kind to Hartley and bemused by his art. "He did paint my shoe once," Forrest recalled. "It was an old shoe and had a hole in it. He painted it, and I think it won a $2500 prize." He remembered that Hartley had also wanted to do one of his old hats, which likewise had a hole in it, but had never gotten around to it. Hartley hoarded the objects he intended to paint, on one occasion hiding a dead crow under a corner of the restaurant until a rotten odor led to its discovery.[8]

Not only was he happy with his work in Corea during the fall of 1940 — "it flows out of me without 'interior' interruptions," he remarked — but he was pleased that *Androscoggin,* his first volume of poetry since 1923, was to be published by the Falmouth Publishing House in Portland.[9] The press was a small one owned by a young man named Leon Tebbetts, who worked hard to produce the book. After several delays, it finally came out that fall, and Hartley was delighted. "I *am* so damned glad the book *is* out — because my poetical career affords me nothing but pure pleasure, and is such a lovely contrast to the painting idea," he wrote to Helen Stein.[10] Most of the poems are about Maine, the Androscoggin River, Lewiston, scenes remembered from Hartley's past, islands in Penobscot Bay, and Robin Hood Cove, near Georgetown. Hartley opened the volume with "Return of the Native," the poem he had first published in 1932 to announce his return from abroad, included this time to signal his complete identification with Maine.

In 1941 Tebbetts would publish another volume, *Sea Burial,* after the success of *Androscoggin,* whose run of three hundred copies sold out quickly. As broad in its scope as the earlier volume was "cohesive," *Sea Burial,* according to Gail Scott, "lacked the firm, lean thrust" of its predecessor. The 1941 volume represented an attempt "to bring together the opposite halves of [Hartley's] experience — his cosmopolitan need of the city, of music, literature and things intellectual, with the simplicity of plain people and isolated nature."[11] What is most noticeable about the poetry in both volumes is its calm tone and mood of acceptance. "The tide comes in, and out goes tide," begins "In Robin Hood Cove":

> it skirts the cliffs, and in their shadow sees
> the remnants of the days that fall
> between a seagull's and a robin's call.
> There is the bridge, and under flows
> the rests of evening with its primulous
> shows.
> It is a river made of listless sea
> after it has explained its fierce integrity.
> No thunder makes, or on rock heaves,
> it learns the place for plain humility,
> and keeps reflection of some mindless
> leaves.[12]

Hartley had at last found peace, despite a restless nature that would keep him from settling down until the end of his days. He grew tired of Bangor during the winter of 1941 and spoke, as he had before, of traveling to the Southwest. But now more than previously he also wanted to be in New York, largely because he liked the idea of basking in the recognition he was receiving. There were more sales of his work: Hudson Walker sold a large sea painting to the Portland Museum in Oregon for $1,440 and himself bought twenty-three paintings for $5,000 after he closed down his gallery. Hartley was secure, finally, as he had never been before. He put the money in a bank but never drew on the account, fearful that he might not have anything to support himself with if sales did not continue to go well.[13]

Even Walker's departure from the gallery business did not disturb Hartley too much. The two of them remained good friends, and Hartley was able to move to the Macbeth Gallery immediately. He was somewhat dismayed by the fact that Macbeth made him pay many of the exhibition costs himself, but that problem would not last long, for in August 1942 the noted dealer Paul Rosenberg would invite him to join his gallery. "Dear Hudson," Hartley exclaimed to his friend,

> I am all of a flutter since yesterday for I received a "Royal Command" request from Mr. Paul Rosenberg himself, inviting me to have an exhibition in his gallery the coming season. . . . I am vain enough or foolish enough to get a thrill out of the idea of seeing a picture of mine put in their grand window, with some Egyptian sculpture, alternating now and then with a Renoir, a Corot, or whatever. It is all too grand Hudson, to turn down and I am just not going to do it.[14]

Excitedly he wrote to other friends about what he considered to be his triumph.

He had arrived. Going to the Rosenberg Gallery was for him the culmination of his increasing success. Most other things, too, now seemed to fall into place. New York was suddenly grand; there were friends to see; he posed for the sculptor Jacques Lipchitz and spent a great deal of time with the noted collector and dealer Dikran Kelekian and the photographer Alfredo Valenti. Milton Avery did a portrait of him, and he enjoyed the company of, among others, Monroe Wheeler and Glenway Wescott, whose friendship dated back to his days in France in the 1920s. There were occasional lectures and more exhibitions in New York as well as in other parts of the country, including one in Cincinnati with Stuart Davis. In December 1942 his painting

Lobster Fishermen won the Fourth Painting Purchase Prize for $2,000 from the Metropolitan Museum of Art.[15]

But his life was not unalloyed by difficulty. He had felt unwell during the fall of 1941 and while still in Corea had found out that he had a serious problem with high blood pressure; it was "far too far over on the dangerous side," the doctor who examined him announced. He was "feeling like hell with it, so I have to keep absolutely quiet, and it alarms me with what I cannot do without being topheavy, not exactly dizzy."[16] He had remained in Corea until his health improved, then returned to New York before Christmas. He continued his patterns of life there, taking so much pleasure in them that he did not depart for Maine — any serious idea of traveling to the Southwest had disappeared with the coming of World War II — until well into the summer of 1942. Although he missed the city, he worked hard, especially after Rosenberg invited him to exhibit with his gallery. In a discarded chicken brooder that the Youngs had provided for him, he painted with a fervor — "I am up to the eyebrows and over with 25 new pictures — & it will take all the time there is to get them done," he wrote to Adelaide Kuntz.[17] His progress was slowed when, walking along the shore, he fell on the rocks and severely bruised his left leg. He had to be driven back to the Youngs' in a car, and it was more than two weeks before he was able to work again.[18] Gamely he told Leon Tebbetts, his publisher, that despite the fact that the leg was a "lovely map of pea green and shit purple," it was healing quickly — a sign that he was "generally in good condition," he was confident.

"I miss people so — up here on the rocks," he declared to Tebbetts. "I don't think I can ever live like this again — I feel it is wrong to be away from one's fellow-kind — and I have made the curious discovery that even nature does not mean what it used to — I begrudge every day — every hour — every moment I am away from the human scene & I shall never leave it again."[19] Although he enjoyed the crowds of servicemen and servicewomen he saw in New York and the few he met in Corea, he was saddened by the war. That and his sense of increasing frailty gave him a feeling of urgency about what he was doing. He stayed in Corea for Christmas with the Youngs, then went back to New York in January and prepared for his first major show at the Rosenberg Gallery (there had been a small exhibition of his paintings the previous November), which opened on February 2, 1943.

The show, which ran for the month of February, was a success in

Hartley's eyes. Nearly two hundred people came to the opening, he reported to a friend.[20] Despite various illnesses, Hartley bustled about the city that spring, thoroughly enjoying the social scene that for so long had driven him to near distraction. Finally, in July, he decided to pull himself away. "I am in the usual throes of assembling my things to get off for Maine early next week — always a job for me," he wrote to Adelaide Kuntz; she had telephoned him that evening at his hotel, but he had been out at the circus with three friends. "Don't feel any too well — caught a grippe cold with the sudden change," he remarked, but that did not prevent him from inviting her to dine with him.[21] When she and her son ran into Hartley several days later and joined him for dinner on the hotel roof, they overlooked the city that he had finally come to love wholeheartedly, once it seemed to have accepted him. It was the last time Kuntz saw him.

From Corea, Hartley wrote to his young friend Richard Sisson that he had hated to leave "the beautiful scene of Broadway at night — God how beautiful — with all the best youth of the nation swaying around in and out of neon glow of the eat places . . . knowing it was the last I should see of the white splendours until next spring & summer." He did not like being back in the village, which was "nothing but rocks — the ocean seagulls."[22] He tried to work but could hardly move about. The Youngs had to help him up and down the stairs to his room, and when he painted he would come in from his chicken coop bathed in sweat. Soon he was so weak that Katie had to hand him his paints. On August 31 the young sculptress Chenoweth Hall visited him at the Youngs'. Hartley, in great pain, asked her to feel one of his legs. It was swollen and hard as wood. He told her that it was like that all the way up his side.[23] The next day it was decided that he must be taken to the hospital in Ellsworth, despite his protestations about going. In the hospital he wanted no one but the Youngs to touch him, and as they left to return to Corea for the night, he called out to Katie, "Now you and Forrest come tomorrow." At 6:00 A.M. on September 2 the hospital called to say that he was sinking. He died at 6:30.[24]

Hartley's body was taken to a funeral home in Ellsworth, where it remained for several days while arrangements were made for the cremation he had wanted. A young artist, Scribner Ames, sat with the body and drew it. "One felt such power there and the courage and integrity," she wrote to Hudson Walker afterward. "The turbulence was gone and only the firmness and determination left."[25] Norma

Berger, as one of the executors of Hartley's estate, was contacted in Ohio and came east as soon as she could. After her uncle's body was cremated in Boston, she took his ashes and scattered them on the Androscoggin River below the falls in Lewiston, as he had requested. No stone was placed in the graveyard above the town overlooking the river.

As he would have hoped, his death was well noted. The *New York Times* for September 3 acknowledged that he was "internationally known" and "had an unusual style." Although he would have laughed ruefully at their description of him as a "short, stocky, gentle-mannered man of simple tastes," the summation of his work and of the places where it was represented would have made him preen.[26] He would have liked even more the eulogy Paul Rosenberg wrote for him two weeks after his death:

> That "gaunt eagle from the hills of Maine," the painter Marsden Hartley — who died September 2, in his sixty-seventh year — was a prodigy. He was an extraordinary, an almost gigantic secondary artist. Had Hartley possessed a passion for perfection, for round, full inclusivity in his work, and somewhat more of the spirit of consecutiveness, he might easily have become a major one. For he was abundantly talented, this very modern American.[27]

He would have liked best of all the assessment of one of his most astute critics, Gail Scott, who wrote about his last work that it is

> the painting of essential reality, in which what is left unsaid, the profoundly empty space behind the image, conveys as much as the actual object. Suspended in this Zen-like emptiness are small mundane objects — a bird, a pair of gloves, a duck decoy or lobster buoy — depicted with a deceptively simple — even, at times, ungainly — directness. But underneath this American backwoods naïveté was the authority of an artist who had used the European modernist tradition to escape provincialism, and then, with astonishing independence, gone on to become, in the words of one critic, "one of the few Americans of his generation to stand whole and free, at once the undeniable citizen of the world and his own imagination."[28]

American, modernist, citizen of the world — nothing could have pleased Hartley more.

Notes and Sources

Full citations for works referred to in the notes may be found in the selected bibliography that follows them. For convenience' sake, I have used the following abbreviations for frequently cited names and sources:

TITLES OF WORKS BY HARTLEY

AIA *Adventures in the Arts*

CP *The Collected Poems of Marsden Hartley, 1904–1943*

OA *On Art*

SAP "Somehow a Past," unpublished manuscript, Hartley Archive, Yale Collection of American Literature, Beinecke Rare Book and Manuscript Library, Yale University

NAMES OF PEOPLE, BOOKS, AND MANUSCRIPT COLLECTIONS

AAA Archives of American Art

AS Alfred Stieglitz. All citations of AS refer to material in the Stieglitz Collection, Yale Collection of American Literature.

ASK Adelaide S. Kuntz. The correspondence of ASK and Hartley is on microfilm at the Archives of American Art.

BH Barbara Haskell, *Marsden Hartley*

EMC Elizabeth McCausland Papers. McCausland collected a great deal of material on Hartley in preparation for a full biography; her papers are on microfilm at the Archives of American Art.

GS Gail R. Scott, *Marsden Hartley*

MH Marsden Hartley

NB Norma Berger. The Berger Papers are in the Yale Collection of American Literature.

RS Rebecca Strand. The correspondence of RS and Hartley is on microfilm at the Archives of American Art.

TL   Townsend Ludington
UCL   Department of Special Collections, University of Chicago Library
YCAL   Yale Collection of American Literature, Beinecke Rare Book and Manu-
        script Library, Yale University

PREFACE

1. Rosenberg, "Marsden Hartley."
2. MH, "Dissertation on Modern Painting"; reprinted in *OA,* p. 68.

PROLOGUE

1. MH to Richard Sisson, 3 August and 16 August 1943; Richard Sisson to TL, 26
   May 1989.
2. AS to Arnold Rönnebeck, 9 September 1943, EMC, Reel 268.
3. MH to Rockwell Kent, [spring 1920], Kent Papers, AAA.
4. Matilde Rice Elliott to TL, 8 July 1982.
5. Rosenfeld, "Paint and Circuses," p. 386.
6. John Paul Kuntz, interview with TL, 4 October 1985.
7. MH to Carl Sprinchorn, EMC, Reel 268.
8. MH to "Dearest Minette" (cat of Elizabeth Nagle), EMC, Reel 268.
9. *Camera Work,* no. 45 (January 1914), pp. 17, 19–20.
10. *AIA*, pp. 116–119; Robinson, *Georgia O'Keeffe: A Life,* p. 136.
11. Unpublished ms. of William Carlos Williams's autobiography, Za. Williams,
    18 (30), YCAL.
12. O'Neill, *Strange Interlude,* p. 581.
13. Ibid., p. 644.
14. Ibid., p. 682.
15. Fairfield Porter to John Brooks Wheelwright, undated and 17 May 1936 (?),
    Wheelwright Papers (MS 79.1, Box 13, Folder 8), Brown University Library.
16. Louise Young to TL, 1 October 1985.
17. Chenoweth Hall to TL, 20 September 1982; the anecdote about his gesturing is
    in BH, p. 122.
18. James Moore to TL, 5 October 1990.
19. MH to William Carlos Williams, 20 February 1937, Poetry/Rare Books Collec-
    tion, University Libraries, SUNY, Buffalo.
20. Williams, *The Autobiography of William Carlos Williams,* p. 171.
21. ASK to Hudson Walker, 31 October 1944, EMC, Reel 268.

CHAPTER ONE

1. MH, "Biographical Note," 9 October 1923, Stieglitz Collection, YCAL.
2. SAP; MH, "Lewiston," *CP,* pp. 254–256.
3. SAP.
4. Ibid.
5. Appendix B, "An Interview between Norma Berger and Gary Gillespie in
   Boston, Massachusetts, October 1, 1973," p. 209 in Gillespie, "A Collateral

Study of Selected Paintings and Poems from Marsden Hartley's Maine Period."

6. MH to ASK, 19 April 1939; MH, "Biographical Note."

7. MH to NB, 13 February 1936.

8. MH, "Biographical Note."

9. *AIA,* p. 4.

10. EMC, Reel D267.

11. SAP.

12. BH, p. 10; SAP.

13. BH, p. 138 n. 9; SAP.

14. SAP.

15. Ibid.

16. *OA,* p. 23.

17. Ibid., p. 24.

18. SAP.

19. Hartley wrote repeatedly about Chase; I have drawn from "Biographical Note"; "Elizabeth Sparhawk Jones," unpublished essay, Hartley-Berger Collection, YCAL; and SAP.

20. MH, "Biographical Note," pp. 2–3.

21. MH to Elizabeth Sparhawk Jones, 29 October 1940, YCAL.

22. Everett, article on MH, *Lewiston Journal,* 2 July 1960.

23. MH to Richard Tweedy, 27 May 1900, Reel NY 59/5, AAA.

24. MH to NB, 3 July 1900.

25. MH to Richard Tweedy, 17 June 1900, Reel NY 59/5, AAA.

26. MH to Richard Tweedy, 16 September 1900, Reel NY 59/5, AAA.

27. SAP.

28. MH to Richard Tweedy, 25 October 1900, Reel NY 59/5, AAA.

29. SAP.

30. MH to Richard Tweedy, 23 November 1900, Reel NY 59/5, AAA.

31. MH to Richard Tweedy, 23 November and 15 December 1900, Reel NY 59/5, AAA.

32. MH to Richard Tweedy, 28 January 1901, Reel NY 59/5, AAA.

33. MH to Richard Tweedy, 10 July 1901, Reel NY 59/5, AAA.

CHAPTER TWO

1. Lynch, "A Gay World After All," p. 3.

2. Gail Scott to TL, 31 October 1988.

3. BH, p. 12.

4. Walt Whitman, "In Paths Untrodden," *Leaves of Grass,* p. 93.

5. Whitman, "Among the Multitude," *Leaves of Grass,* pp. 108–109.

6. Whitman, "Song of Myself," *Leaves of Grass,* pp. 23–29.

7. Whitman, "Spontaneous Me," *Leaves of Grass,* p. 87.

8. MH to Arnold Rönnebeck, 8 November 1936, YCAL.

9. MH to Robert McAlmon, 29 September 1941, YCAL.

10. MH to Arnold Rönnebeck, 29 April 1936, YCAL.

11. MH to Arnold Rönnebeck, 8 November 1936, YCAL.

12. MH to Matilde Rice [Elliott], 11 March 1922, Reel 130, AAA.

13. McAlmon, *Being Geniuses Together*, p. 110.

14. McAlmon, "Distinguished Air," in *Distinguished Air: Grim Fairy Tales*, pp. 9–37.

15. MH to AS, 15 March 1915.

16. MH to AS, 12 January 1922.

17. Field, *Djuna: The Life and Times of Djuna Barnes*, p. 61.

18. Unpublished ms. of William Carlos Williams's autobiography.

19. Williams, *The Autobiography of William Carlos Williams*, pp. 172–173.

20. MH to Robert McAlmon, 3 October 1942, YCAL.

21. MH to Robert McAlmon, 31 August 1942, YCAL.

22. MH to Frank Davison, 17 September 1941, YCAL.

23. Felicia Seyd, interview with TL, 13 February 1986.

24. Helen Stein notes, AAA.

25. MH to Arnold Rönnebeck, 8 November 1936, YCAL.

CHAPTER THREE

1. MH, "Maine Trapper," unpublished essay, Hartley-Berger Collection, YCAL.

2. SAP.

3. MH to RS, 28 October 1928, Reel X3, AAA.

4. MH, "Maine Trapper."

5. Marin, *The Selected Writings of John Marin*, pp. 42, 144.

6. Mavis Gallie, interview with TL, 18 June 1986.

7. SAP.

8. Mellquist, "Marsden Hartley, Visionary Painter," p. 276.

9. Kreymborg, *Troubadour*, pp. 112–113.

10. *CP*, pp. 34–36.

11. Ibid., p. 36.

12. EMC, Reel D267.

13. MH, *Eight Poems and One Essay*, p. 25.

14. Ibid., p. 24.

15. Shaemas O'Sheel, "My Acquaintance with Marsden Hartley," and C. Maclean Savage, "Recollections of Marsden Hartley," Manuscript file (Hartley), Wesleyan University Library.

16. MH, "Vignettes — Peter Doyle," unpublished essay, Hartley-Berger Collection, YCAL.

17. SAP.

18. MH, "On the Subject of the Mountain," unpublished essay, Hartley-Berger Collection, YCAL.

19. MH, "Giovanni Segantini," unpublished essay, Hartley-Berger Collection, YCAL.

20. BH, pp. 12–13.

21. MH, *Heart's Gate*, p. 18.

22. Ibid., p. 20.

23. "Edmund Marsden Hartley of Lewiston, a Student and Painter of Nature."

24. MH to Shaemas O'Sheel, 25 December 1906, EMC, Reel D267.

25. MH to Shaemas O'Sheel, 11 January 1907, YCAL.

26. MH, *Heart's Gate,* pp. 24–25.

27. BH, p. 13.

28. SAP.

29. MH, *Heart's Gate,* p. 84; MH to Shaemas O'Sheel, 10 July 1907, Manuscript file (Hartley), Wesleyan University Library.

30. MH to Shaemas O'Sheel, 10 July 1907.

31. MH to Shaemas O'Sheel, 6 August 1907, Wesleyan.

32. MH, *Heart's Gate,* pp. 32, 36.

33. Ibid., pp. 40, 46–47.

34. Ibid., p. 61.

35. Fairbrother, "Painting in Boston, 1870–1930," in *The Bostonians,* p. 84.

36. SAP.

37. MH, *Heart's Gate,* p. 64.

38. Ibid., pp. 61, 65.

39. Ibid., p. 66.

40. MH to Shaemas O'Sheel, 19 October 1908, YCAL.

41. BH, p. 14.

42. Ibid., p. 17.

43. I am indebted to Laurence Salander for showing me *Landscape No. 16 1909 (?).*

44. I am indebted to Suzanne Vanderwoude, who showed me a transparency of *Resurrection* when I visited the Vanderwoude-Tananbaum Gallery on 30 January 1988. Elizabeth McCausland, not Hartley, applied the title.

45. Homer, *Alfred Stieglitz,* p. 153.

46. SAP.

CHAPTER FOUR

1. AS to MH, 26 October 1923.

2. AS to MH, two letters, 27 October 1923.

3. AS to MH, 27 October 1923.

4. Hartman, "Unphotographic Paint," p. 20.

5. Quoted in Munson, *The Awakening Twenties,* p. 48.

6. MH, "What Is 291?," *OA,* p. 65.

7. See Homer, *Alfred Stieglitz,* pp. 257–259.

8. SAP.

9. MH, "291 — and the Brass Bowl," *OA,* pp. 82–83.

10. SAP.

11. Ibid.

12. MH, "Albert P. Ryder," pp. 94, 96.

13. For this and much else about Ryder, see Broun, *Albert Pinkham Ryder,* p. 140 and passim.

14. MH, "Albert Pinkham Ryder," *OA,* pp. 258–268.

15. Broun, *Albert Pinkham Ryder,* pp. 321–322.
16. Ibid., p. 77.
17. BH, p. 18.
18. EMC, Reel D267.
19. Homer, *Alfred Stieglitz,* p. 296.
20. BH, p. 21.
21. MH, *Eight Poems and One Essay,* p. 20.
22. MH to Horace Traubel, 23 July 1910, reprinted in *Heart's Gate,* p. 72.
23. MH to NB, 15 July 1910.
24. MH to NB, 3 November 1910.
25. MH to NB, December 1910.
26. Homer, *Alfred Stieglitz,* p. 297.
27. MH to NB, 31 January 1911.
28. MH to NB, 18 March 1911.
29. BH, p. 194.
30. MH to NB, 2 April 1911.
31. MH, *Heart's Gate,* p. 78; MH to NB, 3 March 1911.
32. BH, p. 21; EMC, Reel D267.
33. Homer, *Alfred Stieglitz,* p. 154.
34. MH to NB, 14 June 1911.
35. MH to AS, July (?) 1911.
36. In MH to AS, 20 August 1911, Hartley mentions "Meyer-Graefe," which William Innes Homer assumes is Julius Meier-Graefe, *Paul Cézanne* (Munich, 1910). (Homer, *Alfred Stieglitz,* p. 285.)
37. MH to AS, September (?) 1911.
38. MH to AS, 14 October (?) 1911.
39. MH to NB, 13 December 1911.
40. Homer, *Alfred Stieglitz,* p. 154.
41. MH to NB, 16 February 1912.
42. Quoted in *Camera Work,* no. 38 (April 1912), p. 42.
43. MH to NB, 2 March 1912.
44. MH to NB, 4 April 1912.

CHAPTER FIVE

1. MH to NB, 12 April 1912.
2. MH to AS, 13 April 1912.
3. MH to AS, 8 May 1912.
4. MH to NB, 31 July 1912.
5. MH to AS, July 1912.
6. MH to AS, 20 June 1912.
7. MH to AS, 8 May 1912.
8. MH to NB, 31 July 1912.
9. MH to Mrs. Stieglitz, August 1912, Stieglitz Collection, YCAL.
10. MH to Rockwell and Kathleen Kent, 22 August 1912, Kent Papers, AAA.

11. MH to AS, July (?) 1912.

12. MH to AS, July (?) 1912.

13. MH to Rockwell and Kathleen Kent, 22 August 1912.

14. *OA*, pp. 93–94.

15. SAP.

16. Jaffe, *Joseph Stella*, p. 34. Quoted in Mellow, *Charmed Circle*, p. 222.

17. Stein, *The Autobiography of Alice B. Toklas*, p. 100.

18. SAP.

19. Ibid.

20. Ibid.

21. BH, p. 26.

22. MH to AS, 20 June 1912.

23. MH to ASK, 27 July 1932.

24. MH to AS, 30 July 1912.

25. MH to Rockwell Kent, 22 September 1912, Kent Papers, AAA.

26. MH to AS, 2 October 1912.

27. MH to AS, 31 October 1912.

28. MH to AS, 1 September 1912.

29. MH to Rockwell Kent, 22 September 1912.

30. MH to NB, 24 November 1912.

31. MH to AS, December (?) 1912.

32. MH to Rockwell Kent, 22 September 1912; MH to AS, 30 October and early November 1912.

33. MH to AS, July 1912.

34. MH to AS, 1 September 1912.

35. Macke, "Masks," pp. 85, 87.

36. Schönberg, "The Relationship to the Text," pp. 90, 92.

37. MH to AS, received 20 December 1912.

38. BH, p. 29.

39. Ibid., pp. 28–29.

40. MH to AS, received 20 December 1912.

41. Bergson, "An Extract from Bergson," p. 20; Bergson, "What Is the Object of Art?," p. 24.

42. MH to Rockwell Kent, 24 December 1912, Kent Papers, AAA.

43. MH to NB, 30 December 1912.

44. Brown, *The Story of the Armory Show*, p. 205.

45. MH to AS, early November 1912.

46. MH to NB, 30 December 1912.

CHAPTER SIX

1. MH, postcards to NB, 8 January and 11 January 1913.

2. MH to AS, 14 January 1913.

3. The quotation and information about Berlin come from "Berlin 1900–1933: Architecture and Design."

4. Friedrich, *Before the Deluge*, pp. 8–9.

5. MH to AS, 1 February 1913.
6. MH to Gabriel Münter and Franz Marc, February 1913. For copies of these and other letters from MH to Münter and Marc, I am deeply indebted to Professor Thomas Gaehtgens.
7. MH to AS, February 1913.
8. AS to MH, 4 March 1913.
9. MH to AS, 13 March 1913.
10. MH to Rockwell Kent, late March 1913, Kent Papers, AAA.
11. MH to AS, 9 April 1913.
12. AS to MH, 21 April 1913.
13. MH to AS, 29 April and April–May 1913.
14. MH to Wassily Kandinsky and Gabriel Münter, May 1913.
15. MH to AS, May 1913.
16. As transcribed in MH to AS, late May 1913.
17. MH to Franz Marc, 13 May 1913.
18. MH to NB, 18 May 1913.
19. SAP.
20. MH to AS, late May 1913.
21. MH to Franz Marc, 29 May 1913; MH to Gertrude Stein, early June 1913, YCAL.
22. MH to AS, 5 June 1913.
23. MH to Franz Marc, 5 June 1913.
24. MH to AS, early June (?) 1913.
25. MH to Gertrude Stein, 19 June 1913, YCAL.
26. MH to AS, 5 July and 18 July 1913.
27. MH to Gertrude Stein, 7 August 1913, YCAL.
28. MH to AS, August 1913.
29. MH to Gertrude Stein, August 1913, YCAL.
30. BH, p. 33.
31. For a thorough discussion of synchromism, see Levin, *Sychromism and American Color Abstraction.*
32. MH to Emmeline Stieglitz, 19 September 1913, Stieglitz Collection, YCAL.
33. *OA*, p. 135.
34. Erster Deutsche Herbstsalon, catalogue; MH to AS, 20 and 22 September 1913.
35. MH to AS, 28 September 1913.
36. AS to MH, 6 and 11 October 1913.
37. MH to Gertrude Stein, 30 September 1913, YCAL; MH to AS, listed as 18 October 1913 (though that date puts it too close to AS's letter of 20 October; MH's letter was no doubt written several days earlier).
38. AS to MH, 20 October 1913.
39. MH to AS, 22 October 1913.
40. James, *The Varieties of Religious Experience,* p. 398.
41. MH to AS, 22 October 1913.
42. James, *The Varieties of Religious Experience,* pp. 401–402, 419.
43. MH to AS, 29 October 1913.
44. MH to Gertrude Stein, 18, 23, 27, 28, and undated October 1913, YCAL.

CHAPTER SEVEN

1. MH to Gertrude Stein, 7–10 December 1913, YCAL.
2. MH to Gertrude Stein, 16 January 1914, YCAL.
3. *Camera Work,* January 1914, pp. 16–23.
4. For information about the show "Exhibition of Contemporary Scandinavian Art," at the Albright Art Gallery, January 4–26, 1913, I am indebted to Annette Masling, Librarian, the Albright-Knox Art Gallery.
5. MH to AS, February 1914.
6. Luhan, *Movers and Shakers,* p. 255.
7. MH to Gertrude Stein, February 1914, YCAL.
8. MH to Gertrude Stein, 12 March 1914, YCAL.
9. MH to AS, received 14 May 1914.
10. MH to Gertrude Stein, 30 April 1914, YCAL.
11. MH to AS, received 14 May 1914.
12. AS to MH, 14 May 1914.
13. MH to AS, 15 May 1914.
14. Barry, "The Age of Blood and Iron," p. 170; BH, p. 42.
15. MH to AS, 31 May 1914.
16. MH to AS, 31 May 1914.
17. *OA,* pp. 64–65.
18. MH to AS, received 12 June 1914.
19. AS to MH, 16 June 1914.
20. MH to AS, 30 June 1914.
21. MH to AS, 29 July, 30 July, and 31 July–1 August 1914.
22. MH to AS, 2 September 1914.
23. MH to AS, 17 September 1914.
24. AS to MH, 6 October 1914.
25. MH to AS, 23 October 1914.
26. MH to Gertrude Stein, November (?) 1914, YCAL.
27. MH to AS, 29 October 1914; MH, "Letter to Karl von Freyburg," unpublished essay, Hartley-Berger Collection, YCAL.
28. MH to Charles Demuth, fall 1914, Mabel Dodge Luhan Collection, YCAL.
29. MH to AS, 12 November 1914.
30. MH to AS, 15 March 1915.
31. MH to AS, 3 November 1914.
32. MH to Gertrude Stein, November (?) 1914, YCAL.
33. MH to AS, 8 November 1914.
34. MH to AS, 6 April 1915.
35. AS to MH, 12 January 1915.
36. BH, p. 44.
37. Ibid., p. 45.
38. Arnold Rönnebeck to Duncan Phillips, undated [1944], YCAL.
39. MH to AS, 19 May 1915.
40. AS to MH, 21 June 1915.
41. MH to AS, 5 August 1915.

42. "American Artist Astounds Germans."
43. MH to AS, 8 November 1915.
44. Two letters, MH to Lyonel Feininger, undated, Harvard University Library.

CHAPTER EIGHT

1. MH to NB, 9 March 1916.
2. SAP.
3. Luhan, *Movers and Shakers,* p. 460.
4. *The Forum Exhibition of Modern American Painters,* p. 5.
5. MH to NB, 31 March 1916.
6. *OA,* p. 67.
7. MH to AS, 13 July 1916.
8. MH, "The Great Provincetown Summer," unpublished essay, Hartley-Berger Collection, YCAL.
9. MH to AS, July (?) 1916.
10. Hudson Walker, transcript of a discussion about MH, EMC, Reel 268.
11. SAP.
12. BH, pp. 54–55.
13. Ibid., p. 55.
14. MH to AS, 20 November 1916.
15. MH to AS, 26 December 1916.
16. MH to AS, 1 February 1917.
17. MH to AS, 28 February 1917.
18. MH to AS, 8 February 1917, and postcard, February (?) 1917.
19. MH to AS, 8 February 1917; "Art at Home and Abroad."
20. MH to AS, 22 March 1917.
21. BH, p. 55.
22. MH to AS, 8 February 1917.
23. Quoted in BH, pp. 55–56.
24. Coady, "The Indeps."
25. MH to Harriet Monroe, 22 August 1918, UCL.
26. MH to AS, June 1917.
27. MH to AS, 7 September 1917.
28. BH, p. 57.
29. The six are "In the Frail Wood," "Her Daughter," "Spinster," and three under the title "After Battle," *Poetry* 12 (July 1918), pp. 195–201.
30. MH to AS, 24 May 1918.
31. *Poetry* 12, p. 196.
32. Ibid., p. 201.
33. For a full discussion of the poems' publication, see *CP,* pp. 223–226.
34. MH to AS, 13 and 19 June 1918.
35. MH to AS, 20 June 1918.
36. MH to AS, 24 June 1918.
37. MH to AS, 20 July 1918.

38. MH to W. Joseph Fulton, 12 and 13 September 1918, EMC, Reel 272.
39. MH, "America as Landscape" and "Aesthetic Sincerity."
40. MH to AS, 1 August 1918.
41. MH to AS, 19 September 1918.
42. MH to AS, 20 July 1918.
43. MH to AS, 1 August 1918.
44. MH to AS, 13 August 1918.
45. MH to AS, 16 October 1918.
46. MH to AS, 19 September 1918.
47. MH to AS, 21 October 1918.
48. MH to AS, 6 November 1918.
49. MH to AS, 20 November 1918.
50. MH to Harriet Monroe, 19 December 1918, *Poetry* Magazine Papers, UCL.
51. MH, "The Poet of Maine."
52. MH to Harriet Monroe, 26 January 1919, UCL.
53. MH to Harriet Monroe, 12 September 1919, UCL.
54. MH, "The Ivory Woman" and "Sunbathers."
55. MH, "Scaramouche" and "Swallows."
56. MH, "Local Boys and Girls," p. 62.
57. MH to AS, January (?), 8 January, and 11 February 1919, with a copy of a will dated 1 June 1918.
58. MH to AS, 27 February 1919.
59. MH to Harriet Monroe, 3 July 1919, UCL.
60. MH to AS, 12 April 1919.
61. MH to AS, 7 July 1919.
62. MH to AS, 29 September and 9 October 1919.
63. MH to Harriet Monroe, November 1919, UCL.
64. Arnold Rönnebeck to AS, 6 March 1919.
65. Horgan, *Encounters with Stravinsky,* pp. 8–10.
66. MH, "The Red Man," *AIA,* pp. 28–29.

CHAPTER NINE

1. GS, p. 72.
2. MH to AS, 2 August 1920.
3. Ibid.
4. MH to Georgia O'Keeffe, 14 January 1920.
5. *OA,* p. 118.
6. MH to AS, 12 August 1920.
7. MH to AS, 2 September 1920.
8. MH to AS, 6 October 1920.
9. MH to AS, 23 October 1920.
10. MH to AS, 1 November 1920.
11. McBride, "Modern Art."
12. *AIA,* p. 247.

13. *OA*, p. 121.

14. MH to AS, 17 April 1921; Hudson Walker, "Sept. 30, '43," EMC, Reel 268.

15. McBride, "News and Reviews of Art"; unsigned, "James N. Rosenberg and Marsden Hartley."

16. SAP; Hudson Walker, "Sept. 30, '43"; unsigned, "Two 'Modern' Artists Hold Auction Sale."

17. Albert C. Barnes to MH, 2 June 1921, YCAL.

18. Two documents, MH to AS, 7 June 1921; two receipts on "Belmaison Interior Decorations" letterhead, 10 June 1921 and undated.

19. MH to Lillian Baer, 14 October 1921, YCAL.

20. Frederic Sherman to MH, 7 November 1921, YCAL; Seligmann, "The Elegance of Marsden Hartley — Craftsman" and "Hartley Discovers American Civilization"; Rosenfeld, "The Paintings of Marsden Hartley."

21. MH to AS, 14 December 1921.

22. McAlmon, *Being Geniuses Together,* p. 106.

23. Arnold Rönnebeck to Leon Tebbetts, 21 January 1943 and undated, YCAL.

24. Cited in EMC, Reel 268.

25. Quoted in Arnold Rönnebeck to Leon Tebbetts, 1 October 1944, YCAL.

26. McAlmon, *Being Geniuses Together,* p. 108.

27. MH to AS, 24 February 1922.

28. SAP.

29. MH to Matilde Rice [Elliott], 11 March 1922, Reel 130, AAA; MH to ASK, 5 December 1932.

30. MH to AS, 30 November 1921.

31. MH to AS, 12 January 1922.

32. MH to AS, 24 February 1922.

33. MH to AS, 4 September 1922.

34. MH to AS, 14 May 1922.

35. Ibid.

36. Quoted in GS, p. 72.

37. MH to AS, 4 September 1922.

38. MH to AS, 23 January 1923.

39. MH to AS, undated letters datable as February and March 1923.

40. MH to AS, 28 April 1923.

41. MH to AS, 28 May 1923.

42. MH to AS, 28 December 1922.

43. MH, *Twenty-five Poems.* A selection from the volume is included in *CP.*

44. MH to AS, 23 August 1923.

45. MH to AS, 25 September 1923.

46. MH to AS, 16 October 1923.

47. MH to AS, 26 October 1923.

48. For MH's stay in Florence see especially SAP and MH to AS, 24 November 1923.

49. MH, "Some Words on Piero and Masaccio," *OA,* pp. 226–227.

50. MH to AS, 24 November 1923.

51. MH, "Arezzo and Piero," *OA,* pp. 122–125.

52. MH, "Rome and the Ultimate Splendour," *OA,* p. 126.

53. MH, "The Mills of Pleasure," unpublished essay, Hartley-Berger Collection, YCAL.
54. MH to AS, 15 March 1924.

CHAPTER TEN

1. *Vanity Fair* 22 (August 1924).
2. MH to AS, 25 June 1924.
3. MH to NB, 22 July 1924; MH to AS, 23 July and 18 August 1924.
4. MH, "Paris Cafe Terraces," unpublished essay, Hartley-Berger Collection, YCAL.
5. "Modern U.S. Art on View Here."
6. MH to AS, 21 January 1925.
7. Fulton, "Cabbages and Kings," p. 146.
8. Robinson, *Georgia O'Keeffe: A Life,* p. 136; Cowart and Hamilton, *Georgia O'Keeffe: Art and Letters,* pp. 179 and 279–280.
9. MH to NB, 1 September 1924; MH to AS, 18 December 1924.
10. MH to AS, 27 March and 12 April 1925.
11. For a discussion of Provence, see MH, "Impressions of Provence from an American's Point of View," *OA,* pp. 143–147.
12. MH to AS, 1 October 1925.
13. MH to Rogers Bordley, EMC, Reel 268.
14. ASK to Hudson Walker, October 1944, AAA.
15. MH to Gertrude Stein, 27 December 1925, YCAL.
16. MH to AS, 2 February 1926.
17. MH to AS, 31 December 1925 and 2 February 1926.
18. MH to AS, 2 February 1926.
19. MH to AS, 20 July 1926.
20. MH to AS, 2 September 1926.
21. MH to AS, 30 September 1926.
22. MH to ASK, 12 December 1933.
23. MH to AS, 26 October 1926.
24. MH to AS, 19 November 1926.
25. MH to AS, 8 December 1926.
26. BH, p. 75.
27. Debrol, "Marsden Hartley — Painter of Mountains." For a discussion of this essay, see GS, p. 80.
28. MH to AS, 7 January 1927.
29. MH to AS, 16 May and 4 November 1927.
30. MH to AS, 4 October 1927.
31. MH to AS, 4 November 1927.
32. *OA,* pp. 74–76.
33. Ibid., p. 71.
34. Jewell, "What is Imagination? — Doubts Surge Forward as Marsden Hartley Frames New Credo — Six Artists' Work."
35. MH to ASK, 23 June 1928.
36. MH to AS, 2 August 1928.

CHAPTER ELEVEN

1. MH to Isabel Lachaise, 29 August 1928, AAA.
2. MH to AS, 26 September 1928.
3. MH to RS, 25 November 1928.
4. MH to AS, 4 December 1928.
5. MH to AS, 6 January 1929.
6. "Hartley Exhibition, January, 1929."
7. Pemberton, "Soul Exposures," p. xlviii.
8. AS to MH, 5 February 1929.
9. McBride, "Attractions in the Galleries."
10. MH to RS, 6 March 1929.
11. MH to ASK, undated.
12. MH to RS, 27 March 1929.
13. *CP,* p. 101.
14. MH to RS, 7 February 1929.
15. MH to AS, 12 March 1929; AS to MH, 22 March 1929.
16. MH to AS, 12 March 1929.
17. MH to RS, 3 April 1929.
18. MH to AS, 3 April 1929.
19. MH to RS, summer 1929.
20. MH to ASK, summer 1929.
21. MH to AS, 9 November 1929; "St. Thérese of Lisieux," *OA,* pp. 161–162.
22. MH to AS, 9 November 1929.
23. MH to ASK, 21 June, 23 August, and 13 May 1929. Concerning Hart Crane, see also Unterecker, *Voyager,* p. 594.
24. MH to AS, 9 November 1929.
25. *CP,* pp. 109–110.
26. MH to AS, 9 November 1929 and 28 January 1930; MH to Gertrude Stein, 29 January 1930, YCAL.

CHAPTER TWELVE

1. Karl Dworak, interview with TL, 24 September 1988.
2. MH to ASK, spring 1930.
3. MH to AS, 16 April 1930.
4. MH to RS, 10 May 1930.
5. MH, "Eakins, Homer, Ryder," *OA,* pp. 168–172.
6. MH to NB, 25 May and 2 June 1930.
7. MH to Isabel and Gaston Lachaise, 7 June 1930, AAA.
8. MH to AS, 13 July 1930.
9. MH to AS, 7 October 1930.
10. MH to AS, 13 November 1930.
11. Kootz, "Marsden Hartley."
12. McBride, "Marsden Hartley's 'Comeback.'"
13. Jewell, "Metamorphoses."

14. "Marsden Hartley: An American Place."
15. MH to AS, 23 January 1931.
16. *CP,* p. 109.
17. MH to Harriet Monroe, January, March, and 24 March 1931, *Poetry* Magazine Papers, UCL.
18. MH to AS, 4 May 1931.
19. MH to AS, 19 May 1931.
20. Helen Stein notes, AAA.
21. MH to ASK, 16 July 1931.
22. SAP.
23. MH to ASK, 16 July 1931.
24. MH to AS, 12 August 1931.
25. MH to Florine Stettheimer, 17 August 1931, YCAL.
26. *Flaming Pool* is in the YCAL.
27. *CP,* p. 188.
28. MH to ASK, 16 July 1931.
29. MH to Gertrude Stein, 19 July 1931, YCAL.
30. For data about Helen Stein, I am indebted to Jeanne Hokin, who provided me with information she obtained from Jay Friedline, a Gloucester resident and friend of Stein's.
31. MH to Carl Sprinchorn, 3 September 1931, EMC, Reel D268.
32. MH to NB, 31 July 1931.
33. MH to ASK, 24 November 1931.
34. MH to ASK, fall 1931.
35. MH to RS, 31 September 1931.
36. MH to ASK, 22 October 1931.
37. See Scott, "Marsden Hartley at Dogtown Common."
38. MH to AS, 5 November 1931.
39. MH to RS, 12 December 1931.

CHAPTER THIRTEEN

1. MH to ASK, 14 March 1932.
2. MH to ASK, 4 April 1932.
3. Jewell, "Art in Review."
4. MH to Marion Vieth Sampter, 3 May 1932, YCAL.
5. *CP,* p. 251.
6. Crane, *The Letters of Hart Crane, 1916–1932,* pp. 404, 408.
7. Unterecker, *Voyager,* p. 742.
8. Ibid., p. 758.
9. MH, "In Memoriam — Hart Crane," unpublished essay, Hartley-Berger Collection, YCAL.
10. Hart Crane, "Voyages," *Complete Poems,* p. 106.
11. *CP,* pp. 119–127.
12. MH to ASK, 5 December 1932; Cirlot, *A Dictionary of Symbols,* p. 234.

13. For the opportunity to study *Morgenrot, Mexico* in detail, I am indebted to Dr. John Driscoll and the Babcock Gallery.
14. SAP.
15. MH, "Mexican Vignette," unpublished essay, Hartley-Berger Collection, YCAL.
16. MH, "The Bleeding Christs of Mexico," unpublished essay, Hartley-Berger Collection, YCAL.
17. MH to NB, 21 July 1932.
18. MH to ASK, 27 May 1932.
19. MH to ASK, 27 June 1932.
20. MH to ASK, 28 July 1932.
21. MH to NB, 17 February 1933.
22. MH to ASK, 31 December 1932, 5 January, 7 February, and 17 February 1933.
23. MH to ASK, 17 February 1933.
24. MH to NB, 20 September 1933.
25. MH to Donald Greason, 21 March 1933, AAA.
26. MH to Donald Greason, 15 April 1933, AAA.
27. MH to ASK, 25 March 1933.
28. SAP.
29. MH to ASK, 16 May 1933.
30. MH to NB, 18 January 1934.
31. MH to Edith Halpert, 12 July 1933, reprinted in MH, "Letters from Germany," p. 6.
32. MH to ASK, 16 May 1933.
33. MH to ASK, 24 June 1933.
34. MH, "Letters from Germany," pp. 6–7.
35. MH to ASK, 24 June 1933.
36. MH to ASK, 12 July and 19 July 1933.
37. MH to ASK, 15 November 1933.
38. MH to ASK, 11 January 1934.
39. MH to ASK, 3 February 1934.
40. MH to ASK, 12 July 1933.
41. MH to ASK, 24 June 1933.
42. MH to ASK, 12 July 1933.
43. MH to ASK, 19 July 1933.
44. MH to ASK, 22 July 1933.
45. MH to ASK, 7 September 1933.
46. *OA*, p. 46.
47. MH to ASK, 25 December 1933.
48. SAP; also discussed in *OA*, pp. 46–47.
49. MH to ASK, 25 December 1933; MH to NB, 30 December 1933.
50. Stein, *The Autobiography of Alice B. Toklas*, p. 122; MH to Gertrude Stein, 14 November 1933, YCAL.
51. MH to NB, 13 November 1933.
52. MH to NB, 5 December 1933.
53. MH to NB, 14 October 1933.
54. MH to ASK, 11 January and 3 February 1934.

CHAPTER FOURTEEN

1. MH to NB, 23 March and 25 April 1934.
2. MH to NB, 14 January 1935.
3. MH to NB, 5 June 1934.
4. Ibid.
5. Helen Stein notes, AAA.
6. MH to AS, 7, 16, and 27 November 1934; AS to MH, 8 November 1934; MH to NB, 15 and 21 November 1934.
7. MH to AS, 21 November 1934.
8. MH to RS, 29 July 1935; MH to NB, 14 January 1935; Carl Sprinchorn to NB, 29 April 1951, YCAL.
9. MH to Helen Stein, 13 May 1935, AAA.
10. MH, "Letter to Monsieur de Segonzac," in "Letters Never Sent," pp. 66–71.
11. MH to Helen Stein, 31 December 1934, AAA.
12. MH to ASK, 13 August 1935.
13. MH to RS, 29 July 1935.
14. MH to ASK, 4 July 1935.
15. MH to ASK, 13 August 1935.
16. MH to ASK, 6 October 1935.
17. MH to ASK, 16 October 1935.
18. MH to Arnold Rönnebeck, 29 April 1936.
19. MH to ASK, 4 and 6 November 1935.
20. MH to RS, 28 January 1936; MH to NB, 13 February 1936.
21. MH, "Georgia O'Keeffe: A Second Outline in Portraiture," *OA*, pp. 102–108.
22. MH to RS, 3 and 15 January 1936.
23. MH to AS, 1 February 1936.
24. MH to RS, 7 March 1936.
25. MH to ASK, 28 April 1936.
26. MH, "And the Nude Has Descended the Staircase," *OA*, pp. 268–274.
27. MH to RS, 7 March 1936.
28. *OA*, pp. 108–111; *CP*, p. 276.
29. MH to ASK, 28 April 1936; MH to Helen Stein, 17 April 1936, AAA; McBride, "Marsden Hartley Reappears."
30. MH to ASK, 28 April 1936.
31. MH to NB, 13 February and 20 April 1936.
32. Helen Stein notes, AAA.
33. TL interview with Mrs. Pauline Mason, Lunenburg, Nova Scotia, 1 August 1983; MH to ASK, 29 July 1936.
34. MH, "Our Island," in Ferguson, ed., *Marsden Hartley and Nova Scotia,* pp. 78–79; MH, "Suggestion," journal entry, YCAL.
35. MH to AS, 24 August 1936; MH to ASK, 9 September 1936.
36. MH to ASK, 23 September 1936; Stanley Corkum, interview with TL, 1 August 1983.
37. MH to ASK, 23 September 1936.
38. MH to ASK, 5 October 1936; MH to Arnold Rönnebeck, 8 November 1936.
39. MH to ASK, 5 October 1936.

40. MH to ASK, 9 November 1936.

41. MH to ASK, 30 October 1936.

42. MH to ASK, 9 November 1936.

43. Gail R. Scott discusses the creation of the piece in her essay "'Cleophas and His Own': The Making of a Narrative," in Ferguson, ed., *Marsden Hartley and Nova Scotia*, pp. 55–73; the text itself is also included, on pp. 89–122.

44. Ferguson, ed., *Marsden Hartley and Nova Scotia*, pp. 106, 132.

45. Ibid., pp. 126, 127, 130.

46. Yeats, *Collected Poems*, p. 41.

47. MH, "New England Notations," journal entry, YCAL.

48. *OA*, pp. 112–115.

49. MH to ASK, undated [1937].

50. MH to Lloyd Goodrich, two letters, spring 1937, EMC, Reel 268.

51. BH, p. 101.

52. MH to Hudson Walker, 1 October 1937, AAA.

53. MH to ASK, 13 June and 10 September 1937.

54. MH to ASK, 10 September 1937.

55. MH to ASK, 26 September 1937.

56. MH to ASK, 7 November 1937.

57. MH to ASK, undated [spring 1938].

58. MH to ASK, undated [spring 1938].

59. GS, pp. 109–110.

60. BH, p. 115.

61. MH to ASK, 19–20 July 1938.

62. MH to ASK, 25 August 1938.

63. MH to Nick Brigante, 17 September 1938.

64. MH to ASK, 17 November 1938.

65. MH to ASK, [April] 1939.

66. MH to ASK, 19 April 1939.

67. Helen Stein notes, AAA.

68. MH to ASK, [April] 1939.

69. MH to Elizabeth McCausland, [April] 1939, EMC, Reel 270.

70. MH to Helen Stein, 10 September 1939, AAA.

71. MH to Helen Stein, 23 and 30 May 1939, AAA; MH to ASK, spring 1939.

72. MH to Helen Stein, 10 September 1939.

73. MH to Rogers Bordley, 1 August 1939, EMC, Reel 268.

74. MH to Helen Stein, 10 September 1939; MH to ASK, 1 August 1939.

75. MH to Rogers Bordley, 1 August 1939.

76. MH to Helen Stein, 29 September 1939, AAA.

77. MH to Rogers Bordley, 11 August 1939, EMC, Reel 268.

78. For information about Cobbs Camp, I am indebted to Alfred and Susan Cooper, owners of Katahdin Lake Wilderness Camps (formerly Cobbs Camp), who extended every courtesy to me when I talked to them on 5 August 1990. I am also indebted to Gail, Ryder, and Stanley Scott, who led my close friend Don Nice and me into the Coopers' camp, giving us a real sense of Hartley's "ordeal."

79. MH to ASK, 2 February 1940.

80. GS, pp. 134–135.

81. *CP,* pp. 245–246.

82. MH to Elizabeth Sparhawk Jones, 23 October 1939, YCAL.

83. MH to ASK, 11 November 1939.

84. MH to a friend after the Katahdin trip, EMC, Reel X3.

CHAPTER FIFTEEN

1. MH to NB, 20 December 1942.

2. NB to Carl Sprinchorn, 1 June 1951, YCAL.

3. MH to Helen Stein, 26 January 1940, AAA.

4. MH to Helen Stein, 6 and 26 February 1940, AAA.

5. MH to ASK, 10 September 1939; MH to Rogers Bordley, 25 August 1939, EMC, Reel 268.

6. MH to ASK, 4 September 1940.

7. "Joseph Young."

8. Forrest Young, interview with Philip Isaacson, 13 September 1961, EMC, Reel 271.

9. MH to ASK, 13 October 1940.

10. MH to Helen Stein, 4 December 1940, AAA.

11. Gail Scott in *CP,* pp. 347–349.

12. *CP,* p. 282.

13. MH to ASK, undated [spring 1941]; BH, p. 123.

14. MH to Hudson Walker, 25 August 1942, EMC, Reel 268.

15. BH, p. 125.

16. MH to Helen Stein, 12 November 1941, AAA.

17. MH to ASK, undated [summer 1942].

18. MH to Carl Sprinchorn, 30 October 1942, EMC, Reel 268.

19. MH to Leon Tebbetts, 17 October 1942, YCAL.

20. MH to Norwenna McKinnon, [February] 1943, AAA.

21. MH to ASK, undated [July 1943].

22. MH to Richard Sisson, 3 August 1943.

23. TL interviews with Louise Young, 1 October 1985, and Chenoweth Hall, 19 September 1982.

24. Katie Young to Hudson Walker, EMC, Reel 272.

25. Scribner Ames to Hudson Walker, EMC, Reel 268.

26. "Marsden Hartley, Noted Artist, Dies."

27. Rosenberg, "Marsden Hartley."

28. GS, pp. 144–145; Scott quotes Jerome Mellquist, "Marsden Hartley," *Perspectives U.S.A.,* Summer 1953, p. 77.

Selected Bibliography

The following is a selected bibliography of works both by and about Marsden Hartley. If the reader wishes to supplement this listing, invaluable bibliographies may be found in three books, each of which contains full citations for Hartley's monographs and exhibition catalogues:

Hartley, Marsden. *On Art.* Edited by Gail R. Scott. New York: Horizon, 1982.

Haskell, Barbara. *Marsden Hartley.* New York: Whitney Museum of American Art, 1980.

Scott, Gail R. *Marsden Hartley.* New York: Abbeville, 1988.

In addition, extensive discussion of Hartley's poetry may be found in:

Hartley, Marsden. *The Collected Poems of Marsden Hartley, 1904–1943.* Edited by Gail R. Scott. Santa Rosa, Calif.: Black Sparrow Press, 1987.

BOOKS, ARTICLES, AND POEMS BY MARSDEN HARTLEY

Adventures in the Arts: Informal Chapters on Painters, Vaudeville and Poets. New York: Boni and Liveright, 1921.

"Aesthetic Sincerity." *El Palacio* (Santa Fe, N.M.), 9 December 1918, pp. 332–333.

"Albert P. Ryder." *Seven Arts* 2 (May 1917), pp. 94 and 96.

"America as Landscape." *El Palacio* (Santa Fe, N.M.), 21 December 1918, pp. 340–342.

"Art — And the Personal Life." *Creative Art,* June 1928, pp. xxxi–xxxiv.

The Collected Poems of Marsden Hartley, 1904–1943. Edited by Gail R. Scott. Santa Rosa, Calif.: Black Sparrow Press, 1987.

"Dissertation on Modern Painting." *The Nation,* 9 February 1921, pp. 235–236.

Eight Poems and One Essay. Lewiston, Me.: Treat Gallery, Bates College, 1976.

"The Greatest Show on Earth: An Appreciation of the Circus from One of Its Grown-up Admirers." *Vanity Fair,* August 1924.

Heart's Gate. Edited by William Innes Homer. Highlands, N.C.: Jargon Society, 1982.

"The Ivory Woman." *Little Review,* December 1918, pp. 26–27.

"Letters from Germany." Edited by Garnett McCoy. *Archives of American Art Journal* 25 (1985), nos. 1 and 2, pp. 3–28.

"Letters Never Sent." *Northern Lights: Studies in Creativity* 1 (1984), pp. 53–71.

"Local Boys and Girls: Small Town Stuff." In *Others for 1919,* edited by Alfred Kreymborg, pp. 61–62. New York: Nicholas Brown, 1920.

On Art. Edited by Gail R. Scott. New York: Horizon, 1982.

Paintings by Marsden Hartley. Exhibition catalogue. New York: Photo-Secession Galleries, 1914. Reprinted in *Camera Work,* no. 45 (January 1914), pp. 16–23.

"The Poet of Maine." *Little Review,* July 1919, pp. 51–55.

"Scaramouche." *Others,* February 1919, p. 16.

Selected Poems. Edited by Henry W. Wells. New York: Viking, 1945.

"Sunbathers." *Little Review,* December 1918, pp. 27–28.

"Swallows." *Others,* March 1919, p. 14.

Twenty-five Poems. Paris: Contact Publishing, 1923.

SECONDARY SOURCES

"American Artist Astounds Germans." *New York Times,* 19 December 1915, p. 4.

"Art at Home and Abroad: Exhibitions of Modern Painting." *New York Times Magazine,* 28 January 1917, p. 13.

Baigell, Matthew. *The American Scene.* New York: Praeger, 1974.

Barnett, Vivian Endicott. "Marsden Hartley's Return to Maine." *Arts Magazine,* October 1979, pp. 172–176.

Barry, Roxana. "The Age of Blood and Iron: Marsden Hartley in Berlin." *Arts Magazine,* October 1979, pp. 166–171.

Baur, John I. H. *The Inlander: Life and Work of Charles Burchfield, 1893–1967.* New York: Cornwall Books, 1982.

Bergson, Henri. "An Extract from Bergson." *Camera Work,* no. 36 (October 1911), pp. 20–21.

———. "What Is the Object of Art?" *Camera Work,* no. 37 (January 1912), pp. 22–26.

"Berlin 1900–1933: Architecture and Design." Catalogue for an exhibition held at the Cooper-Hewitt Museum, 4 November 1986 to 25 January 1987.

The Blaue Reiter Almanac. Edited by Wassily Kandinsky and Franz Marc. English-language edition edited by Klaus Lankheit. New York: Viking, 1974.

Broun, Elizabeth. *Albert Pinkham Ryder.* Washington: Smithsonian Institution Press, 1989.

Brown, Milton W. *American Painting from the Armory Show to the Depression.* Princeton: Princeton University Press, 1955.

———. *The Story of the Armory Show.* New York: Joseph H. Hirshhorn Foundation, 1963.

Burlingame, Robert Northcutt. "Marsden Hartley: A Study of His Life and Creative Achievement." Ph.D. diss., Brown University, 1953.

Castro, Jan Garden. *The Art and Life of Georgia O'Keeffe.* New York: Crown, 1985.

Chamberlin, Joseph Edgar. "A Return to Primitive Art: Marsden Hartley." *The Evening Mail,* 17 February 1912, p. 8; quoted in *Camera Work,* no. 38 (April 1912), p. 42.

Cirlot, J. E. *A Dictionary of Symbols.* 2d ed. New York: Philosophical Library, 1974.

Coady, R. J. "The Indeps." *The Soil,* July 1917, p. 208.

Conn, Peter. *The Divided Mind: Ideology and Imagination in America, 1891–1917.* Cambridge: Cambridge University Press, 1983.

Cowart, Jack, and Juan Hamilton. *Georgia O'Keeffe: Art and Letters.* Letters selected and annotated by Sarah Greenough. Washington: National Gallery of Art, 1988.

Crane, Hart. *The Letters of Hart Crane, 1916–1932.* Edited by Brom Weber. New York: Hermitage House, 1952.

———. *Complete Poems.* Garden City: Doubleday, 1958.

Debrol, Mme. M. "Marsden Hartley — Painter of Mountains." *Creative Art,* June 1928, pp. xxxv–xxxvi.

Dijkstra, Bram. *The Hieroglyphics of a New Speech.* Princeton: Princeton University Press, 1969.

———. *William Carlos Williams and the American Scene, 1920–1940.* New York: Whitney Museum of American Art, 1978.

"Edmund Marsden Hartley of Lewiston, a Student and Painter of Nature." *Lewiston Journal,* 29 December 1906, p. 9.

Erster Deutsche Herbstsalon. Exhibition catalogue, Berlin 1913.

Everett, Frances Holmes. Piece on Hartley in the *Lewiston Journal,* 2 July 1960, p. 6A (magazine section).

Fairbrother, Trevor J. *The Bostonians: Painters of an Elegant Age, 1870–1930.* Boston: Museum of Fine Arts, 1986.

Ferguson, Gerald, ed. *Marsden Hartley and Nova Scotia.* Halifax: Mount Saint Vincent University Art Gallery, 1987.

Field, Andrew. *Djuna: The Life and Times of Djuna Barnes.* New York: Putnam's, 1983.

The Forum Exhibition of Modern American Painters. 1916. Reprint. New York: Arno Press, 1968.

Friedrich, Otto. *Before the Deluge: A Portrait of Berlin in the 1920s.* New York: Harper and Row, 1972.

Fulton, Deogh. "Cabbages and Kings." *International Studio,* May 1925, pp. 144–147.

Gallup, Donald. "The Weaving of a Pattern: Marsden Hartley and Gertrude Stein." *Magazine of Art,* November 1948, pp. 256–261.

Gillespie, H. Gary. "A Collateral Study of Selected Paintings and Poems from Marsden Hartley's Maine Period." Ph.D. diss., Ohio University, 1974.

Hahn, Emily. *Mabel: A Biography of Mabel Dodge Luhan.* Boston: Houghton Mifflin, 1977.

"Hartley Exhibition, January, 1929." Exhibition catalogue. New York: The Intimate Gallery, 1929.

Hartman, Sadakichi. "Unphotographic Paint: The Texture of Impressionism." *Camera Work,* no. 28 (October 1909), pp. 20–23.

Haskell, Barbara. *Marsden Hartley.* New York: Whitney Museum of American Art, 1980.

———. *Milton Avery.* New York: Harper and Row, 1982.

Hella, Nancy, and Julia Williams. *The Regionalists.* New York: Watson-Guptill, 1976.

Henri, Robert. "The New York Exhibition of Independent Artists." *Craftsman,* May 1910, p. 161.

Homer, William Innes. *Alfred Stieglitz and the American Avant-Garde.* Boston: New York Graphic Society, 1977.

Horgan, Paul. *Encounters with Stravinsky.* New York: Farrar, Straus and Giroux, 1972.

Jaffe, Irma B. *Joseph Stella.* Cambridge: Harvard University Press, 1970.

James, William. *The Varieties of Religious Experience.* New York: Longmans, Green, 1910.

"James N. Rosenberg and Marsden Hartley." *New York Times,* 15 May 1921, sec. 6, p. 8.

Jewell, Edward A. "What Is Imagination? Doubts Surge Forward as Marsden Hartley Frames New Credo — Six Artists' Work." *New York Times,* 17 June 1928, p. 19.

————. "Metamorphoses." *New York Times,* 21 December 1930, sec. 8, p. 15.

————. "Art in Review." *New York Times,* 26 April 1932, p. 24.

"Joseph Young." *Maine Times,* 23 December 1988, p. 22.

Kramer, Hilton. "Hartley and Modern Painting." *Arts Magazine,* February 1961, pp. 42–45.

Kandinsky, Wassily. *On the Spiritual in Art.* New York: Wittenbon, Schultz, 1947.

Kootz, Samuel M. "Marsden Hartley." In *Modern American Painters,* pp. 40–42. New York: Brewer and Martin, 1930.

Kreymborg, Alfred. *Troubadour: An Autobiography.* New York: Liveright, 1925.

Levin, Gail. *Synchromism and American Color Abstraction, 1910–1925.* New York: George Braziller, 1978.

————. "Marsden Hartley and the European Avant-Garde." *Arts Magazine,* September 1979, pp. 158–163.

————. "Hidden Symbolism in Marsden Hartley's Military Pictures." *Arts Magazine,* October 1979, pp. 154–158.

Lowe, Sue Davidson. *Stieglitz: A Memoir/Biography.* New York: Farrar, Straus and Giroux, 1983.

Luhan, Mabel Dodge. *Winter in Taos.* New York: Harcourt, Brace, 1935.

————. *Movers and Shakers.* New York: Harcourt, Brace, 1936.

Lynch, Michael. "A Gay World After All." *Our Image: The Body Politic Review Supplement,* December–January 1976–77, pp. 1–3.

McAlmon, Robert. *Distinguished Air: Grim Fairy Tales.* Paris: Contact Editions at the Three Mountains Press, 1925.

————. *Being Geniuses Together, 1920–1930.* Garden City: Doubleday, 1968.

McBride, Henry. "What Is Happening in the World of Art." *New York Sun,* 18 January 1914, sec. 6, p. 2. Quoted in *Camera Work,* no. 45 (January 1914), pp. 19–21.

————. "Modern Art." *Dial,* January 1921, pp. 113–114.

————. "News and Reviews of Art." *New York Herald,* 8 May 1921, sec. 3, p. 11.

————. "Attractions in the Galleries." *New York Sun,* 5 January 1929, p. 12.

————. "Marsden Hartley's 'Comeback'," *New York Sun,* 20 December 1930, p. 9.

————. "Marsden Hartley Reappears." *New York Sun,* 28 March 1936, p. 32.

McCausland, Elizabeth. *Marsden Hartley.* Minneapolis: University of Minnesota Press, 1952.

————. "The Return of the Native." *Art in America,* Spring 1952, pp. 55–79.

Macke, Auguste. "Masks." In *The Blaue Reiter Almanac,* edited by Wassily Kandinsky and Franz Marc, English-language edition, pp. 83–89.

Marin, John. *The Selected Writings of John Marin.* Edited and with an introduction by Dorothy Norman. New York: Pellegrini and Cudahy, 1949.

Marling, William. *William Carlos Williams and the Painters, 1909–1923.* Athens, Ohio: Ohio University Press, 1982.

"Marsden Hartley: An American Place." *Art News,* 20 December 1930, p. 56.

"Marsden Hartley, Noted Artist, Dies." *New York Times,* 3 September 1943, p. 19.

Martin, Robert K. "Painting and Primitivism: Hart Crane and the Development of an American Expressionist Esthetic." *Mosaic,* Summer 1981, pp. 49–62.

Mellow, James R. *Charmed Circle: Gertrude Stein & Company.* New York: Holt, Rinehart and Winston, 1974.

Mellquist, Jerome. "Marsden Hartley, Visionary Painter." *Commonweal,* 31 December 1943, pp. 276–278.

"Modern U.S. Art on View Here." *Chicago Tribune,* European edition, 20 January 1925, p. 2.

Munson, Gorham. "Homage to Marsden Hartley." *Arts,* February 1961, pp. 33–41.

———. *The Awakening Twenties: A Memoir-History of a Literary Period.* Baton Rouge: Louisiana State University Press, 1985.

Norman, Dorothy. *Alfred Stieglitz: An American Seer.* New York: Random House, 1973.

Olson, Charles. *The Maximus Poems.* New York: Jargon/Corinth, 1960.

O'Neill, Eugene. *Strange Interlude.* In *The Theatre Guild Anthology,* pp. 577–689. New York: Random House, 1936.

Paulson, Ronald. "Marsden Hartley: The Search for the Father(land)." *Bennington Review,* September 1980, pp. 63–68. Reprinted in Ferguson, ed., *Marsden Hartley and Nova Scotia,* pp. 19–33.

Pemberton, Murdock. "Soul Exposures." *Creative Art,* January 1929, pp. xlvii–xlix.

Robinson, Roxana. *Georgia O'Keeffe: A Life.* New York: Harper and Row, 1989.

Rosenberg, Paul. "Marsden Hartley." *The Nation,* 18 September 1943, p. 326.

Rosenfeld, Paul. "Paint and Circuses." *Bookman,* December 1921, pp. 385–388.

———. "The Paintings of Marsden Hartley." *Vanity Fair,* August 1922.

———. *Port of New York.* New York: Harcourt, Brace and Company, 1924. Reprint, with introduction by Sherman Paul. Urbana: University of Illinois Press, 1961.

———. *Men Seen.* New York: Dial Press, 1925.

Schönberg, Arnold. "The Relationship to the Text." In *The Blaue Reiter Almanac,* edited by Wassily Kandinsky and Franz Marc, English-language edition, pp. 90–102.

Scott, Gail R. "Marsden Hartley at Dogtown Common." *Arts Magazine,* October 1979, pp. 159–165.

———. "'Cleophas and His Own': The Making of a Narrative." In Ferguson, ed., *Marsden Hartley and Nova Scotia,* pp. 55–73.

———. *Marsden Hartley.* New York: Abbeville Press, 1988.

Seligmann, Herbert. "The Elegance of Marsden Hartley — Craftsman." *International Studio,* October 1921, pp. li–liii.

———. "Hartley Discovers American Civilization." *Manuscripts,* February 1922, pp. 14–15.

Selz, Peter. *German Expressionist Painting.* Berkeley: University of California Press, 1974.

Stein, Gertrude. "From a Play by Gertrude Stein." *Camera Work,* no. 45 (January 1914), pp. 17–18.

————. *The Autobiography of Alice B. Toklas.* New York: Random House, 1933.

Tashjian, Dickran. *Skyscraper Primitives: Dada and the American Avant-Garde, 1910–25.* Middletown, Conn.: Wesleyan University Press, 1975.

"Two 'Modern' Artists Hold Auction Sale." *New York Herald,* 18 May 1921, p. 8.

Unterecker, John. *Voyager: A Life of Hart Crane.* New York: Farrar, Straus and Giroux, 1969.

Whitman, Walt. *Leaves of Grass.* New York: Modern Library, 1950.

Williams, William Carlos. *The Autobiography of William Carlos Williams.* New York: Random House, 1951.

————. *Selected Letters.* New York: McDowell, Obolensky, 1957.

————. *A Recognizable Image: William Carlos Williams on Art and Artists.* Edited by Bram Dijkstra. New York: New Directions, 1978.

Yeats, William Butler. *Collected Poems.* New York: Macmillan, 1962.

Acknowledgments

Anytime a person undertakes to write a biography, he or she discovers a community of scholars whose expertise and friendship become essential to the completion of the project. I should like to thank in particular Gail Scott, the very finest of scholars and friends; her generosity with her time and knowledge has been remarkable. My special thanks go as well to Gerald Ferguson, Thomas Gaehtgens, and Jeanne Hokin, whose enthusiasm and good will helped me many times. The artistic insights of Don Nice — and his patience with my inability to read maps — meant a great deal to me as I worked to complete this biography.

A would-be Hartley scholar must turn very quickly to the extensive collection of the artist's papers at the Beinecke Rare Book and Manuscript Library at Yale University. For that I am indebted to that giant among Americanists, Donald Gallup. Of great importance also is the work of the late Elizabeth McCausland and of Barbara Haskell. I thank them both.

My cousin Merloyd Lawrence lent her editorial skills to my manuscript at a critical juncture. A lot of whatever stylistic felicity the book has is thanks to her. The rest is thanks to two very fine editors, Ray Roberts and Dorothy Straight, whose care with this biography has been the sort every author dreams of.

Certain places provide a special ambience that makes the work of writing easy. For me the National Humanities Center was one such place. I am deeply indebted to its director at the time, Charles Blitzer, to its entire staff, and to the Lakeview Foundation for their support in 1985–1986. The insights I gained about biography from the noted biographers Charles Carlton, Fred Kaplan, Henry Levinson, and Harold Marcus were significant. Nowhere else could be closer to a heaven on earth than the Center, of that I am certain.

Another important place for me was West Point, New York, where in 1988–89 I had the privilege of serving as a visiting professor in the Department of English at the United States Military Academy. The courtesies extended to me and the openness to ideas there, as well as the beauty of the Hudson Valley region, impressed me deeply. Maryanne Sirotko-Turner took on the task of bringing my manuscript and me into the computer age, for which I am indebted to her.

At the University of North Carolina at Chapel Hill, always a fine place to write, I owe thanks to the late Charles Morrow and the late Cary C. Boshamer, whose support in a variety of ways was essential.

For their insights about Marsden Hartley and their willingness to be interviewed and often to show me their Hartley paintings — and frequently other major American works as well — I want to thank Scribner Ames, Constance Carden, Stanley Corkum, Karl Dworak, Matilde Elliott, Mavis Gallie, Chenoweth Hall, William Innes Homer, Paul Horgan, Philip Isaacson, William and Glenn Janss, Myron Kunin, John Paul and Madelyn Kuntz, Martha Mason, Pauline Mason, Mrs. Baldwin Maull, Dorothy Norman, Françoise and Harvey Rambach, Felizia Seyd, Richard Sisson and Peter Hanson, Leon Tebbetts, Mrs. W. D. Volk, Jonathan Weinberg, Glenway Wescott and Monroe Wheeler, Louise Young, and a group of scholars whose work on Georgia O'Keeffe and her group taught me a great deal: Ellen Bradbury, Sue Davidson Lowe, James Moore, Roxana Robinson, Robert Silberman, and Sharon Udall.

Several people offered encouragement early on: the late Bernard Malamud, Hilton Kramer, James R. Mellow, William Guthrie, and Tiffany Bell. I thank them, as I do Anne and Sam Bell, who enabled me to first meet Marsden Hartley in Maine by sailing into the glorious small harbor of Corea aboard their *Blue Angel.*

For various kinds of help along the way, I wish to thank John I. H. Baur, Isabel Behr, Adelyn Breeskin, William Chambers III, Thadious Davis, Elaine Dietsch, Fred Dillon, Christine Dodds, Maureen Donovan, John Driscoll, Mark Friedl, Emily Goldstein, Elizabeth B. Gordon, Margaret Harmon, William Harmon, Marge Harvey, Louis Hector, Robert Henning, Melissa Herrick, Herbert Hymans, Alfred Kazin, Lyndel King, Virginia King, Marge Kline, Sandra Kunhardt, and Kathryn Hargrove Lattanzi.

Thanks also to William Leuchtenburg, Gail Levin, Garnett McCoy, Patricia McDonnell, Charles Millard, Lillian Miller, Lori Misura, Megan Moynihan, Lisa Nanney, Art Olivas, William O'Reilly, Marc Pachter, James Patterson, Mary Riley, Mark Rosenthal, Helen Rotch and Harry Rose, Larry Salander, David Schoonover, Judith W. Short, Elizabeth Swaim, Nicki Thiras, David and Jackie Thomas, Evan Turner, Suzanne Vanderwoude, Kirk Varnedoe, Berta Walker, Jane Weaver, and Judith Zilczer.

For help in preparing my manuscript, I wish to thank Debbie Simmons-Cahan, Patricia Terry, Diane Chambers, and Emily Baggett.

Finally, but far from least, thanks to all my family for their endurance, support, and gentle prodding with the question "How's the book going?" Now I can answer them, "Well, I think."

Index

1